ATHENAEUS

IV

LCL 235

ATHENAEUS

THE LEARNED BANQUETERS

BOOKS 8–10.420E

EDITED AND TRANSLATED BY

S. DOUGLAS OLSON

HARVARD UNIVERSITY PRESS

CAMBRIDGE, MASSACHUSETTS
LONDON, ENGLAND
2008

s/o Blkwl. 6/08 24010

LOEB CLASSICAL LIBRARY® is a registered trademark
of the President and Fellows of Harvard College

Library of Congress Catalog Card Number 2006041321
CIP data available from the Library of Congress

ISBN 978-0-674-99626-7

Composed in ZephGreek and ZephText by
Technologies 'N Typography, Merrimac, Massachusetts.
Printed on acid-free paper and bound by
Edwards Brothers, Ann Arbor, Michigan

CONTENTS

PREFACE

For a general introduction to Athenaeus and *The Learned Banqueters*, and to my citation conventions, see the beginning of Volumes I and III. I have altered Casaubon's numbering of the text slightly at the beginning of Books 8 and 10, where he chose to repeat certain section-divisions and thus uses 330a, for example, to refer to both one of the final sections of Book 7 and the very beginning of Book 8 (my 8.330d). In addition, I have (like all previous editors) tacitly added a handful of section-divisions at points where they were accidentally omitted from Casaubon's text.

I would like to express again my gratitude to Dean Steven Rosenstone of the College of Liberal Arts at the University of Minnesota for his continuing support of my research, including by means of the award of a Single Semester leave for Spring 2007, during which I completed much of the work on this volume. Funds provided by the University of Minnesota Graduate School in connection with my McKnight Professorship have also been of enormous assistance in this project, and indeed in all my research over the last three years. Thanks are also due my research assistant Timothy Beck, and my undergraduate students Joseph McDonald and William Blessing, for their many hours of reference-checking, proofreading, formatting assistance, and the like. This volume is dedicated to my beautiful daughter Rebekkah, who will probably never read these words, but whom I love and miss more than she will ever know.

ABBREVIATIONS

Berve   H. Berve, *Das Alexanderreich auf prosopographischer Grundlage* ii *Prosopographie* (Munich, 1926)

FGE   D. L. Page (ed.), *Further Greek Epigrams* (Cambridge, 1981)

FGrH   F. Jacoby (ed.), *Die Fragmente der Griechischen Historiker* (Leiden, 1923–69)

FHG   C. and T. Müller, *Fragmenta Historicorum Graecorum* (4 vols.: Paris, 1841–70)

GGM   C. Müller, *Geographi Graeci Minores* (3 vols.: Paris, 1855–61)

GPh   A. S. F. Gow and D. L. Page (eds.), *The Greek Anthology: The Garland of Philip* (Cambridge, 1968)

Grainger   John D. Grainger, *Aitolian Prosopographical Studies* (*Mnemosyne* Suppl. 202: Leiden, Boston and Cologne, 2000)

HE   A. S. F. Gow and D. L. Page (eds.), *The Greek Anthology: Hellenistic Epigrams* (Cambridge, 1965)

IG   *Inscriptiones Graecae*

K–A   see *PCG*

PA   J. Kirchner, *Prosopographia Attica* (Berlin, 1901–3)

PAA	J. Traill (ed.), *Persons of Ancient Athens* (Toronto, 1994–)
PCG	R. Kassel and C. Austin (eds.), *Poetae Comici Graeci* (Berlin and New York, 1983–2001)
PMG	D. L. Page (ed.), *Poetae Melici Graeci* (Oxford, 1962)
Poralla	P. Poralla, *A Prosopography of Lacedaimonians from the Earliest Times to the Death of Alexander the Great (X–323 B.C.)*² (revised by A. S. Bradford: Chicago, 1985)
SH	H. Lloyd-Jones and P. Parsons (eds.), *Supplementum Hellenisticum* (Texte und Kommentare, Band 11: Berlin and New York, 1983)
SSR	G. Giannantoni, *Socratis et Socraticorum Reliquiae* (4 vols.; n.p., 1990)
Stephanis	I. E. Stephanis, Διονυσιακοὶ Τεχνίται (Herakleion, 1988)
SVF	J. van Arnim (ed.), *Stoicorum Veterum Fragmenta* (3 vols.; Leipzig, 1921, 1903)
TrGF	B. Snell *et al.* (eds.), *Tragicorum Graecorum Fragmenta* (Göttingen, 1971–2004)

THE CHARACTERS

ATHENAEUS, the narrator; also a guest at the dinner party

TIMOCRATES, Athenaeus' interlocutor

AEMILIANUS MAURUS, grammarian (e.g. 3.126b)

ALCEIDES OF ALEXANDRIA, musician (1.1f; 4.174b)

AMOEBEUS, citharode (14.622d–e)

ARRIAN, grammarian (3.113a)

CYNULCUS, Cynic philosopher whose given name is Theodorus (e.g. 1.1d; 3.97c)

DAPHNUS OF EPHESUS, physician (e.g. 1.1e; 2.51a)

DEMOCRITUS OF NICOMEDIA, philosopher (1.1e; 3.83c)

DIONYSOCLES, physician (3.96d, 116d)

GALEN OF PERGAMUM, physician (e.g. 1.1e–f, 26c)

LARENSIUS, Roman official and also host of the party (e.g. 1.2b–3c; 2.50f)

LEONIDAS OF ELIS, grammarian (1.1d; 3.96d)

MAGNUS (e.g. 3.74c)

MASURIUS, jurist, poet, musician (e.g. 1.1c; 14.623e)

MYRTILUS OF THESSALY, grammarian (e.g. 3.83a)

PALAMEDES THE ELEATIC, lexicographer (9.379a)

PHILADELPHUS OF PTOLEMAIS, philosopher (1.1d)*

PLUTARCH OF ALEXANDRIA, grammarian (e.g. 1.1c–d; 3.83b)

PONTIANUS OF NICOMEDIA, philosopher (1.1d; 3.109b)

RUFINUS OF NICAEA, physician (1.1f)*

ULPIAN OF TYRE, grammarian and also symposiarch (e.g. 1.1d–e; 2.49a)

VARUS, grammarian (3.118d)

ZOILUS, grammarian (e.g. 1.1d; 7.277c)

* Neither Philadelphus nor Rufinus is said to speak anywhere in the preserved text of *The Learned Banqueters*, and most likely some of the anonymous speeches in 1.2a–3.73e (represented in the Epitome manuscripts only) belong to them.

THE LEARNED BANQUETERS

H

Τὴν κατὰ τὴν Λυσιτανίαν (χώρα δ᾽ ἐστὶν αὕτη τῆς
Ἰβηρίας, ἣν νῦν Ῥωμαῖοι Σπανίαν ὀνομάζουσι) διηγούμενος εὐδαιμονίαν Πολύβιος ὁ Μεγαλοπολίτης,
ἀνδρῶν ἄριστε Τιμόκρατες, ἐν τῇ τετάρτῃ καὶ τριακοστῇ τῶν Ἱστοριῶν φησιν ὡς αὐτόθι ‖ διὰ τὴν τοῦ
ἀέρος εὐκρασίαν καὶ τὰ ζῷα πολύγονα καὶ οἱ ἄνθρωποι, καὶ οἱ ἐν τῇ χώρᾳ καρποὶ οὐδέποτε φθείρονται·
ῥόδα μὲν γὰρ αὐτόθι καὶ λευκόϊα καὶ ἀσπάραγοι καὶ
τὰ παραπλήσια τούτοις οὐ πλεῖον διαλείπει μηνῶν
τριῶν, τὸ δὲ θαλάττιον ὄψον καὶ κατὰ τὸ πλῆθος καὶ
κατὰ τὴν χρηστότητα καὶ κατὰ τὸ κάλλος μεγάλην
ἔχει διαφορὰν πρὸς τὸ γινόμενον ἐν τῇ καθ᾽ ἡμᾶς
θαλάττῃ. καὶ ὁ μὲν τῶν κριθῶν Σικελικὸς μέδιμνός
ἐστι δραχμῆς, ὁ δὲ τῶν πυρῶν ἐννέα ὀβολῶν Ἀλεξαν-
δρεινῶν. τοῦ δ᾽ οἴνου δραχμῆς ὁ μετρητὴς | καὶ ἔριφος
ὁ μέτριος ὀβολοῦ καὶ λαγώς. τῶν δ᾽ ἀρνῶν τριώβολον
καὶ τετρώβολον ἡ τιμή, ὗς δὲ πίων ἑκατὸν μνᾶς ἄγων
πέντε δραχμῶν καὶ πρόβατον δυεῖν, τάλαντον δὲ σύκων τριῶν ὀβολῶν, μόσχος δραχμῶν πέντε καὶ βοῦς
ζύγιμος δέκα. τὰ δὲ τῶν ἀγρίων ζῴων κρέα σχεδὸν
οὐδὲ κατηξιοῦτο τιμῆς, ἀλλ᾽ ἐν ἐπιδόσει καὶ χάριτι

2

BOOK VIII

In his discussion in Book XXXIV (8.4–10) of his *History* of how prosperous Lusitania is—this is part of Iberia, and is referred to nowadays by the Romans as *Spania*, my excellent Timocrates—Polybius of Megalopolis claims that because the climate is so mild, both the animals and the people there produce large numbers of offspring, and the crops in the region never fail. Roses, carnations, asparagus, and the like, for example, are never out of season for more than three months; and the seafood is far better in quantity, quality, and appearance than what is found in the sea near us. A Sicilian *medimnos*[1] of barley costs a drachma; a *medimnos* of wheat costs nine Alexandrian obols[2]; an amphora of wine costs a drachma; and an average-sized kid costs an obol, as does a hare. The price of a lamb is three or four obols; a fat pig that weighs 100 *minas*[3] costs five drachmas, a sheep or goat two; a talent[4] of figs costs three obols, a calf five drachmas, and a yoke-ox ten. Wild-animal meat is considered almost worthless; they give it to one another

[1] An Attic *medimnos* (a dry measure commonly used for grain) was equivalent to about 1 1/3 American bushels; the size of a Sicilian *medimnos* is unknown.   [2] I.e. 1 1/2 drachmas.

[3] About 95 pounds (on the Attic standard).

[4] About 58 pounds (on the Attic standard).

τὴν ἀλλαγὴν ποιοῦνται τούτων. ἡμῖν δὲ ὁ καλὸς Λαρήνσιος τὴν Ῥώμην Λυσιτανίαν ἑκάστοτε παρέχων
ἐμπίπλησι παντοίων ἀγαθῶν ὁσημέραι, μετὰ τοῦ
ἡδέος καὶ μεγαλοφρόνως φιλοτιμούμενος, οὐδὲν φερο-
c μένοις | οἴκοθεν ἢ λογάρια.

Πολλῶν δὲ λεχθέντων ἐπὶ τοῖς ἰχθύσι λόγων δῆλος
μὲν ἦν ἀχθόμενος ὁ Κύνουλκος. καὶ ὁ καλὸς Δημόκριτος αὐτὸν προφθάσας ἔφη· ἀλλὰ μήν, ἄνδρες ἰχθύες
κατὰ τὸν Ἄρχιππον, παρελίπετε (δεῖ γὰρ καὶ ἡμᾶς
μικρὰ προσοψωνῆσαι) τούς τε ὀρυκτοὺς ἰχθύας καλουμένους, οἳ ἐν Ἡρακλείᾳ γίγνονται καὶ περὶ Τίον
τοῦ Πόντου τὴν Μιλησίων ἀποικίαν, ἱστοροῦντος περὶ
αὐτῶν Θεοφράστου. ὁ δ' αὐτὸς οὗτος φιλόσοφος καὶ
περὶ τῶν πηγνυμένων διὰ χειμῶνα τῷ κρυστάλλῳ
ἱστόρησεν, οἳ οὐ πρότερον αἰσθάνονται οὐδὲ κινοῦν-
ται, πρὶν ἂν εἰς τὰς λοπάδας ἐμβληθέντες ἕψωνται.
d ἴδιον δὲ παρὰ τούτους | συμβαίνει τὸ περὶ τοὺς ἐν
Παφλαγονίᾳ ὀρυκτοὺς καλουμένους ἰχθῦς γινόμενον·
ὀρύττεσθαι γὰρ κατὰ βάθους πλέονος τοὺς τόπους
οὔτε ποταμῶν ἐπιχύσεις ἔχοντας οὔτε φανερῶν να-
μάτων, καὶ εὑρίσκεσθαι ἐν αὐτοῖς ἰχθῦς ζῶντας. Μνασέας δὲ ὁ Πατρεὺς ἐν τῷ Περίπλῳ τοὺς ἐν τῷ Κλείτορι
ποταμῷ φησιν ἰχθῦς φθέγγεσθαι, καίτοι μόνους εἰρη-
κότος Ἀριστοτέλους φθέγγεσθαι σκάρον καὶ τὸν ποτάμιον χοῖρον. Φιλοστέφανος δ' ὁ Κυρηναῖος μὲν
γένος, Καλλιμάχου δὲ γνώριμος, ἐν τῷ Περὶ τῶν

[5] Cf. the similar turn of phrase at 1.4b.

as a way of throwing in something extra or doing a favor. The noble Larensius routinely makes Rome into Lusitania for us, by stuffing us with good food of all kinds on a daily basis, and taking a generous pleasure in vigorously pursuing this course, even though we bring nothing from home except the speeches we make.[5]

Numerous remarks had been made on the subject of fish,[6] and Cynulcus was obviously irritated.[7] But before he could say anything, the noble Democritus observed: Well, piscine sirs (to quote Archippus [fr. *30]), you left out— because I need to add a few more fish to our shopping-list!—the so-called excavated fish found in Heracleia and around the Milesian colony of Tius on the Black Sea, despite the fact that Theophrastus (fr. 171 Wimmer) describes them. This same philosopher also offered an account of the fish that are frozen in ice all winter long and do not feel anything or move until they are dumped into casserole-dishes and begin to stew. But even in comparison to them, what happens in the case of the so-called excavated fish in Paphlagonia is peculiar; for deep holes are dug in places that have no rivers emptying into them and no visible springs—and live fish are found in them! Mnaseas of Patras in his *Voyage along the Coast* (fr. 14 Cappelletto) claims that the fish in the Cleitor River produce articulate sounds, although Aristotle (fr. 252) says that the only ones that actually do so are the parrot-wrasse and the river-schall. Philostephanus, whose family was from Cyrene and who was a student of Callimachus, asserts in his *On*

6 The main topic of Book 7.

7 Sc. because eating was constantly deferred in favor of more talk.

e Παραδόξων Ποταμῶν ἐν Ἀόρνῳ φησὶ τῷ ποταμῷ | διὰ
Φενεοῦ ῥέοντι ἰχθῦς εἶναι φθεγγομένους ὁμοίως κί-
χλαις· καλεῖσθαι δ' αὐτοὺς ποικιλίας. Νυμφόδωρος δ'
ὁ Συρακόσιος ἐν τοῖς Περίπλοις ἐν τῷ Ἑλώρῳ ποταμῷ
λάβρακας εἶναί φησι καὶ ἐγχέλεις μεγάλας οὕτω
τιθασοὺς ὡς ἐκ τῶν χειρῶν δέχεσθαι τῶν προσφερόν-
των ἄρτους. ἐγὼ δὲ ἐν τῇ κατὰ Χαλκίδα Ἀρεθούσῃ
τεθέαμαι, ἴσως δὲ καὶ ὑμῶν οἱ πλεῖστοι, κεστρεῖς
χειροήθεις καὶ ἐγχέλεις ἐνώτια ἐχούσας ἀργυρᾶ καὶ
χρυσᾶ, λαμβανούσας τε καὶ λαμβάνοντας παρὰ τῶν
f προσφερόντων τροφὰς τά | τε ἀπὸ τῶν ἱερείων σπλάγ-
χνα καὶ τυροὺς χλωρούς. Σῆμος δ' ἐν ἕκτῳ Δηλιάδος,
Ἀθηναίοις, φησί, θυομένοις ἐν Δήλῳ τὴν χέρνιβα
βάψας ὁ παῖς προσήνεγκε κἂν τῇ φιάλῃ μετὰ τοῦ
ὕδατος ἰχθῦς κατέχεεν· εἰπεῖν οὖν αὐτοῖς τοὺς τῶν
Δηλίων μάντεις ὡς κυριεύσουσι τῆς θαλάσσης. ‖
332 Πολύβιος δ' ἐν τῇ τετάρτῃ καὶ τριακοστῇ τῶν Ἱστοριῶν μετὰ τὴν Πυρήνην φησὶν ἕως τοῦ Νάρβωνος
ποταμοῦ πεδίον εἶναι, δι' οὗ φέρεσθαι ποταμοὺς Ἰλλέ-
βεριν καὶ Ῥόσκυνον ῥέοντας παρὰ πόλεις ὁμωνύμους
κατοικουμένας ὑπὸ Κελτῶν· ἐν οὖν τῷ πεδίῳ τούτῳ
εἶναι τοὺς λεγομένους ἰχθῦς ὀρυκτούς. εἶναί τε τὸ
πεδίον λεπτόγειον καὶ πολλὴν ἄγρωστιν ἔχον πεφυ-
κυῖαν· ὑπὸ δὲ ταύτην διάμμου τῆς γῆς οὔσης ἐπὶ δύο
καὶ τρεῖς πήχεις ὑπορρεῖν τὸ πλαζόμενον ἀπὸ τῶν
b ποταμῶν ὕδωρ· μεθ' οὗ | ἰχθύες κατὰ τὰς παρεκχύσεις
ὑποτρέχοντες ὑπὸ τὴν γῆν χάριν τῆς τροφῆς (φιλη-

6

Strange Rivers that there are fish in the Aornus River, which flows through Pheneus, that produce the same sound as thrushes do; they are known as *poikiliai*.[8] Nymphodorus of Syracuse in his *Voyages along the Coast* (*FGrH* 572 F 8) claims that there are large bass and eels in the Helorus River which are so tame that they take bread from your hand if you offer it to them. I myself have seen— perhaps most of you have as well—gray mullets in the Arethusa spring in Chalcis that are accustomed to being touched, and eels that wear silver and gold earrings; both take the entrails of sacrificial animals and fresh cheese if you offer it to them. Semus says in Book VI of the *History of Delos* (*FGrH* 396 F 12): When some Athenians were making a sacrifice on Delos, the slave scooped up the washing-water and brought it to them, and poured fish into the bowl along with the water. The Delian seers accordingly told them that they would rule the sea. Polybius in Book XXXIV (10.1–4) of his *History* says that a plain extends from Pyrene to the Narbon River, and that the Illeberis and Rhoscynus Rivers flow through it past the Celtic cities that share their names; the so-called excavated fish are found in this plain. The plain has light soil, and a considerable amount of Bermuda grass (*agrōstis*) grows in it. Beneath the grass are three to five feet[9] of sandy earth, and under this flows the water, which has made its way there from the rivers. Fish move underground along with the water that has seeped out of the rivers, in order to

[8] Cf. Paus. 8.21.2, who calls the river the Aroanius and expresses disappointment at not hearing the fish speak, despite waiting into the evening for this to happen.

[9] Literally "two to three cubits".

δοῦσι γὰρ τῇ τῆς ἀγρώστεως ῥίζῃ) πεποιήκασι πᾶν
τὸ πεδίον πλῆρες ἰχθύων ὑπογείων, οὓς ἀνορύττοντες
λαμβάνουσιν. ἐν Ἰνδοῖς δέ φησι Θεόφραστος τοὺς
ἰχθῦς ἐκ τῶν ποταμῶν εἰς τὴν γῆν ἐξιόντας καὶ πη-
δῶντας πάλιν εἰς τὸ ὕδωρ ἀπιέναι καθάπερ τοὺς βατράχους, ὁμοίους ὄντας τὴν ἰδέαν τοῖς μαξείνοις κα-
λουμένοις ἰχθύσιν. οὐκ ἔλαθεν δέ με οὐδὲ Κλέαρχος ὁ
ἀπὸ τοῦ περιπάτου ὅσ᾿ εἴρηκε καὶ περὶ τοῦ ἐξωκοίτου |
c καλουμένου ἰχθύος ἐν τῷ ἐπιγραφομένῳ Περὶ τῶν
Ἐνύδρων. εἴρηκε γὰρ—κρατεῖν δ᾿ οἶμαι καὶ τῆς λέξεως οὕτως ἐχούσης· ὁ ἐξώκοιτος ἰχθύς, ὃν ἔνιοι
καλοῦσιν ἄδωνιν, τοὔνομα μὲν εἴληφε διὰ τὸ πολλάκις
τὰς ἀναπαύσεις ἔξω τοῦ ὑγροῦ ποιεῖσθαι. ἐστὶ δὲ
ὑπόπυρρος καὶ ἀπὸ τῶν βραγχίων ἑκατέρωθεν τοῦ
σώματος μέχρι τῆς κέρκου μίαν ἔχει διηνεκῆ λευκὴν
ῥάβδον. ἐστὶ δὲ στρογγύλος ἀλλ᾿ οὐ πλατὺς ὢν κατὰ
τὸ μέγεθος ἴσος ἐστὶ τοῖς παραιγιαλίταις κεστρι-
d νίσκοις· οὗτοι δ᾿ εἰσὶν ὀκταδάκτυλοι | μάλιστα τὸ
μῆκος. τὸ δὲ σύνολον ὁμοιότατός ἐστι τῷ καλουμένῳ
τράγῳ ἰχθυδίῳ πλὴν τοῦ ὑπὸ τὸν στόμαχον μέλανος,
ὃ καλοῦσι τοῦ τράγου πώγωνα. ἐστὶ δ᾿ ὁ ἐξώκοιτος
τῶν πετραίων καὶ βιοτεύει περὶ τοὺς πετρώδεις τό-
πους· καὶ ὅταν ᾖ γαλήνη, συνεξορούσας τῷ κύματι
κεῖται ἐπὶ τῶν πετριδίων πολὺν χρόνον ἀναπαυόμενος
ἐν τῷ ξηρῷ καὶ μεταστρέφει μὲν ἑαυτὸν πρὸς τὸν
ἥλιον. ὅταν δ᾿ ἱκανῶς αὐτῷ τὰ πρὸς τὴν ἀνάπαυσιν
ἔχῃ, προσκυλινδεῖται τῷ ὑγρῷ, μέχρι οὗ ἂν πάλιν
e ὑπολαβὸν | αὐτὸν τὸ κῦμα κατενέγκῃ μετὰ τῆς ἀναρ-

8

feed—they like the roots of the grass—and have filled the entire plain with subterranean fish, which the locals dig up and catch. In India, according to Theophrastus (fr. 171 Wimmer), the fish leave the rivers and come up onto the land, and then leap back into the water and disappear, like frogs; they look like the so-called *maxeinoi* fish. I am also familiar with what Clearchus the Peripatetic says in his work entitled *On Aquatic Creatures* (fr. 101 Wehrli) on the subject of the so-called *exōkoitos*[10] fish. He says—I believe that I can quote the passage, which runs as follows: The *exōkoitos* fish, which some authorities refer to as an *adōnis*, got its name from the fact that it often rests outside of (*exō*) the water. It is reddish and has a single white stripe that runs the length of its body on both sides from its gills to its tail. It is globular, but not wide across, and is the same size as the small gray mullets caught along the shore, which are six inches[11] long at most. In general it most closely resembles the so-called *tragos* ("billy-goat") fish,[12] except for the dark part beneath its mouth, which is referred to as a "goat's-beard." The *exōkoitos* is a rock-fish and lives in rocky areas; whenever the sea is calm, it rides a wave out of it and lies on the pebbles for a long time, resting on the beach, and turns itself to face the sun. After it has rested enough, it rolls back toward the water until the waves pick it up again and carry it back out to sea as they leave the

10 Literally "out-sleeping".

11 Literally "eight fingers."

12 The male sprat during mating season; cf. Hicesius at 7.328c; Arist. *HA* 607b11–14.

ροίας εἰς τὴν θάλασσαν. ὅταν δ᾽ ἐγρηγορὼς ἐν τῷ
ξηρῷ τύχῃ, φυλάττεται τῶν ὀρνίθων τοὺς παρευδια-
στὰς καλουμένους, ὧν ἐστι κηρύλος, τροχίλος καὶ ὁ
τῇ κρεκὶ προσεμφερὴς ἐρῳδιός· οὗτοι γὰρ ἐν ταῖς
εὐδίαις παρὰ τὸ ξηρὸν νεμόμενοι πολλάκις αὐτῷ περι-
πίπτουσιν, οὓς ὅταν προΐδηται φεύγει πηδῶν καὶ
ἀσπαίρων, ἕως ἂν εἰς τὸ ὕδωρ ἀποκυμβήσῃ. ἔτι ὁ
αὐτὸς Κλέαρχος καὶ ταῦτά φησι σαφέστερον τοῦ
f Κυρηναίου Φιλοστεφάνου, | οὗ πρότερον ἐμνήσθην·
ἐπεί τινες τῶν ἰχθύων οὐκ ἔχοντες βρόγχον φθέγγονται. τοιοῦτοι δ᾽ εἰσὶν οἱ περὶ Κλείτορα τῆς Ἀρκαδίας
ἐν τῷ Λάδωνι καλουμένῳ ποταμῷ· φθέγγονται γὰρ
καὶ πολὺν ἦχον ἀποτελοῦσιν. Νικόλαος δ᾽ ὁ Δαμα-
σκηνὸς ἐν τῇ τετάρτῃ πρὸς ταῖς ἑκατὸν τῶν Ἱστοριῶν,
περὶ Ἀπάμειαν, φησί, τὴν Φρυγιακὴν κατὰ τὰ Μιθρι-
δατικὰ σεισμῶν γενομένων ἀνεφάνησαν περὶ τὴν χώραν αὐτῶν λίμναι τε πρότερον[1] οὐκ οὖσαι καὶ ποταμοὶ
καὶ ἄλλαι πηγαὶ ὑπὸ τῆς κινήσεως ἀνοιχθεῖσαι, πολλαὶ δὲ καὶ ἠφανίσθησαν, τοσοῦτόν τε ἄλλο ἀνέβλυ-
σεν αὐτῶν ἐν τῇ γῇ πικρόν τε καὶ γλαυκὸν ὕδωρ,
πλεῖστον ὅσον ἀπεχούσης τῶν τόπων τῆς θαλάσσης,
ὥστε ὀστρέων πλησθῆναι τὸν πλησίον τόπον ἅπαντα
καὶ ἰχθύων τῶν τε ἄλλων ὅσα τρέφει ἡ θάλασσα. ‖
333 οἶδα δὲ καὶ πολλαχοῦ ὕσαντα τὸν θεὸν ἰχθύσι· Φαινίας γοῦν ἐν δευτέρῳ Πρυτάνεων Ἐρεσίων ἐν Χερ-
ρονήσῳ φησὶν ἐπὶ τρεῖς ἡμέρας ὗσαι τὸν θεὸν ἰχθύας.
καὶ Φύλαρχος δ᾽ ἐν τετάρτῃ ἑωρακέναι τινὰς πολλαχοῦ τὸν θεὸν ὕσαντα ἰχθύσι, πολλάκις δὲ καὶ γυρίνοις

10

shore. As it lies awake on the beach, it keeps an eye out for the so-called fair-weather birds, which include the *kērulos*, the Egyptian plover, and the type of heron that resembles a *krēx*. Because when the weather is good, these birds feed along the coast and often attack the *exōkoitos*; when it spies them, it tries to get away by flopping and thrashing about, until it finally jumps into the water. The same Clearchus (fr. 104 Wehrli) also says the following, expressing himself more clearly than Philostephanus of Cyrene, whom I mentioned earlier (8.331d–e): since some fish produce articulate sounds, despite lacking a windpipe. Those found around Arcadian Cleitor in what is known as the Ladon River are an example; they produce sounds and in fact generate considerable noise. Nicolaus of Damascus says in Book CIV of his *History* (*FGrH* 90 F 74): When earthquakes occurred around Apameia in Phrygia during the Mithridatic Wars, lakes that previously had not existed appeared throughout their country, as did rivers and other water-sources that had been opened up by the earth's movement, while many others disappeared. On top of that, so much gray saltwater gushed out onto their land that, although the sea was quite a long way from the region, the entire area around there was filled with shellfish, fish, and every other kind of sea-creature. I am also aware that it has rained fish in many places. Phaenias in Book II of *The Rulers of Eresus* (fr. 17a Wehrli), for example, claims that it rained fish for three days in the Chersonese. So too Phylarchus in Book IV (*FGrH* 81 F 4) (reports) that people have seen it rain fish in a number of places, and that some-

---

1 λίμναι τε αἱ πρότερον A: λίμνας πρότερον tantum CE: αἱ del. Kaibel

11

τοῦ αὐτοῦ συμβαίνοντος². Ἡρακλείδης γοῦν ὁ Λέμ-
βος ἐν τῇ πρώτῃ καὶ εἰκοστῇ τῶν Ἱστοριῶν, περὶ τὴν
Παιονίαν καὶ Δαρδανίαν βατράχους, φησίν, ὗσεν ὁ
θεὸς καὶ τοσοῦτο αὐτῶν ἐγένετο τὸ πλῆθος ὡς τὰς |
b   οἰκίας καὶ τὰς ὁδοὺς πλήρεις εἶναι. τὰς μὲν οὖν
πρώτας ἡμέρας κτείνοντες τούτους καὶ συγκλείοντες
τὰς οἰκίας διεκαρτέρουν· ὡς δ᾽ οὐδὲν ἤνυον, ἀλλὰ τά τε
σκεύη ἐπληροῦτο καὶ μετὰ τῶν ἐδεσμάτων εὑρίσκοντο
συνεψόμενοι καὶ συνοπτώμενοι οἱ βάτραχοι καὶ πρὸς
τούτοις οὔτε τοῖς ὕδασιν ἦν χρῆσθαι οὔτε τοὺς πόδας
ἐπὶ τὴν γῆν θεῖναι συσσεσωρευμένων αὐτῶν, ἐν-
οχλούμενοι δὲ καὶ ὑπὸ τῆς τῶν τετελευτηκότων ὀδμῆς
ἔφυγον τὴν χώραν. οἶδα δὲ καὶ Ποσειδώνιον τὸν ἀπὸ
τῆς στοᾶς εἰπόντα καὶ περὶ πλήθους ἰχθύων τάδε· ὅτε
c   Τρύφων | ὁ Ἀπαμεὺς ὁ τὴν τῶν Σύρων βασιλείαν
ἁρπάσας ἐπολεμεῖτο ὑπὸ Σαρπηδόνος τοῦ Δημητρίου
στρατηγοῦ περὶ Πτολεμαΐδα πόλιν καὶ ὡς ὁ Σαρπη-
δὼν ληφθεὶς ἀνεχώρησεν εἰς τὴν μεσόγαιαν μετὰ τῶν
ἰδίων στρατιωτῶν, οἱ δὲ τοῦ Τρύφωνος ὤδευον κατὰ τὸ
πλησίαλον νικήσαντες τῇ μάχῃ, ἐξαίφνης πελάγιον
κῦμα ἐξαρθὲν μετέωρον εἰς ὕψος ἐξαίσιον ἐπῆλθεν τῇ
γῇ καὶ πάντας αὐτοὺς ἐπέκλυσεν διέφθειρέν τε ὑπο-
βρυχίους, ἰχθύων τε πολὺν σωρὸν ἀναχωροῦν τὸ κῦμα
d   μετὰ τῶν νεκρῶν κατέλιπε. καὶ οἱ περὶ | τὸν Σαρπη-
δόνα ἀκούσαντες τὴν συμφορὰν ἐπελθόντες τοῖς μὲν

---

² συμβαίνοντος καὶ ἐπὶ βατράχων A: καὶ ἐπὶ βατράχων
del. Dobree

thing similar often occurs with tadpoles. Heracleides of Lembos, for example, says in Book XXI of his *History* (fr. 3, *FHG* iii.168): Around Paeonia and Dardania it rained frogs, and there were so many of them that they filled the houses and the streets. For the first few days the people coped by killing them and keeping the doors of their houses shut. But this got them nowhere: their pots and jars were full of frogs; they found frogs being stewed and roasted along with their food; on top of this, it became impossible to drink the water, or even to put their feet on the ground, because of the heaps of frogs; and since the stench of the dead ones was making them miserable, they abandoned the place. I am also aware that Posidonius the Stoic (*FGrH* 87 F 29 = fr. 226 Edelstein–Kidd) said the following about a large quantity of fish: After Tryphon of Apameia seized the Syrian throne, he was attacked by Demetrius' general Sarpedon near the city of Ptolemais.[13] When Sarpedon was defeated, he withdrew into the interior with his troops; meanwhile, Tryphon's men, who had won the battle, were traveling along the coastal road. Suddenly a huge wave towering extraordinarily high in the air hit the shore, submerging and drowning them; when the wave withdrew, it left an enormous heap of fish behind, along with the corpses. Sarpedon's men heard about the disaster, and came and gloated over their enemies' bodies;

[13] The events described here probably took place *c*.144/3 BCE. The Demetrius in question is Demetrius II Nicator. Strabo 16.758 offers a shorter version of the same anecdote.

τῶν πολεμίων σώμασιν ἐφήσθησαν, ἰχθύων δὲ ἀφθο-
νίαν ἀπηνέγκαντο καὶ ἔθυσαν Ποσειδῶνι Τροπαίῳ
πρὸς τοῖς προαστείοις τῆς πόλεως. οὐ κατασιωπήσο-
μαι δὲ οὐδὲ τοὺς ἐν Λυκίᾳ ἰχθυομάντεις ἄνδρας, περὶ
ὧν ἱστορεῖ Πολύχαρμος ἐν δευτέρῳ Λυκιακῶν γράφων
οὕτως· ὅταν γὰρ διέλθωσι πρὸς τὴν θάλασσαν, οὗ τὸ
ἄλσος ἐστὶ πρὸς τῷ αἰγιαλῷ τοῦ Ἀπόλλωνος, ἐν ᾧ
ἐστιν ἡ δῖνα ἐπὶ τῆς ἀμάθου, παραγίνονται ἔχοντες οἱ
e μαντευόμενοι ὀβελίσκους δύο | ξυλίνους, ἔχοντας ἐφ'
ἑκατέρῳ σάρκας ὀπτὰς ἀριθμῷ δέκα. καὶ ὁ μὲν ἱερεὺς
κάθηται πρὸς τῷ ἄλσει σιωπῇ, ὁ δὲ μαντευόμενος
ἐμβάλλει τοὺς ὀβελίσκους εἰς τὴν δῖναν καὶ ἀποθεω-
ρεῖ τὸ γινόμενον. μετὰ δὲ τὴν ἐμβολὴν τῶν ὀβελίσκων
πληροῦται θαλάσσης ἡ δῖνα καὶ παραγίνεται ἰχθύων
πλῆθος τοσοῦτον ὥστ᾽[3] ἐκπλήττεσθαι τὸ ἀόρατον τοῦ
πράγματος, τῷ δὲ μεγέθει ⟨τοιούτων⟩[4] ὥστε καὶ εὐλα-
βηθῆναι. ὅταν δὲ ἀπαγγείλῃ τὰ εἴδη τῶν ἰχθύων ὁ
προφήτης, οὕτως τὸν χρησμὸν λαμβάνει παρὰ τοῦ
f ἱερέως ὁ μαντευόμενος περὶ | ὧν ηὔξατο. φαίνονται δὲ
ὀρφοί, γλαῦκοι, ἐνίοτε δὲ φάλλαιναι ἢ πρίστεις, πολλοὶ δὲ καὶ ἀόρατοι ἰχθῦς καὶ ξένοι τῇ ὄψει. Ἀρτεμίδωρος δ᾽ ἐν τῷ δεκάτῳ τῶν Γεωγραφουμένων λέγεσθαί
φησιν ὑπὸ τῶν ἐπιχωρίων πηγὴν ἀναδίδοσθαι γλυ-
κέος ὕδατος, ὅθεν συμβαίνειν δίνας γίνεσθαι· γίνεσθαι δὲ καὶ ἰχθύας ἐν τῷ δινάζοντι τόπῳ μεγάλους.
τούτοις δὲ οἱ θυσιάζοντες ἐμβάλλουσιν ἀπαρχὰς τῶν
θυσιαζομένων ἐπὶ ξυλίνων ὀβελίσκων ἀναπείροντες

but they also took away an enormous quantity of fish and sacrificed them to Poseidon Tropaios ("Giver of Victory") on the city's outskirts. Nor will I will neglect to mention the Lycian fish-prophets described by Polycharmus in Book II of the *History of Lycia* (*FGrH* 770 F 1), where he writes as follows: When they get to the sea, to the spot on the shore where Apollo's sacred grove (which contains the whirlpool, set on the dune) is located, the individuals seeking an oracle are there holding two wooden spits, each of which has ten pieces of roasted meat on it. The priest sits silently in the grove, and the person seeking an oracle tosses the spits into the whirlpool and watches to see what happens. After the spits are thrown in, the pool fills with seawater, and fish appear in such numbers that the oddness of the situation inspires astonishment, while the fish themselves are big enough to make one wary of them. The interpreter announces what the fish look like, which is how the individual seeking an oracle gets a response from the priest to the questions he prayed about. Sea-perch, *glaukoi*, and occasionally whales and sawfish appear, along with many unusual, rarely-seen fish. Artemidorus in Book X of his *Geography*[14] says that the locals claim that a fresh-water spring emerges and produces whirlpools; he also reports that large fish are found in the place that features the whirlpool. The people who make offerings to these fish put bits of stewed and roasted meat, barley-cakes, and loaves

---

[14] Not necessarily referring to the same whirlpool (despite the implication of Athenaeus' organization).

---

[3] τοσοῦτον καὶ τοιοῦτον ὥστ᾽ A: τοσοῦτον ὥστε tantum CE: καὶ τοιοῦτον del. Kaibel   [4] add. Kaibel

334 κρέα ἑφθὰ καὶ ὀπτὰ καὶ ‖ μάζας καὶ ἄρτους. ὀνομάζε-
ται δὲ ὁ λιμὴν καὶ ὁ τόπος οὗτος Δῖνος. οἶδα δὲ καὶ
Φύλαρχον εἰρηκότα που περὶ μεγάλων ἰχθύων καὶ τῶν
συμπεμφθέντων αὐτοῖς σύκων χλωρῶν, ὅτι αἰνιττόμε-
νος Πάτροκλος ὁ Πτολεμαίου στρατηγὸς Ἀντιγόνῳ
τῷ βασιλεῖ ἔπεμψεν[5], ὡς Δαρείῳ Σκύθαι ἐπερχομένῳ
αὐτῶν τῇ χώρᾳ· ἔπεμψαν γὰρ οὗτοι μέν, ὥς φησιν
Ἡρόδοτος, ὄρνιν καὶ ὀιστὸν καὶ βάτραχον· ἀλλ᾽ ὅ γε
Πάτροκλος, ὡς διὰ τῆς τρίτης τῶν Ἱστοριῶν φησιν ὁ
Φύλαρχος, πεμφθέντων τῶν προειρημένων σύκων |
b καὶ ἰχθύων. ἐτύγχανεν δὲ κωθωνιζόμενος ὁ βασιλεὺς
καὶ ὡς πάντες διηποροῦντο ἐπὶ τοῖς δώροις, ὁ Ἀντίγονος γελάσας πρὸς τοὺς φίλους ἔφη γινώσκειν τί
βούλεται τὰ ξένια· "ἢ γὰρ θαλαττοκρατεῖν ἡμᾶς φησι
Πάτροκλος ἢ τῶν σύκων τρώγειν." οὐ λανθάνει δέ με
καὶ ὅτι κοινῶς πάντες οἱ ἰχθύες καμασῆνες ὑπὸ Ἐμπε-
δοκλέους ἐλέχθησαν τοῦ φυσικοῦ οὕτως·

πῶς καὶ δένδρεα μακρὰ καὶ εἰνάλιοι καμασῆνες,

καὶ ὅτι ὁ τὰ Κύπρια ποιήσας ἔπη, εἴτε Κυπρίας[6] τις |
c ἐστὶν ἢ Στασῖνος ἢ ὅστις δή ποτε χαίρει ὀνομαζό-

───────────

[5] ἔπεμψεν Olson: ἔπεμπεν A
[6] Κυπρίας Olson, cf. 15.682e: Κύπριος A

───────────

[15] The incident described took place during the Chremoni-
dean War (c.267–261 BCE), and the kings in question are Ptolemy
II Philadelphus (backing Athens) and Antigonus Gonatas. De-

of bread on wooden spits as first-fruits of the victims. The name of the harbor and of the spot itself is Dinos ("Whirl-pool"). I am also aware that Phylarchus somewhere discusses large fish and the green figs sent along with them, saying that Ptolemy's general Patroclus sent these items to King Antigonus as a sort of riddle,[15] in the same way the Scythians sent Darius gifts when he was about to invade their country; because according to Herodotus (4.131.1) they sent him a bird, an arrow, and a frog.[16] Patroclus, on the other hand, according to Phylarchus in Book III of his *History* (*FGrH* 81 F 1), was sent the figs and fish mentioned above. The king was getting drunk; and when everyone was puzzled by the gifts, Antigonus laughed and told his friends that he recognized the point of the presents: "Patroclus is saying that either we control the sea or we eat figs." Nor am I unaware that all fish were referred to generically as *kamasēnes* by the scientist Empedocles (31 B 72 D–K), as follows:

and how tall trees and *kamasēnes* in the sea.

(I am) also (aware) that the author of the epic poem the *Cypria*, whether this is a certain Cyprias, or Stasinus, or

spite Patroclus' brave words, the Athenians and their allies were ultimately forced to capitulate to Macedon.

[16] *c*.512 BCE. Herodotus (4.131–2) says that a mouse was included as well, and that Gobryes (one of the Persian leaders) recognized that the intended message was: "Unless you turn into fish and fly off into the air, or into mice and burrow beneath the earth, or into frogs and jump into the marshes, you will be shot by these arrows and will not get back home."

μενος, τὴν Νέμεσιν ποιεῖ διωκομένην ὑπὸ Διὸς καὶ εἰς
ἰχθὺν μεταμορφουμένην διὰ τούτων·

> τοὺς δὲ μέτα τριτάτην Ἑλένην τέκε, θαῦμα
> βροτοῖσι·
> τήν ποτε καλλίκομος Νέμεσις φιλότητι μιγεῖσα
> Ζηνὶ θεῶν βασιλῆι τέκε κρατερῆς ὑπ’ ἀνάγκης·
> φεῦγε γὰρ οὐδ’ ἔθελεν μιχθήμεναι ἐν φιλότητι |

d
> πατρὶ Διὶ Κρονίωνι· ἐτείρετο γὰρ φρένας αἰδοῖ
> καὶ νεμέσει· κατὰ γῆν δὲ καὶ ἀτρύγετον μέλαν
> ὕδωρ
> φεῦγε, Ζεὺς δ’ ἐδίωκε—λαβεῖν δ’ ἐλιλαίετο
> θυμῷ—
> ἄλλοτε μὲν κατὰ κῦμα πολυφλοίσβοιο θαλάσσης
> ἰχθύι εἰδομένην πόντον πολὺν ἐξορόθυνων,
> ἄλλοτ’ ἀν’ Ὠκεανὸν ποταμὸν καὶ πείρατα γαίης,
> ἄλλοτ’ ἀν’ ἤπειρον πολυβώλακα· γίγνετο δ’ αἰνὰ
> θηρί, ὅσ’ ἤπειρος πολλὰ τρέφει, ὄφρα φύγοι
> νιν. |

e οἶδα δὲ καὶ τὰ περὶ τὴν ἀπόπυριν καλουμένην περὶ
τὴν Βόλβην λίμνην, περὶ ἧς Ἡγήσανδρος ἐν τοῖς
Ὑπομνήμασι φησὶν οὕτως· Ἀπολλωνίαν τὴν Χαλκιδι-

---

[17] For the disputed authorship of the *Cypria*, cf. 15.682d.
Stasinus was supposedly Homer's son-in-law, to whom, according
to some authorities, he gave the poem as his daughter's dowry
(*Cypr.* test. 1–3 Bernabé).

whatever name he prefers to be called,[17] represents Nemesis as being chased by Zeus and turning into a fish, in the following passage (*Cypr.* fr. 9 Bernabé):

> After them she bore her third child, Helen, a wonder
>   to mortal eyes.
> Fair-haired Nemesis bore her after having sex
> with Zeus, the king of the gods, under harsh
>   compulsion;
> for she tried to escape and was unwilling to have sex
> with Father Zeus, son of Cronus; because her mind
>   was oppressed by shame
> and resentment. She tried to flee over the earth and
>   the barren
> black water, but Zeus pursued her—his heart was
>   eager to catch her—
> sometimes through the waves of the much-surging
>   sea,
> stirring up the immense billows, when she took the
>   form of a fish;
> sometimes over the river Ocean and the earth's
>   edges;
> sometimes over the mainland with its rich soil. She
>   became all
> the many terrible beasts the mainland nurses, in
>   order to escape him.

I am also aware of the stories told about the so-called *apopuris*[18] near Lake Bolbe, about which Hegesander in his *Commentaries* (fr. 40, *FHG* iv.420–1) says the follow-

---

[18] Small-fry of some sort, presumably called after the fact that they were roasted and eaten directly "off the fire".

19

κὴν δύο ποταμοὶ περιρρέουσιν Ἀμμίτης καὶ Ὀλυνθια-
κός· ἐμβάλλουσι δ' ἀμφότεροι εἰς τὴν Βόλβην λίμνην.
ἐπὶ δὲ τοῦ Ὀλυνθιακοῦ μνημεῖόν ἐστιν Ὀλύνθου τοῦ
Ἡρακλέους καὶ Βόλβης υἱοῦ. κατὰ δὲ τὸν Ἀνθεστη-
ριῶνα καὶ Ἐλαφηβολιῶνα λέγουσιν οἱ ἐπιχώριοι διότι
πέμπει ἡ Βόλβη τὴν ἀπόπυριν Ὀλύνθῳ, καὶ κατὰ τὸν
f   καιρὸν τοῦτον ἀπέραντον πλῆθος ἰχθύων | ἐκ τῆς
λίμνης εἰς τὸν Ὀλυνθιακὸν ἀναβαίνει⁷ ποταμόν. ἐστὶ
δὲ βραχύς, ὥστε μόλις κρύπτειν τὸ σφυρόν· ἀλλ'
οὐδὲν ἧττον τοσοῦτον ἔρχεται πλῆθος ἰχθύων ὥστε
τοὺς περιοίκους ἅπαντας ἱκανὸν εἰς τὴν ἑαυτῶν χρείαν
συντιθέναι τάριχος. θαυμαστὸν δέ ἐστι τὸ μὴ παραλ-
λάττειν τὸ τοῦ Ὀλύνθου μνημεῖον. πρότερον μὲν οὖν
φασι τοὺς κατὰ τὴν Ἀπολλωνίαν Ἐλαφηβολιῶνος τὰ
νόμιμα συντελεῖν τοῖς τελευτήσασι, νῦν δ' Ἀνθεστη-
ριῶνος· διὰ ταύτην οὖν τὴν αἰτίαν μόνοις τούτοις τοῖς
μησὶ τοὺς ἰχθῦς τὴν ἀνάβασιν ποιεῖσθαι, ἐν οἷς τοὺς
τετελευτηκότας εἰώθασι τιμᾶν.

Καὶ ταῦτα μὲν ταύτῃ, ἄνδρες ἰχθύες· ὑμεῖς γὰρ
335   πάντα συναθροίσαντες βορὰν ἡμᾶς ‖ τοῖς ἰχθύσι
παραβεβλήκατε καὶ οὐκ ἐκείνους ἡμῖν, τοσαῦτα εἰπόντες ὅσα οὐδὲ Ἰχθύας ὁ Μεγαρικὸς φιλόσοφος οὐδ'
Ἰχθύων· ὄνομα δὲ καὶ τοῦτο κύριον, οὗ μνημονεύει
Τηλεκλείδης ἐν Ἀμφικτύοσι. δι' ὑμᾶς δὲ καὶ τῷ παιδὶ
παρακελεύσομαι κατὰ τοὺς Φερεκράτους Μυρμηκαν-
θρώπους·

⁷ ἀναβαίνει Olson: ἀναβαίνειν A

20

ing: Two rivers, the Ammites and the Olynthiacus, flow on either side of Chalcidic Apollonia; both empty into Lake Bolbe. A monument to Olynthus, the son of Heracles and Bolbe, is located on the banks of the Olynthiacus. The locals claim that in Anthesterion and Elaphebolion[19] Bolbe sends the *apopuris* to Olynthus, and during this period an enormous number of fish move upstream from the lake into the Olynthiacus River. The river is shallow, barely deep enough to cover one's ankles; nevertheless so many fish appear that all the inhabitants of the area can produce as much saltfish as they need. An astonishing fact is that the fish do not go past Olynthus' monument. In the past, the story goes, the people who live around Apollonia celebrated their rites for the dead in Elaphebolion, but nowadays they do so in Anthesterion. This is accordingly why the fish migrate upstream only during these months, when it is the locals' custom to honor their dead.

That is how matters stand, my piscine sirs:[20] although you have assembled food of every type, you have thrown us to the fish rather than the other way around, by making speeches longer than those of the Megarian philosopher Ichthyas[21] (fr. 47 Döring) or Ichthyon; this too is a personal name[22] and is mentioned by Teleclides in *Amphictyonies* (fr. 9). Because of you, I intend to order my slave, to quote Pherecrates' *Ant-People* (fr. 125):

[19] I.e. in late winter/early spring.
[20] Another allusion to the passage of Archippus' *Fish* referred to at 8.331c; cf. Archipp. fr. 28 (cited at 8.343c) for the comment that follows.   [21] The second master of the school, after its founder Eucleides (fr. 33 Döring).
[22] Both names are cognate with *ichthus* ("fish").

μηδέποτ᾽ ἰχθύν, ὦ Δευκαλίων, μηδ᾽ ἢν αἰτῶ
παραθῇς μοι.

καὶ γὰρ ἐν Δήλῳ φησὶ Σῆμος ὁ Δήλιος ἐν δευτέρῃ
Δηλιάδος ὅταν θύωσι τῇ Βριζοῖ—αὕτη δ᾽ ἐστὶν ἡ
ἐνυπνιόμαντις· βρίζειν δ᾽ οἱ ἀρχαῖοι λέγουσι τὸ κα-
θεύδειν· |

b   ἔνθα δ᾽ ἀποβρίξαντες ἐμείναμεν ἠῶ δῖαν—

ταύτῃ οὖν ὅταν θύωσιν αἱ Δηλιάδες, προσφέρουσιν
αὐτῇ σκάφας πάντων πλήρεις ἀγαθῶν πλὴν ἰχθύων
διὰ τὸ εὔχεσθαι ταύτῃ περί τε πάντων καὶ ὑπὲρ τῆς
τῶν πλοίων σωτηρίας. Χρύσιππον δ᾽, ἄνδρες φίλοι,
τὸν τῆς στοᾶς ἡγεμόνα κατὰ πολλὰ θαυμάζων ἔτι
μᾶλλον ἐπαινῶ τὸν πολυθρύλητον ἐπὶ τῇ Ὀψολογίᾳ
Ἀρχέστρατον αἰεί ποτε μετὰ Φιλαινίδος κατατάττον-
τα, εἰς ἣν ἀναφέρεται τὸ περὶ ἀφροδισίων ἀκόλαστον
c   σύγγραμμα, ὅπερ φησὶ | ποιῆσαι Αἰσχρίων ὁ Σάμιος
ἰαμβοποιὸς Πολυκράτη τὸν σοφιστὴν ἐπὶ διαβολῇ
τῆς ἀνθρώπου σωφρονεστάτης γενομένης. ἔχει δὲ
οὕτως τὰ ἰαμβεῖα·

ἐγὼ Φιλαινὶς ἡ ᾽πίβωτος ἀνθρώποις
ἐνταῦθα γήρᾳ τῷ μακρῷ κεκοίμημαι.
μή μ᾽, ὦ μάταιε ναῦτα, τὴν ἄκραν κάμπτων
χλεύην τε ποιεῦ καὶ γέλωτα καὶ λάσθην.

---

23 *PAA* 779380 (late 5th/early 4th century BCE); among his
works was a prosecution speech supposedly delivered at Socrates'

Never serve me a fish, Deucalion, even if I ask for one!

For on Delos, according to Semus of Delos in Book II of the *History of Delos* (*FGrH* 396 F 4), when they sacrifice to Brizo—this is a goddess who supplies prophecies via dreams; the ancients use *brizein* to mean "to sleep" (*Od.* 12.7):

And going to sleep (*apobrizantes*) there we awaited
    bright dawn—

when the women of Delos sacrifice to her, at any rate, they bring her bowls full of everything good except fish; because they pray to her about matters of all sorts, including the safety of their ships. Although I respect Chrysippus (xxviii fr. 5, *SVF* iii.199), the head of the Stoa, for many reasons, my friends, I commend him in particular for always putting Archestratus (test. 5 Olson–Sens), who is notorious for his *Cookbook*, in the same category as Philaenis, to whom the perverted essay on sex is attributed—although according to the iambic poet Aeschrio of Samos she was completely chaste, and the sophist Polycrates[23] wrote it to slander her. The iambs in question run as follows (*AP* 7.345 = *HE* 1–9 = *SH* 4):

I, the notorious Philaenis,
    have been laid to rest here by extended old age.
As you round the cape, flippant sailor, do not
    make me a source of mockery, laughter, or insult.

trial in 399. Aeschrio of Mytilene (Berve i #34) was a student of Aristotle and a friend of Alexander the Great; another fragment of his poetry is preserved at 7.296e–f.

οὐ γὰρ μὰ τὸν Ζῆν᾽, οὐ μὰ τοὺς κάτω κούρους, |
d οὐκ ἦν ἐς ἄνδρας μάχλος οὐδὲ δημώδης.
Πολυκράτης δὲ τὴν γενὴν Ἀθηναῖος,
λόγων τι παιπάλημα καὶ κακὴ γλῶσσα,
ἔγραψεν οἷ᾽ ἔγραψ᾽· ἐγὼ γὰρ οὐκ οἶδα.

ἀλλ᾽ οὖν ὅ γε θαυμασιώτατος Χρύσιππος ἐν τῷ πέμπτῳ Περὶ τοῦ Καλοῦ καὶ τῆς Ἡδονῆς φησι· καὶ
βιβλία τά τε Φιλαινίδος καὶ τὴν τοῦ Ἀρχεστράτου
Γαστρονομίαν καὶ δυνάμεις ἐρωτικὰς καὶ συνουσι-
αστικάς, ὁμοίως δὲ καὶ τὰς θεραπαίνας ἐμπείρους
τοιῶνδε κινήσεών τε καὶ σχημάτων καὶ περὶ τὴν
e τούτων μελέτην γινομένας. καὶ πάλιν· ἐκμανθάνειν | τ᾽
αὐτοὺς τὰ τοιαῦτα καὶ κτᾶσθαι τὰ περὶ τούτων γεγραμμένα Φιλαινίδι καὶ Ἀρχεστράτῳ καὶ τοῖς τὰ
ὅμοια γράψασιν. κἂν τῷ ἑβδόμῳ δέ φησι· καθάπερ
γὰρ οὐκ ἐκμανθάνειν τὰ Φιλαινίδος καὶ τὴν Ἀρχεστράτου Γαστρονομίαν ἔστιν ὡς φέροντά τι πρὸς τὸ
ζῆν ἄμεινον. ὑμεῖς δὲ πολλάκις τοῦ Ἀρχεστράτου
τούτου μνημονεύσαντες ἀκολασίας ἐπληρώσατε τὸ
συμπόσιον. τί γὰρ τῶν ἐπιτρῖψαι δυναμένων παρέλι-
πεν ὁ καλὸς οὗτος ἐποποιὸς καὶ μόνος ζηλώσας τὸν
f Σαρδαναπάλλου | τοῦ Ἀνακυνδαράξεω βίον, ὃν ἀδια-
νοητότερον εἶναι ⟨ἢ⟩[8] κατὰ τὴν προσηγορίαν τοῦ
πατρὸς Ἀριστοτέλης ἔφη, ἐφ᾽ οὗ τοῦ τάφου ἐπιγε-
γράφθαι φησὶ Χρύσιππος τάδε· ||

[8] add. Madvig

24

For, by Zeus and his sons in the Underworld,
I was never loose with men or a whore.
Polycrates the Athenian,
a sly talker and a vicious tongue,
wrote what he wrote; I know nothing of this.

But the admirable Chrysippus, at any rate, says in Book V
of his *On the Good and Pleasure* (xxviii fr. 5, *SVF* iii.199 =
Archestr. test. 5 Olson–Sens, continued): and Philaenis'
books and Archestratus' *Gastronomy*, and other forces
that encourage sex and partying, and likewise slave-girls
who have experience in movements and positions of this
sort and are involved in practicing them. And again: that
they learn such material by heart and acquire what has
been written on these topics by Philaenis, Archestratus,
and the authors of similar works. So too in Book VII (xxviii
fr. 5, *SVF* iii.199, continued) he says: Just as one cannot
memorize the works of Philaenis or Archestratus' *Gastronomy* on the ground that they contribute something to
living a better life. But you, by repeatedly mentioning this
Archestratus,[24] filled our party with ugly behavior. For
what possible source of ruin was omitted by this noble
epic poet, the most notorious aspirant to the life-style of
Sardanapallus[25] son of Anacyndaraxes, a man Aristotle
(fr. 5) said was even more foolish than his father's name
would lead one to expect. Chrysippus (xxviii fr. 11, *SVF*
iii.200) claims that the following was inscribed on his tomb
(= Choerilus Iasius? *SH* 335):

[24] E.g. at 7.293f, 326f–7a, 328a. For related material on Sardanapallus, see 12.529e–30c.

[25] The Greek name for the Assyrian king Ashurbanipal.

336   εὖ εἰδὼς ὅτι θνητὸς ἔφυς σὸν θυμὸν ἄεξε
       τερπόμενος θαλίῃσι· θανόντι τοι οὔτις ὄνησις.
       καὶ γὰρ ἐγὼ σποδός εἰμι, Νίνου μεγάλης
           βασιλεύσας.
       ταῦτ᾽ ἔχω ὅσσ᾽ ἔφαγον καὶ ἐφύβρισα καὶ μετ᾽
           ἔρωτος
       τέρπν᾽ ἔπαθον· τὰ δὲ πολλὰ καὶ ὄλβια κεῖνα
           λέλειπται.
       ἥδε σοφὴ βιότοιο παραίνεσις, οὐδέ ποτ᾽ αὐτῆς |
   b   λήσομαι· ἐκτήσθω δ᾽ ὁ θέλων τὸν ἀπείρονα
           χρυσόν.

   καὶ ἐπὶ τῶν Φαιάκων δὲ ὁ ποιητὴς ἔφη·

       αἰεὶ δ᾽ ἡμῖν δαίς τε φίλη κίθαρίς τε χοροί τε
       εἵματά τ᾽ ἐξημοιβὰ λοετρά τε θερμὰ καὶ εὐναί.

   καὶ ἄλλος δέ τίς φησι τῷ Σαρδαναπάλλῳ παραπλή-
   σιος, ὑποτιθέμενος καὶ οὗτος τοῖς μὴ σωφρονοῦσι
   τοιάδε·

       πᾶσιν δὲ θνητοῖς βούλομαι παραινέσαι
       τοὐφήμερον ζῆν ἡδέως· ὁ γὰρ θανών
       τὸ μηδέν ἐστι καὶ σκιὰ κατὰ χθονός· |
   c   μικροῦ δὲ βιότου ζῶντ᾽ ἐπαυρέσθαι χρεών.

   καὶ Ἄμφις δ᾽ ὁ κωμῳδιοποιὸς ἐν Ἰαλέμῳ φησί·

Keep in mind that you are mortal, and make yourself
    happy
by enjoying feasts; nothing is any use to you once you
    are dead.
For I am dust, even though I was king of great
    Ninevah.
What is mine is what I ate, and the malicious fun I
    had, and the pleasure
I got in bed, whereas my enormous, well-known
    wealth has perished.
This is wise advice for living, and I will never
forget it; let anyone who wishes acquire endless gold.

In regard to the Phaeacians as well Homer[26] said (*Od.*
8.248–9):

We always enjoy feasts, the lyre, dances,
changes of clothing, warm baths, and bed.

Another individual who resembles Sardanapallus, and who
is likewise offering advice to reckless individuals, says
something like the following (adesp. tr. fr. 95):

I would like to offer all mortals a bit of advice,
which is to enjoy their day-to-day existence; because
    a dead man's
nothing—just a shadow under the earth.
You need to enjoy the brief life you have while you're
    alive.

The comic poet Amphis as well says in *Ialemus* (fr. 21):

[26] Literally "the poet".

27

ὅστις δὲ θνητὸς γενόμενος μὴ τῷ βίῳ
ζητεῖ τι τερπνὸν προσφέρειν, τὰ δ' ἄλλ' ἐᾷ,
μάταιός ἐστιν ἔν γ' ἐμοὶ καὶ τοῖς σοφοῖς
κριταῖς ἅπασιν ἐκ θεῶν τε δυστυχής.

καὶ ἐν τῇ ἐπιγραφομένῃ δὲ Γυναικοκρατίᾳ τὰ ὅμοια
λέγει·

πῖνε, παῖζε· θνητὸς ὁ βίος, ὀλίγος οὑπὶ γῇ
   χρόνος·
ἀθάνατος ὁ θάνατός ἐστιν, ἂν ἅπαξ τις ἀποθάνῃ.

d καὶ Βακχίδας δέ τις τὸν αὐτὸν | Σαρδαναπάλλῳ ζήσας
βίον ἀποθανὼν ἐπὶ τοῦ τάφου ἐπιγεγραμμένον ἔχει·

πιέν, φαγὲν καὶ πάντα τᾷ ψυχᾷ δόμεν·
κἠγὼ γὰρ ἔστακ' ἀντὶ Βακχίδα λίθος.

Ἄλεξις δ' ἐν Ἀσωτοδιδασκάλῳ, φησὶ Σωτίων ὁ
Ἀλεξανδρεὺς ἐν τοῖς Περὶ τῶν Τίμωνος Σίλλων· ἐγὼ
γὰρ οὐκ ἀπήντησα τῷ δράματι· πλείονα τῆς μέσης
καλουμένης κωμῳδίας ἀναγνοὺς δράματα τῶν ὀκτα-
κοσίων καὶ τούτων ἐκλογὰς ποιησάμενος οὐ περιέτυ-
e χον τῷ Ἀσωτοδιδασκάλῳ, | ἀλλ' οὐδ' ἀναγραφῆς
ἀξιωθέν τινι σύνοιδα· οὔτε γὰρ Καλλίμαχος οὔτε
Ἀριστοφάνης αὐτὸ ἀνέγραψαν, ἀλλ' οὐδ' οἱ τὰς ἐν
Περγάμῳ ἀναγραφὰς ποιησάμενοι. ὁ δὲ Σωτίων φη-

Any mortal who doesn't try to add
some pleasure to his life and let everything else go
is a fool in my eyes and those of wise
judges generally, and the gods have sent him bad
    luck.

He makes similar remarks in his play entitled *Women in Power* (fr. 8):

Drink! Have fun! Life's mortal, and our time on
    earth's limited;
whereas death's immortal, once you're dead.

A certain Bacchidas, who died after living a life like Sardanapallus', also has inscribed on his tomb (*GVI* 1368):

Drink! Eat! Indulge your soul!
For I am a stone that stands here in Bacchidas'
    place.

According to Sotion of Alexandria in his *On Timo's Silloi* (fr. 1 Wehrli), Alexis in *The Instructor in Profligacy*—I never encountered the play myself; despite reading over 800 so-called Middle Comedies and compiling extracts from them, I never came upon *The Instructor in Profligacy*, and I know of no one who thought it deserved to be catalogued; because neither Callimachus nor Aristophanes[27] catalogued it, and neither did the cataloguers working in Pergamum[28]—but Sotion claims that in the play a

---

[27] Both working in the Library in Alexandria, in the first half of the 3rd and the 2nd centuries BCE, respectively.

[28] The site of another great library; cf. 1.3a with n. Most likely *The Instructor in Profligacy* (or at least the supposed excerpt from it cited by Sotion) is an ancient forgery.

σὶν ἐν τῷ δράματι Ξανθίαν τινὰ οἰκέτην πεποιῆσθαι
προτρεπόμενον ἐπὶ ἡδυπάθειαν ὁμοδούλους ἑαυτοῦ
καὶ λέγοντα·

   τί ταῦτα ληρεῖς, φληναφῶν ἄνω κάτω
   Λύκειον, Ἀκαδήμειαν, Ὠιδείου πύλας,
   λήρους σοφιστῶν; οὐδὲ ἓν τούτων καλόν.
   πίνωμεν, ἐμπίνωμεν, ὦ Σίκων, ⟨Σίκων⟩, |

f   χαίρωμεν, ἕως ἔνεστι τὴν ψυχὴν τρέφειν.
   τύρβαζε, Μάνη· γαστρὸς οὐδὲν ἥδιον.
   αὕτη πατήρ σοι καὶ πάλιν μήτηρ μόνη,
   ἀρεταὶ δὲ πρεσβεῖαί τε καὶ στρατηγίαι
   κόμποι κενοὶ ψοφοῦσιν ἀντ᾽ ὀνειράτων.
   ψύξει σε δαίμων τῷ πεπρωμένῳ χρόνῳ·
   ἕξεις δ᾽ ὅσ᾽ ἂν φάγῃς τε καὶ πίῃς μόνα,
   σποδὸς δὲ τἆλλα, Περικλέης, Κόδρος, Κίμων.

κρεῖττον δ᾽ ἂν εἶχε, φησὶν ὁ Χρύσιππος, εἰ μετελήφθη
τὰ ἐπὶ τοῦ Σαρδαναπάλλου οὕτως· ‖

337   εὖ εἰδὼς ὅτι θνητὸς ἔφυς σὺν θυμὸν ἄεξε,
   τερπόμενος μύθοισι· φαγόντι σοι οὔτις ὄνησις.

---

[29] The Lyceum and the Academy were the locations of the
schools of Aristotle and Plato, respectively. But the Odeion (a
multi-columned, roofed building used for concerts and musical
contests) is not known to have been used for philosophical instruction before Chrysippus (D.L. 7.184), who arrived in Athens
around 260 BCE and became head of the Stoa in 232, a fact that
counts against assigning this fragment to Alexis (d. c.275)

[30] Pericles (PAA 772645) and Cimon (PAA 569795) were

slave named Xanthias is represented as encouraging his
fellow slaves to live luxuriously and as saying (Alex. fr. 25):

> Why do you talk like this, mixing up
> the Lyceum, the Academy, and the gates of the
>   Odeion,[29]
> sophists' nonsense? None of this is any good.
> Let's drink! Let's really drink, Sicon, Sicon!
> Let's enjoy ourselves as long as we can stay happy!
> Have a wild time, Manes! Nothing produces more
>   pleasure than the belly.
> It's your only father, and your only mother too,
> whereas personal distinctions—I mean
>   ambassadorships and generalships—
> are empty boasts that ring as hollow as dreams.
> Some god will bring about your death at the fated
>   time.
> All you'll have is what you eat and drink;
> everything else—Pericles, Codrus, Cimon[30]—it's
>   dust!

It would have been better, says Chrysippus (xxviii fr. 11,
SVF iii.200, continued), if Sardanapallus' epitaph had
been emended to the following:[31]

> Keep in mind that you are mortal, and make yourself
>   happy
> by taking pleasure in conversation; nothing is any use
>   to you after you eat it.

prominent 5th-century Athenian generals and politicians, while
the mythical Codrus was one of the city's last kings.

[31] Reworking the opening section of the text quoted at 8.335f–
6b (also from Chrysippus).

καὶ γὰρ ἐγὼ ῥάκος εἰμί, φαγὼν ὡς πλεῖστα καὶ
 ἡσθείς.
ταῦτ' ἔχω ὅσσ' ἔμαθον καὶ ἐφρόντισα καὶ μετὰ
 τούτων
ἔσθλ' ἔπαθον· τὰ δὲ λοιπὰ καὶ ἡδέα πάντα
 λέλειπται.

παγκάλως δὲ καὶ ὁ Τίμων ἔφη·

πάντων μὲν πρώτιστα κακῶν ἐπιθυμίη ἐστί.

Κλέαρχος δὲ ἐν τοῖς Περὶ Παροιμιῶν καὶ διδάσκα-
b λον | τοῦ Ἀρχεστράτου γενέσθαι φησὶν Τερψίωνα, ὃν
καὶ πρῶτον Γαστρολογίαν γράψαντα διακελεύεσθαι
τοῖς μαθηταῖς τίνων ἀφεκτέον. ἀπεσχεδιακέναι τε τὸν
Τερψίωνα καὶ περὶ τῆς χελώνης τάδε·

ἢ κρῆ χελώνης χρὴ φαγεῖν ἢ μὴ φαγεῖν.

ἄλλοι δ' οὕτως λέγουσιν·

ἢ δεῖ χελώνης κρέα φαγεῖν ἢ μὴ φαγεῖν.

πόθεν δὲ ὑμῖν, ὦ σοφώτατοι, ἐπῆλθε καὶ ὁ ὀψολόγος
Δωρίων ὡς καὶ συγγραφεύς τις γενόμενος; ὃν ἐγὼ
κρουματοποιὸν οἶδα ὀνομαζόμενον καὶ φίλιχθυν, συγ-
c γραφέα δὲ οὔ. ὡς μὲν οὖν κρουματοποιοῦ | μνημονεύει
Μάχων ὁ κωμῳδιοποιὸς οὕτως·

---

[32] Terpsion is otherwise unknown, but is perhaps to be identified with the Terpsicles whose On Sex Athenaeus cites at 7.325d;
9.391e–f; both fragments are gastronomic in character. Whether

For I am a tattered bit of nothing, even though I ate
      and enjoyed myself as much as I could.
What is mine is what I learned and thought, and the
      excellent
experiences that came with this, whereas everything
      else, pleasant though it all was, has perished.

Timo (*SH* 845) was absolutely right when he said:

Of all evils, desire is the foremost.

Clearchus in his *On Proverbs* (fr. 78 Wehrli = Archestr. test. 3 Olson–Sens) says that Archestratus was taught by Terpsion, the first person to write a *Gastrology* and to give his pupils instructions about which foods to avoid.[32] He also claims that Terpsion improvised the following verse about the tortoise:

Either it's meet to eat tortoise meat or it's not meet.

Others quote it as follows:

You should either eat tortoise meat or not eat it.

But how, my enormously wise friends, did the fish-expert Dorion get a reputation among you for being a prose-author? I am aware that he is referred to as a musician[33] and as someone who loved seafood, but not as a prose-author. The comic poet Macho (53–63 Gow) refers to him as a musician, as follows:

Terpsion/Terpsicles was actually Archestratus' teacher is impossible to say, but doubt is called for.

[33] Stephanis #805; cf. 10.435b–c with n. The alleged confusion is with the author of the *On Fish* cited repeatedly by Athenaeus' characters (e.g. 7.282c, 330a).

ὁ κρουματοποιὸς Δωρίων ποτ᾽ εἰς Μυλῶν
ἐλθὼν κατάλυσιν οὐδαμοῦ μισθωσίμην
δυνάμενος εὑρεῖν, ἐν τεμένει καθίσας τινί
ὃ πρὸ τῶν πυλῶν ἦν κατὰ τύχην ἱδρυμένον
ἰδών τ᾽ ἐκεῖ θύοντα τὸν νεωκόρον,
"πρὸς τῆς Ἀθηνᾶς καὶ θεῶν, τίνος, φράσον,
ἐστὶν ὁ νεώς, βέλτιστε," φησίν, "οὑτοσί;"
ὁ δ᾽ εἶπεν αὐτῷ, "Ζηνοποσειδῶνος, ξένε." |

d   ὁ Δωρίων δέ, "πῶς ἂν οὖν ἐνταῦθ᾽," ἔφη,
"δύναιτο καταγωγεῖον ἐξευρεῖν τις, οὗ
καὶ τοὺς θεοὺς φάσκουσιν οἰκεῖν σύνδυο;"

Λυγκεὺς δ᾽ ὁ Σάμιος, ὁ Θεοφράστου μὲν μαθητής,
Δούριδος δὲ ἀδελφὸς τοῦ τὰς Ἱστορίας γράψαντος καὶ
τυραννήσαντος τῆς πατρίδος, ἐν τοῖς Ἀποφθέγμασιν·
Δωρίωνι τῷ αὐλητῇ φάσκοντός τινος ἀγαθὸν ἰχθὺν
εἶναι βατίδα, "ὥσπερ ἂν εἴ τις", ἔφη, "ἐφθὸν τρίβωνα
ἐσθίοι." ἐπαινοῦντος δ᾽ ἄλλου τὰ τῶν θύννων ὑπογάστρια, "καὶ μάλα," ἔφη· "δεῖ μέντοι γε ἐσθίειν
e   αὐτά, | ὥσπερ ἐγὼ ἐσθίω." εἰπόντος δέ, "πῶς;",
"ἡδέως", ἔφη. τοὺς δὲ καράβους ἔφη τρία ἔχειν, δια-
τριβὴν καὶ εὐωχίαν καὶ θεωρίαν. ἐν Κύπρῳ δὲ παρὰ
Νικοκρέοντι δειπνῶν ἐπήνεσε ποτήριόν τι. καὶ ὁ Νικο-
κρέων ἔφη· "ἐὰν βούλῃ, ὁ αὐτὸς τεχνίτης ποιήσει σοι
ἕτερον." "σοί γε," ἔφη, "ἐμοὶ δὲ τοῦτο δός," οὐκ ἀνοή-

---

34 "Zeus-Poseidon".
35 Sc. because they must be shelled before being eaten.

34

The musician Dorion visited Mylae
once and was unable to find a room
for rent anywhere. He sat down in a sacred precinct
that happened to be located before the gates,
and when he saw the person in charge of the temple
        making a sacrifice there,
he said: "By Athena and the other gods—tell me,
sir: whose temple is this?"
The man said to him: "It belongs to Zenoposeidon[34],
        stranger."
And Dorion said: "How could anyone
find a place to stay here, where
they say that even the gods share a house?"

Lynceus of Samos, who was Theophrastus' student and the
brother of the Duris (*FGrH* 76 T 2) who wrote the *History*
and was tyrant of his native country, in his *Witty Remarks*
(fr. 32 Dalby): When someone observed to the pipe-player
Dorion that the skate was a nice fish, he said: "Yeah—it's
like eating a stewed cloak." When someone else spoke
highly of tuna underbellies, he said: "Absolutely; but you
have to eat them like I do." When the other man asked:
"How's that?", he said: "With great pleasure." He claimed
that crayfish have three virtues: they occupy your time,[35]
provide a fine meal, and are nice to look at. He was having
dinner on Cyprus with Nicocreon[36] and expressed his ad-
miration for a cup. Nicocreon said: "If you like, the same
craftsman will make one for you." Dorion responded: "He
can make it for *you*; give this one to me!" This was quite a

36 Berve i #568; he became king of Cyprian Salamis in 332/1
BCE and was later supported by Ptolemy. Cf. 8.349e n.

τως γε τοῦτο φήσας ὁ αὐλητής· λόγος γὰρ παλαιὸς ὡς
ὅτι·

f

    ἀνδρὶ μὲν αὐλητῆρι θεοὶ νόον οὐκ ἐνέφυσαν, |
    ἀλλ᾽ ἅμα τῷ φυσῆν χὠ νόος ἐκπέταται.

Ἡγήσανδρος δ᾽ ἐν τοῖς Ὑπομνήμασι τάδε φησὶ περὶ
αὐτοῦ· Δωρίων ὁ ὀψοφάγος τοῦ παιδὸς οὐκ ἀγοράσαν-
τος ἰχθῦς μαστιγῶν αὐτὸν ἐκέλευεν τῶν ἀρίστων
ἰχθύων ὀνόματα λέγειν. τοῦ δὲ παιδὸς ὀρφὸν καὶ
338 γλαυκίσκον || καὶ γόγγρον καὶ τοιούτους ἑτέρους
καταριθμοῦντος, "ἰχθύων σε", φησίν, "ἐκέλευον ὀνόματα λέγειν, οὐ θεῶν." ὁ αὐτὸς Δωρίων καταγελῶν τοῦ
ἐν τῷ Τιμοθέου Ναυτίλῳ χειμῶνος ἔφασκεν ἐν κακ-
κάβᾳ ζεούσᾳ μείζονα ἑωρακέναι χειμῶνα. Ἀριστόδημος δὲ ἐν δευτέρῳ Γελοίων Ἀπομνημονευμάτων
φησί· Δωρίωνος τοῦ κρουματοποιοῦ κυλλόποδος ὄντος
ἀπώλετο ἐν συμποσίῳ τοῦ χωλοῦ ποδὸς τὸ βλαυτίον.
καὶ ὅς, "οὐθέν", ἔφη, "πλεῖον καταράσομαι τῷ κλέψαν-
b τι ἢ ἁρμόσαι αὐτῷ τὸ | σανδάλιον." ὅτι δ᾽ ἦν ὁ Δωρίων
οὗτος ἐπὶ ὀψοφαγίᾳ διαβόητος φανερὸν ἐξ ὧν λέγει
Μνησίμαχος ὁ κωμῳδιοποιὸς ἐν Φιλίππῳ δράματι·

    οὐκ ἀλλὰ καὶ τῆς νυκτός ἐστι Δωρίων
    ἔνδον παρ᾽ ἡμῖν λοπαδοφυσητής.

οἶδα δὲ καὶ ἃ ὁ Ἑρμιονεὺς Λᾶσος ἔπαιξε περὶ ἰχθύων,
ἅπερ Χαμαιλέων ἀνέγραψεν ὁ Ἡρακλεώτης ἐν τῷ περὶ
αὐτοῦ τοῦ Λάσου συγγράμματι λέγων ὧδε· τὸν Λᾶσόν

clever remark by the pipe-player, despite the ancient saying (anon. *FGE* 1550–1 = *SH* 1010):

> The gods gave pipe-players no sense;
> > when they blow into their instrument, their brains
> > fly out.

Hegesander in his *Commentaries* (fr. 14, *FHG* iv.416) has the following to say about him: When his slave failed to purchase any fish, the glutton Dorion whipped him and simultaneously ordered him to name the best varieties. The slave listed sea-perch, *glaukiskos*, conger eel, and the like; and Dorion said: "I asked you to give me the names of *fish*, not gods!" The same Dorion ridiculed the storm in Timotheus' *The Sailor* (*PMG* 785)[37] by claiming to have seen a bigger storm in a pot of boiling water. Aristodemus says in Book II of the *Humorous Memoirs* (fr. 8, *FHG* iii.310): The musician Dorion had a club-foot, and when the slipper for his bad foot disappeared at a party, he said: "The extent of my curse on the thief is going to be that I hope my shoe fits him." That this Dorion was a notorious glutton is apparent from the comic poet Mnesimachus' remarks in his play *Philip* (fr. 10):

> No; even at night we've got Dorion
> the casserole-dish-player in our house with us.

I am also aware of the jokes Lasus of Hermione made about fish, and which Chamaeleon of Heraclea (fr. 30 Wehrli) recorded in his treatise on Lasus himself, in which he says the following: Lasus, he reports, used to refer to

[37] The poem is otherwise lost.

φησι τὸν ὠμὸν ἰχθὺν ὀπτὸν εἶναι φάσκειν. θαυμα-
ζόντων δὲ πολλῶν ἐπιχειρεῖν λέγοντα ὡς ὃ ἔστιν |
c ἀκοῦσαι τοῦτό ἐστιν ἀκουστὸν καὶ ὃ ἔστιν νοῆσαι
τοῦτό ἐστιν νοητόν· ὡσαύτως οὖν καὶ ὃ ἔστιν ἰδεῖν
τοῦτ᾽ εἶναι ὀπτόν· ὥστ᾽ ἐπειδὴ τὸν ἰχθὺν ἦν ἰδεῖν,
ὀπτὸν αὐτὸν εἶναι. καὶ παίζων δέ ποτε ἰχθὺν παρά
τινος τῶν ἁλιέων ὑφείλετο καὶ λαβὼν ἔδωκέ τινι τῶν
παρεστώτων. ὁρκίζοντος δὲ ὤμοσεν μήτ᾽ αὐτὸς ἔχειν
τὸν ἰχθὺν μήτ᾽ ἄλλῳ συνειδέναι λαβόντι, διὰ τὸ λαβεῖν μὲν αὐτόν, ἔχειν δὲ ἕτερον, ὃν ἐδίδαξεν ἀπομόσαι
πάλιν ὅτι οὔτ᾽ αὐτὸς ἔλαβεν οὔτ᾽ ἄλλον ἔχοντα οἶδεν·
d εἰλήφει μὲν γὰρ ὁ Λᾶσος, εἶχεν δὲ αὐτός. τοιαῦτα | δὲ
καὶ Ἐπίχαρμος παίζει, ὥσπερ ἐν Λόγῳ καὶ Λογίνᾳ·

(Α.) ὁ Ζεύς μ᾽ ἐκάλεσε, Πέλοπί γ᾽ ἔρανον ἱστιῶν.
(Β.) ἦ παμπόνηρον ὄψον, ὦ ᾽τάν, ὁ γέρανος.
(Α.) ἀλλ᾽ οὔτι γέρανον, ἀλλ᾽ ἔρανόν <γα> τοι
λέγω.

Ἄλεξις δ᾽ ἐν Δημητρίῳ Φαύλλόν τινα κωμῳδεῖ ὡς
φίλιχθυν ἐν τούτοις·

πρότερον μὲν εἰ πνεύσειε βορρᾶς ἢ νότος
ἐν τῇ θαλάττῃ λαμπρός, ἰχθῦς οὐκ ἐνῆν
οὐδενὶ φαγεῖν· νυνὶ δὲ πρὸς τοῖς πνεύμασι
τούτοις Φαύλλος προσγέγονε χειμὼν τρίτος. |

---

38 The adjective would normally be taken to mean "roasted".

a raw fish as *optos*.[38] When many people repeatedly expressed puzzlement, he attempted to explain that what one can hear (*estin akousai*) is audible (*akoustos*); what one can imagine (*estin noēsai*) is conceivable (*noētos*); and so too, therefore, what one can see (*estin idein*)[39] is *optos*— and since the fish could be seen, it was accordingly *optos*! So too, he once stole a fish from a fisherman as a joke, and after he took it, he handed it to one of the bystanders. When the fisherman demanded that he swear to his innocence, he took an oath that he did not have the fish himself and was not aware that anyone else had taken it—because he had taken it himself, but someone else was in possession of it—and he coached the other man to swear for his part that he had not taken it himself and was unaware of anyone else having it—because Lasus had taken it, and he himself was in possession of it. Epicharmus also makes jokes of this sort, as for example in *Male and Female Logos* (fr. 76):

> (A.) Zeus was giving a pot-luck dinner (*g' eranon*) for
>   Pelops, and he invited me.
> (B.) A crane (*geranon*)—that's quite a nasty dish, sir!
> (A.) I'm talking about a pot-luck dinner, not a crane!

Alexis in *Demetrius* (fr. 47) mocks a certain Phayllus for his love of fish in the following passage:

> Previously, if a brisk north or south wind
> blew in the sea, no one had any
> fish to eat. But nowadays Phayllus has been added
> to these winds as storm number three.

[39] Several of the principal parts of *idein* are formed from the root *op-*, hence the pun. Cf. 3.97a.

e ἐπὰν γὰρ ἐκνεφίας καταιγίσας τύχῃ
 ἐς τὴν ἀγοράν, τοὖψον πριάμενος οἴχεται
 φέρων ἅπαν τὸ ληφθέν· ὥστε γίγνεται
 ἐν τοῖς λαχάνοις τὸ λοιπὸν ἡμῖν ἡ μάχη.

 Ἀντιφάνης δ᾽ ἐν Ἁλιευομένῃ φιληδοῦντάς τινας καταλέγων ἰχθύσιν φησί·

  τὰς σηπίας δὸς πρῶτον. Ἡράκλεις ἄναξ,
  ἅπαντα τεθολώκασιν. οὐ βαλεῖς πάλιν
  εἰς τὴν θάλατταν καὶ πλυνεῖς; μὴ φῶσί σε
  † Δωριάς, ἀλλ᾽ ὀνε † σηπίας εἰληφέναι. |
f   τὸν κάραβον δὲ τόνδε πρὸς τὰς μαινίδας
  ἀπόδος· παχύς γε νὴ Δί᾽. ὦ Ζεῦ, τίς ποτε,
  ὦ Καλλιμέδων, σὲ κατέδετ᾽ ἄρτι τῶν φίλων;
  οὐδεὶς ὃς ἂν μὴ κατατιθῇ τὰς συμβολάς.
  ὑμᾶς δ᾽ ἔταξα δεῦρο πρὸς τὰ δεξιά,
  τρίγλας, ἔδεσμα τοῦ καλοῦ Καλλισθένους·
  κατεσθίει γοῦν ἐπὶ μιᾷ τὴν οὐσίαν.
  καὶ τὸν Σινώπης γόγγρον ἤδη παχυτέρας ‖
339   ἔχοντ᾽ ἀκάνθας τουτονὶ τίς λήψεται
  πρῶτος προσελθών; Μισγόλας γὰρ οὐ πάνυ

---

40 A fish-monger (presumably sorting the eponymous fisher-woman's catch for sale) is speaking.

41 For Callimedon "the Crayfish" (*PAA* 558185), see 3.104d–e; 6.242d; 8.339e–40e, 364e.   42 A prominent Athenian politician of the second half of the 4th century BCE (*PAA* 559815); *Triglē* (literally "red mullet") was presumably the name of a courtesan on whom he was spending large amounts of money.

40

Because whenever he roars into the marketplace
like a hurricane, he buys the fish and disappears,
carrying off everything he grabbed. As a result,
we're left to fight it out in the vegetable-market.

Antiphanes in *The Fisher-Woman* (fr. 27) lists some people
who are fond of fish, saying:[40]

First give me the cuttlefish. Lord Heracles—
they're all covered with ink! Throw 'em back
in the sea and wash 'em off! Otherwise people might
          say you've
caught † Doric [corrupt] † cuttlefish.
Hand me this crayfish, along with
the sprats. It's a fat one, by Zeus! Zeus! Which
of your friends, Callimedon,[41] is going to gulp you
          down any minute now?
No one who doesn't contribute his share of the
          dinner expenses!
I stationed you here on the right,
red mullets, as the noble Callisthenes'[42] favorite food;
he's spending everything he's got, at any rate, on just
          one of you!
As for this conger eel here now, that's got spines
sturdier than Sinope's[43]—who'll be the first
to step up and take it? Because Misgolas[44] doesn't eat

[43] A courtesan also mentioned at e.g. Anaxil. fr. 22.12 (preserved at 13.558b).

[44] A prominent late 4th-century Athenian (*PAA* 654265; also mentioned in a number of comic fragments preserved at 8.339a–c) discussed below (where his father's name and deme are also given).

τούτων ἐδεστής. ἀλλὰ κίθαρος οὑτοσί,
ὃν ἂν ἴδῃ τὰς χεῖρας οὐκ ἀφέξεται.
καὶ μὴν ἀληθῶς τοῖς κιθαρῳδοῖς ὡς σφόδρα
ἅπασιν οὗτος ἐπιπεφυκὼς λανθάνει.
ἀνδρῶν δ' ἄριστον Κωβιὸν πηδῶντ' ἔτι
πρὸς Πυθιονίκην τὴν καλὴν πέμψαι με δεῖ· |
b   ἁδρὸς γάρ ἐστιν. ἀλλ' ὅμως οὐ γεύσεται·
ἐπὶ τὸ τάριχός ἐστιν ὡρμηκυῖα γάρ.
ἀφύας δὲ λεπτὰς τάσδε καὶ τὴν τρυγόνα
χωρὶς Θεανοῖ δεῦρ' ἔθηκ' ἀντιρρόπους.

πιθανώτατα ἐν τούτοις ὁ Ἀντιφάνης καὶ τὸν Μισγό-
λαν κεκωμῴδηκεν ὡς ἐσπουδακότα περὶ κιθαρῳδοὺς
καὶ κιθαριστὰς ὡραίους. φησὶ γὰρ καὶ ὁ ῥήτωρ
Αἰσχίνης ἐν τῷ Κατὰ Τιμάρχου λόγῳ περὶ αὐτοῦ
τάδε· Μισγόλας ἐστὶν Ναυκράτους, ἄνδρες Ἀθηναῖοι,
Κολλυτεύς, ἀνὴρ τὰ μὲν ἄλλα καλὸς καὶ ἀγαθός, καὶ
c   οὐδαμῇ ἄν τις αὐτὸν μέμψαιτο, περὶ | δὲ τὸ πρᾶγμα
τοῦτο δαιμονίως ἐσπουδακὼς καὶ ἀεί τινας εἰωθὼς
ἔχειν περὶ αὐτὸν κιθαρῳδοὺς ἢ κιθαριστάς. ταυτὶ δὲ
λέγω οὐ τοῦ φορτικοῦ ἕνεκα, ἀλλ' ἵνα γνωρίσητε
αὐτὸν ὅστις ἐστίν. καὶ Τιμοκλῆς δ' ἐν Σαπφοῖ φησιν·

---

[45] "Goby" (*PAA* 588990); also mentioned in Alex. frr. 102.4
(preserved at 4.134d); 173.2 (preserved at 6.242d). See 8.339e.

[46] A courtesan (*PAA* 793690) mentioned also in the comic
fragments quoted below and at 13.567e–f, 595c–d, as well as by
the historian Theopompus in passages preserved at 13.586c,

these at all! But here's a *kitharos*;
if he sees *this*, he won't keep his hands off it!
The fact is, no one realizes how much time
this guy actually spends with all the citharodes!
I've got to send the distinguished Cobius[45] off
to the lovely Pythionice[46] while he's still flopping
    around;
because he's a fat one.[47] But she won't taste him
    anyway;
she's after saltfish.
As for these tiny small-fry and the sting-ray, they're
the same weight as Theano[48], so I've set them aside
    here for her.

Antiphanes is mocking Misgolas in a very convincing fashion for his interest in handsome young citharodes and *cithara*-players. Because the orator Aeschines in his speech *Against Timarchus* (1.41) says the following about him: Misgolas son of Naucrates of the deme Collyte, men of Athens, is an excellent person in other respects, and no one would criticize him for anything. But he's oddly enthusiastic about this business, and he makes it a habit to constantly surround himself with citharodes and *cithara*-players. I'm telling you this not to be vulgar, but so that you understand what he's like. Timocles as well says in *Sappho* (fr. 32):

594d–5d (associated with Harpalus). For her supposed love of saltfish, see 8.339c–d.

    47 I.e. "rich".

    48 A courtesan (*PAA* 501887) also mentioned in Anaxil. fr. 22.20–1 (preserved at 13.558c).

43

ὁ Μισγόλας οὐ προσιέναι σοι φαίνεται
ἀνθοῦσι τοῖς νέοισιν ἠρεθισμένος.

Ἄλεξις δ' ἐν Ἀγωνίδι ἢ Ἱππίσκῳ·

ὦ μῆτερ, ἱκετεύω σε, μὴ 'πίσειέ μοι
τὸν Μισγόλαν· οὐ γὰρ κιθαρῳδός εἰμ' ἐγώ.

Πυθιονίκην δέ φησι φιληδεῖν ταρίχῳ, ἐπεὶ ἐραστὰς |
d εἶχε τοὺς Χαιρεφίλου τοῦ ταριχοπώλου υἱούς, ὡς
Τιμοκλῆς ἐν Ἰκαρίοις φησίν· † Ἄνυτος ὁ παχὺς πρὸς
Πυθιονίκην ὅταν ἐλθὼν φάγῃ τι. καλεῖ γὰρ αὐτόν, ὥς
φασιν, ὁπόταν Χαιρεφίλου τοὺς δύο σκόμβρους ξε-
νίσῃ μεγάλους ἡδομένη. † καὶ πάλιν·

ἡ Πυθιονίκη δ' ἀσμένως σε δέξεται,
καί σου κατέδεται τυχὸν ἴσως ἃ νῦν ἔχεις
λαβὼν παρ' ἡμῶν δῶρ'· ἄπληστός ἐστι γάρ. |
e ὅμως δὲ δοῦναί σοι κέλευσον σαργάνας
αὐτήν· ταρίχους εὐπόρως γὰρ τυγχάνει
ἔχουσα καὶ σύνεστι σαπέρδαις δυσίν,
καὶ ταῦτ' ἀνάλτοις καὶ πλατυρρύγχοις τισί.

πρὸ τούτων δ' ἦν ἐραστὴς αὐτῆς Κωβιός τις ὄνομα.
περὶ δὲ Καλλιμέδοντος τοῦ Καράβου ὅτι καὶ φίλιχθυς

---

49 PA 15187; cf. 3.119f.

50 Athenaeus refers to the play as *Icarians* again at 8.342a (as
does Didymus when he cites fr. 19), but calls it *Icarian Satyrs* at
9.407f.

51 PAA 139455; probably to be identified with the wealthy

Misgolas doesn't seem to be approaching you,
even though he gets excited by handsome boys.

Alexis in *Agonis or The Brooch* (fr. 3):

Please, Mother—don't sic Misgolas
on me! I'm not a citharode.

As for Pythionice, he claims that she has a taste for salt-fish because the sons of the saltfish-dealer Chaerephilus[49] were her lovers, as Timocles says in *Icarians*[50] (fr. 15, un-metrical): † whenever the fat Anytus[51] visits Pythionice and eats something. Because people say she invites him whenever she entertains the two big mackerel of Chaere-philus she's so fond of. † Again (fr. 16):

Pythionice'll be happy to have you as a guest,
and she'll probably gobble up the gifts
you got from us; since she's insatiable.
All the same, tell her to give you
some baskets; because she's got lots of
saltfish and spends her time with a pair of
     saperdai[52]—
and unsalted ones with broad snouts at that!

Before them, her lover was someone named Cobius[53]. As for the fact that Callimedon the Crayfish loved fish and was

Anytus of the deme Euonymon (*PAA* 139465), and thus most likely a descendant of the man by the same rare name who prose-cuted Socrates (*PAA* 139460); cf. J. K. Davies, *Athenian Proper-tied Families 600–300* B.C. (Oxford, 1971) 40–1.
   [52] An unidentified fish also described as raw material for saltfish by Archestratus (fr. 39.3–4 Olson–Sens = *SH* 169.3–4, pre-served at 3.116f–17a).   [53] See 8.339a with n.

f ἦν καὶ διάστροφος τοὺς ὀφθαλμούς, | Τιμοκλῆς ἐν
Πολυπράγμονι·

        εἶθ' ὁ Καλλιμέδων ἄφνω
ὁ Κάραβος προσῆλθεν. ἐμβλέπων δ' ἐμοί,
ὡς γοῦν ἐδόκει, πρὸς ἕτερον ἄνθρωπόν τινα
ἐλάλει· συνιεὶς δ' οὐδὲν εἰκότως ἐγὼ

340   ὧν ἔλεγεν ἐπένευον διακενῆς. || τῷ δ' ἄρα
βλέπουσι χωρὶς καὶ δοκοῦσιν αἱ κόραι.

Ἄλεξις δ' ἐν Κρατείᾳ ἢ Φαρμακοπώλῃ·

   (Α.) τῷ Καλλιμέδοντι γὰρ θεραπεύω τὰς κόρας
ἤδη τετάρτην ἡμέραν. (Β.) ἦσαν κόραι
θυγατέρες αὐτῷ; (Α.) τὰς μὲν οὖν τῶν ὀμμάτων,
ἃς οὐδ' ὁ Μελάμπους, ὃς μόνος τὰς Προιτίδας |

b   ἔπαυσε μαινομένας, καταστήσειεν ἄν.

ὁμοίως αὐτὸν σκώπτει κἀν τοῖς ἐπιγραφομένοις Συν-
τρέχουσιν. εἰς δὲ ὀψοφαγίαν ἐν μὲν Φαίδωνι ἢ Φαι-
δρίᾳ οὕτως·

   (Α.) ἀγορανομήσεις, ἂν θεοὶ θέλωσι, σύ,
ἵνα Καλλιμέδοντ' εἰς τοὔψον, εἰ φιλεῖς ἐμέ,
παύσῃς καταιγίζοντα δι' ὅλης ἡμέρας.
(Β.) ἔργον τυράννων, οὐκ ἀγορανόμων λέγεις.
μάχιμος γὰρ ἀνήρ, χρήσιμος δὲ τῇ πόλει. |

---

[54] Proetus was king of Argos, and paid the seer Melampus a

cross-eyed, Timocles (says) in *The Busybody* (fr. 29):

> Then Callimedon the Crayfish
> abruptly arrived. He appeared to be
> looking at me, but he was talking to
> someone else. Naturally I didn't understand
> a word he was saying; but I kept nodding my head
>   vacantly. His eyes (*korai*)
> look in a different direction than they seem to.

Alexis in *Crateia or The Pharmacist* (fr. 117):

> (A.) I've been looking after Callimedon's *korai*
> for three days now. (B.) You mean he's got
> daughters (*korai*)? (A.) No—the *korai* of his eyes.
> Not even Melampus, the only person who could cure
> Proetus' daughters of their madness,[54] could fix them.

He also makes fun of him in a similar way in his play entitled *Men Who Agree* (fr. 218). But he attacks his gluttony in *Phaedo or Phaedrias* (fr. 249), as follows:

> (A.) If the gods permit, you'll be a market-official,
> so you can prove you're my friend, by stopping
>   Callimedon
> from roaring through the fish-market all day long like
>   a hurricane.
> (B.) That's a job for a tyrant, not a market-official,
>   you're talking about;
> the man's a fighter—but useful to the city.

share of his kingdom to cure his daughters and the other Argive women of madness sent by Hera; cf. Hes. frr. 270–9; Pherecyd. *FGrH* 3 F 114; Bacch. 11.43–112; Hdt. 9.34.

c τὰ αὐτὰ ἰαμβεῖα φέρεται κἂν τῇ ἐπιγραφομένῃ Εἰς τὸ
Φρέαρ. ἐν δὲ Μανδραγοριζομένῃ·

       εἴ τινας μᾶλλον φιλῶ
ξένους ἑτέρους ὑμῶν, γενοίμην ἔγχελυς,
ἵνα Καλλιμέδων ὁ Κάραβος πρίαιτό με.

ἐν δὲ Κρατείᾳ·

καὶ Καλλιμέδων μετ᾽ Ὀρφέως ὁ Κάραβος.

Ἀντιφάνης δ᾽ ἐν Γοργύθῳ·

ἧττόν τ᾽ ἀποσταίην ἂν ὧν προειλόμην
ἢ Καλλιμέδων γλαύκου πρόοιτ᾽ ἂν κρανίον. |

d Εὔβουλος δ᾽ ἐν Ἀνασῳζομένοις·

ἕταιροι δὲ † θεοῖσι † συμπεπλεγμένοι
μετὰ Καράβου σύνεισιν, ὃς μόνος βροτῶν
δύναται καταπιεῖν ἐκ ζεόντων λοπαδίων
ἄθρους τεμαχίτας, ὥστ᾽ ἐνεῖναι μηδὲ ἕν.

Θεόφιλος δ᾽ ἐν Ἰατρῷ ἅμα σκώπτων αὐτοῦ καὶ τὸ ἐν
λόγοις ψυχρόν·

πᾶς δὲ φιλοτίμως πρὸς αὐτὸν τῶν νεανίσκων
      ⟨ . . . ⟩
⟨   . . .   ⟩ ἐγχέλειον παρατέθεικε τῷ πατρί.
e "τευθὶς ἦν χρηστή, πατρίδιον. πῶς ἔχεις | πρὸς
    κάραβον;"

BOOK VIII

The same lines appear in the play entitled *Into the Well* (fr. 87). And in *The Woman Who Ate Mandrake* (fr. 149):

> If I love any other foreigners
> more than you, may I turn into an eel—
> and may Callimedon the Crayfish buy me!

In *Crateia*[55] (fr. 118):

> and Callimedon the Crayfish, along with Orpheus.

Antiphanes in *Gorgythus* (fr. 77):

> I'd no more abandon the people I chose
> than Callimedon would give up a *glaukos*-head.

Eubulus in *Men Who Were Trying to Get Home Safe* (fr. 8):

> Comrades entangled with † gods †
> are accompanying me, along with Crayfish, the only
>   mortal
> capable of gulping down whole slabs of fish
> out of boiling-hot casserole-dishes, leaving them
>   empty.

Theophilus in *The Physician* (fr. 4) simultaneously makes fun of him for the stiffness[56] of his language:

> All the young men are trying to imitate him . . .
> . . . He's served his father an eel.
> "The squid was excellent, Dad. How do you feel
>   about the crayfish?"

[55] More often referred to as *Crateia or The Pharmacist* (e.g. 8.340a).
[56] Literally "frigidity", a conventional term of aesthetic disapprobation; see Austin–Olson on Ar. *Th.* 168–70.

"ψυχρός ἐστιν, ἄπαγε", φησί· "ῥητόρων οὐ
γεύομαι."

Φιλήμονος δ᾽ ἐν Μετιόντι εἰπόντος·

Ἀγύρριος δὲ παρατεθέντος καράβου
ὡς εἶδεν αὐτὸν "χαῖρε πάππα φίλτατε"
εἶπας, "τί ἐποίει;", τὸν πατέρα κατήσθιεν,

Ἡρόδικος δ᾽ ὁ Κρατήτειος ἐν τοῖς Συμμίκτοις Ὑπομνήμασι τοῦ Καλλιμέδοντος υἱὸν ὄντα ἀπέδειξε τὸν
Ἀγύρριον.

Γεγόνασι δὲ καὶ οἵδε ὀψοφάγοι. Ἀνταγόρας μὲν ὁ
f ποιητὴς οὐκ εἴα τὸν παῖδα | ἀλεῖψαι τὸν ἰχθὺν ἀλλὰ
λοῦσαι, ὥς φησιν Ἡγήσανδρος. ἐν δὲ στρατοπέδῳ
ἕψοντι, φησίν, αὐτῷ γόγγρων λοπάδα καὶ περι-
εζωσμένῳ Ἀντίγονος ὁ βασιλεὺς παραστάς, "ἆρά γε,"
εἶπεν, "ὦ Ἀνταγόρα, τὸν Ὅμηρον οἴει τὰς τοῦ Ἀγα-
μέμνονος πράξεις ἀναγράψαι γόγγρους ἕψοντα;"
κἀκεῖνον οὐ φαύλως εἰπεῖν· "σὺ δὲ οἴει", φησί, "τὸν
Ἀγαμέμνονα τὰς πράξεις ἐκείνας ἐργάσασθαι πολυ-
πραγμονοῦντα τίς ἐν τῷ στρατοπέδῳ γόγγρους ἕψει;"
ὄρνιν δὲ ἕψων ποτὲ ὁ Ἀνταγόρας οὐκ ἔφη βαδιεῖσθαι
εἰς τὸ βαλανεῖον, εὐλαβούμενος μή ποτε οἱ παῖδες τὸν
341 ζωμὸν ἐκροφήσωσι. Φιλοκύδους ‖ δ᾽ εἰπόντος ὅτι ἡ

---

57 *PAA* 107665; a prominent late 5th-/early 4th-century Athenian politician.

58 Herodicus' conjecture is confirmed by inscriptional evidence; see *Hesperia* 7 (1938) 100 #18.

"It's cold and stiff;" he says, "get it out of here! I've
got no appetite for politicians."

Because Philemon said in *The Man Who Was in Pursuit*
(fr. 43):

A crayfish was served, and when Agyrrhius[57]
saw it, he said: "Hi, Daddy dear;
how are you doing?"—and gobbled down his father,

Herodicus the Cratetaean in his *Miscellaneous Notes*
(p. 126 Düring) accordingly identified Agyrrhius as Callimedon's son.[58]

The following individuals were also gluttons. The poet
Antagoras[59] did not let his slave pour oil on his fish, but
made him "give it a bath", according to Hegesander (fr. 15,
FHG iv.416). He was wearing an apron and stewing a casserole-dish full of conger eels in camp, Hegesander reports; and King Antigonus[60] stood beside him and said:
"So, Antagoras; do you think Homer produced his account
of Agamemnon's accomplishments by stewing conger
eels?" Antagoras offered a clever reply: "Do *you* think", he
said, "that Agamemnon produced those accomplishments
by worrying about who in his camp was stewing conger
eels?"[61] Once when Antagoras was stewing a chicken, he
refused to visit the bathhouse, since he was worried that
his slaves might drink the broth. When Philocydes[62] told

---

59 Antagoras of Rhodes (3rd century BCE); only three fragments of his work survive (pp. 120–1 Powell).

60 Antigonus Gonatas (reigned *c.*277–239 BCE).

61 Plutarch preserves a virtually identical anecdote at *Mor.*
668c–d.

62 Unidentified.

μήτηρ τηρήσει, "ἐγὼ οὖν", εἶπε, "τῇ μητρὶ ὀρνίθειον
ζωμὸν πιστεύσω;" καὶ Ἀνδροκύδης δ᾽ ὁ Κυζικηνὸς
ζωγράφος φίλιχθυς ὤν, ὡς ἱστορεῖ Πολέμων, ἐπὶ
τοσοῦτον ἦλθεν ἡδυπαθείας ὡς καὶ τοὺς περὶ τὴν
Σκύλλαν ἰχθῦς κατὰ σπουδὴν γράψαι. περὶ δὲ Φιλοξένου τοῦ Κυθηρίου διθυραμβοποιοῦ Μάχων ὁ κωμῳδιοποιὸς τάδε γράφει·

    ὑπερβολῇ λέγουσι τὸν Φιλόξενον
    τῶν διθυράμβων τὸν ποιητὴν γεγονέναι |
b   ὀψοφάγον. εἶτα πουλύποδα πηχῶν δυεῖν
    ἐν ταῖς Συρακούσαις ποτ᾽ αὐτὸν ἀγοράσαι
    καὶ σκευάσαντα καταφαγεῖν ὅλον σχεδὸν
    πλὴν τῆς κεφαλῆς, ἁλόντα δ᾽ ὑπὸ δυσπεψίας
    κακῶς ἔχειν σφόδρ᾽· εἶτα δ᾽ ἰατροῦ τινος
    πρὸς αὐτὸν εἰσελθόντος ὃς φαύλως πάνυ
    ὁρῶν φερόμενον αὐτὸν εἶπεν, "εἴ τί σοι
    ἀνοικονόμητόν ἐστι, διατίθου ταχύ,
    Φιλόξεν᾽· ἀποθανῇ γὰρ ὥρας ἑβδόμης." |
c   κἀκεῖνος εἶπε, "τέλος ἔχει τὰ πάντα μοι,
    ἰατρέ," φησί, "καὶ δεδιῴκηται πάλαι.
    τοὺς διθυράμβους σὺν θεοῖς καταλιμπάνω
    ἠνδρωμένους καὶ πάντας ἐστεφανωμένους,

---

63 Plin. *Nat*. 35.64 calls Androcydes a contemporary of Zeuxis
and Parrhasius, placing him at the very end of the 5th century
BCE. For the anecdote, cf. Plu. *Mor*. 665d, 668c.
64 Cf. 1.5e–6b with 1.5b n.

him that his mother would keep an eye on it, Antagoras said: "So I'm supposed to trust my mother with chicken broth?" The painter Androcydes of Cyzicus[63] also loved seafood, according to Polemon (fr. 66 Preller), and was so devoted to a luxurious life-style that he meticulously depicted the fish surrounding Scylla. The comic poet Macho (64–86 Gow) writes the following about the dithyrambic poet Philoxenus of Cythera:[64]

> They say that the dithyrambic poet
> Philoxenus was an extraordinary
> glutton. So once when he was in Syracuse,
> he bought an octopus that was three feet[65] long,
> and prepared it and ate almost the entire thing
> except for the head. He got a stomach-ache
> and was in terrible shape. A doctor
> came to visit him, saw that he was doing
> very badly, and said: "If you've got
> any business that needs to be taken care of, do it
>   right away,
> Philoxenus; because you'll be dead by mid-
>   afternoon[66]."
> He responded: "My affairs are all in order,
> doctor," he said, "and have been settled for a while
>   now.
> With the gods' help, the dithyrambs I'm leaving
>   behind
> have all grown up and been awarded garlands,[67]

[65] Literally "two cubits".
[66] Literally "the seventh hour".
[67] I.e. have taken the prize in poetic competitions.

53

οὓς ἀνατίθημι ταῖς ἐμαυτοῦ συντρόφοις
Μούσαις. Ἀφροδίτην καὶ Διόνυσον ἐπιτρόπους—
ταῦθ᾽ αἱ διαθῆκαι διασαφοῦσιν. ἀλλ᾽ ἐπεὶ
ὁ Τιμοθέου Χάρων σχολάζειν οὐκ ἐᾷ, |

d   οὐκ τῆς Νιόβης, χωρεῖν δὲ πορθμὸν ἀναβοᾷ,
καλεῖ δὲ μοῖρα νύχιος ἧς κλύειν χρεών,
ἵν᾽ ἔχων ἀποτρέχω πάντα τἀμαυτοῦ κάτω,
τοῦ πουλύποδός μοι τὸ κατάλοιπον ἀπόδοτε."

κἂν ἄλλῳ δὲ μέρει φησί·

Φιλόξενός ποθ᾽, ὡς λέγουσ᾽, ὁ Κυθήριος
ηὔξατο τριῶν σχεῖν τὸν λάρυγγα πήχεων,
"ὅπως καταπίνω", φησίν, "ὅτι πλεῖστον χρόνον
καὶ πάνθ᾽ ἅμα μοι τὰ βρώμαθ᾽ ἡδονὴν ποῇ." |

e   καὶ Διογένης δὲ ὁ κύων ὠμὸν πολύποδα καταφαγὼν
ἐπιθεμένης αὐτῷ τῆς γαστρὸς ἀπέθανε. περὶ δὲ τοῦ
Φιλοξένου καὶ ὁ παρῳδὸς Σώπατρος λέγων φησί·

δισσαῖς γὰρ ἐν μέσαισιν ἰχθύων φοραῖς
ἧσται, τὸν Αἴτνης ἐς μέσον λεύσσων σκοπόν.

καὶ Ὑπερείδης δὲ ὁ ῥήτωρ ὀψοφάγος ἦν, ὥς φησι

---

[68] This allusion to the dithyrambic poet Timotheus = *PMG*
786.

[69] Literally "three cubits".

[70] I.e. since numerous different foods will be passing down
different parts of his now radically elongated gullet at the same
time. Cf. 1.6b.

[71] Cf. D.L. 6.76.

and I'm entrusting them to the care of the Muses I
    grew
up with. That Aphrodite and Dionysus are my
    executors,
my will makes clear. But since
Timotheus' Charon, the one from his *Niobe*,[68]
is not allowing me to linger, but is shouting for me to
    proceed to the ferry,
and my night-dark fate, which I must heed, is
    calling—
so that I can run off to the Underworld with
    everything that's mine:
give me the rest of that octopus!"

So too, he says elsewhere (Macho 87–90 Gow):

They say that Philoxenus of Cythera once
prayed to have a throat five feet[69] long,
"So that I can make my eating", he said, "last as long
    as possible,
and everything I eat can give me pleasure
    simultaneously."[70]

Diogenes the Cynic likewise died when his stomach
turned on him after he ate a raw octopus.[71] The parodist
Sopater (fr. 23) also says about Philoxenus:

For he sits between two loads
of fish, gazing at the central spot on Aetna.[72]

The orator Hyperides was also a glutton, according to the

[72] For Philoxenus on Sicily, see 1.6e–7a; but the point of
Sopater's remark is unclear.

Τιμοκλῆς ὁ κωμικὸς ἐν Δήλῳ διηγούμενος τοὺς παρὰ
f Ἁρπάλου δωροδοκήσαντας. γράφει | δὲ οὕτως·

(A.) Δημοσθένης τάλαντα πεντήκοντ᾿ ἔχει.
(B.) μακάριος, εἴπερ μεταδίδωσι μηδενί.
(A.) καὶ Μοιροκλῆς εἴληφε χρυσίον πολύ.
(B.) ἀνόητος ὁ διδούς, εὐτυχὴς δ᾿ ὁ λαμβάνων.
(A.) εἴληφε καὶ Δήμων τι καὶ Καλλισθένης.
(B.) πένητες ἦσαν, ὥστε συγγνώμην ἔχω.
(A.) ὅ τ᾿ ἐν λόγοισι δεινὸς Ὑπερείδης ἔχει. ||
342 (B.) τοὺς ἰχθυοπώλας οὗτος ἡμῶν πλουτιεῖ·
† ὀψοφάγος † γὰρ ὥστε τοὺς λάρους εἶναι
Σύρους.

καὶ ἐν Ἰκαρίοις δὲ ὁ αὐτὸς ποιητής φησι·

τόν τ᾿ ἰχθυόρρουν ποταμὸν Ὑπερείδην πέρα,
ὃς ἠπίαις φωναῖσιν ἔμφρονος λόγου
κόμποις παφλάζων † ἠπίοις † πυκνώμασι
πρὸς † παν ‹   . . .   › δυσας † ἔχει
μισθωτὸς ἄρδει πεδία τοῦ δεδωκότος.

b Φιλέταιρος δ᾿ ἐν Ἀσκληπιῷ[9] πρὸς | τῷ ὀψοφαγεῖν καὶ
κυβεύειν αὐτόν φησι, καθάπερ καὶ Καλλίαν τὸν ῥήτο-

---

[9] Ἀσκληπιῷ τὸν Ὑπερείδην A: τὸν Ὑπερείδην del. Wilamowitz

---

[73] See 6.245f–6a n. Of the men mentioned by Timocles,
Hyperides (*PA* 13912), Demosthenes (*PAA* 318625), Moerocles
(*PAA* 658480), and Callisthenes (*PAA* 559815) were prominent

comic author Timocles in *Delos* (fr. 4), in his discussion of the people Harpalus bribed.[73] He writes as follows:

(A.) Demosthenes has 50 talents.
(B.) He's a lucky guy—provided he's not offering
    anyone else a share.
(A.) Moerocles also got a lot of gold.
(B.) The fellow doing the giving is an idiot; but the
    one doing the getting is lucky!
(A.) Demon also got something; Callistratus too.
(B.) They were poor, so I forgive them.
(A.) And Hyperides the clever speech-writer got a
    bit.
(B.) He'll make our fish-sellers rich;
because he's enough of † a glutton † to make the
    seagulls look like Syrians![74]

So too in *Icarians*[75] (fr. 17) the same poet says:

and beyond the Hyperides River, rich in fish,
which with mild words of thoughtful speech,
blustering with constant † mild † boasts
turns toward [corrupt] . . .
is paid to water the plains of anyone who hires him.

Philetaerus in *Asclepius* (fr. 2) claims that Hyperides spent his time eating and shooting dice, which is exactly what

late 4th-century Athenian politicians. Demon (*PAA* 322735), on the other hand, is otherwise known only for proposing the motion that recalled his cousin Demosthenes from exile (Plu. *Dem.* 27.6; [Plu.] *Mor.* 846d).

74 For the Syrians' refusal to eat fish, cf. 8.346c–d.
75 For the title, see 8.339d n.

ρα Ἀξιόνικος ἐν Φιλευριπίδῃ·

    ἄλλον δ᾽ ἰχθὺν
      μεγέθει πίσυνόν τινα τοῖσδε τόποις
      ἥκει κομίσας
    Γλαῦκός τις ἐν πόντῳ † γαλούς †.
    σῖτον ὀψοφάγων
      καὶ λίχνων ἀνδρῶν ἀγάπημα φέρω κατ᾽ ὤμων.
    τίνα τῷδ᾽ ἐνέπω τὴν σκευασίαν;
      πότερον χλωρῷ τρίμματι βρέξας
      ἢ τῆς ἀγρίας
    ἅλμης πάσμασι σῶμα λιπάνας
      πυρὶ παμφλέκτῳ παραδώσω;
    ἔφα τις ὡς ἐν ἅλμῃ
    θερμῇ τοῦτο φάγοι γ᾽ ἑφθὸν ἀνὴρ
c   Μοσχίων | φίλαυλος.
    βοᾷ δ᾽ ὄνειδος ἴδιον, ὦ Καλλία.
    "ἢ σὺ μὲν ἀμφί ‹τε› σῦκα καὶ ἀμφὶ ταρίχι᾽
      ἀγάλλῃ,
    τοῦ δ᾽ ἐν ἅλμῃ παρεόντος
    οὐ γεύῃ χαρίεντος ὄψου,"

τὰ μὲν σῦκα, ὡς ἂν συκοφάντην λοιδορῶν, τὰ δὲ
ταρίχη, μήποτε καὶ ὡς αἰσχροποιοῦντος. καὶ Ἕρμιπ-
πος δέ φησιν ἐν τρίτῳ Περὶ τῶν Ἰσοκράτους Μαθη-
τῶν· ἑωθινὸν τὸν Ὑπερείδην ποιεῖσθαι νῦν τοὺς περι-
πάτους ἐν τοῖς ἰχθύσι. Τίμαιος δ᾽ ὁ Ταυρομενίτης καὶ

Axionicus in *The Man Who Loved Euripides* (fr. 4) says
about the orator Callias:[76]

> A certain maritime Glaucus [corrupt]
> has come, bringing
>   another fish confident in its size
>   to this place.
> I bear on my shoulders
>   food for gluttons and a source of delight for the
>   greedy.
> What style of preparation do I propose for it?
>   Ought I to douse it in an herb-sauce
>   or anoint its body
> with a sprinkling of rough brine, before I
>   turn it over to the all-blazing fire?
> A certain Moschion[77], a man
> devoted to the pipes, claimed he would eat it
> stewed in hot broth.
> He cries out a personal insult, Callias:
> "You certainly take delight in figs and saltfish;
> but when a lovely dish in broth
> is available, you've got no taste for it."

He mentions figs (*suka*) as a way of attacking him for
being a sycophant, and saltfish perhaps to imply that he be-
haved shamefully.[78] So too Hermippus says in Book III of
On Isocrates' Students (fr. 68a II Wehrli): that Hyperides
is now taking walks in the fish-market at dawn. Timaeus

---

76 *PAA* 553610; otherwise unidentified.

77 *PAA* 659185; see Gow on Macho 46, and cf. 6.242c.

78 The point is obscure, but the shameful behavior in question
is presumably sexual in nature.

Ἀριστοτέλη τὸν φιλόσοφον ὀψοφάγον φησὶ γεγο-
d νέναι. καὶ Μάτων | δ᾽ ὁ σοφιστὴς ὀψοφάγος ἦν· δηλοῖ
δὲ τοῦτο Ἀντιφάνης ἐν Κιθαρῳδῷ, οὗ ἡ ἀρχή·

οὐ ψεῦδος οὐδέν φησιν.

ὀφθαλμὸν ὤρυττέν τις ὥσπερ ἰχθύος
Μάτων προσελθών.

Ἀναξίλας δ᾽ ἐν Μονοτρόπῳ·

τοῦ κεστρέως κατεδήδοκεν τὸ κρανίον
ἀναρπάσας Μάτων· ἐγὼ δ᾽ ἀπόλλυμαι.

ὑπερβολὴ γαστριμαργίας τὸ καὶ ἁρπάζειν ἐσθίοντα |
e καὶ ταῦτα κρανίον κεστρέως, εἰ μὴ ἄρα οἱ περὶ ταῦτα
δεινοὶ ἴσασιν ἐνόν τι χρήσιμον ἐν κεστρέως κρανίῳ,
ὅπερ ἐστὶ τῆς Ἀρχεστράτου λιχνείας ἐμφανίσαι ἡμῖν.
Ἀντιφάνης δ᾽ ἐν Πλουσίοις κατάλογον ποιεῖται ὀψο-
φάγων ἐν τούτοις·

Εὔθυνος δ᾽ ἔχων
σανδάλια καὶ σφραγῖδα καὶ μεμυρισμένος
ἐλογίζετο † τῶν πραγμάτων οὐκ οἶδ᾽ ὅ τι· |
f Φοινικίδης δὲ Ταυρέας θ᾽ ὁ φίλτατος,
ἄνδρες † πάλαι ὀψοφάγοι τοιοῦτοί † τινες

---

[79] Drawing on Polybius.
[80] PAA 635840; otherwise unknown.
[81] Quoted also at 7.307c.

of Tauromenium (*FGrH* 566 F 156)[79] claims that the philosopher Aristotle was also a glutton. The sophist Maton[80] was a glutton as well; Antiphanes makes this clear in *The Citharode*, which begins (fr. 116):

> He tells no lies.

> Someone came up and gouged out his eye,
> like Maton does with a fish. (Antiph. fr. 117)

Anaxilas in *The Recluse* (fr. 20):[81]

> Maton grabbed the head of the gray mullet
> and gobbled it down; but I'm ruined.

Snatching and eating food—and a gray mullet's head at that!—is the height of gluttony, unless the experts in such matters know of any value in a mullet's head, a point it would take Archestratus' greed to reveal to us. Antiphanes in *Wealthy Men* (fr. 188) offers a list of gluttons in the following passage:

>   Euthynus,[82] wearing
> sandals and a seal-ring, and soaked in perfume,
> was calculating † some sort of business;
> and Phoenicides and my good friend Taureas,[83]
> certain † for a long time now gluttons of such a sort †
> men,

[82] *PAA* 433922; also mentioned (and described as a saltfish-vendor) in Antiph. fr. 126 (preserved at 3.120a).

[83] Mentioned together again in Antiph. fr. 50 (preserved at 8.343d). Taureas (otherwise unknown) is also referred to as a glutton in Philetaer. fr. 3 (preserved at 10.416e–f).

οἷοι καταβροχθίζειν ἐν ἀγορᾷ τὰ τεμάχη,
ὁρῶντες ἐξέθνησκον ἐπὶ τῷ πράγματι
ἔφερόν τε δεινῶς τὴν ἀνοψίαν πάνυ.
κύκλους δὲ συναγείροντες ἔλεγον † τάδε
ὡς οὐ βιωτόν ἐστιν οὐδ᾽ ἀνασχετὸν
"τῆς μὲν θαλάττης ἀντιποιεῖσθαί τινας ‖
ὑμῶν ἀναλίσκειν τε πολλὰ χρήματα,
ὄψου δὲ μηδὲ < . . . > εἰσπλεῖν μηδὲ γρῦ.
τί οὖν ὄφελος τῶν νησιάρχων; ἔστι δὴ
νόμῳ κατακλεῖσαι τοῦτο, παραπομπὴν ποεῖν
τῶν ἰχθύων. νυνδὶ Μάτων συνήρπακεν
τοὺς ἁλιέας, καὶ <δὴ> Διογείτων νὴ Δία
ἅπαντας ἀναπέπεικεν ὡς αὑτὸν φέρειν,
κοὐ δημοτικόν γε τοῦτο δρᾷ τοιαῦτα φλῶν.
γάμοι δ᾽ ἐκεῖνοι καὶ πότοι νεανικοὶ |
ἦσαν."

343

b

Εὐφάνης[10] δὲ ἐν Μούσαις·

Φοινικίδης δ᾽ ὡς εἶδεν ἐν πλήθει νέων
μεστὴν ζέουσαν λοπάδα Νηρείων τέκνων,

[10] Εὔφρων Schweighäuser

---

[84] *PAA* 325590; unidentified.

[85] According to *Suda* ε 3815, Athenaeus assigned plays entitled *Aeschra* (7.307e), *Muses*, *Fellow Ephebes* (9.377d), and *Sacred Ambassadors* (9.399b–c) to Euphro; as the manuscript contains no reference to Euphro and instead assigns this fragment to Euphanes' otherwise unattested *Muses*, Schweighäuser emended

the type who gulp down slabs of fish in the
    marketplace,
practically passed out when they saw what was going
    on,
and got extremely upset about the lack of fish.
They gathered a crowd around them and said † the
    following:
that life was not worth living, and that it was
    unbearable
"that some of you lay claim to
the sea and spend loads of money—
but not a speck of fish enters the harbor!
What's the use of having island-commissioners, then?
    It's legally possible,
you know, to require that the fish be escorted
by a convoy! But as it is, Maton has captured
the fishermen, and Diogeiton[84], by Zeus,
has convinced them all to bring their catch to him.
And he's not behaving *democratically* by gobbling
    food like this!
Those were wedding feasts and young men's
drinking parties!"

Euphanes in *Muses* (fr. 1):[85]

When Phoenicides was in a crowd of young men
and saw a boiling hot casserole-dish full of Nereus'
    children,

the poet's name. But Euphro probably belongs to the 3rd century
BCE, whereas inscriptional evidence places Euphanes in the 4th,
and (following K–A) I retain the reading in A.

ATHENAEUS

ἐπίσχετ᾽ ὀργῇ χεῖρας ἠρεθισμένας·
"τίς φησιν εἶναι δεινὸς ἐκ κοινοῦ φαγεῖν;
τίς ἐκ μέσου τὰ θερμὰ δεινὸς ἁρπάσαι;
ποῦ Κόρυδος, ἢ Φυρόμαχος, ἢ Νείλου βία;
ἴτω πρὸς ἡμᾶς, καὶ τάχ᾽ οὐδὲν μεταλάβοι." |

c τῆς αὐτῆς ἰδέας καὶ Μελάνθιος ἦν ὁ τῆς τραγῳδίας
ποιητής· ἔγραψε δὲ καὶ ἐλεγεῖα. κωμῳδοῦσι δ᾽ αὐτὸν
ἐπὶ ὀψοφαγίᾳ Λεύκων ἐν Φράτερσιν, Ἀριστοφάνης ἐν
Εἰρήνῃ, Φερεκράτης ἐν Πετάλῃ. ἐν δὲ τοῖς Ἰχθύσιν
Ἄρχιππος τῷ δράματι ὡς ὀψοφάγον δήσας παρα-
δίδωσι τοῖς ἰχθύσιν ἀντιβρωθησόμενον. ἀλλὰ μὴν
καὶ Ἀρίστιππος ὁ Σωκρατικὸς ὀψοφάγος ἦν· ὅστις καὶ
ὑπὸ Πλάτωνός ποτε ὀνειδιζόμενος ἐπὶ τῇ ὀψοφαγίᾳ,
ὥς φησι Σωτίων καὶ Ἡγήσανδρος, < . . . > γράφει δὲ
οὕτως ὁ Δελφός· Ἀρίστιππος Πλάτωνος ἐπιτιμήσαν-
d τος | αὐτῷ διότι πολλοὺς ἰχθῦς ἠγόρασε, δυεῖν ὀβο-
λοῖν ἔφησεν ἐωνῆσθαι. τοῦ δὲ Πλάτωνος εἰπόντος
διότι καὶ "αὐτὸς ἂν ἠγόρασα τοσούτου", "ὁρᾷς οὖν,"
εἶπεν, "ὦ Πλάτων, ὅτι οὐκ ἐγὼ ὀψοφάγος, ἀλλὰ σὺ
φιλάργυρος." Ἀντιφάνης δ᾽ ἐν Αὐλητρίδι ἢ Διδύμαις
Φοινικίδην τινὰ ἐπ᾽ ὀψοφαγίᾳ κωμῳδῶν φησιν·

---

86 Corydos ("Lark"; his real name was Eucrates, *PAA* 437510;
cf. the numerous anecdotes and comic fragments quoted at
6.240e–2c), Phyromachus, and Neilus (*PAA* 705855; cf. Timocl. fr.
10.4, quoted at 6.240f) were all notorious 4th-century Athenian
gluttons.   87 *PAA* 638275; he belongs to the second half of
the 5th century BCE.
88 Aristippus of Cyrene (*SSR* IV A; the anecdote that follows is

he restrained his hands, stirred though they were
    with passion.
"Who claims he's a terror when it comes to eating
    from a shared pot?
Or a terror at snatching hot food from the midst?
Where is Corydos, or Phyromachus, or mighty
    Neilus?[86]
Let him confront me—and I wouldn't be surprised if
    he gets nothing!"

The tragic poet Melanthius[87] (*TrGF* 23 T 2)—he also
wrote elegiac verse—was the same sort of person: Leucon
in *Phratries* (fr. 3), Aristophanes in *Peace* (803–13), and
Pherecrates in *Petale* (fr. 148) make fun of him for being a
glutton. And in his play *Fish* (fr. 28) Archippus puts him
in chains and turns him over to the fish to be eaten in
compensation, on the ground that he is a glutton. But Socrates' student Aristippus[88] was also a glutton; according to
Sotion (fr. 4 Wehrli) and Hegesander (fr. 17, *FHG* iv.416–
17), Plato once criticized him for his gluttony . . . The
Delphian[89] writes as follows: When Plato attacked him for
buying a large number of fish, Aristippus informed him
that he had paid only two obols. When Plato said "I would
have bought them myself at that price," Aristippus responded: "So you see, Plato: it's not that I'm a glutton—it's
that you're a miser!" Antiphanes in *The Pipe-Girl or Twin
Girls* (fr. 50) makes fun of a certain Phoenicides[90] for being
a glutton and says:

one of a number of similar tales about him preserved in late
sources); cf. 11.507b; 12.544a–f.
   [89] Hegesander.   [90] See 8.342f n.

ὁ <μὲν> Μενέλεως ἐπολέμησ᾽ ἔτη δέκα
τοῖς Τρωσὶ διὰ γυναῖκα τὴν ὄψιν καλήν,
Φοινικίδης δὲ Ταυρέᾳ δι᾽ ἔγχελυν. |

e Δημοσθένης δ᾽ ὁ ῥήτωρ Φιλοκράτην, ἐπειδὴ ἐκ τοῦ
προδοτικοῦ χρυσίου πόρνας καὶ ἰχθῦς ἠγόραζεν, εἰς
ἀσέλγειαν καὶ ὀψοφαγίαν λοιδορεῖ. Διοκλῆς δὲ ὁ
ὀψοφάγος, ὥς φησιν Ἡγήσανδρος, πυθομένου τινὸς
αὐτοῦ πότερος χρηστότερος ἰχθύς, γόγγρος ἢ λά-
βραξ, "ὁ μὲν ἐφθός," ἔφη, "ὁ δὲ ὀπτός." ὀψοφάγος δ᾽
ἦν καὶ Λεοντεὺς ὁ Ἀργεῖος τραγῳδός, Ἀθηνίωνος μὲν
μαθητής, οἰκέτης δὲ γενόμενος Ἰόβα τοῦ Μαυρουσίων
βασιλέως, ὥς φησιν Ἀμάραντος ἐν τοῖς Περὶ Σκηνῆς,
f γεγραφέναι φάσκων | εἰς αὐτὸν τόδε τὸ ἐπίγραμμα
τὸν Ἰόβαν, ὅτε κακῶς τὴν Ὑψιπύλην ὑπεκρίνατο·

μή με Λεοντῆος τραγικοῦ κιναρηφάγον ἦχος
    λεύσσων Ὑψιπύλης ἐς κακὸν ἦτορ ὅρα.
ἤμην γάρ ποτ᾽ ἐγὼ Βάκχῳ φίλος, οὐδέ τιν᾽ ὧδε
    γῆρυν χρυσολόβοις οὔασιν ἠγάσατο·
νῦν δέ με χυτρόποδες κέραμοι καὶ ξηρὰ τάγηνα ||
344   χήρωσαν φωνῆς γαστρὶ χαριζόμενον.

---

91 See 8.342f n.
92 A late 4th-century Athenian politician (*PA* 14599).
93 Cf. 8.344b; otherwise unknown.
94 Stephanis #1534.
95 Stephanis #73; perhaps to be identified with the comic poet
by the same name quoted at 14.660e–1d (drawn from Juba!).

Menelaus waged war on the Trojans
    for ten years for the sake of a beautiful woman,
whereas Phoenicides wages war on Taureas[91] for the
    sake of an eel.

The orator Demosthenes (19.229) criticizes Philocrates[92]
for being a dissolute glutton because he spent the gold he
got for his treachery on whores and fish. According to
Hegesander (fr. 16, *FHG* iv.416), when someone asked
the glutton Diocles[93] which fish was better, a conger eel
or a sea-bass, he said: "The former's better stewed, but
the latter's better roasted." The Argive tragic actor Leonteus[94]—he was a student of Athenion[95] and a slave of Juba
the king of Mauretania[96]—was also a glutton, according to
Amarantus in his *On the Stage*, in which he claims that
Juba wrote the following epigram about Leonteus when he
did a bad job of acting in the *Hypsipyle*[97] (*FGrH* 275 F 104
= Juba Rex *FGE* 239–44):

When you behold me, the cardoon-eating[98] voice of
    the tragic actor
    Leonteus, do not believe that you look upon
    Hypsipyle's ugly heart.
For I was once Bacchus' friend, nor did his gold-
    spangled ears
    get as much pleasure from any other voice.
But now earthenware pots and dry frying-pans
    have taken away my voice, since I paid more
    attention to my belly.

96 Reigned 25 BCE–*c*.23 CE, *FGrH* 275; Athenaeus cites his
historical and linguistic works repeatedly (e.g. 3.83b–c; 4.170e–f,
175d).   97 Sc. of Euripides.

Φόρυσκον δέ φησιν Ἡγήσανδρος τὸν ἰχθυοφάγον οὐ
δυνηθέντα ὅσον ἤθελεν ἀφελεῖν τοῦ ἰχθύος, ἀλλ᾽ ἀκο-
λουθήσαντος αὐτῷ πλείονος εἰπεῖν·

τὰ δ᾽ ἀντιτείνοντ᾽ αὐτόπρεμν᾽ ἀπόλλυται,

καὶ ὅλον τὸν ἰχθὺν ἀναλῶσαι. Βίων δὲ προαρπάσαν-
τός τινος τὰ ἐπάνω τοῦ ἰχθύος στρέψας καὶ αὐτὸς καὶ
δαψιλῶς φαγὼν ἐπεῖπεν·

Ἰνὼ δὲ τἀπὶ θάτερ᾽ ἐξηργάζετο. |

b   Θεόκριτος δ᾽ ὁ Χῖος τελευτησάσης τῆς γυναικὸς Διο-
κλεῖ τῷ ὀψοφάγῳ, ἐπειδὴ ποιῶν αὐτῇ τὸ περίδειπνον
πάλιν ὠψοφάγει κλαίων ἅμα, "παῦσαι", φησί, "κλαίων, ὦ πόνηρε·

οὐδὲν γὰρ πλέον ὀψοφαγῶν ποιήσεις."

τοῦ δ᾽ αὐτοῦ καὶ τὸν ἀγρὸν καταβεβρωκότος εἰς ὀψοφαγίαν, ἐπειδὴ θερμόν ποτε καταβροχθίσας ἰχθὺν
ἔφησε τὸν οὐρανὸν κατακεκαῦσθαι, "λοιπόν", ἔφησεν,
"ἐστίν", ὁ Θεόκριτος, "σοι καὶ τὴν θάλασσαν ἐκπιεῖν,
καὶ ἔσῃ τρία τὰ μέγιστα ἠφανικώς, γῆν καὶ θάλατταν
c   καὶ οὐρανόν." | Κλέαρχος δ᾽ ἐν τοῖς Περὶ Βίων φι-

---

98 For cardoon (*kinara*; also known as artichoke thistle), see
2.70a–1c. There appear to be no other references to its allegedly
deleterious effect on the voice.   99 Otherwise unknown.

100 Presumably the philosopher Bion of Borysthenes (*c*.335–
c.245 BCE).

Hegesander (fr. 19, *FHG* iv.417) reports that when Pho-
ryscus[99], who ate large amounts of seafood, was unable to
rip off as large a piece of a fish as he wanted, because most
of it stuck to the bone, he said (S. *Ant.* 714):

but those that resist are destroyed root and branch,

and consumed it whole. When someone else grabbed the
part of the fish that was facing up before Bion[100] (fr. 81
Kindstrand) could get to it, he flipped it over, ate a large
piece himself, and then said (E. *Ba.* 1129):

And Ino completed the work on the other side.[101]

When the wife of the glutton Diocles[102] died and he began
eating aggressively again as he was hosting her funeral dinner, crying all the while, Theocritus of Chios[103] said: "Stop
crying, wretch;

for you'll gain no advantage by being a glutton."[104]

The same man had consumed his property in the country
by behaving like a glutton; once when he gobbled up a hot
fish and said that he had burned the roof of his mouth
(*ouranos*), Theocritus responded: "All that's left for you is
to swallow the sea, and you'll have made the three largest
objects there are disappear: the earth, the sea, and the sky
(*ouranos*)." Clearchus in his *On Lives* (fr. 58 Wehrli) offers

---

[101] A virtually identical anecdote about the Stoic philosopher
Zeno is preserved at 5.186d.

[102] Cf. 8.343e with n.   [103] Active in the second half of
the 4th century BCE; see 1.21c n.

[104] Apparently a witty adaptation of part of an otherwise unattested dactylic hexameter line; cf. 12.540a.

λιχθύν τινα ἀναγράφων φησὶν οὕτως· Τέχνων ὁ παλαιὸς αὐλητὴς Χάρμου τοῦ αὐλητοῦ τελευτήσαντος
(ἦν δὲ φίλιχθυς) ἀποπυρίδας ἐπὶ τοῦ μνήματος ἐνήγι-
ζεν αὐτῷ. καὶ Ἄλεξις δ᾽ ὁ ποιητὴς ἦν ὀψοφάγος, ὡς ὁ
Σάμιός φησι Λυγκεύς· καὶ σκωπτόμενος ὑπό τινων
σπερμολόγων εἰς ὀψοφαγίαν ἐρομένων τε ἐκείνων τί
ἂν ἥδιστα φάγοι, ὁ Ἄλεξις σπερμολόγους ἔφη πε-
φρυγμένους. Νόθιππον δὲ τὸν τραγῳδιοποιόν, ὃν Ἕρ-
d   μιππος ἐν ταῖς | Μοίραις φησίν·

   εἰ δ᾽ ἦν τὸ γένος τῶν ἀνθρώπων τῶν νῦν τοιόνδε
       μάχεσθαι,
   καὶ βατὶς αὐτῶν ἡγεῖτ᾽ ὀπτὴ μεγάλη καὶ πλευρὸν
       ὕειον,
   τοὺς μὲν ἄρ᾽ ἄλλους οἰκουρεῖν χρῆν, πέμπειν δὲ
       Νόθιππον ἑκόντα·
   εἷς γὰρ μόνος ὢν κατεβρόχθισεν ἂν τὴν
       Πελοπόννησον ἅπασαν.

ὅτι δὲ οὗτός ἐστιν ὁ ποιητὴς σαφῶς παρίστησι Τηλεκλείδης ἐν Ἡσιόδοις. Μυννίσκος ὁ τραγικὸς ὑποκρι-
τὴς κωμῳδεῖται ὑπὸ Πλάτωνος ἐν Σύρφακι ὡς ὀψο-
φάγος οὕτως· |

e   (Α.) ὁδὶ μὲν Ἀναγυράσιος ὀρφώς ἐστί σοι.

---

105 Stephanis #2621; cf. 1.4a–c with n.
106 Stephanis #2404.
107 Literally "seed-gatherers", i.e. "rooks" (*spermologoi*—the
word also used colloquially above to mean "gossips").

the following account of a man who loved seafood: When
the pipe-player Charmus[105] (who loved seafood) died, the
ancient pipe-player Technon[106] dedicated small-fry to him
at his tomb. The poet Alexis was also a glutton, according
to Lynceus of Samos (fr. 33 Dalby = Alex. test. 12); when
some wiseacres poked fun at him for this at one point and
asked what his favorite food was, Alexis said: "Roasted
wag-tongues[107]." Also the tragic poet Nothippus[108] (*TrGF*
26 T 1), mentioned by Hermippus in his *Fates* (fr. 46):

> If people today could fight like this,
> and a large roasted skate, accompanied by a side of
>   pork, was their commander,
> the others would have to stay at home, and
>   Nothippus would be sent as a volunteer;
> because even alone he could gulp down the entire
>   Peloponnese.

Teleclides in *Hesiods* (fr. 17) establishes beyond any
doubt that this is the poet. The tragic actor Mynniscus[109] is
mocked by Plato in *The Rabble* (fr. 175) for being a glutton,
as follows:

> (A.) Here's a sea-perch for you from Anagyrus.

108 *PAA* 720940. His name is probably to be restored in the list
of Athenian tragic victors at *IG* II² 2325.4 (470 BCE; victorious
only once). No fragments of his plays survive.
109 Stephanis #1757; *PAA* 661940. He was victorious in the actors' competition at the City Dionysia first sometime in the mid-
440s BCE (*IG* II² 2325.24) and again at least once (unless this was
his homonymous son) in 422 (*IG* II² 2318.119).

(B.) οἶδ᾽, ᾧ φίλος Μυννίσκος ἔσθ᾽ ὁ Χαλκιδεύς.
(A.) καλῶς λέγεις.

καὶ Λάμπωνα δὲ τὸν μάντιν ἐπὶ τοῖς ὁμοίοις κωμῳδοῦσι Καλλίας Πεδήταις καὶ Λύσιππος Βάκχαις. Κρατῖνος δ᾽ ἐν Δραπέτισιν εἰπὼν περὶ αὐτοῦ·

Λάμπωνα, τὸν οὐ βροτῶν
ψῆφος δύναται φλεγυρὰ δείπνου φίλων
ἀπείργειν,

ἐπιφέρει·

νῦν δ᾽ αὖτις ἐρυγγάνει·
βρύχει γὰρ ἅπαν τὸ παρόν, τρίγλῃ | δὲ κἂν
μάχοιτο.

Ἡδύλος δ᾽ ἐν Ἐπιγράμμασιν ὀψοφάγους καταλέγων
Φαίδωνος μέν τινος ἐν τούτοις μέμνηται·

Φαίδων δὲ < . . . > φυκί ἐνεῖκαι
χορδάς <θ᾽> ὁ ψάλτης, ἐστὶ γὰρ ὀψοφάγος.

Ἄγιδος δ᾽ ἐν τούτοις·

ἐφθὸς ὁ κάλλιχθυς· νῦν ἔμβαλε τὴν
βαλανάγραν ||

---

110 *PAA* 601665; he belongs to the mid-5th century BCE.
111 Stephanis #2454; otherwise unknown.
112 Perhaps an alternative name for the wrasse-variety elsewhere called a *phukis*.

(B.) I know him—he's friends with Mynniscus of
        Chalcis.
(A.) You're right.

Callias in *Men in Shackles* (fr. 20) and Lysippus in *Bacchants* (fr. 6) also make fun of the seer Lampon[110] for similar reasons. Cratinus in *Runaway Women* (fr. 62, encompassing both quotations) first says about him:

Lampon, whom no flaming
vote cast by mortals can bar from a dinner given by
        his friends,

and then continues:

But now he's burping again;
because he's gobbling everything that's there, and
        he'd even fight with a red mullet.

Hedylus in the *Epigrams* (*HE* 1863–4) offers a list of gluttons, and mentions a certain Phaedo[111] in the following
passage:

and the harp-player Phaedo . . . to bring
phukia[112] and sausages, since he's a glutton.

And (he mentions) Agis[113] in the following passage (*HE*
1865–70):

The beauty-fish[114] has been stewed. Now bolt the
        door

113 Perhaps the cookbook-author referred to at 12.516c.
114 Obscure; cf. 7.282c–e.

73

345   ἔλθῃ μὴ Πρωτεὺς Ἆγις ὁ τῶν λοπάδων.
γίνεθ᾽ ὕδωρ καὶ πῦρ καὶ ὃ βούλεται· ἀλλ᾽
ἀπόκλειε

*   *   *

ἥξει γὰρ τοιαῦτα μεταπλασθεὶς τυχὸν ὡς Ζεὺς
χρυσορόης ἐπὶ τήνδ᾽ Ἀκρισίου λοπάδα.

καὶ γυναῖκα δέ τινα Κλειὼ ἐπὶ τοῖς ὁμοίοις σκώπτων
φησίν·

  ὀψοφάγει, Κλειώ· καταμύομεν. ἢν δὲ θελήσῃς, |
b   ἔσθε μόνη. δραχμῆς ἐστιν ὁ γόγγρος ἅπας.
  θὲς μόνον ἢ ζώνην ⟨ἢ⟩ ἐνώτιον ἤ τι τοιοῦτον
  σύσσημον † τὸ δ᾽ ὁρᾶν μὴ μόνον οὐ
  λέγομεν.†
  ἡμετέρη σὺ Μέδουσα· λιθούμεθα † πάντα πάλαι
  που †
  οὗ Γοργοῦς γόγγρου δ᾽ οἱ μέλεοι λοπάδι.

Ἀριστόδημος δ᾽ ἐν τοῖς Γελοίοις Ἀπομνημονεύμασιν
c Εὐφρανόρα φησὶ τὸν ὀψοφάγον ἀκούσαντα | ὅτι ἄλ-
λος ἰχθυοφάγος ἀπέθανε θερμὸν ἰχθύος τέμαχος
καταπιὼν ἀναφωνῆσαι, "ἱερόσυλος ὁ θάνατος." Κίν-

---

[115] A reference to the sea-divinity encountered by Homer's
Menelaus, who could turn into anything he wished, including
water and fire (*Od.* 4.417–18, 455–8).

[116] Sc. when he visited Danae, the daughter of Acrisius.

[117] Clearly a courtesan, given that she is dining with a group of
men; cf. 10.440d.

to keep Agis, the Proteus[115] of casserole-dishes,
    from coming!
He turns into water, or fire, or whatever he wants.
    But lock him out!

*   *   *

Because after he transforms himself, perhaps, like
    Zeus did,[116] he'll come
    as a shower of gold to this casserole-dish of
      Acrisius.

He makes fun of a woman named Cleio[117] for similar reasons, saying (*HE* 1871–6):

Act like a glutton, Cleio! We've got our eyes closed.
    But if you don't mind—
    eat by yourself! The entire conger eel costs a
      drachma.
Just offer your belt, or your earring, or something like
    that
    as your contribution † the seeing not only we don't
      say. †
You're our Medusa; we're turned to stone †
    everything long ago somehow, †
    miserable us, not by a casserole-dish of Gorgon,
      but by one of conger eel (*gongros*).

Aristodemus in his *Humorous Memoirs* (fr. 10, *FHG* iii.310) reports that when the glutton Euphranor[118] heard that another seafood-eater passed away after gulping down a hot fish-steak, he cried: "Death is a sacrilegious

---

[118] Otherwise unknown.

δων δὲ ὁ ὀψοφάγος καὶ Δημύλος (ὀψοφάγος δὲ καὶ
οὗτος) γλαύκου παρατεθέντος, ἄλλου δ᾽ οὐδενός, ὁ μὲν
τὸν ὀφθαλμὸν κατελάβετο, καὶ ὁ Δημύλος ἐπὶ τὸν
ἐκείνου ὀφθαλμὸν ἐπιβαλὼν ἐβιάζετο φωνῶν, "ἄφες
καὶ ἀφήσω." ἐν δείπνῳ δέ ποτε καλῆς λοπάδος ὄψου
παρατεθείσης ὁ Δημύλος οὐκ ἔχων ὅπως αὐτὴν μόνος
καταφάγῃ ἐνέπτυσεν εἰς αὐτήν. Ζήνων δ᾽ ὁ Κιτιεὺς ὁ
τῆς στοᾶς κτίστης πρὸς τὸν ὀψοφάγον ᾧ συνέζη ἐπὶ
d   πλείονα χρόνον, καθά φησιν | Ἀντίγονος ὁ Καρύστιος
ἐν τῷ Ζήνωνος Βίῳ, μεγάλου τινὸς κατὰ τύχην ἰχθύος
παρατεθέντος, ἄλλου δ᾽ οὐδενὸς παρεσκευασμένου,
λαβὼν ὅλον ὁ Ζήνων ἀπὸ τοῦ πίνακος οἷος ἦν κατ-
εσθίειν. τοῦ δ᾽ ἐμβλέψαντος αὐτῷ, "τί οὖν", ἔφη, "τοὺς
συζῶντάς σοι οἴει πάσχειν, εἰ σὺ μίαν ἡμέραν μὴ
δεδύνησαι ἐνεγκεῖν ὀψοφαγίαν;" Ἴστρος δέ φησι Χοι-
ρίλον τὸν ποιητὴν παρ᾽ Ἀρχελάου τέσσαρας μνᾶς ἐφ᾽
ἡμέρᾳ λαμβάνοντα ταύτας καταναλίσκειν εἰς ὀψοφαγίαν, γενόμενον ὀψοφάγον. οὐκ ἀγνοῶ δὲ καὶ τοὺς
e   ἰχθυοφάγους παῖδας, ὧν Κλέαρχος μνημονεύει | ἐν τῷ
Περὶ Θινῶν φάσκων Ψαμμήτιχον τὸν Αἰγυπτίων βα-

---

[119] Sc. because he would have liked to have had a chance of
getting some of the food for himself instead.

[120] Neither man is known from any other source (but cf. Sosip.
fr. 1.2, preserved at 9.377f, where a braggart cook's interlocutor is
named Demylus).

[121] D.L. 7.19 preserves a very similar anecdote.

[122] Choerilus of Samos, the epic poet; 22 lines or partial lines
of his poetry, supplemented by some dubiously attributed papy-

thief!"[119] As for Cindon the glutton and Demylus (who
was also a glutton),[120] when a *glaukos*—but nothing else—
was served, Cindon grabbed its eye. Demylus jammed
his thumb into Cindon's eye and tried to strong-arm him,
shouting: "You let go, and I'll let go!" Once when a nice casserole-dish of fish was served at a dinner party, Demylus
could see no way to eat it all himself—so he spat in it. According to Antigonus of Carystus in his *Life of Zeno* (pp.
119–20 Wilamowitz = fr. 38A Dorandi = Zeno fr. 290, *SVF*
i.66), Zeno of Citium, the founder of the Stoa, shared a
house for a long time with a glutton; when a large fish happened to be served, but no other food had been prepared,
Zeno grabbed the entire fish from the platter and managed
to wolf it down. The other man glowered in his direction,
and Zeno said: "What do you think your housemates go
through, if you can't put up with someone else's gluttony
for a single day?"[121] Istrus (*FGrH* 334 F 61) claims that the
poet Choerilus[122] got four *minas*[123] per day from Archelaus
and spent the money gorging himself, since he was a glutton. I also know about the fish-eating slaves Clearchus
mentions in his *On Deserts* (fr. 98 Wehrli), where he reports that the Egyptian king Psammetichus[124] bred fish-

rus fragments, survive. Archelaus king of Macedon (reigned 413–
399 BCE) lured numerous famous poets, including Euripides and
Agathon, to his court with gifts of large amounts of money.

[123] I.e. 400 drachmas, as much as a skilled workman earned in
a year.

[124] Presumably Psammetichus I (reigned 664–610 BCE),
founder of the 26th (Saite) dynasty, rather than his grandson
Psammetichus II (reigned 595–589); cf. Herodotus' story at 2.2
about his experiments involving the ontogony of human speech.

σιλέα παῖδας θρέψαι ἰχθυοφάγους, τὰς πηγὰς τοῦ
Νείλου βουλόμενον εὑρεῖν· καὶ ἄλλους δὲ ἀδίψους
ἀσκῆσαι τοὺς ἐρευνησομένους τὰς ἐν Λιβύῃ ψάμμους,
ὧν ὀλίγοι διεσώθησαν. οἶδα δὲ καὶ τοὺς περὶ Μόσ-
συνον τῆς Θρᾴκης βοῦς, οἳ ἰχθῦς ἐσθίουσι παραβαλ-
λομένους αὐτοῖς εἰς τὰς φάτνας. Φοινικίδης δὲ τοὺς
ἰχθῦς παρατιθεὶς τοῖς τὰς συμβολὰς δεδωκόσι τὴν
μὲν θάλασσαν ἔλεγε κοινὴν εἶναι, τοὺς δ' ἐν αὐτῇ
ἰχθῦς τῶν ὠνησαμένων.

f   Εἴρηται δὲ καὶ ὁ ὀψοφάγος, ὦ ἑταῖροι, καὶ | τὸ
ὀψοφαγεῖν. Ἀριστοφάνης ἐν Νεφέλαις δευτέραις·

    οὐδ' ὀψοφαγεῖν οὐδὲ κιχλίζειν.

Κηφισόδωρος Ὑΐ·

    οὐδ' ὀψοφάγος οὐδ' ἀδολέσχης.

Μάχων Ἐπιστολῇ·

    ὀψοφάγος εἰμί, τοῦτο δ' ἐστὶ τῆς τέχνης ‖
346 θεμέλιος ἡμῖν. προσπεπονθέναι τι δεῖ
    τὸν μὴ τὰ παραδοθέντα λυμανούμενον·
    πεφροντικὼς αὐτοῦ γὰρ οὐκ ἔσται κακός.
    ἔπειτ' ἐπὰν ᾖ καθαρὰ τὰσθητήρια,
    οὐκ ἂν διαμάρτοις. ἕψε καὶ γεύου πυκνά.

---

[125] The idea is that the diet to which they were accustomed
would allow them to live off the river's produce, no matter how far
they followed it upstream.

[126] Cf. Hdt. 5.16.4.

eating slaves because he wanted to discover the sources of the Nile.[125] He also trained other slaves to go without water, so that they could explore the deserts in Libya; only a few survived. In addition, I am familiar with the cattle found around Mossynus in Thrace, which eat any fish that are thrown into their mangers.[126] When Phoenicides[127] served fish to the people who had contributed to the dinner expenses, he used to say that the sea belonged to everyone, but the fish it contained were the property of those who paid for them.

The word *opsophagos* ("glutton") is used, my friends, as is *opsophagein* ("to be a glutton"). Aristophanes in *Clouds II*[128] (983):

> not *opsophagein* or to giggle.

Cephisodorus in *The Pig* (fr. 9):

> not an *opsophagos* or a chatterer.

Macho in *The Letter* (fr. 2):

> I'm an *opsophagos*, and this is the fundamental basis
> of our business. If you don't want to ruin
> your raw materials, you have to be sympathetic to
>   them;
> no one who's self-aware will abuse them.
> Also, when your sense-organs are clear,
> you won't make mistakes. Taste what you're cooking
>   repeatedly!

[127] See 8.342f n.
[128] I.e. the preserved version of the play, rather than the original (staged in 423 BCE and a failure).

ἄλας οὐκ ἔχει· προσένεγκ'. ⟨ἔτ'⟩ ἐπιδεῖταί τινος
ἑτέρου· πάλιν γεύου σύ, μέχρι ἂν ἡδὺς ᾖ,
ὥσπερ λύραν ἐπίτειν' ἕως ⟨ἂν⟩ ἁρμόσῃ. |
b   εἶθ' ὁπόταν ἤδη πάντα συμφωνεῖν δοκῇς,
εἴσαγε διὰ πασῶν † Νικολαΐδας Μυκόνιος.†

πρὸς τούτοις τοῖς ὀψοφάγοις, ἄνδρες ἑταῖροι, οἶδα καὶ
τὸν παρ' Ἠλείοις τιμώμενον Ὀψοφάγον Ἀπόλλωνα·
μνημονεύει δὲ αὐτοῦ Πολέμων ἐν τῇ Πρὸς Ἄτταλον
Ἐπιστολῇ. οἶδα δὲ καὶ τὴν ἐν τῇ Πισάτιδι γραφὴν
ἀνακειμένην ἐν τῷ τῆς Ἀλφειώσας Ἀρτέμιδος ἱερῷ
(Κλεάνθους δ' ἐστὶ τοῦ Κορινθίου), ἐν ᾗ Ποσειδῶν
c   πεποίηται θύννον τῷ Διὶ | προσφέρων ὠδίνοντι, ὡς
ἱστορεῖ Δημήτριος ἐν ὀγδόῳ Τρωικοῦ Διακόσμου.

Καὶ τοσαῦτα μέν, ἔφη ὁ Δημόκριτος, καὶ αὐτὸς
ὑμῖν προσοψωνήσας οὐκ ὀψοφαγήσων παρῆλθον διὰ
τὸν πάντα ἄριστον Οὐλπιανόν, ὃς διὰ τὰ Σύρων
πάτρια καὶ ἡμᾶς τῶν ἰχθύων ἀπεστέρησεν ἕτερ' ἐκ
Συρίας παρεισφέρων. καίτοι γε Ἀντίπατρος ὁ Ταρ-
σεὺς ὁ ἀπὸ τῆς στοᾶς ἐν τετάρτῳ Περὶ Δεισιδαιμονίας
λέγεσθαί φησι πρός τινων ὅτι Γάτις ἡ τῶν Σύρων
d   βασίλισσα οὕτως ἦν ὀψοφάγος ὥστε κηρῦξαι | ἄτερ
Γάτιδος μηδένα ἰχθὺν ἐσθίειν· ὑπ' ἀγνοίας δὲ τοὺς

---

129 Sc. to Athena, from his head; cf. Str. 8.343, who mentions a
second painting by Cleanthes, a Sack of Troy, in the same temple.
Cleanthes was a very early Greek painter (perhaps early 7th century BCE); cf. Plin. *Nat.* 35.16. The point of the reference here

It needs salt? Add some! It still needs something
else? Taste it again until it's delicious,
and tweak it like a lyre until it's right!
Then, once you think everything's in tune,
take it in among all † Nicolaidas of Myconos †.

In addition to these gluttons, gentlemen, I am also familiar with Apollo Opsophagos ("the Glutton"), who is worshipped in Elis; Polemon mentions him in his *Letter to
Attalus* (fr. 70 Preller). I also know about the painting dedicated in the temple of Artemis Alpheiosa in Pisa (the artist
is Cleanthes of Corinth), which shows Poseidon offering a
tuna to Zeus as Zeus gives birth,[129] according to Demetrius
in Book VIII of the *Trojan Battle-Order* (fr. 5 Gaede).

Although I personally offered you all this additional
seafood, said Democritus, I did not come here to be a glutton, on account of the excellent Ulpian, who has followed
his ancestral Syrian customs by depriving us of our fish,
while still offering us other Syrian goods.[130] Nevertheless
the Stoic Antipater of Tarsus in Book IV of *On Superstition*
(fr. 64, *SVF* iii.257) reports that some authorities claim that
the Syrian queen Gatis was such a glutton that she announced that no one was to eat fish except (*ater*) Gatis; so
out of ignorance many people began to refer to her as

must be that Zeus was—allegedly—represented as a typical fish-
loving glutton. But doubtless the fish in Poseidon's hand was
merely a bit of crude standard iconography, designed to identify
him as the god of the sea.

[130] At 7.275c, Ulpian suspends the serving of the fish so that
the guests can speak freely. The "other Syrian goods" in question
probably include frankincense, which was routinely burned at
sacrifices and dinner parties.

πολλοὺς αὐτὴν μὲν Ἀταργάτιν ὀνομάζειν, ἰχθύων δὲ
ἀπέχεσθαι. Μνασέας δ᾽ ἐν δευτέρῳ Περὶ Ἀσίας φησὶν
οὕτως· ἐμοὶ μὲν ἡ Ἀταργάτις δοκεῖ χαλεπὴ βασίλισ-
σα γεγονέναι καὶ τῶν λαῶν σκληρῶς ἐπεστατηκέναι,
ὥστε καὶ ἀπονομίσαι αὐτοῖς ἰχθὺν μὴ ἐσθίειν, ἀλλὰ
πρὸς αὐτὴν ἀναφέρειν διὰ τὸ ἀρέσαι αὐτῇ τὸ βρῶμα.
καὶ διὰ τόδε νόμιμον ἔτι διαμένειν, ἐπὰν εὔξωνται τῇ
θεῷ, ἰχθῦς ἀργυροῦς ἢ χρυσοῦς ἀνατιθέναι· τοὺς δὲ
e ἱερεῖς | πᾶσαν ἡμέραν τῇ θεῷ ἀληθινοὺς ἰχθῦς ἐπὶ τὴν
τράπεζαν ὀψοποιησαμένους παρατιθέναι, ἑφθούς τε
ὁμοίως καὶ ὀπτούς, οὓς δὴ αὐτοὶ καταναλίσκουσιν οἱ
τῆς θεοῦ ἱερεῖς. καὶ μικρὸν προελθὼν πάλιν φησίν· ἡ
δέ γε Ἀταργάτις, ὥσπερ Ξάνθος λέγει ὁ Λυδός, ὑπὸ
Μόψου τοῦ Λυδοῦ ἁλοῦσα κατεποντίσθη μετὰ Ἰχθύος
τοῦ υἱοῦ ἐν τῇ περὶ Ἀσκάλωνα λίμνῃ διὰ τὴν ὕβριν
καὶ ὑπὸ τῶν ἰχθύων κατεβρώθη. τάχα δὲ καὶ ὑμεῖς,
ἄνδρες φίλοι, ἑκόντες παρελίπετε ὡς ἱερόν τινα ἰχθὺν
f τὸν παρ᾽ Ἐφίππῳ | τῷ κωμῳδιοποιῷ, ὅν φησι τῷ
Γηρυόνῃ σκευάζεσθαι ἐν τῷ ὁμωνύμῳ δράματι διὰ
τούτων λέγων·

τούτῳ δ᾽ ὁπόταν ναέται χώρας
ἰχθύν τιν᾽ ἕλωσ᾽ οὐχ ἡμέριον,
τῆς περικλύστου δ᾽ ἁλίας Κρήτης
μείζω μεγέθει, λοπάς ἐστ᾽ αὐτῷ
δυνατὴ τούτους χωρεῖν ἑκατόν.
347 καὶ περιοίκους ‖ εἶναι ταύτῃ

Atargatis[131] and to avoid fish. Mnaseas in Book II of *On Asia* (fr. 31 Cappelletto) says the following: In my opinion, Atargatis was a cruel queen who ruled harshly over her people, to the extent that she even refused to allow them to eat fish, and instead ordered that they bring it to her, because this was her favorite food. As a consequence, it is still their practice to dedicate silver or gold fish when they pray to the goddess; and all day long the priests cook real fish and serve them, both stewed and roasted, to the goddess on her cult-table—although the goddess' priests themselves, of course, consume them. And a little further on again he says: According to Xanthus of Lydia (*FGrH* 765 F 17a), Atargatis was captured by Mopsus of Lydia and was drowned in the lake near Ascalon, along with her son Ichthys[132], because of her outrageous behavior, and was eaten by the fish. But perhaps you too, my friends, deliberately passed over the fish found in the comic poet Ephippus on the ground that it was sacred. He claims that it was prepared for Geryon[133], in the following passage from the play by the same name (fr. 5):

> Whenever the inhabitants of the country catch
> an exceptional fish for him,
> one larger in size than Crete, which rests
> in the middle of the sea, he has a casserole-dish
> capable of holding 100 of these.
> The people who live on its edge

[131] The goddess known in the Roman world as the *Dea Syria* ("Syrian goddess").　　[132] "Fish"; cf. 7.301d.

[133] A mythical king of Erythrae, killed by Heracles ([Apollod.] *Bib*. 2.5.10).

Σίνδους, Λυκίους, Μυγδονιώτας,
Κραναούς, Παφίους. τούτους δ᾽ ὕλην
κόπτειν, ὁπόταν βασιλεὺς ἕψῃ
τὸν μέγαν ἰχθύν· καὶ προσάγοντας,
καθ᾽ ὅσον πόλεως ἕστηκεν ὄρος,
τοὺς δ᾽ ὑποκαίειν. λίμνην δ᾽ ἐπάγειν
ὕδατος μεστὴν εἰς τὴν ἅλμην,
τοὺς δ᾽ ἅλας αὐτῷ ζεύγη προσάγειν
μηνῶν ὀκτὼ συνεχῶς ἑκατόν. |
περιπλεῖν δ᾽ ἐπὶ τοῖς ἄμβωσιν ἄνω
πέντε κέλητας πεντασκάλμους
περιαγγέλλειν τ᾽· "οὐχ ὑποκαίεις,
Λυκίων πρύτανι; ψυχρὸν τουτί."
"παύου φυσῶν, Μακεδὼν ἄρχων."
"σβέννυ, Κέλθ᾽, ὡς μὴ προσκαύσῃς."

οὐκ ἀγνοῶ δ᾽ ὅτι τὰ αὐτὰ ταῦτα εἴρηκεν ὁ Ἔφιππος
κἂν Πελταστῇ τῷ δράματι, ἐν ᾧ καὶ ταῦτα | ἐκείνοις
ὑποτέτακται·

τοιαῦθ᾽ ὑθλῶν δειπνεῖ καὶ ζῇ
θαυμαζόμενος μετὰ μειρακίων,
οὐ γινώσκων ψήφων ἀριθμούς,
σεμνὸς σεμνῶς χλανίδ᾽ ἕλκων.

εἰς τίνα δὲ ταῦτ᾽ ἀποτεινόμενος ὁ Ἔφιππος εἴρηκεν
ὥρα σοι ζητεῖν, καλὲ Οὐλπιανέ, καὶ διδάσκειν ἡμᾶς.
καὶ τῶν εἰρημένων τούτων

are Sindians, Lycians, Mygdoniotae,
Cranaoi, and Paphians. They chop
wood when the king is cooking
his big fish, and bring as
much as the city's walls can hold,
and set fire to it. They also bring a lake
full of water for the stewing-brine;
100 teams of oxen work continuously for eight
months to transport the salt for it.
Five fast little boats[134]
sail about on top of the rim
and carry his orders around: "Light the fire,
Lycian commander! This part's cold!"
"Stop blowing on it, ruler of Macedon!"
"Quench that flame, Celt—watch you don't burn it!"

I am well aware that Ephippus makes exactly the same remarks in his play *The Peltast* (fr. 19), in which the following
lines come after the ones just quoted:

This is the nonsense he talks as he eats dinner and
        lives
in enviable style with the boys;
although he can't work an abacus,
    he's proud and wears a fancy wool garment
        proudly.

It is time for you, my good Ulpian, to take up the question
of the object of these remarks by Ephippus, and to offer us
some instruction. And if any of my remarks

---

[134] Literally "five-tholed yachts".

εἴ τί σοι ψελλόν τε καὶ δυσεύρετον,
ἐπανδίπλαζε καὶ σαφῶς ἐκμάνθανε·
σχολὴ δὲ πλείων ἢ θέλω πάρεστί μοι,

κατὰ τὸν Αἰσχύλου Προμηθέα. καὶ ὁ Κύνουλκος |
d ἀνεβόησε· καὶ τίν' ἂν τῶν μεγάλων οὗτος οὐκ ἰχθύων,
ἀλλὰ ζητήσεων ἐπὶ νοῦν λάβοι; ὃς τὰς ἀκάνθας ἀεὶ
ἐκλέγει ἑψητῶν τε καὶ ἀθερίνων καὶ εἴ τι τούτων
ἀτυχέστερόν ἐστιν ἰχθύδιον, τὰ μεγάλα τεμάχη παρα-
πεμπόμενος. καθάπερ γὰρ

ἐν ταῖς γεννικαῖς εὐωχίαις,

φησὶν ἐν Ἰξίονι Εὔβουλος,

ἀμύλων παρόντων ἐσθίουσ' ἑκάστοτε
ἄνηθα καὶ σέλινα καὶ φλυαρίας
καὶ κάρδαμ' ἐσκευασμένα,

οὕτω μοι δοκεῖ καὶ ὁ λεβητοχάρων Οὐλπιανός, κατὰ |
e τὸν ἐμὸν Μεγαλοπολίτην Κερκιδᾶν, μηδὲν μὲν ἐσθίειν
τῶν ἀνδρὶ προσηκόντων, τηρεῖν δὲ τοὺς ἐσθίοντας εἰ
παρεῖδον ἢ ἄκανθαν ἢ τῶν τραγανῶν τι ἢ χονδρῶδες
τῶν παρατεθέντων, οὐδ' ἐπὶ νοῦν βαλλόμενος τὸ τοῦ
καλοῦ καὶ λαμπροῦ Αἰσχύλου, ὃς τὰς αὑτοῦ τραγῳδίας τεμάχη εἶναι ἔλεγεν τῶν Ὁμήρου μεγάλων δείπνων. φιλόσοφος δὲ ἦν τῶν πάνυ ὁ Αἰσχύλος, ὃς καὶ

---

[135] A glancing allusion to one of Athenaeus' favorite common-
places (3.97c–d with n.; 6.228c; 9.385b; 15.671c), as again below.

> seem unintelligible or obscure to you,
> return to the point and achieve a clear
> understanding;
> I have more free time than I wish,

to quote Aeschylus' *Prometheus* (816–18). Cynulcus bellowed: But what large questions—not large fish—would interest this fellow? He is always collecting the backbones[135] of stewing-fish and herring, or of any little fish more miserable than these, and rejecting the large steaks. For just as

> at aristocratic banquets,

as Eubulus puts it in *Ixion* (fr. 35, including what follows),

> although wheat-paste cakes are available, they
>   routinely eat
> anise and celery and similar nonsense
> and cress that's been prepared for them,

that is how, it seems to me, our cauldron-friend (to quote my countryman Cercidas of Megalopolis [fr. 11, p. 212 Powell]) Ulpian behaves: he eats none of the foods that are appropriate for a man, but keeps an eye on the people who are dining, to see if they overlooked a backbone, a bit of gristle, or a cartilaginous part of what has been served! He fails to keep in mind the comment by the noble and distinguished Aeschylus (test. 112a), who used to claim that his own tragedies were steaks cut from Homer's great banquets. Aeschylus was a first-rate philosopher; once when

ἡττηθεὶς ἀδίκως ποτέ, ὡς Θεόφραστος ἢ Χαμαιλέων
f ἐν τῷ Περὶ Ἡδονῆς εἴρηκεν, ἔφη Χρόνῳ | τὰς τραγῳ-
δίας ἀνατιθέναι, εἰδὼς ὅτι κομιεῖται τὴν προσήκουσαν
τιμήν. πόθεν δὲ καὶ εἰδέναι δύναται, ἅπερ εἶπεν Στρατόνικος ὁ κιθαριστὴς εἰς Πρόπιν τὸν Ῥόδιον κιθαρῳδόν; Κλέαρχος γὰρ ἐν τοῖς Περὶ Παροιμιῶν φησιν ὡς
ὁ Στρατόνικος θεασάμενος τὸν Πρόπιν ὄντα τῷ μὲν
μεγέθει μέγαν, τῇ δὲ τέχνῃ κακὸν καὶ ἐλάττονα τοῦ
σώματος, ἐπερωτώντων αὐτόν, "ποῖός τίς ἐστιν;", ‖
348 εἶπεν, "οὐδεὶς κακὸς μέγας ἰχθύς," αἰνισσόμενος ὅτι
πρῶτον μὲν οὐδείς ἐστιν, εἶθ᾽ ὅτι κακός, καὶ πρὸς
τούτοις μέγας μέν, ἰχθὺς δὲ διὰ τὴν ἀφωνίαν. Θεόφραστος δ᾽ ἐν τῷ Περὶ Γελοίου λεχθῆναι μέν φησι τὴν
παροιμίαν ὑπὸ τοῦ Στρατονίκου, ἀλλ᾽ εἰς Σιμύκαν τὸν
ὑποκριτήν, διελόντος τὴν παροιμίαν "μέγας οὐδεὶς
σαπρὸς ἰχθύς." Ἀριστοτέλης δ᾽ ἐν τῇ Ναξίων Πολιτείᾳ περὶ τῆς παροιμίας οὕτως γράφει· τῶν παρὰ
b Ναξίοις εὐπόρων οἱ | μὲν πολλοὶ τὸ ἄστυ ᾤκουν, οἱ δὲ
ἄλλοι διεσπαρμένοι κατὰ κώμας. ἐν οὖν δή τινι τῶν
κωμῶν, ᾗ ὄνομα ἦν Ληϊστάδαι, Τελεσταγόρας ᾤκει,
πλούσιός τε σφόδρα καὶ εὐδοκιμῶν καὶ τιμώμενος
παρὰ τῷ δήμῳ τοῖς τ᾽ ἄλλοις ἅπασι καὶ τοῖς καθ᾽
ἡμέραν πεμπομένοις. καὶ ὅτε καταβάντες ἐκ τῆς πόλεως δυσωνοῖντό τι τῶν πωλουμένων, ἔθος ἦν τοῖς
πωλοῦσι λέγειν ὅτι μᾶλλον ἂν προέλοιντο Τελεστα-
γόρᾳ δοῦναι ἢ τοσούτου ἀποδόσθαι. νεανίσκοι οὖν

136 Stephanis #2310.

he was cheated out of the prize (test. 113a), according to Theophrastus (fr. 553 Fortenbaugh) or Chamaeleon in his *On Pleasure* (fr. 7 Wehrli), he said that he dedicated his tragedies to Time, since he knew that it would give him the honor he deserved. And how can Ulpian understand what the *cithara*-player Stratonicus[136] said about the citharode Propis of Rhodes?[137] Because Clearchus in his *On Proverbs* (fr. 80 Wehrli) reports that Stratonicus saw that Propis was physically imposing, but bad at his craft, and thus looked better than he played; and when people asked him "What do you think of this guy?", he said: "No bad fish can be described as big," implying first of all that Propis was a nobody, second that he was no good, and in addition that he might be big, but was a fish, since he had no voice. Theophrastus in his *On the Ridiculous* (fr. 710 Fortenbaugh) claims that the proverb was coined by Stratonicus, but was aimed at the actor Simycas[138] and was a reworking of the proverb "No rotten fish can be described as big" (p. 85 Strömberg). Aristotle in his *Constitution of the Naxians* (fr. 566) writes as follows about the proverb: Many rich Naxians lived in the city, while the rest were scattered about in villages. In one village, known as Leïstadae, lived Telestagoras, who was extremely wealthy and well-respected, and whom the people honored in many ways, including by sending him gifts every day. And whenever people went down to the harbor from the city and tried to drive down the price of some merchandise, the vendors routinely said that they would rather give it to Telestagoras than sell it for so little. Some young

137 Stephanis #2151.
138 Stephanis #2276.

ATHENAEUS

c τινες ὠνούμενοι μέγαν ἰχθὺν εἰπόντος | τοῦ ἁλιέως τὰ
αὐτὰ λυπηθέντες τῷ πολλάκις ἀκούειν ὑποπιόντες
ἐκώμασαν πρὸς αὐτόν. δεξαμένου δὲ τοῦ Τελεστα-
γόρου φιλοφρόνως αὐτοὺς οἱ νεανίσκοι αὐτόν τε ὕβρι-
σαν καὶ δύο θυγατέρας αὐτοῦ ἐπιγάμους. ἐφ᾽ οἷς
ἀγανακτήσαντες οἱ Νάξιοι καὶ τὰ ὅπλα ἀναλαβόντες
ἐπῆλθον τοῖς νεανίσκοις, καὶ μεγίστη τότε στάσις
ἐγένετο προστατοῦντος τῶν Ναξίων Λυγδάμιδος, ὃς
ἀπὸ ταύτης τῆς στρατηγίας τύραννος ἀνεφάνη τῆς
πατρίδος.

Οὐκ ἄκαιρον δ᾽ εἶναι νομίζω[11] ἔτι καὶ αὐτός, |
d ἐπειδήπερ ἐμνήσθην τοῦ κιθαριστοῦ Στρατονίκου,
λέξαι τι περὶ τῆς εὐστοχίας αὐτοῦ τῶν ἀποκρίσεων.
διδάσκων γὰρ κιθαριστάς, ἐπειδὴ ἐν τῷ διδασκαλείῳ
εἶχεν ἐννέα μὲν εἰκόνας τῶν Μουσῶν, τοῦ δὲ Ἀπόλλωνος μίαν, μαθητὰς δὲ δύο, πυνθανομένου τινὸς
πόσους ἔχοι μαθητάς, ἔφη, "σὺν τοῖς θεοῖς δώδεκα."
εἰς Μύλασα δ᾽ ἐπιδημήσας καὶ κατιδὼν ναοὺς μὲν
πολλούς, ἀνθρώπους δὲ ὀλίγους στὰς ἐν μέσῃ τῇ
e ἀγορᾷ ἔφη, "ἀκούετε νεώ." Μάχων δ᾽ αὐτοῦ | ἀνα-
γράφει τάδε ἀπομνημονεύματα·

Στρατόνικος ἀπεδήμησεν εἰς Πέλλαν ποτὲ
παρὰ πλειόνων ἔμπροσθε τοῦτ᾽ ἀκηκοώς

11 νομίζω εἰπεῖν A: εἰπεῖν del. Schweighäuser

139 According to Hdt. 1.64.2 and [Arist.] *Ath.* 15.3, Lygdamis
became tyrant of Naxos probably in the late 540s BCE. He was

90

men were trying to buy a large fish; when the fisherman said the usual thing, they became annoyed at hearing this again and again, and got drunk and went in a group to visit him. Although Telestagoras welcomed them amiably, the young men beat him up and abused his two marriageable daughters. The Naxians were appalled at this behavior, and seized their weapons and attacked the young men. The result was a major civic crisis, in which Lygdamis served as the Naxians' leader; he emerged from this command as tyrant of his native land.[139]

Given that I mentioned the *cithara*-player Stratonicus (8.347f–8a), I consider this an appropriate occasion to say something further myself about how aptly he responded to questions. He was offering lessons on the *cithara*, and had nine pictures of the Muses in his school, one of Apollo— and two students. When someone asked him how many pupils he had, he said: "Thanks be to the gods,[140] a dozen!" When he was visiting Mylasa and saw a large number of temples, but not many people, he stood in the middle of the marketplace and said *"Akouete neōi!"*[141] Macho (91– 167 Gow) records the following witty remarks by him:

> Stratonicus visited Pella at one point,
> having heard beforehand from many sources

overthrown by the Spartans most likely in 524 (Plu. *Mor.* 859d).

[140] The phrase (literally "with the gods") normally means— and would be understood—"thanks to the gods, with the assistance of the gods". But Stratonicus uses it to mean "counting the gods".

[141] "Attention, temples!" (a parody of the standard formula *Akouete laōi*, "Attention, people!", used to introduce public announcements of all sorts).

ὡς σπληνικοὺς εἴωθεν ἡ πόλις ποεῖν.
ἐν τῷ βαλανείῳ καταμαθὼν οὖν πλείονας
γυμναζομένους τῶν μειρακίων παρὰ τῷ πυρὶ
κομψοὺς τό τε χρῶμα καὶ τὸ σῶμ᾽ ἠσκηκότας,
διαμαρτάνειν ἔφασκε τοὺς εἰρηκότας
αὐτῷ. καταμαθὼν δ᾽ ἡνίκ᾽ ἐξῄει πάλιν
τῆς κοιλίας τὸν σπλῆν᾽ ἔχοντα διπλάσιον |

* * *

f "καθήμενος γὰρ ἐνθάδ᾽ οὗτος φαίνεται
τά ⟨θ᾽⟩ ἱμάτια τῶν εἰσιόντων λαμβάνων
τηρεῖν ἅμα καὶ τοὺς σπλῆνας εὐθέως ἵνα
μηδ᾽ ἡτισοῦν τοῖς ἔνδον ᾖ στενοχωρία."
ψάλτης κακὸς Στρατόνικον ἑστιῶν ποτε
ἐπεδείκνυτ᾽ αὐτῷ τὴν τέχνην παρὰ τὸν πότον.
οὔσης δὲ λαμπρᾶς καὶ φιλοτίμου τῆς δοχῆς
ψαλλόμενος ⟨ὁ⟩ Στρατόνικος οὐκ ἔχων δ᾽ ὅτῳ
διαλέξεθ᾽ ἑτέρῳ συγκατέθλα τὸ ποτήριον. ‖
349 ᾔτησε μεῖζον καὶ κυάθους πολλοὺς λαβὼν
τῷ θ᾽ ἡλίῳ τὴν κύλικα δείξας συντόμως
πιὼν καθεῦδε ταῦτ᾽ ἐπιτρέψας τῇ Τύχῃ.
ἐπὶ κῶμον ἐλθόντων δὲ τῷ ψάλτῃ τινῶν
ἑτέρων κατὰ τύχην, ὡς ἔοικε γνωρίμων,

---

142 A sign of chronic malaria.
143 The bath-attendant, as the verses that follow the lacuna
make clear.
144 The next six lines do not fit easily into the anecdote and
may belong elsewhere.

that the city had a tendency to produce people with
     enlarged spleens.[142]
At the bathhouse he noticed a large number of
young men exercising naked beside the fire
who had healthy-looking skin and and were well-
     built;
and he commented that his informants must have
     been
in error. As he was going out again, however, he
     noticed
someone[143] whose spleen was twice as large as his
     belly

* * *

"because this guy apparently sits here
and takes people's robes when they go in,
and keeps an eye on them, as well as their spleens,
so there won't be any shortage of space inside."
A bad harp-player had Stratonicus to dinner at one
     point
and began demonstrating his skill on the instrument
     to him as they drank.[144]
Although the hospitality was brilliant and lavish,
Stratonicus had no one else to talk to as he
listened to the music, so he broke his cup;
asked for a larger one; took numerous ladlesful of
     wine;
quickly toasted the sun;
and after he finished drinking, fell asleep, trusting his
     luck.
Some other people—acquaintances of the harp-
     player,
apparently—happened to visit to join the party.

ἔξοινος ὁ Στρατόνικος ἐγένετ᾽ εὐθέως,
προσπυνθανομένων δ᾽ ὅ τι πολὺν πίνων ἀεὶ
οἶνον ἐμεθύσθη συντόμως, ἀπεκρίνατο,
"ὁ γὰρ ἐπίβουλος κἀναγὴς ψάλτης", ἔφη,
"ὡς βοῦν ἐπὶ φάτνῃ δειπνίσας ἀπέκτονεν." |

b   Στρατόνικος εἰς Ἄβδηρ᾽ ἀποδημήσας ποτὲ
ἐπὶ τὸν ἀγῶνα τὸν τιθέμενον αὐτόθι,
ὁρῶν ἕκαστον τῶν πολιτῶν κατ᾽ ἰδίαν
κεκτημένον κήρυκα κηρύττοντά τε
ἕκαστον αὐτῶν ὅτε θέλοι νουμηνίαν
σχεδόν τε τοὺς κήρυκας ἐν τῷ χωρίῳ
ὄντας πολὺ πλείους κατὰ λόγον τῶν δημοτῶν,
ἐπ᾽ ἄκρων ἐβάδιζε τῶν ὀνύχων ἐν τῇ πόλει
σχέδην, δεδορκὼς ἀτενὲς εἰς τὴν γῆν κάτω.
πυνθανομένου δὲ τῶν ξένων αὐτοῦ τινος |

c   τὸ πάθος τὸ γεγονὸς ἐξαπίνης περὶ τοὺς πόδας
τοῦτ᾽ εἶπε, "τοῖς ὅλοις μὲν ἔρρωμαι, ξένε,
καὶ τῶν κολάκων πολὺ μᾶλλον ἐπὶ δεῖπνον
    τρέχω,
ἀγωνιῶ δὲ καὶ δέδοικα παντελῶς
μή ποτ᾽ ἐπιβὰς κήρυκι τὸν πόδ᾽ ἀναπαρῶ."
αὐλεῖν ἐπὶ τοῖς ἱεροῖσιν αὐλητοῦ κακοῦ
μέλλοντος ὁ Στρατόνικος, "εὐφήμει μέχρι

---

[145] An adaptation of *Od.* 4.534–5; 11.410–11 (of Agamemnon's death at Aegisthus' hands).
[146] Both "herald" and "whelk".

Stratonicus was thoroughly smashed.
and when they asked him why, if he always drank a
    lot
of wine, he had got drunk so quickly, he replied:
"Because the treacherous and defiled harp-player",
    he said,
"fed me like an ox at a manger and then slaughtered
    me."[145]
Stratonicus visited Abdera at one point
for a competition that was being held there.
When he saw that every citizen had a private
herald, and that each of them was issuing a
    proclamation
about when he wanted the new moon celebrated,
and that the heralds in the place were, by his count,
almost more numerous than the citizens,
he walked slowly around the city
on tiptoe, staring intently down at the ground.
When someone visiting from out of town asked him
what sudden injury he had suffered to his feet,
he said the following: "I'm by and large healthy,
    stranger,
and I can outrace the flatterers to dinner.
But I'm thoroughly anxious and terrified
that I'm going to step on a *kērux*[146] and injure my
    foot."
A bad pipe-player was about to perform at
a sacrifice, and Stratonicus said: "Maintain a holy
    silence until

σπείσαντες εὐξώμεσθά", φησι, "τοῖς θεοῖς."
Κλέων τις ἦν κιθαρῳδός, ὃς ἐκαλεῖτο Βοῦς,
δεινῶς ἀπᾴδων τῇ λύρᾳ τ᾽ οὐ χρώμενος· |

d   τούτου διακούσας ὁ Στρατόνικος εἶφ᾽ ὅτι
"ὄνος λύρας ἐλέγετο, νῦν δὲ Βοῦς λύρας."
Στρατόνικος ὁ κιθαρῳδὸς ὡς Βηρισάδην
ἔπλευσεν εἰς τὸν Πόντον ὄντα βασιλέα.
πολλοῦ χρόνου δ᾽ ἤδη γεγονότος ἀποτρέχειν
ἠβούλετο Στρατόνικος εἰς τὴν Ἑλλάδα.
ὡς δ᾽ αὐτόν, ὡς ἔοικεν, οὐ προσίετο
τοῦτ᾽, ἀποκριθῆναί φασι τῷ Βηρισάδῃ,
"σὺ γὰρ διανοεῖ", φησίν, "αὐτοῦ καταμένειν;"
ἐν τῇ Κορίνθῳ παρεπεδήμησέν ποτε |

e   Στρατόνικος ὁ κιθαρῳδός, εἶτα γρᾴδιον
ἐνέβλεπεν αὐτῷ κοὐκ ἀφίστατ᾽ οὐδαμοῦ.
κᾆθ᾽ ὁ Στρατόνικος, "πρὸς θεῶν, μῆτερ, φράσον
τί ἔσθ᾽ ὃ βούλει καὶ τί μ᾽ εἰσβλέπεις ἀεί."
"διηπόρησά," φησιν· "ἡ μήτηρ σε ⟨γὰρ⟩
δέκα μῆνας εἶχε κἀκράτει τῆς κοιλίας,
πόλις δ᾽ ἔχουσά σ᾽ ἡμέραν ἀλγεῖ μίαν."

---

147 "Holy silence", intended to avoid words of ill omen, was generally requested of all participants in a sacrifice—except the pipe-player!   148 Stephanis #1456.

149 Macar. 6.39; said of an individual unable to appreciate something good.   150 King of Thrace 358–357/6 BCE.

151 Cf. 8.350f. The Greeks (whose months were slightly shorter than ours, and who tended to count inclusively in any case) regularly refer to a full-term pregnancy as lasting ten months.

we've poured a libation and prayed to the gods!"[147]
Cleon,[148] a citharode whose nickname was Ox,
was singing horribly off-key, unaccompanied by his
　　lyre.
After Stratonicus listened to him perform, he said:
"The saying used to be 'A donkey (listening to) a
　　lyre'[149]—but now it's 'An Ox (listening to) a
　　lyre'".
The citharode Stratonicus sailed to the
Black Sea to visit Berisades[150], the local king.
After a long time had passed, Stratonicus
wanted to return to Greece.
When Berisades, apparently, didn't want
to let him do so, people say, he responded:
"Do *you*", he said, "actually intend to stay here?"
The citharode Stratonicus was visiting
Corinth at one point, and an old woman
kept staring at him and refused to leave him alone.
So Stratonicus said: "By the gods, madam—tell me
what it is you want and why you're constantly staring
　　at me!"
"I'm puzzled," she said; "because your mother carried
you for ten months without miscarrying—
but our city's suffering by having you around for a
　　single day."[151]

152 For Nicocreon, see 8.337e n. At 8.352c–d Athenaeus (citing Phaenias) claims that Stratonicus was not drowned (below),
but ordered to drink poison, and not by Nicocreon, but by another
king of Cyprus, Nicocles, who dates to a generation earlier. Which
account—if either—is correct, is impossible to say.

ATHENAEUS

ἡ Νικοκρέοντος εἰσιοῦσα Βιοθέα
γυνὴ μετὰ παιδίσκης ἁβρᾶς εἰς τὸν πότον
ἀπεψόφησε, κᾆτα τῷ Σικυωνίῳ |
f ἀμυγδάλην ἐπιβᾶσα συνέτριβεν ταχύ.
Στρατόνικος εἶπεν, "οὐχ ὅμοιος ὁ ψόφος."
ὑπὸ νύκτα τῆς φωνῆς δὲ ταύτης οὕνεκα
ἐν τῷ πελάγει διέλυσε τὴν παρρησίαν.
ἐπιδεικνυμένου πόθ᾽, ὡς ἔοικεν ἐν Ἐφέσῳ,
ἀφυοῦς κιθαρῳδοῦ τὸν μαθητὴν τοῖς φίλοις,
παρὼν κατὰ τύχην ὁ Στρατόνικος τοῦτ᾽ ἔφη·
"ὃς αὐτὸς αὑτὸν οὐ κιθ‹αρίζει φαῦλος ὢν›
ἄλλους κιθ‹αρίζων φαυλότατος ὢν δείκνυται›."

Κλέαρχος δ᾽ ἐν δευτέρῳ Περὶ Φιλίας, Στρατόνικος,
φησίν, ὁ κιθαριστὴς ἀναπαύεσθαι μέλλων ἐκέλευεν
ἀεὶ τὸν παῖδα προσφέρειν αὐτῷ πιεῖν· "οὐχ ὅτι διψῶ,"
φησίν, "ἵνα δὲ μὴ διψήσω." ἐν δὲ Βυζαντίῳ κιθαρῳ-
350 δοῦ ‖ τὸ μὲν προοίμιον ᾄσαντος εὖ, ἐν δὲ τοῖς λοιποῖς
ἀποτυγχάνοντος, ἀναστὰς ἐκήρυξεν, "ὃς ἂν κατα-
μηνύσῃ τὸν τὸ προοίμιον ᾄσαντα κιθαρῳδόν, λήψεται
χιλίας δραχμάς." ἐρωτηθεὶς δ᾽ ὑπό τινος τίνες εἰσὶν οἱ
μοχθηρότατοι, τῶν ἐν Παμφυλίᾳ Φασηλίτας μὲν ἔφησε μοχθηροτάτους εἶναι, Σιδήτας δὲ τῶν ἐν τῇ οἰκου-
μένῃ. πάλιν δ᾽ ἐπερωτηθείς, ὥς φησιν Ἡγήσανδρος,

153 Which thus by implication excluded Pamphylia.

98

Nicocreon's[152] wife Biothea entered
a drinking party, accompanied by a delicate little
    slave-girl;
passed some gas; and then quickly stepped on an
    almond
with her Sicyonian shoe and cracked it.
Stratonicus said: "That didn't sound the same."
He paid for his outspokenness in the sea
one night as a result of this remark.
At one point, apparently in Ephesus, an untalented
    citharode
was showing off his pupil to his friends.
Stratonicus happened to be there and said the
    following:
"The same guy who won't perform in public because
    he's no good
makes other people perform and thus proves he's
    terrible."

Clearchus says in Book II of *On Friendship* (fr. 18 Wehrli):
When the *cithara*-player Stratonicus was about to go to
sleep, he always ordered his slave to bring him a drink,
"Not because I'm thirsty," he said, "but so I don't *get* thirsty."
In Byzantium a citharode sang his prelude well, but the
performance was otherwise a failure. (Stratonicus) stood
up and announced: "If anyone can identify the citharode
who sang the prelude, he will receive a reward of 1000
drachmas!" When someone asked him who the nastiest
people were, he said that the inhabitants of Phaselis were
the nastiest people in Pamphylia, but that the inhabitants
of Side were the nastiest people in the civilized world.[153]
Again, according to Hegesander (fr. 11, *FHG* iv.415), when

99

ATHENAEUS

πότερα Βοιωτοὶ βαρβαρώτεροι τυγχάνουσιν ὄντες ἢ
b Θετταλοί, Ἠλείους ἔφησεν. ἀναστήσας δέ | ποτε καὶ
τρόπαιον ἐν τῇ διατριβῇ ἐπέγραψε "κατὰ τῶν κακῶς
κιθαριζόντων." ἐρωτηθεὶς δὲ ὑπό τινος τίνα τῶν πλοίων ἀσφαλέστατά ἐστι, τὰ μακρὰ ἢ τὰ στρογγύλα, τὰ
νενεωλκημένα εἶπεν. ἐν Ῥόδῳ δ' ἐπίδειξιν ποιούμενος,
ὡς οὐδεὶς ἐπεσημήνατο, καταλιπὼν τὸ θέατρον ἐξῆλθεν εἰπών, "ὅπου τὸ ἀδάπανον οὐ ποιεῖτε, πῶς ἐγὼ
ἐλπίζω παρ' ὑμῶν ἔρανον λήψεσθαι;" < . . . > "γυμνι-
κοὺς δὲ ἀγῶνας", ἔφη, "διατιθέτωσαν Ἠλεῖοι, Κορίν-
c θιοι δὲ θυμελικούς, | Ἀθηναῖοι δὲ σκηνικούς. εἰ δέ τις
τούτων πλημμελοίη, μαστιγούσθωσαν Λακεδαιμόνιοι", ἐπισκώπτων τὰς παρ' αὐτοῖς ἀγομένας μαστι-
γώσεις, ὥς φησι Χαρικλῆς ἐν τῷ πρώτῳ Περὶ τοῦ
Ἀστικοῦ Ἀγῶνος. Πτολεμαίου δὲ τοῦ βασιλέως περὶ
κιθαριστικῆς πρὸς αὐτὸν διαλεγομένου φιλονικότε-
ρον, "ἕτερόν ἐστιν," εἶπεν, "ὦ βασιλεῦ, σκῆπτρον", ὥς
φησι Καπίτων ὁ ἐποποιὸς ἐν τετάρτῳ τῶν Πρὸς Φιλό-
παππον Ὑπομνημάτων. παρακληθεὶς δ' ἀκοῦσαί ποτε
κιθαρῳδοῦ μετὰ τὴν ἀκρόασιν ἔφη· |

d   τῷ δ' ἕτερον μὲν ἔδωκε πατήρ, ἕτερον δ'
       ἀνένευσεν·

---

154 Where the Olympic Games—at which Stratonicus had apparently not done well recently—were held.
155 Sc. and had thus been defeated, allowing Stratonicus to
erect his monument; cf. the very similar anecdote at 8.351f.

100

he was asked whether the Boeotians or the Thessalians were the more barbaric, he said he was voting for the inhabitants of Elis.[154] He once set up a victory monument in his school and inscribed on it "In condemnation of those who play the *cithara* badly."[155] When someone asked him which ships were the safest, warships or merchantships, he said it was the ones that had been hauled up onto the shore. He put on a show in Rhodes, and when no one applauded, he said on his way out of the theater: "Why do I think I'm going to get money out of you, when you won't do something that's yours for free?" . . . "Let the inhabitants of Elis organize athletic competitions," he said, "the Corinthians musical competitions, and the Athenians dramatic competitions. And if any of them makes a mistake, let the Spartans be whipped," as a way of making fun of the floggings they celebrate, according to Charicles in Book I of *On the City Contest* (*FGrH* 367 F 1). When King Ptolemy[156] was discussing *cithara*-playing with him in a combative way, he said: "A sceptre (*skēptron*) is one thing, your majesty,"[157] according to the epic poet Capito in Book IV of his *Commentaries Directed to Philopappus*. Once when he was invited to listen to a citharode, he said after the performance (*Il.* 16.250):

> The father granted him one request, but refused the other.

[156] Ptolemy I Soter only assumed the title "King" in 305 BCE, and this anecdote is thus much too late for the historical Stratonicus and must have been told originally of some other famous and witty musician.

[157] Sc. "but a lyre-pick (*plēktron*) is another".

ATHENAEUS

καί τινος εἰπόντος "τὸ ποῖον;" ἔφη, "κακῶς μὲν κιθαρίζειν ἔδωκεν, ᾄδειν δὲ καλῶς ἀνένευσε." δοκοῦ δέ ποτε
καταπεσούσης καὶ ἀποκτεινάσης ἕνα τῶν πονηρῶν,
"ἄνδρες," ἔφη, "δοκῶ, εἰσὶ θεοί· εἰ δὲ μή εἰσι, δοκοί
εἰσιν." ἀναγράφει δὲ καὶ τάδε μετὰ τὰ προειρημένα
τοῦ Στρατονίκου ἀπομνημονευμάτων οὕτως. Στρατόνικος πρὸς τὸν Χρυσογόνου πατέρα λέγοντα ὅτι πάντα
e αὐτῷ ὑπάρχει | οἰκεῖα· αὐτὸς μὲν γὰρ ἐργολάβος
εἶναι, τῶν δὲ υἱῶν ὁ μὲν διδάξει, ὁ δὲ αὐλήσει, "προσ-
δεῖ γ'", ἔφη ὁ Στρατόνικος, "ἔτι ἑνός." εἰπόντος δὲ
"τίνος;", "θεάτρου", ἔφη, "οἰκείου." ἐρομένου δέ τινος ὅ
τι τὴν Ἑλλάδα πᾶσαν περινοστεῖ, ἀλλ' οὐκ ἐν μιᾷ
πόλει διαμένει, παρὰ τῶν Μουσῶν ἔφη εἰληφέναι
τέλος τοὺς Ἕλληνας ἅπαντας, παρ' ὧν πράττεσθαι
μισθὸν ἀμουσίας. τὸν Φάωνα δὲ ἔφη αὐλεῖν οὐχ
ἁρμονίαν, ἀλλὰ τὸν Κάδμον. προσποιουμένου δὲ εἶναι
f Φάωνος αὐλητικοῦ | καὶ ἔχειν φάσκοντος Μεγαροῖ
χορόν, "ληρεῖς," ἔφη· "ἐκεῖ μὲν γὰρ οὐκ ἔχεις, ἀλλ'
ἔχει." μάλιστα δὲ θαυμάζειν ἔφη τὴν τοῦ σοφιστοῦ

158 Or (punningly) "they appear to".
159 Thus the lemma in A, based on what evidence, we do not know.
160 Chrysogonus (Stephanis #2637) was a pipe-player who was victorious at the Pythian games sometime in the late 5th century (12.535d ~ Plu. Alc. 32.2); cf. 14.648d, where he is accused of being the author of a poem falsely attributed to Epicharmus.
161 Literally "their Muselessness", the point perhaps being that they now belonged to him, not the Muses.

102

When someone asked "What do you mean?", he said: "He granted him the ability to play the *cithara* badly, but refused him the ability to sing well." At one point a roof-beam (*dokos*) collapsed and killed a bad person, and he said: "Gentlemen, I believe (*dokō*) the gods exist. And if they don't, there are roof-beams."[158] He also records the following along with the other witty sayings by Stratonicus mentioned above (= Callisthenes, *FGrH* 124 F 5)[159], as follows. When Chrysogonus'[160] father said that he had everything he needed right in his own house, because he himself was a theatrical producer, and one of his sons would direct the plays, while the other would play the pipes, Stratonicus said: "You're still short one item." When the man asked "What?", Stratonicus said: "Your own private audience." When someone asked why he traveled all over Greece, rather than settling down in one city, he told him that the Muses had awarded him all the Greeks as his source of support, and that he was allowed to extract pay from them as a consequence of their lack of musical talent.[161] He said that it wasn't harmony (*harmonia*) that Phaon[162] played on his pipes, but Cadmus.[163] When Phaon claimed to be good at playing the pipes and said that he had a chorus in Megara, Stratonicus said: "That's nonsense. You don't have anything there; *they* have *you*." He claimed to be absolutely astonished by the mother of the sophist Satyrus[164],

162 Stephanis #2465; nothing is known of him except what is preserved here.

163 The husband of the legendary Queen Harmonia of Thebes.

164 The name is common, and the individual in question cannot be identified.

Σατύρου μητέρα, ὅτι ὃν οὐδεμία πόλις ἐνεγκεῖν οἷά τε
δέκα ἡμέρας, ἐκείνη δέκα μῆνας ἤνεγκε. πυνθανό-
μενος δὲ ἐν Ἰλίῳ ἐπιδημεῖν αὐτὸν τοῖς Ἰλιείοις[12],

351 "αἰεί", ἔφησεν, "Ἰλίῳ κακά." ‖ Μυννάκου δ' αὐτῷ περὶ
μουσικῆς διαμφισβητοῦντος οὐ προσέχειν αὐτῷ ἔφη,
ὅτι ἀνώτερον τοῦ σφυροῦ λέγει. τὸν δὲ φαῦλον ἰατρὸν
ἀπαυθημερίζειν ἔφη ποιεῖν εἰς Ἅιδου τοὺς θεραπευ-
ομένους. ἀπαντήσας δέ τινι τῶν γνωρίμων ὡς εἶδεν
ἐσπογγισμένα τὰ ὑποδήματα καλῶς συνηχθέσθη ὡς
πράττοντι κακῶς, νομίζων οὐκ ἂν οὕτως ἐσπογγίσθαι
καλῶς, εἰ μὴ αὐτὸς ἐσπόγγισεν. ἐν Τειχιοῦντι δὲ τῆς
Μιλήτου μιγάδων οἰκούντων ὡς ἑώρα πάντας τοὺς

b τάφους | ξενικοὺς ὄντας, "ἀπίωμεν," ἔφη, "παῖ· ἐνταῦ-
θα γὰρ οἱ ξένοι ἐοίκασιν ἀποθνῄσκειν, τῶν δ' ἀστῶν
οὐδείς." Ζήθου δὲ τοῦ κιθαριστοῦ διεξιόντος περὶ μουσικῆς, μόνῳ δὲ οὐκ ἔφη προσήκειν περὶ μουσικῆς
λαλεῖν, "ὅς γε", ἔφη, "τὸ ἀμουσότατον τῶν ὀνομάτων
εἵλου, εἰ σεαυτὸν ἀντ' Ἀμφίονος Ζῆθον καλεῖς." Μακε-
δόνα δέ τινα κιθαρίζειν διδάσκων ἐπικρανθεὶς ἐπὶ τῷ
μηδὲν αὐτὸν ποιεῖν τῶν δεόντων "εἰς Μακεδονίαν"
ἔφη. πρὸς βαλανείῳ ψυχρῷ καὶ φαύλῳ κεκοσμημένον

---

[12] ἐν τοῖς Ἰλιείοις ACE: ἐν del. Kaibel

165 Cf. 10.349e (another variant of the same joke) with n.
166 I.e. "above his pay-grade". Mynnacus was apparently a
well-known shoemaker; cf. Poll. 7.89.
167 As if this rapidity were a mark of some distinction.
168 Stephanis #1018.   169 Amphion and Zethus were

because no city could endure him for even ten days, whereas she carried him for ten months.[165] When he heard that Satyrus was visiting Troy for the Ilieian Games, he said: "It's always trouble for Troy." When Mynnacus was arguing with him about music, he said that he wasn't paying him any attention, because Mynnacus was speaking above his ankle.[166] He observed that an incompetent physician required only one day to get his patients to Hades.[167] When he ran into an acquaintance and saw that the man's shoes had been carefully polished, he expressed condolences for his poverty, since he assumed that his shoes would not have been so well-polished unless he had done the job himself. When he was in Milesian Teichious, which had a mixed population, and saw that all the graves belonged to people who came from elsewhere, he said: "Let's get out of here, slave! Apparently foreigners die in this city, and none of the locals do!" When the *cithara*-player Zethus[168] was lecturing on music, Stratonicus remarked that he was the one individual *not* entitled to speak on the subject, "Since," he said, "you chose the least musical name possible, if you call yourself Zethus rather than Amphion."[169] In the course of teaching a Macedonian to play the lyre, he grew bitter at his pupil's failure to do anything he was supposed to, and said: "What a Messadon!"[170] As he left a nasty bath-house that offered only

mythical kings of Thebes. Amphion was devoted to music, but Zethus held the art in contempt, until his brother built his portion of the city's wall by charming the stones with his lyre (AR. 1.735–41; [Apollod.] *Bib*. 3.5.5; Paus. 9.5.7–8).   [170] Literally *eis Makedonian* ("[Go] to Macedon!"), a punning variation on *eis makarian* ("[Go] to your reward!" i.e. "to hell!"; e.g. Ar. *Eq*. 1151).

c ἰδὼν ἥρῳον | λαμπρῶς ὡς ἐξῆλθεν λελουμένος κακῶς,
"οὐ θαυμάζω", ἔφη, "ὅτι πολλοὶ ἀνάκεινται πίνακες·
ἕκαστον γὰρ τῶν λουομένων ὡς σωθέντα ἀνατιθέναι."
ἐν Αἴνῳ δὲ ἔφη τοὺς μὲν ὀκτὼ μῆνας εἶναι ψῦχος, τοὺς
δὲ τέτταρας χειμῶνα· τοὺς δὲ Ποντικοὺς ἐκ τοῦ πολλοῦ ἥκειν πόντου, ὥσπερ ἐκ τοῦ ὀλέθρου. τοὺς δὲ
Ῥοδίους ἐκάλει λευκοὺς Κυρηναίους καὶ μνηστήρων
πόλιν, τὴν δ' Ἡράκλειαν Ἀνδροκόρινθον καὶ τὸ Βυ-
ζάντιον μασχάλην τῆς Ἑλλάδος, τοὺς δὲ Λευκαδίους
d ἐώλους | Κορινθίους, τοὺς δ' Ἀμβρακιώτας Μεμβρα-
κιώτας. ἐκ τῆς δ' Ἡρακλείας ὡς ἐξῄει τὰς πύλας καὶ
περιεσκόπει, ἐρομένου τινὸς τί περισκοπεῖ, αἰσχύνε-
σθαι ἔφη, μὴ ὀφθῇ, ὥσπερ ἐκ πορνείου ἐξιών. ἰδὼν δ'
ἐν τῷ κύφωνι δεδεμένους δύο, "ὡς μικροπολιτικόν",
ἔφη, "τὸ μὴ δύνασθαι συμπληρῶσαι." πρὸς δὲ ἁρμο-
νικόν τινα, κηπουρὸν ὄντα πρότερον, ἀμφισβητοῦντ'
αὐτῷ περὶ ἁρμονίας ἔφη·

   ἄρδοι τις ἦν ἕκαστος εἰδείη τέχνην.

e ἐν Μαρωνείᾳ | δὲ συμπίνων τισὶν ἐθέλειν ἔφη γνῶναι
κατὰ τίνα τόπον ἐστὶ τῆς πόλεως, ἐὰν κατακαλύψαντες
ἄγωσιν. εἶθ' ὡς ἦγον καὶ ἠρώτων, "κατὰ τὸ καπη-

---

171 Presumably referring to the behavior of Penelope's suitors
in the *Odyssey*. The same anecdote appears again, but with ex-
planatory glosses, at 8.352b–c.   172 "Man-Corinth", i.e. a
place where the male population was as actively involved in prosti-
tution as the women were said to be in Corinth, with a pun on
"Acrocorinth" (the name of the city's citadel).

cold water, having had an unpleasant experience there, he saw a lavishly decorated hero-shrine next door and said: "I'm not surprised that lots of plaques are dedicated here; everyone who takes a bath offers one as thanks for having escaped alive." He observed that there were eight months of cold weather in Aenus—and the other four were winter; also that the people of Pontus had emerged from the depths of the sea (*pontos*) and thus, as it were, from the realm of death. He referred to the people of Rhodes as Cyreneans without a tan, and as a city of suitors;[171] to Heracleia as Androcorinth;[172] to Byzantium as the armpit of Greece; to the Leucadians as leftover Corinthians;[173] and to the Ambraciotes as Membraciotes.[174] He used to look both ways when he went out through the gates of Heracleia; when someone asked why he did this, he said that he was ashamed to be seen, because it was like leaving a whorehouse. When he noticed two men locked up in the stocks, he said: "How typical of a small town, to operate below capacity!" To a musician who had previously been a gardener and was arguing with him about a scale, he said:

Everyone should water the craft he knows.[175]

When he was drinking with some people in Maroneia, he said that he was willing to identify where he was in the city, if they led him there blindfolded. So they took him somewhere and asked him to name the spot; and he said

---

173 Leucas was a Corinthian colony (Hdt. 8.45).

174 Punning on *membras* ("sprat", a small, inexpensive fish).

175 A punning allusion to Ar. V. 1431, which has *erdoi* ("work at") for Stratonicus' *ardoi* ("water").

ATHENAEUS

λεῖον," ἔφη, ὅτι καπηλεῖα ἐδόκει εἶναι ἡ Μαρώνεια.
τὸν δὲ Τηλεφάνην, ἐπεὶ ἀναφυσᾶν ἤρχετο παρακατα-
κείμενος, "ἄνω", ἔφη, "ὡς οἱ ἐρυγγάνοντες." τοῦ δὲ
βαλανέως ἐν Καρδίᾳ ῥύμμα γῆν μοχθηρὰν καὶ ὕδωρ
ἁλμυρὸν παρέχοντος, πολιορκεῖσθαι ἔφη κατὰ γῆν
καὶ κατὰ θάλατταν. νικήσας δ' ἐν Σικυῶνι τοὺς ἀντα-
f γωνιστὰς ἀνέθηκεν | εἰς τὸ Ἀσκληπιεῖον τρόπαιον
ἐπιγράψας· Στρατόνικος ἀπὸ τῶν κακῶς κιθαριζόντων.
ᾄσαντος δέ τινος, ἤρετο ⟨τίνος⟩[13] τὸ μέλος· εἰπόντος
δ' ὅτι Καρκίνου, "πολύ γε μᾶλλον", ἔφη, "ἢ ἀνθρώπου." ἐν Μαρωνείᾳ δ' ἔφη οὐ γίνεσθαι ἔαρ, ἀλλ'
ἀλέαν. ἐν Φασήλιδι δὲ πρὸς τὸν παῖδα διαμφισβητοῦντος τοῦ βαλανέως περὶ τοῦ ἀργυρίου (ἦν γὰρ
352 νόμος πλείονος λούειν || τοὺς ξένους), "ὦ μιαρέ", ἔφη,
"παῖ, παρὰ χαλκοῦν με[14] Φασηλίτην ἐποίησας." πρὸς
δὲ τὸν ἐπαινοῦντα ἵνα λάβῃ τι, αὐτὸς ἔφη μείζων εἶναι
πτωχός. ἐν μικρᾷ δὲ πόλει διδάσκων ἔφη, "αὕτη οὐ
πόλις ἐστίν, ἀλλὰ μόλις." ἐν Πέλλῃ δὲ πρὸς φρέαρ
προσελθὼν ἠρώτησεν εἰ πότιμόν ἐστιν. εἰπόντων δὲ
τῶν ἱμώντων, "ἡμεῖς γε τοῦτο πίνομεν," "οὐκ ἄρ'", ἔφη,
"πότιμόν ἐστιν"· ἐτύγχανον δ' οἱ ἄνθρωποι χλωροὶ

[13] add. Casaubon
[14] με μικροῦ ACE: πικροῦ del. Wilamowitz

[176] Stephanis #2408; cf. D. 21.17; Nicarch. AP 7.159 = HE
2747–50; [Plu.] Mor. 1138a.
[177] Literally "low-quality earth"; cf. 9.409e.
[178] Cf. 8.350b.

"Near the bar" (because Maroneia is, apparently, nothing but bars). When Telephanes[176], who was lying beside him on a couch, started playing the pipes, he said: "People who burp are supposed to sit up!" When a bathman in Cardia supplied him with a dirty piece of soap[177] for washing and some saltwater, he said that he was under seige by land and by sea. When he defeated the other competitors in Sicyon, he dedicated the trophy in the sanctuary of Asclepius with the inscription: "Stratonicus, from the spoils of bad *cithara*-players."[178] Someone sang a song, and he asked who the composer was; when the man told him that it was by Carcinus[179], he responded: "That's a lot more likely than it being by a human being!" He claimed that there was no spring in Maroneia; the temperature just went up. When a bathman in Phaselis argued with his slave about the money (it was the law that foreigners paid more for a bath), he said: "Damn you, slave! For one *chalkous*[180] you turned me into a Phaselite!" When someone praised him in the hope of getting a reward, he said that he himself was even more of a beggar. When he was giving lessons in a small city, he said: "This isn't a state (*polis*)—it's an understatement (*molis*)[181]!" In Pella he went up to a well and asked if the water was drinkable. When the people drawing water answered "*We* drink it," he said: "I guess not, then" (they looked a bit green). After he listened to

179 Presumably the 4th-century tragic poet (*TrGF* 70; *PAA* 564130), rather than his homonymous grandfather. His name is literally "Crab", hence Stratonicus' witticism.

180 A small bronze coin, and apparently the amount that the argument was about.

181 Literally "an almost".

ὄντες. ἐπακούσας δὲ τῆς Ὠδῖνος τῆς Τιμοθέου, "εἰ δ'
ἐργολάβον", ἔφη, "ἔτικτεν καὶ μὴ θεόν, ποίας ἂν ἠφίει
b φωνάς." Πολυΐδου δὲ | σεμνυνομένου ὡς ἐνίκησε Τιμό-
θεον ὁ μαθητὴς αὐτοῦ Φιλωτᾶς, θαυμάζειν ἔφη, "εἰ
ἀγνοεῖς ὅτι αὐτὸς μὲν ψηφίσματα ποιεῖ, Τιμόθεος δὲ
νόμους." πρὸς Ἄρειον δὲ τὸν ψάλτην ὀχλοῦντά τι
αὐτόν, "ψάλλ᾽ ἐς κόρακας" ἔφη. ἐν Σικυῶνι δὲ πρὸς
νακοδέψην γεγενημένος, ἐπεὶ ἐλοιδορεῖτό τι αὐτῷ
⟨καὶ⟩[15] κακόδαιμον ἔφη, "νακόδαιμον" ἔφη. τοὺς δὲ
Ῥοδίους ⟨ὁ⟩ αὐτὸς Στρατόνικος σπαταλῶνας καὶ θερ-
μοπότας θεωρῶν ἔφη αὐτοὺς λευκοὺς εἶναι Κυρηναίους, καὶ αὐτὴν δὲ τὴν Ῥόδον ἐκάλει μνηστήρων
c πόλιν, χρώματι μὲν εἰς ἀσωτίαν | διαλλάττειν ἐκείνων
ἡγούμενος αὐτούς, ὁμοιότητι δ᾽ εἰς καταφέρειαν ἡδονῆς τὴν πόλιν μνηστήρων εἰκάζων. ζηλωτὴς δὲ ⟨διὰ⟩[16]
τῶν εὐτραπέλων λόγων τούτων ἐγένετο ὁ Στρατόνικος
Σιμωνίδου τοῦ ποιητοῦ, ὥς φησιν Ἔφορος ἐν δευτέρῳ
Περὶ Εὑρημάτων, φάσκων καὶ Φιλόξενον τὸν Κυθή-
ριον περὶ τὰ ὅμοια ἐσπουδακέναι. Φαινίας δ᾽ ὁ περιπατητικὸς ἐν δευτέρῳ Περὶ Ποιητῶν, Στρατόνικος,

[15] add. Dindorf
[16] add. Wilamowitz

[182] Sc. of Semele, mortal mother of the god Dionysus. Nothing else of the poem survives.
[183] A dithyrambic poet (*TrGF* 78, although there is no firm evidence that he wrote tragedies). Only one fragment of his poetry, a

110

Timotheus' *Birth-Pangs*[182] (*PMG* 792), he said: "Imagine
the shrieks she would've let loose, if she'd given birth to a
theatrical producer instead of a god!" When Polyidus[183]
was acting proud because his student Philotas defeated
Timotheus, he said that he was astonished "if you're unaware that he merely produces decrees, whereas Timotheus produces *nomoi*[184]." When the harp-player (*psaltēs*)
Areius[185] was annoying him somehow, he said: "*Psall' es
korakas*."[186] He was with a leather-worker (*nakodepsēs*)
in Sicyon; when the man spoke rudely to him and called
him *kakodaimōn* ("ill-starred, accursed"), he called him
nakodaimōn. When the same Stratonicus saw that the
Rhodians were self-indulgent and liked to drink hot wine,
he said that they were Cyreneans without the suntan. He
also referred to Rhodes itself as a city of suitors; because he
took their complexion to indicate that they lived more
profligately than the Cyreneans did, and compared them
to a city of suitors, because they were similarly devoted
to pleasure.[187] Stratonicus imitated the poet Simonides
with these witticisms, according to Ephorus in Book II
of *On Inventions* (*FGrH* 70 F 2), where he claims that
Philoxenus of Cythera made similar efforts. Phaenias the
Peripatetic says in Book II of *On Poets* (fr. 32 Wehrli):

prose summary of his account of Perseus' encounter with Atlas,
survives (*PMG* 837). His student Philotas is otherwise unknown.

184 "Laws" (which were more general and authoritative than
psēphismata, "decrees"), but also "citharodic compositions" *vel
sim.*   185 Stephanis #295; otherwise unknown.

186 "Play the harp to the ravens!", i.e. "to hell!"; punning on the
colloquial curse *Ball' es korakas*, "Throw (yourself) to the ravens!"

187 Cf. 8.351c n.

φησίν, ὁ Ἀθηναῖος δοκεῖ τὴν πολυχορδίαν εἰς τὴν ψιλὴν κιθάρισιν πρῶτος εἰσενεγκεῖν καὶ πρῶτος | d μαθητὰς τῶν ἁρμονικῶν ἔλαβε καὶ διάγραμμα συνεστήσατο. ἦν δὲ καὶ ἐν τῷ γελοίῳ οὐκ ἀπίθανος. φασὶ δὲ καὶ τελευτῆσαι αὐτὸν διὰ τὴν ἐν τῷ γελοίῳ παρρησίαν ὑπὸ Νικοκλέους τοῦ Κυπρίων βασιλέως φάρμακον πιόντα διὰ τὸ σκώπτειν αὐτοῦ τοὺς υἱούς.

Τοῦ δ' Ἀριστοτέλους τεθαύμακα, ὃν πολυθρύλητον πεποιήκασιν οἱ σοφοὶ οὗτοι, καλέ μου Δημόκριτε, (καὶ σὺ τῶν λόγων αὐτοῦ πρεσβεύεις ὡς καὶ τῶν ἄλλων φιλοσόφων τε καὶ ῥητόρων) τῆς ἀκριβείας πότε μα- e θὼν | ἢ παρὰ τίνος ἀνελθόντος ἐκ τοῦ βυθοῦ Πρωτέως ἢ Νηρέως, τί ποιοῦσιν οἱ ἰχθύες ἢ πῶς κοιμῶνται ἢ πῶς διαιτῶνται. τοιαῦτα γὰρ συνέγραψεν ὡς εἶναι κατὰ τὸν κωμῳδιοποιὸν

θαύματα μωροῖς.

φησὶν γὰρ ὅτι κήρυκες μὲν καὶ πάντα τὰ ὀστρακόδερμα ἀνόχευτον αὐτῶν ἐστι τὸ γένος καὶ ὅτι ἡ πορφύρα καὶ ὁ κῆρυξ μακρόβια. ζῆν γὰρ τὴν πορφύραν ἔτη ἓξ πόθεν τοῦτο οἶδε; καὶ ὅτι ἐπὶ πλεῖστον χρόνον ἐν ὀχείᾳ γίγνεται ἡ ἔχιδνα; καὶ ὅτι μέγιστον μέν ἐστιν f ἡ φάττα, δεύτερον | δὲ ἡ οἰνάς, ἐλάχιστον δὲ ἡ τρυγών; πόθεν δ' ὅτι ὁ μὲν ἄρρην ἵππος ζῇ ἔτη πέντε

---

188 Nicocles (reigned 374/3–c.360 BCE) was the son and successor of Evagoras of Salamis. See 8.349e n.
189 Two "Old Men of the Sea"; cf. 1.6e; 8.345a with n.

Stratonicus of Athens appears to have been the first to introduce multiple tunings to unaccompanied *cithara*-playing, as well as the first to take on students in musical theory and to produce a visual representation of a scale. He was also good at making people laugh; they say that he actually died as a result of his outspoken willingness to make jokes, when the Cyprian king Nicocles[188] forced him to drink poison, because he poked fun at the king's sons.

I am astonished, my noble Democritus, at the precise information provided by Aristotle, whom these clever people cite constantly—you too show as much respect for his remarks as for those of other philosophers and orators—and I would like to know when and from what Proteus or Nereus[189] arisen from the depths he learned what activities fish engage in, and how they sleep and pass their time. Because he wrote books fit to be, to quote the comic poet (adesp. com. fr. 113),

marvels for fools.

For he claims that (*HA* 537ᵇ22–31) whelks and all testaceans reproduce asexually, and that (*HA* 547ᵇ8) purple shellfish and whelks live for a long time. But how does he know that (*HA* 547ᵇ9) purple shellfish live for six years?[190] Or that poisonous snakes take longer to have sex than any other animal? Or that (*HA* 544ᵇ5–7) the ringdove is the largest bird of its class, the rock-pigeon second, and the turtledove the smallest?[191] What is his source for the

190 At *HA* 547ᵇ9–11 Aristotle explains his basis for this assertion, which is that each year's growth can be detected in the physical structure of the shell.

191 Cf. 9.394a.

καὶ τριάκοντα, ἡ δὲ θήλεια πλείω τῶν τεσσαράκοντα,
βιῶσαι φήσας τινὰ καὶ ἑβδομήκοντα πέντε; ἱστορεῖ δ᾽
ὅτι καὶ ἐκ τῆς τῶν φθειρῶν ὀχείας αἱ κονίδες γεννῶν-
ται καὶ ὅτι ἐκ τοῦ σκώληκος μεταβάλλοντος γίνεται
κάμπη, ἐξ ἧς βομβυλιός, ἀφ᾽ οὗ ὁ νεκύδαλλος ὀνομα-
ζόμενος· ἀλλὰ μὴν καὶ τὰς μελίσσας βιοῦν φησι
μέχρι ἐτῶν ἕξ, τινὰς δὲ καὶ ἑπτά. οὐκ ὦφθαι δέ φησιν
353 οὔτε μέλισσαν οὔτε κηφῆνα ὀχεύοντας, ὅθεν ‖ οὐκ
εἶναι διιδεῖν πότερα αὐτῶν ἄρρενα ἢ θήλεα. πόθεν δ᾽
ὅτι οἱ ἄνθρωποι ἥσσονες μελισσῶν; αἰεὶ γὰρ αὗται
τὴν ἰσότητα τοῦ βίου τηροῦσιν, οὐ μεταβαλλόμεναι,
ἀλλ᾽ ἀγείρουσαι καὶ ἀδιδάκτως ποιοῦσι· οἱ δ᾽ ἄνθρωποι ἥσσονες μελισσῶν καὶ πλήρεις οἰήσεως ὡς ἐκεῖ-
ναι μέλιτος. πόθεν δ᾽ ἐτήρησεν; ἐν δὲ τῷ Περὶ Μακρο-
βιότητός φησιν ὅτι ὦπταί τις μυῖα ἔτη ἓξ ἢ ἑπτὰ
ζήσασα. τίς γὰρ τούτων ἡ ἀπόδειξις; ποῦ δὲ εἶδεν ἐκ
κέρατος ἐλάφου κισσὸν ἀναφύντα; γλαῦκες δέ, φησί,
b   καὶ κόρακες ἡμέρας ἀδυνατοῦσι | βλέπειν· διὸ νύκτωρ
τὴν τροφὴν ἑαυτοῖς θηρεύουσι καὶ οὐ πᾶσαν νύκτα
ἀλλὰ τὴν ἀκρέσπερον· καὶ τὰς ἰδέας δὲ τῶν ὀφθαλμῶν
αὐτῶν οὐκ ἐμφερεῖς εἶναι· τοῖς μὲν γὰρ γλαυκαί, τοῖς
δὲ μέλαιναι, τοῖς δὲ χαροποί. ἀνθρώποις δὲ ὅτι παν-
τοῖος ὁ ὀφθαλμὸς ἠθῶν τε διαφορὰς εἶναι περὶ τοὺς
ὀφθαλμοὺς λέγει· τοὺς μὲν γὰρ αἰγωποὺς τῶν ἀνθρώ-

---

192 The material that follows, which takes Aristotle's claims
seriously, must be from a different source than what precedes (=
Arist. fr. 253), which is otherwise bitterly and sarcastically hostile.

claim that (*HA* 545^{b}18–20) a stallion lives for 35 years and a mare for more than 40, adding that one lived to be 75? He reports that (*HA* 539^{b}10–11) nits are produced when lice mate, and that (*HA* 551^{b}10–12) larvae change into caterpillars, which become a cocoon, from which the so-called *nekudallos* ("pupa") emerges. He also claims that (*HA* 554^{b}6–7) honeybees live for up to six years, and some even seven; and he denies that (*GA* 759^{b}21–3) any honeybee or drone has ever been seen mating, so that, as a result, it is impossible to tell which of them are male and which female. What is his source for the claim that human beings are inferior to honeybees?[192] Because bees always maintain an even balance in life rather than changing; they accumulate property; and they do what they do without being taught. Human beings, on the other hand, are inferior to bees, and as full of foolish ideas as bees are of honey. What is his source for this observation? In his *On Longevity* he claims that individual flies have been observed to live for six or seven years. What proof is there of this? And where did he see (*Mir.* 831^{a}2–3) ivy growing from a deer's horn? He claims that (*HA* 619^{b}18–21) owls and ravens are unable to see during the day, which is why they hunt at night, and not all night, but at dusk; also that (*HA* 492^{a}2–12)[193] their eyes do not look the same, because some have gray eyes, others black, others yellowish-brown. And he says that human beings have eyes of all sorts, and that their character varies along with their eyes: people with

[193] Aristotle is here discussing animals generally, not owls and ravens only.

πων πρὸς ὀξύτητα μὲν ὄψεως εὖ πεφυκέναι, τὰ δ' ἤθη
βελτίστους εἶναι· καὶ τῶν ἄλλων τοὺς μὲν ἐκτὸς ἔχειν
τοὺς ὀφθαλμούς, τοὺς δὲ ἐντός, ἄλλους δὲ μέσως· καὶ |
c τοὺς μὲν ἐντὸς ὀξυωπεστάτους εἶναι, τοὺς δ' ἐκτὸς
κακοηθεστάτους· οἱ δὲ μέσως, φησίν, ἔχοντες ἐπιεικεῖς.
εἶναι δέ τινας καὶ σκαρδαμυκτικούς, τοὺς δ'
ἀτενεῖς, τοὺς δὲ μέσους· ἀβεβαίους δ' εἶναι τοὺς
σκαρδαμυκτικούς, ἀναιδεῖς δ' εἶναι τοὺς ἀτενεῖς· τοὺς
δὲ μέσους βελτίστων ἠθῶν. μόνον τε ἄνθρωπον τῶν
ζῴων τὴν καρδίαν ἔχειν ἐν τοῖς ἀριστεροῖς μέρεσι, τὰ
δ' ἄλλα ζῷα ἐν τῷ μέσῳ. καὶ τοὺς ἄρρενας τῶν
θηλειῶν πλείονας ὀδόντας ἔχειν· τετηρῆσθαί φησι
τοῦτο καὶ ἐπὶ προβάτου καὶ ἐπὶ συὸς καὶ ἐπὶ αἰγός.
d τῶν δὲ ἰχθύων οὐδένα γεννᾶσθαι ὄρχεις | ἔχοντα·
μαστοὺς δὲ οὔτ' ἰχθὺν ἔχειν οὔτε ὄρνιθας, δελφῖνα δὲ
μόνον οὐκ ἔχειν χολήν. ἔνιοι δέ, φησίν, ἐπὶ μὲν τῷ
ἥπατι οὐκ ἔχουσιν χολὴν ἀλλὰ πρὸς τοῖς ἐντέροις, ὡς
ἔλοψ καὶ συναγρὶς καὶ σμύραινα καὶ ξιφίας καὶ χελιδών.
ἡ δὲ ἀμία παρ' ὅλον τὸ ἔντερον παρατεταμένην
ἔχει τὴν χολήν, ἱέραξ δὲ καὶ ἰκτῖνος πρὸς τῷ ἥπατι
καὶ τοῖς ἐντέροις· ὁ δ' αἰγοκέφαλος πρὸς τῷ ἥπατι καὶ
τῇ κοιλίᾳ, περιστερὰ δὲ καὶ ὄρτυξ καὶ χελιδὼν οἱ μὲν
πρὸς τοῖς ἐντέροις, οἱ δὲ πρὸς τῇ κοιλίᾳ. τὰ δὲ |

---

194 Literally "goat-like".
195 Aristotle actually says that the dolphin is "the only sea-creature with lungs" that lacks a gall-bladder.

116

yellow[194] eyes have excellent vision and the best characters. As for the others, some have bulging eyes, others
sunken eyes, and the rest fall somewhere in between; people with sunken eyes have the best vision, while those with
bulging eyes have the worst character, and those in the
middle, he says, are decent individuals. Also that some
people tend to blink their eyes, others stare fixedly, and
others fall in between; those who blink are unreliable,
those who stare are shameless, and those who fall in the
middle have the best character. (He also asserts) that (*HA*
496ᵃ14–17; cf. 506ᵇ33–7ᵃ2) human beings are the only animal with its heart on the left side, and that other animals
have it in the middle. Also (*HA* 501ᵇ19–21) that males have
more teeth than females; he claims that this has been
observed in the case of sheep, pigs, and goats. Also that
(*HA* 509ᵇ3; *GA* 716ᵇ15–16, 717ᵃ18–19) no fish is born with
testicles; that (*HA* 521ᵇ25–6) fish and birds lack breasts;
and that (*HA* 506ᵇ4–5) the dolphin is the only animal[195]
that lacks a gall-bladder. Some animals, he reports (*HA*
506ᵇ15–17), have a gall-bladder that is attached not to
their liver, but to their intestines, for example the *elops*,
sunagris, moray eel, swordfish, and flying fish.[196] (*HA*
506ᵇ13–14) The bonito's gall-bladder extends the full
length of its intestines, while (*HA* 506ᵇ23–4) hawks and
kites have one that is attached to their liver and their intestines. (*HA* 506ᵇ22–3) The horned owl's gall-bladder is
attached to its liver and its stomach; and (*HA* 506ᵇ20–2)
as for doves, quail, and swallows, some have it attached
to their intestines, others to their stomach. He asserts

196 The traditional text of Aristotle contains a slightly different
list of fish.

e μαλακόδερμά φησι καὶ τὰ ὀστρακόδερμα καὶ τὰ σε-
λαχώδη καὶ τὰ ἔντομα πλείονα χρόνον ὀχεύειν· δελφῖνα δὲ καί τινας τῶν ἰχθύων παρακατακλινομένους
ὀχεύειν, καὶ εἶναι τῶν μὲν δελφίνων βραδεῖαν τὴν
μῖξιν, τῶν δὲ ἰχθύων ταχεῖαν. ἔτι ὁ λέων, φησί,
στερέμνια ἔχει τὰ ὀστᾶ, καὶ κοπτομένων αὐτῶν ὥσπερ
ἐκ τῶν λίθων πῦρ ἐκλάμπειν. δελφὶς δὲ ὀστᾶ μὲν ἔχει
καὶ οὐκ ἄκανθαν, τὰ δὲ σελάχη καὶ χόνδρον καὶ
ἄκανθαν, τῶν δ᾽ ἰχθύων ‹ . . . › τὰ μὲν εἶναι χερσαῖα,
f τὰ δὲ ἔνυδρα, τὰ δὲ πυριγενῆ· | εἶναι δέ τινα καὶ
ἐφήμερα καλούμενα, ἃ μίαν μόνην ἡμέραν ζῆν. τὰ δὲ
ἀμφίβια εἶναι ὡς τὸν ποτάμιον ἵππον καὶ κροκόδειλον
καὶ ἔνυδριν. πάντα τε τὰ ζῷα δύο ἡγεμόνας ἔχειν
πόδας, καρκίνον δὲ τέσσαρας. ὅσα δ᾽ ἔναιμά ἐστι,
φησί, τῶν ζῴων ἢ ἄποδά ἐστιν ἢ δίποδα ‹ἢ τετράπο-
δα›[17], ὅσα δὲ τῶν τεσσάρων πλείονας ἔχει πόδας
ἄναιμά ἐστι. διὸ καὶ πάντα τὰ κινούμενα τέτταρσι
σημείοις κινεῖται· ἄνθρωπος μὲν δύο ποσὶ καὶ ‹δύο›[18]
χερσί, ὄρνις δὲ δύο ποσὶ καὶ δύο πτέρυξιν, ἔγχελυς
354 καὶ γόγγρος δύο πτερυγίοις καὶ δύο καμπαῖς. ‖ ἔτι
τῶν ζῴων τὰ μὲν ἔχει χεῖρας, ὡς ἄνθρωπος, τὰ δὲ
δοκεῖ, ὡς πίθηκος· οὐδὲν γὰρ τῶν ἀλόγων ζῴων δίδωσι καὶ λαμβάνει, πρὸς ἅπερ αἱ χεῖρες ὄργανα δέδον-
ται. πάλιν τῶν ζῴων τὰ μὲν ἄρθρα ἔχει, ὡς ἄνθρωπος,
ὄνος, βοῦς, τὰ δὲ ἄναρθρά ἐστιν, οἷον ὄφεις, ὄστρεα,

[17] add. Musurus
[18] add. Kaibel, ducente Musuro

that (cf. *HA* 565^{b}20–2; *GA* 755^{b}32–5) soft-skinned animals, testaceans, sharks and rays and the like, and insects take a long time to mate; also that (*HA* 540^{b}22–4) dolphins and some fish mate lying side-by-side, and that dolphins have sex slowly, whereas fish do it quickly.[197] Moreover, he maintains that (*HA* 516^{b}9–11) lions have solid bones, and that when their bones are struck together, sparks leap out as if from stones. (*HA* 516^{b}11–12) The dolphin has bones, but no backbone; (*PA* 655^{a}23) sharks and rays have both cartilage and a backbone; and of fish . . . (*HA* 487^{a}15–16) that some are terrestrial, others aquatic, others (cf. *HA* 552^{b}11–14) born from fire; there are also creatures known as *ephēmera* that live for only one day. (Cf. *HA* 487^{a}19–22) Amphibious creatures include, for example, the hippopotamus, crocodile, and otter. Also that (cf. *HA* 489^{a}30–4; *MA* 704^{a}11–18) all living creatures have two feet in front, except that the crab has four. All animals that contain blood, he claims, have either no feet or two or four, while those with more than four feet have no blood. This is why (cf. *MA* 707^{b}5–9) everything that moves does so in units of four: human beings do this with two feet and two hands, birds with two feet and two wings, and eels and conger eels with two fins and two flexures. Some animals, moreover, have hands, for example (cf. *PA* 687^{a}6–12) human beings, while others merely appear to, for example monkeys; because no irrational creature gives or takes anything, which are the functions for which hands have been provided as instruments. Again, some animals have joints, for example human beings, donkeys, and cows, whereas others lack them,

---

[197] Aristotle actually says that the dolphin's mating takes "neither a short nor a particularly long time".

πλεύμονες. πολλά τε τῶν ζῴων οὐ κατὰ πᾶσαν ὥραν
φαίνεται, οἷον τὰ φωλεύοντα, καὶ ὅσα δὲ μὴ φωλεύει
οὐκ αἰεὶ φαίνεται, οἷον χελιδόνες καὶ πελαργοί.

    Πολλὰ δὲ ἔχων ἔτι λέγειν περὶ ὧν ἐλήρησεν ὁ
b φαρμακοπώλης | παύομαι, καίτοι εἰδὼς καὶ Ἐπίκου-
ρον τὸν φιλαληθέστατον ταῦτ᾽ εἰπόντα περὶ αὐτοῦ ἐν
τῇ Περὶ Ἐπιτηδευμάτων Ἐπιστολῇ, ὅτι καταφαγὼν
τὰ πατρῷα ἐπὶ στρατείαν ὥρμησε καὶ ὅτι ἐν ταύτῃ
κακῶς πράττων ἐπὶ τὸ φαρμακοπωλεῖν ἦλθεν· εἶτα
ἀναπεπταμένου τοῦ Πλάτωνος περιπάτου, φησί,
παραβαλὼν ἑαυτὸν προσεκάθισε τοῖς λόγοις, οὐκ ὢν
ἀφυής, καὶ κατὰ μικρὸν εἰς τὴν θεωρουμένην ἐξῆλθεν.
οἶδα δὲ ὅτι ταῦτα μόνος Ἐπίκουρος εἴρηκεν κατ᾽ |
c αὐτοῦ, οὔτε δ᾽ Εὐβουλίδης, ἀλλ᾽ οὐδὲ Κηφισόδωρος
τοιοῦτόν τι ἐτόλμησεν εἰπεῖν κατὰ τοῦ Σταγειρίτου,
καίτοι καὶ συγγράμματα ἐκδόντες κατὰ τἀνδρός. ἐν δὲ
τῇ αὐτῇ ἐπιστολῇ ὁ Ἐπίκουρος καὶ Πρωταγόραν φησὶ
τὸν σοφιστὴν ἐκ φορμοφόρου καὶ ξυλοφόρου πρῶτον
μὲν γενέσθαι γραφέα Δημοκρίτου· θαυμασθέντα δ᾽
ὑπ᾽ ἐκείνου ἐπὶ ξύλων τινὶ ἰδίᾳ συνθέσει ἀπὸ ταύτης
τῆς ἀρχῆς ἀναληφθῆναι ὑπ᾽ αὐτοῦ καὶ διδάσκειν ἐν
d κώμῃ τινὶ γράμματα, ἀφ᾽ ὧν ἐπὶ | τὸ σοφιστεύειν

---

198 Both migratory.

199 Eubulides of Megara (mid-4th century BCE), one of Aristotle's most outspoken ancient critics.

200 Cephisodorus of Athens (*PAA* 568030; mid-4th century
BCE); Athenaeus cites his *Against Aristotle* (from which it is

such as snakes, oysters, and jellyfish. And many animals cannot be seen in every season, such as those that retreat into burrows; so too those that do not retreat into burrows are not always visible, such as swallows and storks.[198]

Although I have much more to say about the nonsense the drug-peddlar talked, I am bringing my remarks to a close, despite my awareness that Epicurus (who was deeply devoted to the truth) said about him in his *Letter on Life-Styles* (fr. 171 Usener) that after he gobbled up his inheritance, he tried military service; and when he failed at that, he moved on to selling drugs. Then when Plato's school opened, he says, he took himself off there and sat in on the lectures; he was no fool, and gradually embarked on the contemplative path. I realize that only Epicurus attacks him this way, and that neither Eubulides[199] (fr. 61 Döring = *SSR* II B 10) nor Cephisodorus[200] was reckless enough to say anything like this against the Stagirite,[201] even though they published treatises directed against him. In the same letter, Epicurus (fr. 172 Usener = Democr. 68 A 9 D–K) claims that the sophist Protagoras, who originally worked as a porter and transporting firewood, was initially Democritus' scribe. Democritus was struck by a peculiar way Protagoras had of stacking wood;[202] he started there, was taken on by him, and taught reading and writing in some village; from there he moved on to be a

tempting to believe that the hostile material at 8.352e–3a is drawn) at 2.60d–e; 3.122b.

[201] Aristotle (called here after his place of birth, Stagira in Chalcidice).

[202] Cf. D.L. 9.53–4.

ὁρμῆσαι. κἀγὼ δέ, ἄνδρες συνδαιταλῆς, ἀπὸ τῶν πολλῶν τούτων λόγων τὴν ὁρμὴν ἔχω ἐπὶ τὸ ἤδη γαστρίζεσθαι.

Εἰπόντος οὖν τινος ἔτι παρασκευάζεσθαι τοὺς μαγείρους διὰ τὴν πολλὴν τῶν λόγων ἑστίασιν, ἵνα μὴ ψυχρὰ παρατιθῶσιν—

οὐδεὶς γὰρ ἂν φάγοι ψυχρῶν—

ὁ Κύνουλκος ἔφη· κατὰ τὸν Ἀλέξιδος τοῦ κωμῳδιοποιοῦ Μίλκωνα·

ἐγώ (φησιν),
κἂν μὴ παραθῶσι θερμά. τἀγαθὸν Πλάτων
ἁπανταχοῦ φησ᾽ ἀγαθὸν εἶναι, μανθάνεις;
τό θ᾽ ἡδὺ πάντως ἡδὺ κἀκεῖ κἀνθάδε. |

e οὐκ ἀχαρίτως δὲ καὶ Σφαῖρον τὸν συσχολάσαντα μὲν Χρυσίππῳ παρὰ Κλεάνθει, μετάπεμπτον δὲ γενόμενον εἰς Ἀλεξάνδρειαν ὑπὸ τοῦ βασιλέως Πτολεμαίου, κηρίνων ποτὲ ἐν τῷ δείπνῳ παρατεθεισῶν ὀρνίθων ἐκτείναντα τὰς χεῖρας ἐπισχεθῆναι ὑπὸ τοῦ βασιλέως, ὡς ψεύδει συγκατατιθέμενον. τὸν δ᾽ εὐστόχως ἀποφήνασθαι εἰπόντα οὐ τούτῳ συγκατατίθεσθαι ὅτι εἰσὶν ὄρνεις, ἀλλ᾽ ὅτι εὔλογόν ἐστι ταύτας ὄρνεις εἶναι.

f διαφέρειν δὲ τὴν καταληπτικὴν φαντασίαν | τοῦ εὐλόγου· τὴν μὲν γὰρ ἀδιάψευστον εἶναι, τὸ δ᾽ εὔλογον

---

203 Part of an adespota iambic trimeter.

sophist. And I myself, my fellow dinner-guests, am moving on from these long remarks to stuffing myself now.

Someone observed that, as a consequence of our enormous feast of speeches (cf. Pl. *Ti.* 27b), the cooks were still working on the meal, so as to avoid serving us cold food—

because no one prefers cold food[203]—

and Cynulcus said: To quote the *Milcon* of the comic poet Alexis (fr. 98):

> I (he says),
> even if they don't serve warm food. Plato claims that
> the Good is good everywhere, do you understand?
> And that what's nice is nice in all circumstances,
> whether here or there.

A witty remark is attributed to Sphaerus[204] (Sphaerus 624, SVF i.140–1 = 40F Long–Sedley), who studied with Cleanthes at the same time Chrysippus did, and was invited to Alexandria by King Ptolemy. Once during a dinner party, when some birds made of wax were set on the table, he reached for them and was stopped by the king, on the ground that he was assenting to a lie. Sphaerus offered a clever response, saying that he was not assenting to the notion that they *were* birds, but to the notion that it was *probable* that they were birds. Apparent truth based on sensory perception is different from what is probable; the former cannot deceive, whereas probability can turn out other-

[204] Sphaerus of Borysthenes (3rd century BCE); according to D.L. 7.177, who offers a slightly fuller and more coherent version of the anecdote, the Ptolemy in question is Ptolemy III Philopator (reigned 221–204 BCE).

⟨κἂν⟩[19] ἄλλως ἀποβαίνειν. καὶ ἡμῖν οὖν κατὰ τὴν
καταληπτικὴν φαντασίαν καὶ τῶν κηρίνων περιεν-
εχθήτω, ἵνα κἂν κατὰ τὴν ὄψιν πλανᾶσθαι δυνώμεθα
μὴ[20] πάντα λαλῶμεν. ||

355   Καὶ μελλόντων ἤδη δειπνεῖν ἐπισχεῖν ἐκέλευσεν ὁ
Δάφνος, ἐπειπὼν τὸ ἐκ Μαμμακύθου ἢ Αὐρῶν Μετα-
γένους ἰαμβεῖον·

      ὥσπερ ἐπειδὰν δειπνῶμέν που, τότε πλεῖστα
        λαλοῦμεν ἅπαντες.

κἀγώ φημι ἐνδεῶς εἰρῆσθαι τὸν περὶ ἰχθύων λόγον,
πολλὰ εἰρηκότων καὶ Ἀσκληπιαδῶν παίδων, Φυλοτί-
μου λέγω ἐν τοῖς Περὶ Τροφῆς καὶ Μνησιθέου τοῦ
Ἀθηναίου, ἔτι δὲ Διφίλου τοῦ Σιφνίου. οὗτος γὰρ ἐν
τῷ ἐπιγραφομένῳ Περὶ τῶν Προσφερομένων τοῖς
b Νοσοῦσι καὶ τοῖς | Ὑγιαίνουσί φησιν ὅτι τῶν θαλασ-
σίων ἰχθύων οἱ μὲν πετραῖοί εἰσιν εὔφθαρτοι, εὔχυλοι,
σμηκτικοί, κοῦφοι, ὀλιγότροφοι, οἱ δὲ πελάγιοι
δυσφθαρτότεροι, πολύτροφοι, δυσοικονόμητοι. καὶ
τῶν πετραίων ὁ φύκης καὶ ἡ φυκίς, ἁπαλώτατα ἰχθύδια ὄντα, ἄβρωμα καὶ εὔφθαρτά ἐστιν, ἡ δὲ πέρκη
τούτοις προσεοικυῖα κατὰ τόπους ὀλίγῳ διαλλάττει. οἱ
δὲ κωβιοὶ ἀναλογοῦσι τῇ πέρκῃ· ὧν οἱ μικροὶ καὶ οἱ
λευκοὶ ἁπαλοί εἰσιν, ἄβρωμοι, εὔχυλοι, εὔπεπτοι· οἱ δὲ
c χλωροὶ (καλοῦνται δὲ καυλίναι) ξηροί | εἰσι καὶ ἁλι-

19 add. Wilamowitz
20 ἵνα μὴ A: ἵνα del. Kaibel

wise than anticipated. So let something our senses can appreciate—even if it is made of wax—be brought around to us, so that even if our eyes may be taken in, we can do more than talk!

We were at last about to begin dinner; but Daphnus ordered us to wait, quoting the iambic line from Metagenes' *The Dunce or Breezes* (fr. 3):[205]

Just as, whenever we have dinner, that's when we all
       talk the most.

Thus I too insist that our discussion of fish is deficient,[206] since the sons of Asclepius[207] have had a great deal to say on the topic; I am referring to Phylotimus in his *On Food* (fr. 14 Steckerl) and Mnesitheus of Athens (fr. 35 Bertier), as well as to Diphilus of Siphnos. For the latter asserts in his work entitled *On the Food Offered to the Sick and the Healthy* that, of the saltwater fish, rockfish are easily broken down, produce good *chulē*,[208] and are purgative, light, and not very nourishing, whereas deep-sea fish are more difficult to break down, very nourishing, and difficult to assimilate. Of rockfish, the *phukēs*- and *phukis*-wrasses, which are extremely tender little fish, have no odor and are easily broken down, whereas the perch resembles them, but varies a bit by place. Gobies are similar to perch; the small, white varieties are tender and odorless, produce good *chulē*, and are easily digested. But the pale variety (referred to as *kaulinai*) are dry and lack fat. Sea-perch

---

[205] Actually an anapestic tetrameter catalectic; from the same speech as fr. 2 (quoted at 9.385c).   [206] Cf. Democritus at 8.331c.   [207] I.e. the physicians.   [208] "Digestive juice" *vel sim.* (one of Diphilus' favorite technical terms).

πεῖς. αἱ δὲ χάνναι ἀπαλόσαρκοι, σκληρότεραι δὲ τῆς
πέρκης. ὁ δὲ σκάρος ἀπαλόσαρκος, ψαθυρός, γλυκύς,
κοῦφος, εὔπεπτος, εὐανάδοτος, εὐκοίλιος. τούτων δὲ ὁ
πρόσφατος ὕποπτος, ἐπειδὴ τοὺς θαλαττίους λαγὼς
θηρεύοντες σιτοῦνται· διὸ καὶ τὰ ἐντὸς χολέρας ποιη-
τικὰ ἔχει. ἡ δὲ καλουμένη κηρὶς ἀπαλόσαρκος, εὐκοίλιος, εὐστόμαχος· ὁ δὲ χυλὸς αὐτῆς παχύνει καὶ
σμήχει. ὀρφὸς ἢ ὀρφὼς εὔχυλος, πολύχυλος, γλί-
d σχρος, δύσφθαρτος, | πολύτροφος, οὐρητικός· τὰ δὲ
πρὸς τῇ κεφαλῇ αὐτοῦ γλίσχρα, εὔπεπτα, τὰ δὲ σαρκώδη δύσπεπτα, βαρύτερα· ἀπαλώτερον δὲ τὸ οὐραῖον. φλέγματος δ᾽ ἐστὶ δραστικὸς ὁ ἰχθὺς καὶ
δύσπεπτος. αἱ δὲ σφύραιναι τῶν γόγγρων εἰσὶ τροφι-
μώτεραι. ἡ δὲ λιμναία ἔγχελυς τῆς θαλασσίας ἐστὶν
εὐστομωτέρα καὶ πολυτροφωτέρα. τῷ δὲ μελανούρῳ
ἀναλογεῖ ὁ χρύσοφρυς. σκορπίοι δὲ οἱ πελάγιοι καὶ
e κιρροὶ τροφιμώτεροι | τῶν τεναγωδῶν τῶν ἐν τοῖς
αἰγιαλοῖς τῶν μεγάλων. σπάρος δὲ δριμύς, ἀπαλόσαρκος, ἄβρωμος, εὐστόμαχος, οὐρητικός, οὐκ ἄπεπτος, ταγηνιστὸς δὲ δύσπεπτος. τρίγλη εὐστόμαχος,
παραστύφουσα, σκληρόσαρκος, δύσφθαρτος, ἐφεκτι-
κὴ κοιλίας καὶ μάλιστα ἡ ἐξ ἀνθράκων· ἡ δὲ ἀπὸ
τηγάνου βαρεῖα καὶ δύσπεπτος, κοινῶς δὲ πᾶσα αἵματος ἐκκριτική. συνόδους καὶ χάραξ τοῦ μὲν αὐτοῦ
γένους εἰσί, διαφέρει δ᾽ ὁ χάραξ. φάγρος γίνεται μὲν
καὶ ποτάμιος, καλλίων δ᾽ ἐστὶν ὁ θαλάττιος. καπρί-

---

[209] Said to be poisonous at 7.325c.

(*channai*) have tender flesh, but are tougher than perch. The parrot-wrasse has tender flesh and is flaky, sweet, light, easily digested and assimilated, and easy on the intestines. If any of these is fresh-caught, it should be regarded as suspect, since they hunt and feed on sea-hares;[209] as a result, their entrails produce nausea and vomiting. The so called *kēris* has tender flesh and is easy on the intestines and the stomach; the liquid it releases is fattening and purgative. *Orphos* or *orphōs* ("sea-perch") produces large quantities of good *chulē*, is tough, difficult to break down, and very nourishing, and encourages urination. The sections nearest its head are tough and easily digested, whereas the fleshy portions are difficult to digest and heavier; the tail-section is more tender. The fish also produces phlegm and is hard to digest. Spet are more nourishing than conger eels. Lake-eels are tastier and more nourishing than marine eels. The gilthead resembles the *melanouros*. Bullheads and *kirroi* caught in the open sea are more nourishing than the large ones caught in the shallows along the coast. *Sparos*-bream has a pungent flavor, tender flesh, and no odor, is easy on the stomach, promotes urination, and is quite digestible, although it is difficult to digest when pan-fried. Red mullet is easy on the stomach, astringent, tough-fleshed, and difficult to break down, and has a tendency to arrest the movement of the intestines, particularly when cooked directly on the coals. When pan-fried, it is heavy and difficult to digest; but in general it encourages the secretion of blood, no matter how it is prepared. Four-toothed sea-bream and sargue (*charax*) belong to the same family, but the sargue is better. There is a river-variety of sea-bream, but the marine variety is preferable. The

f σκος καλεῖται | μὲν καὶ μῦς, βρωμώδης δ' ἐστὶ καὶ
σκληρός, κιθάρου δ' ἐστὶ δυσπεπτότερος· δέρμα δ'
ἔχει εὔστομον. ῥαφὶς ἢ βελόνη (καλεῖται δὲ καὶ
ἀβλεννής) δύσπεπτος, ὑγρός, εὐκοίλιος. θρίσσα καὶ
τὰ ὁμογενῆ, χαλκὶς καὶ ἐρίτιμος, εὐανάδοτα. κεστρεὺς
δὲ γίνεται μὲν καὶ θαλάσσιος καὶ λιμναῖος καὶ
ποτάμιος· οὗτος δέ, φησί, καλεῖται καὶ ὀξύρυγχος. ‖
356 κορακῖνος δ' ὁ ἐκ τοῦ Νείλου· ἥττων δ' ὁ μέλας τοῦ
λευκοῦ καὶ ὁ ἑφθὸς τοῦ ὀπτοῦ· οὗτος γὰρ καὶ εὐστόμαχος καὶ εὐκοίλιος. σάλπη σκληρά, ἄστομος. κρείσσων δ' ἡ ἐν Ἀλεξανδρείᾳ καὶ ἡ τῷ φθινοπώρῳ γινο-
μένη· ὑγρόν τι γὰρ καὶ λευκόν, ἔτι δὲ καὶ ἄβρωμον
ἀνίησιν. ὁ γρύλλος ὅμοιος μέν ἐστιν ἐγχέλει, ἄστομος
δέ. ὁ δὲ ἱέραξ σκληροσαρκότερος μὲν κόκκυγος, τοῖς
δ' ἄλλοις ὅμοιος· καὶ ὁ κόραξ ἱέρακος σκληρότερος.
οὐρανοσκόπος δὲ καὶ ὁ ἁγνὸς καλούμενος ἢ καὶ καλ-
λιώνυμος βαρεῖς. βῶξ δὲ ἑφθὸς εὔπεπτος, εὐανάδοτος,
b ὑγρὸν ἀνιείς, εὐκοίλιος· ὁ δ' ἀπ' | ἀνθράκων γλυκύτε-
ρος καὶ ἁπαλώτερος. βάκχος εὔχυλος, πολύχυλος,
εὔτροφος. τράγος οὐκ εὔχυλος, ἄπεπτος, βρωμώδης.
ψῆττα, βούγλωσσοι εὔτροφοι καὶ ἡδεῖαι· τούτοις ἀναλογεῖ καὶ ὁ ῥόμβος. λευκίσκοι, κέφαλοι, κεστρεῖς,
μυξῖνοι, χελλῶνες ὅμοιοί εἰσι κατὰ τὴν προσφοράν,
τοῦ δὲ κεφάλου καταδεέστερός ἐστιν ὁ κεστρεύς, ἧσ-

---

210 Hence presumably the name, literally "little boar".
211 Normally "sturgeon".

kapriskos is also referred to as a *mus*; it has a strong odor[210] and is tough, and is more difficult to digest than a *kitharos*; but its skin is delicious. Garfish or gar-pike (also referred to as an *ablennēs*) is difficult to digest, moist, and easy on the intestines. Herring and related species, sardines, and *eritimoi* are easily assimilated. There are marine, marsh-, and river-varieties of gray mullet; the latter, he reports, is also referred to as an *oxurhunchos*.[211] The Nile *korakinos*:[212] the dark variety is inferior to the white variety, and it is worse stewed than roasted; because when roasted, it is easy on the stomach and the intestines. Saupe is tough and does not taste good, although it is better when caught in Alexandria or in the fall; for it emits a white liquid that does not smell bad. The *grullos* resembles an eel, but is unpalatable. The flying gurnard has tougher flesh than the gurnard, but is like the others; the *korax* is even tougher than the flying gurnard. *Ouranoskopos* and the so-called sacred fish or beauty-name are rich. Stewed bogue is easily digested and assimilated, yields juice, and is easy on the intestines; when cooked on the coals, it is sweeter and more tender. *Bacchos* produces large quantities of good *chulē* and is nourishing. *Tragos* produces bad *chulē*, is difficult to digest, and smells bad. Flounder and sole are nourishing and delicious; the turbot resembles them. *Leukiskoi*, *kephalos*-mullets, gray mullets, *muxinoi*, and *chellōnes* are equally valuable as food; but the gray mullet is inferior to the *kephalos*-mullet, the *muxinos* is even worse, and the

[212] Cf. 7.309a (also from a diaetetic source, probably Hicesius).

[213] According to Hesychius *a* 2283, *akarnax* (presumably a variant of *akarnan*) is another name for the sea-bass (*labrax*).

ATHENAEUS

σων δὲ ὁ μυξῖνος, τελευταῖος ὁ χελλών. θυννὶς δὲ καὶ
θύννος βαρεῖς καὶ πολύτροφοι. ὁ δὲ καλούμενος ἀκαρ-
c νὰν γλυκύς ἐστι | καὶ παραστύφων, τρόφιμος δὲ καὶ
εὐέκκριτος. ἡ δὲ ἀφύη βαρεῖα ἐστι καὶ δύσπεπτος· ὧν
ἡ λευκὴ καλεῖται κωβῖτις. καὶ ὁ ἑψητὸς δέ, τὸ μικρὸν
ἰχθύδιον, τοῦ αὐτοῦ γένους ἐστί. τῶν δὲ σελαχίων ὁ
μὲν βοῦς κρεώδης, ὁ δὲ γαλεὸς κρείσσων ὁ ἀστερίας
λεγόμενος. ὁ δὲ ἀλωπεκίας ὅμοιός ἐστι τῇ γεύσει τῷ
χερσαίῳ ζῴῳ, διὸ καὶ τοῦ ὀνόματος ἔτυχε. καὶ ἡ βατὶς
δὲ εὔστομος, ἡ δὲ ἀστερία βατὶς ἁπαλωτέρα καὶ
εὔχυλος. ὁ δὲ λειόβατος δυσκοιλιώτερος καὶ βρωμώ-
d δης. ἡ δὲ νάρκη δύσπεπτος οὖσα τὰ μὲν κατὰ | τὴν
κεφαλὴν ἁπαλά τε καὶ εὐστόμαχα ἔχει, ἔτι δὲ εὔπεπτα, τὰ δὲ ἄλλα οὔ· κρείττονες δέ εἰσιν αἱ μικραὶ
καὶ μάλιστα αἱ λιτῶς ἑψόμεναι. ἡ δὲ ῥίνη καὶ αὐτὴ
τῶν σελαχίων οὖσα εὔπεπτός ἐστι καὶ κούφη· ἡ δὲ
μείζων καὶ τροφιμωτέρα. κοινῶς δὲ πάντα τὰ σελάχια
φυσώδη ἐστὶ καὶ κρεώδη καὶ δυσκατέργαστα πλεονα-
ζόμενά τε τὰς ὄψεις ἀμβλύνει. ἡ δὲ σηπία καὶ ἑψομένη
μὲν ἁπαλὴ καὶ εὔστομος καὶ εὔπεπτος, ἔτι δ᾽ εὐκοί-
λιος· ὁ δ᾽ ἀπ᾽ αὐτῆς χυλὸς λεπτυντικός ἐστιν αἵματος |
e καὶ κινητικὸς τῆς δι᾽ αἱμορροίδων ἐκκρίσεως. τευθὶς
δὲ εὐπεπτοτέρα καὶ τρόφιμος, καὶ μᾶλλον ἡ μικρά· ἡ
δὲ ἐφθὴ σκληροτέρα ἐστὶ καὶ οὐκ εὔστομος. ὁ δὲ
πῶλυψ συνεργεῖ μὲν ἀφροδισίοις, σκληρὸς δ᾽ ἐστὶ καὶ
δύσπεπτος· ὁ δὲ μείζων τροφιμώτερος. παρυγραίνει δὲ
καὶ κοιλίαν ἑψόμενος ἐπὶ πλεῖον καὶ τὸν στόμαχον

130

chellōn comes last. *Thunnis* and tuna are rich and nourishing. The so-called *akarnan*[213] is sweet and astringent, as well as nourishing and easily excreted. Small-fry are rich and difficult to digest; the white variety is referred to as *kōbitis*. Stewing fish (that is, tiny little fish) belong to the same family. Among the sharks and rays, the horned ray is meaty, but the dogfish known as an *asterias* is better. The thresher shark (*alōpekias*) tastes like the land-animal,[214] which is how it got its name. The skate also tastes good, but the *asteria*-skate is tenderer and produces good *chulē*. The *leiobatos* is harder on the intestines and has a smell. Although the electric ray is difficult to digest, the parts closer to its head are tender and easy on the stomach, as well as easily digested, whereas the rest is not; the small ones are better, particularly when lightly stewed. The monkfish, which is another member of the shark and ray family, is easily digested and light; the larger variety is more nourishing. All sharks and rays generally produce gas, are meaty and difficult to break down, and damage the vision when eaten in large quantities. Even when stewed, the cuttlefish is tender, tasty, and easily digested, as well as easy on the intestines; the liquid it yields thins the blood and assists excretion when hemorrhoids are present. Squid is more easily digested and is nourishing, especially the small variety; it is tougher when stewed and does not taste good. Octopus is an aphrodisiac, but is tough and difficult to digest; the larger variety is more nourishing. When stewed for a long time, it relaxes the intestines and settles the stomach.

214 I.e. the fox (*alōpēx*).

ἵστησιν. ἐμφανίζει δὲ καὶ Ἄλεξις ἐν Παμφίλῃ τοῦ
πολύποδος τὸ χρήσιμον λέγων ὧδε·

ἐρῶντι δέ, Κτήσων, τί μᾶλλον συμφέρει
ὧν νῦν φέρων πάρειμι; κήρυκας, κτένας, |
f   βολβοὺς μέγαν τε πουλύπουν ἰχθῦς θ᾽ ἁδρούς.

ἡ δὲ πηλαμὺς πολύτροφος μέν ἐστι καὶ βαρεῖα, οὐρη-
τικὴ δὲ καὶ δύσπεπτος· ταριχευθεῖσα δὲ κυβίῳ ὁμοίως
εὐκοίλιος καὶ λεπτυντική. ἡ δὲ μείζων συνοδοντὶς
καλεῖται. ἀναλογῶν μέντοι ὁ χελιδονίας τῇ πηλαμύδι
σκληρότερός ἐστιν. ἡ δὲ χελιδὼν ἡ τῷ πουλύπῳ ἐοι-
κυῖα ἔχει τὸ ἀφ᾽ αὑτῆς ὑγρὸν εὔχροιαν ποιοῦν καὶ
357   κινοῦν αἷμα. ‖ ὁ δὲ ὄρκυνος βορβορώδης· καὶ ὁ
μείζων προσέοικε τῷ χελιδονίᾳ κατὰ τὴν σκληρότητα,
τὰ δὲ ὑπογάστρια αὐτοῦ καὶ ἡ κλεὶς εὔστομα καὶ
ἁπαλά. οἱ δὲ κοσταὶ λεγόμενοι ταριχευθέντες εἰσὶ
μέσοι. ξανθίας δ᾽ ἐπὶ ποσὸν βρωμώδης ἐστὶν καὶ
ἁπαλώτερος τοῦ ὀρκύνου. ταῦτα μὲν οὖν ὁ Δίφιλος
εἴρηκεν.

Ὁ δὲ Ἀθηναῖος Μνησίθεος ἐν τῷ Περὶ Ἐδεστῶν
τῶν μειζόνων φησὶν ἰχθύων γένος ὑφ᾽ ὧν μὲν καλεῖσθαι τμητόν, ὑπ᾽ ἄλλων δὲ πελάγιον, οἷον χρυσόφρυς
καὶ γλαύκους καὶ φάγρους. εἰσὶ δὲ δυσκατέργαστοι·
b   κατεργασθέντες | δὲ πολλαπλασίαν τροφὴν παρ-
έχουσι. τὸ δὲ τῶν λεπιδωτῶν γένος, οἷον θύννων,
σκόμβρων, θυννίδων, γόγγρων καὶ τῶν τοιούτων,
συμβαίνει τούτοις καὶ ἀγελαίοις εἶναι. τὰ μὲν οὖν
μήτε καθ᾽ αὑτὰ φαινόμενα μήτ᾽ ἐν ταῖς ἀγέλαις ἐκ-

Alexis in *Pamphile* (fr. 175) indicates the use to which the octopus is put,[215] saying the following:

> What's more useful for a man who's in love, Cteson,
> than what I've brought you now? Whelks, scallops,
> hyacinth-bulbs, a big octopus, and some nice fat fish!

Immature tuna are very nourishing and rich, but encourage urination and are difficult to digest; when salted, they are as easy on the intestines as cube-saltfish, and thin the blood. The larger variety is referred to as a *sunodontis*. Although the *chelidonias* resembles the immature tuna, it is not as tender. The flying fish that is similar to an octopus yields a juice that produces a good skin-tone and energizes the blood. The *orkunos* is muddy; the larger variety is as tough as the *chelidonias*, but its belly-sections and its key[216] are tasty and tender. What are referred to as *kostai* are moderately valuable when salted. *Xanthias* has a bit of a smell and is tenderer than the *orkunos*. This, then, is what Diphilus has to say.

Mnesitheus of Athens in his *On Foods* (fr. 38 Bertier) reports that some authorities refer to larger fish as *tmētos*[217], while others call them deep-sea fish; examples are giltheads, *glaukoi*, and sea-breams. They are difficult to break down; but once digested, they provide considerable nourishment. As for scaly fish (for example tuna, mackerel, *thunnides*, conger eels, and the like), they happen to be gregarious. Those that are not seen alone, then, but that also do not travel in schools, are more easily di-

---

[215] Sc. as an aphrodisiac, like the other foods the speaker mentions.　　[216] See 7.315d n.

[217] "Cut", i.e. "cut into steaks to be sold and cooked".

φερόμενα μᾶλλόν ἐστιν εὔπεπτα, οἷον γόγγροι καὶ
καρχαρίαι καὶ τὰ τοιαῦτα. τὰ δὲ ἀγελαῖα γένη τῶν
ἰχθύων τούτων τὴν μὲν ἐδωδὴν ἡδεῖαν ἔχει (πίονα
γάρ ἐστι), βαρεῖαν δὲ καὶ δυσκατέργαστον· διὸ καὶ
ταριχεύεσθαι δύναται μάλιστα καί ἐστι τῶν ταριχη-
c ρῶν βέλτιστα γένη ταῦτα. | χρήσιμοι δ' εἰσὶν ὀπτοί·
τήκεται γὰρ τὸ πιμελῶδες αὐτῶν. τὰ δὲ καλούμενα
δαρτὰ τὸ μὲν ὅλον ἐστὶν ὅσα τραχεῖαν ἔχει τὴν
ἐπίφυσιν τοῦ δέρματος, οὐ λεπίσιν, ἀλλ' οἷον ἔχουσιν
αἱ βατίδες καὶ ῥῖναι. ταῦτα δὲ πάντα ἐστὶ μὲν εὔθρυ-
πτα, οὐκ εὐώδη δέ. καὶ τροφὰς ἐμποιεῖ τοῖς σώμασιν
ὑγράς, ὑπάγει δὲ καὶ τὰς κοιλίας μάλιστα πάντων τῶν
ἑψομένων ἰχθύων· τὰ δὲ ὀπτώμενα χείρονα. τὸ δὲ τῶν
μαλακίων γένος, οἷον πολυπόδων τε καὶ σηπιῶν καὶ
τῶν τοιούτων, τὴν μὲν σάρκα δύσπεπτον ἔχει. διὸ καὶ
d πρὸς ἀφροδισιασμοὺς | ἁρμόττουσιν· αὐτοὶ μὲν γάρ
εἰσι πνευματώδεις, ὁ δὲ τῶν ἀφροδισιασμῶν καιρὸς
πνευματώδους προσδεῖται διαθέσεως. βελτίω δὲ ταῦτα γίνεται ἑψηθέντα· τὰς γὰρ ὑγρότητας ἔχει πονη-
ράς. ἰδεῖν γοῦν ἔστιν οἵας ἀφίησιν πλυνόμενα. ταύτας
οὖν ἡ ἕψησις ἐκκαλεῖται τῆς σαρκός· μαλακῆς γὰρ
τῆς πυρώσεως καὶ μεθ' ὑγροῦ διδομένης οἰονεὶ πλύσις
τις αὐτῶν γίνεται, τὰ δ' ὀπτώμενα καταξηραίνει τὰς
ὑγρότητας· ἔτι δὲ καὶ τῆς σαρκὸς αὐτῶν φύσει σκλη-
e ρᾶς οὔσης κατὰ λόγον οὕτως ἔχει | γίνεσθαι αὐτά.
ἀφύαι δὲ καὶ μεμβράδες καὶ τριχίδες καὶ τἆλλα ὅσων
συγκατεσθίομεν τὰς ἀκάνθας, ταῦτα πάντα τὴν πέψιν
φυσώδη ποιεῖ, τὴν δὲ τροφὴν δίδωσιν ὑγράν. τῆς οὖν

gested (for example conger eels, sharks, and the like). The schooling varieties of these fish make pleasant eating (because they are fatty), although they are heavy and difficult to break down; this is why they are particularly suited to salting and produce the best varieties of saltfish. They are good roasted, because the fat they contain melts. What are referred to as *darta* are in general fish with a rough exterior that lack scales, but have something like what is seen on skates and rays. These are all flaky, but have an unappealing smell. They produce moist nourishment inside the body and have the strongest purgative effect on the intestines of all stewed fish; they are worse when roasted. Cephalopod molluscs (for example octopi, cuttlefish, and the like) have flesh that is difficult to digest. This is why they function as aphrodisiacs: they themselves have a flatulent character, and orgasm requires a pneumatic condition. These are better stewed, because they contain low-quality juices. One can see, at any rate, the sort of juices they release when washed. Stewing draws the juice out of their flesh; because when the fire is kept low and plenty of liquid is provided, they are, as it were, washed clean, whereas when they are roasted, the juices dry up inside them. Furthermore, since their flesh is naturally tough, it is logical that they be the same themselves. Small-fry, sprats, pilchards, and any other fish that we consume bones and all, all produce gas as part of the digestive process, but provide moist nourishment. Since the digestive process is

πέψεως οὐχ ὁμαλιζούσης, ἀλλὰ τῶν μὲν σαρκῶν ἄγαν
ταχὺ πεττομένων, τῆς δὲ ἀκάνθης σχολῇ διαλυομένης
(καὶ γὰρ ἅμα αἱ ἀφύαι καθ᾽ αὑτὰς ἀκανθώδεις) ἐμπο-
δισμὸς αὐτῶν ἑκατέρου γίγνεται περὶ τὴν κατερ-
γασίαν, εἶτα φῦσαι μὲν ἀπὸ τῆς πέψεως, ὑγρασίαι δὲ
f   ἀπὸ τῆς τροφῆς | συμβαίνουσι. βελτίω δ᾽ ἐστὶν ἑψό-
μενα, τῆς δὲ κοιλίας ἐστὶν ἀνωμάλως ὑπακτικά. τὰ δὲ
καλούμενα πετραῖα, κωβιοὶ καὶ σκορπίοι καὶ ψῆτται
καὶ τὰ ὅμοια, τοῖς τε σώμασιν ἡμῶν ξηράν τε δίδωσι
τροφήν (εὔογκα δ᾽ ἐστὶ καὶ τρόφιμα καὶ πέττεται
ταχέως καὶ οὐκ ἐγκαταλείπει περιττώματα πολλά)
πνευμάτων τε οὔκ ἐστι περιποιητικά. γίνεται δ᾽ εὐ-
πεπτότερον ἅπαν ὄψον ταῖς σκευασίαις ἁπλῶς ἀρτυ-
θέν· τὰ δὲ πετραῖα καὶ < . . . > τῇ ἡδονῇ ἁπλῶς
σκευασθέντα. τούτοις δ᾽ ὅμοιόν ἐστι γένος τὸ καλούμενον μαλακόσαρκον, κίχλαι καὶ κόσσυφοι καὶ τὰ
358   ὅμοια· ἐστὶ δὲ ὑγρότερα μὲν ταῦτ᾽ ἐκείνων, ‖ πρὸς δὲ
τὰς ἀναλήψεις ἀπόλαυσιν ἔχει πλείω. τῆς μὲν κοιλίας
καὶ τῆς οὐρήσεως ὑπακτικώτερα ταῦτ᾽ ἐστὶν ἐκείνων
διὰ τὸ καὶ τὰς σάρκας ὑγροτέρας καὶ πλείους ἔχειν
τῶν προειρημένων. χρὴ δὲ ἐὰν μὲν τὴν κοιλίαν βούλη-
ταί τις ὑπάγειν, ἕψοντα διδόναι· μετρίως δὲ ἐχούσης
ὀπτηθέντα γίνεται τρόφιμα. πρὸς δὲ τὰς οὐρήσεις
ἀμφοτέρως σκευασθέντα χρήσιμα. οἱ δὲ τόποι τῆς
θαλάσσης ὅπου ποταμοὶ καὶ λίμναι συμβάλλουσιν,
ἔτι δὲ τενάγη[21] μεγάλα καὶ κόλποι θαλάττης εἰσίν,
b   ἐνταῦθα μὲν πάντες οἱ ἰχθύες | εἰσὶν ὑγρότεροι καὶ
μᾶλλον πίονες ὑπάρχουσι· καὶ ἐσθίεσθαι μέν εἰσιν

not uniform, then, but the flesh is digested very rapidly, whereas the bones dissolve slowly—and uncleaned small-fry are in fact full of bones—each portion prevents the other from being broken down, and the result is flatulence that results from the digestive process, while the food itself generates moisture. They are better stewed, and purge the intestines to different degrees. What are referred to as rockfish (gobies, bullheads, flounders, and the like) provide our bodies with dry nourishment—they have dense flesh, are nourishing and quickly digested, and do not leave much excess behind[218]—and do not produce gas. Seafood of all types is more easily digested if it is seasoned simply when prepared; rockfish and . . . in flavor when prepared simply. Similar to these are what are referred to as the soft-fleshed group (thrush-wrasses, blackbird-wrasses, and the like); these are moister than the varieties discussed above, and provide more pleasure during assimilation. They purge the intestines and the urinary tract more effectively than the other varieties, and provide more pleasure during assimilation, because they have moister and more abundant flesh than those mentioned earlier. If you want to purge the intestines, you should serve them stewed; if the intestines are in a balanced condition, they are nourishing when roasted. But they encourage urination when prepared either way. Spots in the sea where rivers or marshes have outlets, or where there are large shallow areas or gulfs in the sea—the fish in these areas are all moister and fatter; they also have a better flavor, but are not as easily digested

218 Sc. to be excreted.

---

21 τενάγη Casaubon: πελάγη ACE

ἡδίους, πρὸς δὲ τὴν πέψιν καὶ τροφὴν γίνονται χείρους. ἐν δὲ τοῖς αἰγιαλοῖς τοῖς κειμένοις πρὸς τὰ πελάγη καὶ λίαν ἀναπεπταμένοις σκληροὶ καὶ λεπτοὶ καὶ κυματοπλῆγές εἰσιν οἱ πλείους. περὶ δὲ τὰς ἀγχιβαθεῖς, ἐν αἷς μὴ λίαν ἔγκειται μεγάλα πνεύματα, πρὸς δὲ τούτοις εἴ που καὶ πόλεις σύνεγγύς εἰσιν, ἐνταῦθα δ᾽ ἔστι τὰ πλεῖστα γένη τῶν ἰχθύων ὁμαλῶς ἄριστα καὶ πρὸς ἡδονὴν καὶ πρὸς εὐπεψίαν καὶ πρὸς τὴν τροφὴν τοῦ σώματος. δύσπεπτοι δὲ καὶ βαρύc τατοι | τῶν θαλασσίων εἰσὶν οἱ μετεκβαίνοντες ἐκ τῆς θαλάσσης εἴς τε ποταμοὺς καὶ λίμνας, οἷον κεστρεὺς καὶ συλλήβδην τῶν ἰχθύων ὅσοι δύνανται βιοτεύειν ἐν ἀμφοτέροις τοῖς ὕδασι. τῶν δὲ τελείως ἐν τοῖς ποταμοῖς καὶ λίμναις βιοτευόντων ἀμείνους εἰσὶν οἱ ποτάμιοι· σῆψις γὰρ ὕδατος τὸ λιμναῖόν ἐστι. καὶ τῶν ποταμίων δ᾽ αὐτῶν βέλτιστοί εἰσιν οἱ ἐν τοῖς ὀξυτάτοις τῶν ποταμῶν ὄντες οἵ τε πυροῦντες· οὗτοι γὰρ οὐ γίνονται, ἐὰν μὴ ποταμὸς ὀξὺς ᾖ καὶ ψυχρός, διαφέρουσι δὲ τῶν ποταμίων ἰχθύων εὐπεψίᾳ.

d　　Ταῦτα καὶ | παρ᾽ ἡμῶν ἔχετε, ἄνδρες φίλοι, ὀψωνησάντων κατὰ δύναμιν τὴν ἑαυτῶν ὑγιεινῶς. κατὰ γὰρ τὸν Ἀντιφάνους Παράσιτον·

ἐγὼ περὶ τὴν ὀψωνίαν μὲν οὐ πάνυ
ἐσπούδακ᾽, οὐδ᾽ αὖ συνέτεμον λίαν πάνυ,
ὡς ἄν τις ἄλλως ἐξενεχθεῖσιν † ὅπου
τοῦ διαλάβοι † κραιπάλην Ἑλληνικῶς.

ἀλλὰ μὴν οὐδὲ οὕτως εἰμὶ φίλιχθυς ὡς ὁ παρὰ τῷ

138

and are less nourishing. Most fish caught along shores that face wide expanses of water and are overly exposed are tough, thin, and wave-beaten. Whereas in areas where the sea-floor drops off rapidly and the winds are not particularly strong, if cities are anywhere in the area, most of the fish there are uniformly the best, be it in flavor, digestibility, or the physical nourishment they provide. Saltwater fish that migrate from the sea into rivers or marshes (for example gray mullets and, in short, any fish capable of living in both types of water) are difficult to digest and extremely rich. Of fish that live exclusively in rivers or marshes, the river-fish are better; because marshes consist of putrefied water. Of the river-fish themselves, the best are those found in the most turbulent rivers, as well as the *purountes*[219]; because these are only present if a river is turbulent and cold, and are more easily digested than other river-fish.

That is what I have to offer you, my friends; I have bought you the healthiest fish I could. For to quote Antiphanes' *Parasite* (fr. 182):

I wasn't particularly serious about my grocery-
    shopping;
but on the other hand, I didn't cut it too short,
as someone might for pointlessly brought forth †
    where
of this he could get hold † a Greek-style party.

Even so, I am not as much of a fish-lover as the character in

219 Literally "burning (fish)"; perhaps "red (fish)"?

αὐτῷ ποιητῇ ἐν Βουταλίωνι, ὅπερ δρᾶμα τῶν Ἀγροί-
κων ἐστὶν ἑνὸς διασκευή. φησὶ γάρ· |

e   (Α.) καὶ μὴν ἑστιάσω τήμερον
ὑμᾶς ἐγώ· σὺ δ᾽ ἀγοράσεις ἡμῖν λαβών,
Πίστ᾽, ἀργύριον. (Πι.) ἄλλως γὰρ οὐκ ἐπίσταμαι
χρηστῶς ἀγοράζειν. (Α.) φράζε δή, Φιλούμενον,
ὄψῳ τίνι χαίρεις; (Φι.) πᾶσι. (Α.) καθ᾽ ἕκαστον
    λέγε,
ἰχθὺν τίν᾽ ἡδέως φάγοις ἄν; (Φι.) εἰς ἀγρὸν
ἦλθεν φέρων ποτ᾽ ἰχθυοπώλης μαινίδας
καὶ τριγλίδας, καὶ νὴ Δί᾽ ἤρεσεν σφόδρα
ἡμῖν ἅπασιν. (Α.) εἶτα καὶ νῦν, εἰπέ μοι,
τούτων φάγοις ἄν; (Φι.) κἄν τις ἄλλος μικρὸς
    ᾖ· |

f τοὺς γὰρ μεγάλους τούτους ἅπαντας νενόμικα
ἀνθρωποφάγους ἰχθῦς. (Α.) τί φῄς, ὦ φιλτάτη;
ἀνθρωποφάγους, πῶς; (Πι.) οὓς ⟨ἂν⟩ ἄνθρωπος
    φάγοι,
δῆλον ὅτι· ταῦτα δ᾽ ἐστὶν Ἑλένης βρώματα,
ἅ φησιν οὗτος, μαινίδας καὶ τριγλίδας.

ἐν δὲ τῷ Ἀγροίκῳ Ἑκάτης βρώματα ἔφη τὰς μαινίδας
εἶναι καὶ τὰς τριγλίδας. ἐκφαυλίζων δὲ καὶ Ἔφιππος
τοὺς μικροὺς τῶν ἰχθύων ἐν Φιλύρᾳ φησί·

---

[220] The final five lines are quoted also at 7.313b–c, where
see n.

the same poet's *Boutalion* (a play that is a revised version of one of his *Rustics*). For he says (Antiph. fr. 69):[220]

> (A.) I'm certainly going to offer you guys a
> feast today. Pistis—you're going to take some money
> and do our shopping. (Pistis) Sure; I don't know any
>   other way
> to shop properly. (A.) Tell me, Philoumenon—
> what kind of seafood do you like? (Philoumenon) All
>   of it. (A.) Be specific:
> what fish would you enjoy eating? (Philoumenon) A
>   fish-seller
> came out to the country once with sprats
> and red-mullet minnows, and, by Zeus, he really
>   made us
> all happy! (A.) So tell me: would you like to eat
> some of those now? (Philoumenon) Yes—and
>   anything else that's small!
> Because I consider all these big
> fish people-eaters. (A.) What are you talking about,
>   my dear?
> People-eaters—how so? (Pistis) She means the type
>   that people eat,
> obviously. But the ones this guy's referring to
> are Helen's food: sprats and red-mullet minnows.

In his *Rustic*, on the other hand, he said that sprats and red-mullet minnows are Hecate's food.[221] Ephippus in *Philyra* (fr. 21) shows no respect for small fish when he says:

---

[221] Thus the version of the fragment quoted at 7.313b–c.

141

(A.) παππία, βούλει δραμὼν ‖

359 εἰς τὴν ἀγορὰν κᾆτ᾽ ἀγοράσαι μοι— (Β.) φράζε
τί.
(Α.) ἰχθῦς φρονοῦντας, ὦ πάτερ. μή μοι βρέφη.
(Β.) οὐκ οἶσθ᾽ ὁτιὴ τἀργύριόν ἐστ᾽ ἰσάργυρον;

ἥδιστος δ᾽ ἐστὶ καὶ ὁ παρὰ τῷ αὐτῷ ποιητῇ ἐν τοῖς
Ὀβελιαφόροις νεανίσκος κατασμικρύνων ἅπαντα τὰ
περὶ τὴν ὀψωνίαν καὶ λέγων ὧδε·

(Α.) ἀλλ᾽ ἀγόρασον εὐτελῶς·
ἅπαν γὰρ ἱκανόν ἐστι. (Β.) φράζ᾽, δέσποτα.
(Α.) μὴ πολυτελῶς, ἀλλὰ καθαρείως, ὅ τι ἂν ᾖ, |
b ὁσίας ἕνεκ᾽· ἀρκεῖ τευθίδια, σηπίδια,
κἂν κάραβός τις ᾖ λαβεῖν, εἷς ἀρκέσει
ἢ δύ᾽ ἐπὶ τὴν τράπεζαν. ἐγχελύδια
Θήβηθεν ἐνίοτ᾽ ἔρχεται· τούτων λαβέ.
ἀλεκτρυόνιον, φάττιον, περδίκιον,
τοιαῦτα. δασύπους ἄν τις εἰσέλθῃ, φέρε.
(Β.) ὡς μικρολόγος εἶ. (Α.) σὺ δέ γε λίαν
πολυτελής.
πάντως κρέ᾽ ἡμῖν ἔστι. (Β.) πότερ᾽ ἔπεμψέ τις;
c (Α.) οὐκ ἀλλ᾽ ἔθυσεν ἡ γυνή· | τὸ μοσχίον
τὸ τῆς Κορώνης αὔριον δειπνήσομεν.

ὁ δὲ παρὰ Μνησιμάχῳ ἐν τῷ ὁμωνύμῳ δράματι δύ-

---

222 Or perhaps (punningly) "How addicted to diminutives".
223 The name means literally "Crow", and at 13.583e is said to
be the nickname of the courtesan Theocleia (*PAA* 507884).

(A.) Daddykins, would you be willing to run
to the marketplace and buy me—(B.) Tell me what
        you want.
(A.) Some thoughtful fish, Pops. No babies, please!
(B.) Don't you realize that money's worth its weight
        in silver?

The young man in the same poet's *Spit-Bearers* (Ephipp.
fr. 15) is quite appealing when he belittles everything that
shopping involves and says the following:

(A.) But do the shopping without spending too
        much;
anything's acceptable. (B.) Give me my orders,
        master.
(A.) Don't be extravagant. Keep it simple; whatever's
        available,
for appearances' sake. Little squid and cuttlefish are
        OK;
and if a crayfish is for sale, one or two'll
be enough for our table. Sometimes little eels
come from Thebes; buy some of them.
A little rooster, a little ringdove, a little partridge—
stuff like that. If a hare appears, bring it home.
(B.) How stingy[222] you are! (A.) But *you're* too
        extravagant.
In any case, we've got meat. (B.) Did someone send
        it?
(A.) No; the lady of the house made a sacrifice.
        Tomorrow
we're dining on Corone's[223] little calf!

The unpleasant man in Mnesimachus' play by the same

σκολος φιλάργυρος ὢν σφόδρα πρὸς τὸν ἀσωτευό-
μενον νεανίσκον φησίν·

   (Α.) ἀλλ᾿ ἀντιβολῶ σ᾿, ἐπίταττέ μοι μὴ πόλλ᾿
      ἄγαν
   μηδ᾿ ἄγρια λίαν μηδ᾿ ἐπηργυρωμένα,
   μέτρια δέ, τῷ θείῳ σεαυτοῦ. (Β.) πῶς ἔτι
   μετριώτερ᾿, ὦ δαιμόνιε; (Α.) πῶς; σύντεμνε καὶ
   ἐπεξαπάτα με. τοὺς μὲν ἰχθῦς μοι κάλει |
d   ἰχθύδι᾿· ὄψον δ᾿ ἂν λέγῃς ἕτερον, κάλει
   ὀψάριον. ἥδιον γὰρ ἀπολοῦμαι πολύ.

ἐπεὶ δὲ κατὰ θεὸν ἐν τοῖς προκειμένοις, φίλτατε Οὐλπιανέ, ἢ ὑμεῖς, γραμματικῶν παῖδες, εἴπατέ μοι τίνι
ἐννοίᾳ ὁ Ἔφιππος ἐν τοῖς προειρημένοις ἔφη·

                 τὸ μοσχίον
   τὸ τῆς Κορώνης αὔριον δειπνήσομεν.

ἐγὼ γὰρ οἴομαι ἱστορίαν τινὰ εἶναι καὶ ποθῶ μαθεῖν.
καὶ ὁ Πλούταρχος ἔφη Ῥοδιακὴν εἶναι λεγομένην
e ἱστορίαν, ἣν ἐπὶ τοῦ παρόντος ἀποστοματίζειν | οὐ
δύνασθαι τῷ πάνυ πρὸ πολλοῦ ἐντετυχηκέναι τῷ ταῦτα περιέχοντι βιβλίῳ. οἶδα δὲ Φοίνικα τὸν Κολοφώ-
νιον ἰαμβοποιὸν μνημονεύοντά τινων ἀνδρῶν ὡς ἀγει-
ρόντων τῇ κορώνῃ, καὶ λέγοντα ταῦτα·

   ἐσθλοί, κορώνη χεῖρα πρόσδοτε κριθέων,

name (fr. 3) is an extraordinary miser and says to the young man who's a spendthrift:

> (A.) Please—don't ask me for way too much,
> or give me overly brutal orders, or far too expensive
>   ones!
> Make modest demands—I'm your uncle! (B.) How
>   could they be any
> more modest, you kook? (A.) How? Dice them up
>   and
> try to trick me! Describe the fish to me as
> "little fish"; and if you mention any other delicacy,
>   refer to it as
> a "little delicacy". That way I'll be ruined a lot more
>   happily.

But since this was, by chance, included in the passage quoted earlier, my beloved Ulpian—or perhaps you grammarians can tell us what Ephippus meant when he said in the passage quoted above (fr. 15.12–13, quoted at 8.359c):

>   Tomorrow
> we're dining on Corone's little calf!

Because I suspect that there is a story here, and I would like to learn it. Plutarch responded that there was a story told on Rhodes, but that he was at the moment unable to repeat it, because he had encountered the book that included it so long ago. But I am aware (he said) that the iambic poet Phoenix of Colophon (fr. 2, p. 233 Powell) mentions men who make a collection "for the crow (korōnē)" and says the following:

> Noble sirs, contribute a handful of barley to a crow,

145

τῇ παιδὶ τἀπόλλωνος, ἢ λέκος πυρῶν
ἢ ἄρτον ἢ ἤμαιθον ἢ ὅτι τις χρῄζει.
δότ᾽, ὦγαθοί, ⟨τι⟩ τῶν ἕκαστος ἐν χερσὶν
ἔχει κορώνῃ· χάλα λήψεται χονδρόν· |
f   φιλεῖ γὰρ αὕτη πάγχυ ταῦτα δαίνυσθαι·
ὁ νῦν ἅλας δοὺς αὖθι κηρίον δώσει.
ὦ παῖ, θύρην ἄγκλινε, Πλοῦτος ἔκρουσε,
καὶ τῇ κορώνῃ παρθένος φέροι σῦκα.
θεοί, γένοιτο πάντ᾽ ἄμεμπτος ἡ κούρη,
κἀφνειὸν ἄνδρα κὠνομαστὸν ἐξεύροι,
καὶ τῷ γέροντι πατρὶ κοῦρον εἰς χεῖρας
καὶ μητρὶ κούρην εἰς τὰ γοῦνα κατθείη, ||
360   θάλος τρέφειν γυναῖκα τοῖς κασιγνήτοις.
ἐγὼ δ᾽, ὅκοι πόδες φέρωσιν, ὀφθαλμοὺς

           *   *   *

ἀμείβομαι Μούσῃσι πρὸς θύρῃς ἄδων,
καὶ δόντι καὶ μὴ δόντι, πλεῦνα τῶν ⟨Γύ⟩γεω.

καὶ ἐπὶ τέλει δὲ τοῦ ἰάμβου φησίν·

ἀλλ᾽, ὦγαθοί, ᾽πορέξαθ᾽ ὧν μυχὸς πλουτεῖ·
δός, ὦ ἄναξ, δὸς καὶ σὺ πότνα μοι νύμφη·
νόμος κορώνῃ χεῖρα δοῦν᾽ ἐπαιτούσῃ.
τοσαῦτ᾽ ἀείδω· δός τι καὶ καταχρήσει. |

b κορωνισταὶ δὲ ἐκαλοῦντο οἱ τῇ κορώνῃ ἀγείροντες, ὥς

---

224 A fabulously wealthy mid-7th-century BCE king of Lydia.

Apollo's child; or a dish of wheat,
or a loaf of bread, or half an obol, or whatever you
    like!
Gentlemen—give a bit of whatever each of you has in
his hands to a crow! She'll also accept a lump of salt,
for she's very fond of dining on this;
whoever gives her salt now will give honeycomb some
    other time.
Slave! Open the door—Wealth knocked!
Let an unmarried girl bring figs for the crow!
Gods, may this girl never be faulted for anything;
may she find a rich husband with a good reputation,
and set a boy in her old father's
hands, and a girl on her mother's knees,
a child to raise to be a wife for her brothers!
But as for me, wherever my feet take me, eyes

* * *

By singing at doors I trade with the Muses for
more than Gyges[224] had, both for him who gives and
    him who does not.

And at the end of his iambic poem he says:

But, good sirs, offer me some of the wealth your
    house has deep within.
Give me something, lord! And you too, young lady!
The law requires that you give a handful to a crow
    when she asks.
That's the end of my song. Give something; it will be
    enough.

The people who made a collection for the crow (*korōnē*)
were referred to as *korōnistai*, according to Pamphilus

147

φησι Πάμφιλος ὁ Ἀλεξανδρεὺς ἐν τοῖς Περὶ Ὀνο-
μάτων· καὶ τὰ ᾀδόμενα δὲ ὑπ᾽ αὐτῶν κορωνίσματα
καλεῖται, ὡς ἱστορεῖ Ἀγνοκλῆς ὁ Ῥόδιος ἐν Κορω-
νισταῖς. καὶ χελιδονίζειν δὲ καλεῖται παρὰ Ῥοδίοις
ἀγερμός τις ἄλλος, περὶ οὗ φησι Θέογνις ἐν δευτέρῳ
Περὶ τῶν Ἐν Ῥόδῳ Θυσιῶν γράφων οὕτως· εἶδος δέ τι
τοῦ ἀγείρειν χελιδονίζειν Ῥόδιοι καλοῦσιν, ὃ γίνεται
τῷ Βοηδρομιῶνι μηνί. χελιδονίζειν δὲ λέγεται διὰ τὸ |
c   εἰωθὸς ἐπιφωνεῖσθαι·

ἦλθ᾽ ἦλθε χελιδὼν
καλὰς ὥρας ἄγουσα,
καλοὺς ἐνιαυτούς,
ἐπὶ γαστέρα λευκά,
ἐπὶ νῶτα μέλαινα.
παλάθαν σὺ προκύκλει
ἐκ πίονος οἴκου
οἴνου τε δέπαστρον
τυροῦ τε κάννυστρον.
καὶ πύρνα χελιδὼν
καὶ λεκιθίταν
οὐκ ἀπωθεῖται· πότερ᾽ ἀπίωμες ἢ λαβώμεθα;
εἰ μέν τι δώσεις· εἰ δὲ μή, οὐκ ἐάσομες·
ἢ τὰν θύραν φέρωμες ἢ τὸ ὑπέρθυρον
ἢ τὰν γυναῖκα τὰν ἔσω καθημέναν· |

---

225 In Athens, Boedromion came at the very end of summer.
But the song quoted below belongs at the beginning of spring,

of Alexandria in his *On Names* (fr. XV Schmidt); and
their songs are referred to as *korōnismata*, according to
Hagnocles of Rhodes in *Korōnistai*. The Rhodians use the
term *chelidonizein* for another type of collection, which is
discussed by Theognis in Book II of *On the Sacrifices on
Rhodes* (*FGrH* 526 F 1), where he writes as follows: The
Rhodians refer to a type of collection that occurs during
the month of Boedromion[225] with the word *chelidonizein*.
The term *chelidonizein* is used because it is their custom to
cry out (carm. pop. *PMG* 848):

> The swallow (*chelidōn*) is come, is come,
> bringing good weather
> and a good year,
> white on her belly
> and black on her back!
> You—roll a cake of dried fruit out
> of your wealthy house,
> and a cup of wine,
> and a basket of cheese!
> The swallow rejects
> neither wheat
> nor pea-cake. Should we leave or should we take
>   something?
> If you'll give us something, (fine); but if not, we won't
>   leave you alone.
> We'll carry off your door, or your lintel,
> or your wife who's sitting inside!

when the swallows return to Greece; so presumably that is when
Badromios (the actual local name for the month) came on the
Rhodian calendar.

149

d   μικρὰ μέν ἐστι, ῥᾳδίως νιν οἴσομες.
     ἂν δὴ † φέρῃς τι, μέγα δή τι † φέροις·
     ἄνοιγ' ἄνοιγε τὰν θύραν χελιδόνι·
     οὐ γὰρ γέροντές ἐσμεν, ἀλλὰ παιδία.

τὸν δὲ ἀγερμὸν τοῦτον κατέδειξε πρῶτος Κλεόβουλος
ὁ Λίνδιος ἐν Λίνδῳ χρείας γενομένης συλλογῆς χρημάτων. ἐπεὶ δὲ Ῥοδιακῶν ἱστοριῶν ἐμνήσθημεν, ἰχθυ-
ολογήσων καὶ αὐτὸς ὑμῖν ἔρχομαι ἀπὸ τῆς καλῆς
Ῥόδου, ἣν εὔιχθυν εἶναί φησιν ὁ ἥδιστος Λυγκεύς.

e Ἐργείας οὖν ὁ Ῥόδιος | ἐν τοῖς περὶ τῆς πατρίδος
προειπών τινα περὶ τῶν κατοικησάντων τὴν νῆσον
Φοινίκων φησὶν ὡς οἱ περὶ Φάλανθον ἐν τῇ Ἰαλυσῷ
πόλιν ἔχοντες ἰσχυροτάτην τὴν Ἀχαΐαν καλουμένην
καὶ ὕδατος²² ἐγκρατεῖς ὄντες χρόνον πολὺν ἀντεῖχον
Ἰφίκλῳ πολιορκοῦντι. ἦν γὰρ αὐτοῖς καὶ θέσφατον ἐν
χρησμῷ τινι λελεγμένον ἕξειν τὴν χώραν, ἕως κόρακες λευκοὶ γένωνται καὶ ἐν τοῖς κρατῆρσιν ἰχθύες
φανῶσιν. ἐλπίζοντες οὖν τοῦτ' οὐδέποτε ἔσεσθαι καὶ
τὰ πρὸς τὸν πόλεμον ῥαθυμοτέρως εἶχον. ὁ δ' Ἴφι-
f κλος | πυθόμενος παρά τινος τὰ τῶν Φοινίκων λόγια
καὶ ἐνεδρεύσας τοῦ Φαλάνθου πιστόν τινα πορευόμενον ἐφ' ὕδωρ, ᾧ ὄνομα ἦν Λάρκας, καὶ πίστεις πρὸς
αὐτὸν ποιησάμενος, θηρεύσας ἰχθύδια ἐκ τῆς κρήνης

---

²² ὕδατος Kaibel: δαιτὸς ACE

²²⁶ One of the Seven Sages, and thus to be dated to the early
6th century BCE; cf. 10.445a.

150

She's small—so we'll carry her off with no trouble!
But if in fact † you bring something, something big in
    fact † might you bring!
Open your door, open it, to a swallow!
For we're not old men, but children.

The pioneer of this type of collection was Cleobulus of
Lindus,[226] at a time when money had to be collected on
Lindus. But since I mentioned Rhodian history, I am here
to personally offer you fish-stories from beautiful Rhodes,
which the delightful Lynceus (fr. 11 Dalby) claims has
excellent seafood. Thus Ergeias of Rhodes in his essay on
his fatherland (*FGrH* 513 F 1) begins with some remarks
about the Phoenicians who settled the island, and then reports that because Phalanthus' people[227] controlled the
powerful citadel in Ialysus known as Achaea and had ac-
cess to drinking water, they held out for a long time when
Iphiclus had them under seige. They had a prophecy expressed in an oracle of some sort to the effect that they
would control the place until ravens turned white and fish
appeared in their mixing-bowls; they accordingly expected
that this would never happen and were less concerned
about the war. Someone told Iphiclus about the Phoenicians' prophecies, and he ambushed a man Phalanthus
trusted, whose name was Larcas, as he was going to fetch
water. After coming to an understanding with him, he
caught some small fish in the well and put them into a

---

[227] Perhaps simply a way of saying "Phalanthus", with the plu-
rals that follow all accordingly to be translated as singulars. The
events described here took place in the early (legendary) period of
the island's history.

καὶ ἐμβαλὼν εἰς ὑδρεῖον ἔδωκε τῷ Λάρκᾳ καὶ ἐκέλευσε φέροντα τὸ ὕδωρ τοῦτο ἐγχέαι εἰς τὸν κρατῆρα
ὅθεν τῷ Φαλάνθῳ ᾠνοχοεῖτο. καὶ ὁ μὲν ἐποίησε ταῦτα·
ὁ δὲ Ἴφικλος κόρακας θηρεύσας καὶ ἀλείψας γύψῳ
361   ἀφῆκεν. ‖ Φάλανθος δ᾽ ἰδὼν τοὺς κόρακας ἐπορεύετο
καὶ ἐπὶ τὸν κρατῆρα· ὡς δὲ καὶ τοὺς ἰχθῦς εἶδεν,
ὑπέλαβε τὴν χώραν οὐκέτι αὐτῶν εἶναι καὶ ἐπεκηρυ-
κεύσατο πρὸς τὸν Ἴφικλον, ὑπόσπονδος ὑπεξελθεῖν
ἀξιῶν μετὰ τῶν σὺν αὑτῷ. συγκαταθεμένου δὲ τοῦ
Ἰφίκλου ἐπιτεχνᾶται ὁ Φάλανθος τοιόνδε τι· κατα-
βαλὼν ἱερεῖα καὶ τὰς κοιλίας ἐκκαθάρας ἐν ταύταις
ἐπειρᾶτο ἐξάγειν χρυσίον καὶ ἀργύριον. αἰσθόμενος
b   δὲ ὁ Ἴφικλος διεκώλυε· προφέροντός τε τοῦ | Φαλάν-
θου τὸν ὅρκον ὃν ὤμοσεν, ἐάσειν ἐξάγεσθαι ὅ τι κα τᾷ
γαστρὶ αἴρωνται, ἀντισοφίζεται πλοῖα αὐτοῖς διδοὺς
ἵνα ἀποκομισθῶσιν, παραλύσας τὰ πηδάλια καὶ τὰς
κώπας καὶ τὰ ἱστία, ὁμόσαι φήσας πλοῖα παρέξειν,
ἄλλο δὲ οὐδέν. ἐν ἀπορίᾳ δὲ οἱ Φοίνικες ἐχόμενοι
πολλὰ μὲν τῶν χρημάτων κατώρυσσον ἐπισημαινό-
μενοι τοὺς τόπους, ἵν᾽ ὕστερόν ποτε ἀνέλωνται ἀφικό-
μενοι, πολλὰ δὲ τῷ Ἰφίκλῳ κατέλειπον. ἀπαλλαγέν-
των οὖν τούτῳ τῷ τρόπῳ ἐκ τῆς χώρας τῶν Φοινίκων
c   κατέσχον | τὰ πράγματα οἱ Ἕλληνες. τὰ δ᾽ αὐτὰ
ἱστορήσας καὶ Πολύζηλος ἐν τοῖς Ῥοδιακοῖς τὰ περὶ
τῶν ἰχθύων φησί· καὶ τῶν κοράκων μόνοι ᾔδεσαν ὁ
Φακᾶς καὶ ἡ θυγάτηρ αὐτοῦ Δορκία. αὕτη δ᾽ ἐρασθεῖ-
σα τοῦ Ἰφίκλου καὶ συνθεμένη περὶ γάμου διὰ τῆς

water-jar. He then gave the jar to Larcas, and told him to take this water and pour it into the mixing-bowl from which Phalanthus' wine was served. Larcas did what he was ordered; in the meantime, Iphiclus caught some ravens, smeared them with gypsum, and let them go. When Phalanthus saw the ravens, he went to his mixing-bowl; and when he saw the fish, he concluded that the place was no longer theirs, and sent an embassy to Iphiclus, proposing that he be allowed to withdraw under the protection of a truce, along his people. When Iphiclus agreed, Phalanthus came up with the following trick: he slaughtered and gutted some sacrificial animals, and tried to take out gold and silver coins inside the animals. Iphiclus realized what he was doing and attempted to stop him; when Phalanthus cited the terms of the oath he had sworn, which were that Iphiclus would allow them to remove whatever they had in their bellies, he came up with a clever response: he gave them ships so they could remove their property, but took off the rudders, oars, and sails, and claimed that he had sworn to supply ships, but nothing else. The Phoenicians were at a loss as to what to do, and accordingly buried much of the money, marking the spots, in order that they could come back someday and retrieve it; but they also left a large amount behind for Iphiclus. After the Phoenicians left the area in this way, the Greeks took control of the situation. Polyzelus in his *History of Rhodes* (*FGrH* 521 F 6) tells the same story about the fish and then says: Phacas[228] and his daughter Dorcia were the only people who knew about the ravens. But she fell in love with Iphiclus and agreed to marry him; and using

---

[228] I.e. the man Ergeias called Phalanthus.

τροφοῦ ἔπεισε τὸν φέροντα τὸ ὕδωρ ἰχθῦς ἀγαγεῖν καὶ
ἐμβαλεῖν εἰς τὸν κρατῆρα, καὶ αὐτὴ δὲ τοὺς κόρακας
λευκάνασα ἀφῆκεν.

Κρεώφυλος δ᾽ ἐν τοῖς Ἐφεσίων Ὥροις· οἱ τὴν
Ἔφεσον, φησί, κτίζοντες καὶ πολλὰ ταλαιπωρηθέντες
d ἀπορίᾳ τόπου | τὸ τελευταῖον πέμψαντες εἰς θεοῦ
ἠρώτων ὅπου τὸ πόλισμα θῶνται. ὁ δ᾽ αὐτοῖς ἔχρησεν
ἐνταῦθα οἰκίζειν πόλιν ᾗ ἂν ἰχθὺς δείξῃ καὶ ὗς ἄγριος
ὑφηγήσηται. λέγεται οὖν ὅπου νῦν ἡ κρήνη ἐστὶν
Ὑπέλαιος καλουμένη καὶ ὁ ἱερὸς λιμὴν ἁλιέας ἀρι-
στοποιεῖσθαι, καὶ τῶν ἰχθύων τινὰ ἀποθορόντα σὺν
ἀνθρακιᾷ εἰσπεσεῖν εἰς φορυτόν, καὶ ἀφθῆναι ὑπ᾽
αὐτοῦ λόχμην, ἐν ᾗ ἔτυχε σῦς ἄγριος ὤν· ὃς ὑπὸ τοῦ
πυρὸς θορυβηθεὶς ἐπέδραμε τοῦ ὄρους ἐπὶ πολύ, ὃ δὴ
e καλεῖται | Τρηχεῖα, καὶ πίπτει ἀκοντισθεὶς ὅπου νῦν
ἐστιν ὁ τῆς Ἀθηνᾶς ναός. καὶ διαβάντες οἱ Ἐφέσιοι ἐκ
τῆς νήσου, ἔτεα εἴκοσιν οἰκήσαντες, τὸ δεύτερον[23]
κτίζουσι Τρηχεῖαν καὶ τὰ ἐπὶ Κορησσόν, καὶ ἱερὸν
Ἀρτέμιδος ἐπὶ τῇ ἀγορῇ ἱδρύσαντο Ἀπόλλωνός τε τοῦ
Πυθίου ἐπὶ τῷ λιμένι.

Τοιούτων οὖν ἔτι πολλῶν λεγομένων τότε ἐξάκου-
στος ἐγένετο κατὰ πᾶσαν τὴν πόλιν αὐλῶν τε βόμβος
καὶ κυμβάλων ἦχος ἔτι τε τυμπάνων κτύπος μετὰ

---

[23] τὸ δεύτερον εἴκοσι A: εἴκοσι del. Kaibel

her nurse as an intermediary, she convinced the man who fetched their water to bring some fish and throw them into the mixing-bowl, while she herself colored the ravens white and let them go.

Creophylus (says) in his *Annals of the Ephesians* (*FGrH* 417 F 1): The people who were trying to found Ephesus had a great deal of trouble, because they were unable to locate a site. Finally they sent to the god's oracle[229] and asked where they should put their city, and he prophesied to them (Delphic Oracle L54 Fontenrose) that they should found a city in a place a fish would show them and to which a wild boar would lead the way. The story goes, then, that some fishermen were having lunch in the spot where the so-called Hypelaeus spring and the sacred lake are located today, and that one of their fish jumped out of the fire with an ember struck to it, and fell into some dry brush. This set fire to a thicket in which a wild boar happened to be; it was thrown into a panic by the fire and ran for a long distance along the mountain, which is known as Trēcheia. After it was hit by a javelin, it collapsed in the spot where the temple of Athena is now located. The Ephesians crossed over from the island where they had been living for 20 years, and settled Trēcheia and the area around Coressus for a second time; they also established a temple of Artemis in the marketplace and a temple of Pythian Apollo by the harbor.

Although many long speeches along these lines were still being made, the buzzing of pipes, the clash of cymbals, and the pounding of drums, accompanied by singing,

---

[229] In Delphi (hence the temple dedicated to Pythian Apollo referred to below).

f   ᾠδῆς ἅμα γινόμενος. ἔτυχεν | δὲ οὖσα ἑορτὴ τὰ Παρί-
λια[24] μὲν πάλαι καλουμένη, νῦν δὲ Ῥωμαῖα, τῇ τῆς
πόλεως Τύχῃ ναοῦ καθιδρυμένου ὑπὸ τοῦ πάντα ἀρίστου καὶ μουσικωτάτου βασιλέως Ἀδριανοῦ· ἐκείνην
τὴν ἡμέραν κατ' ἐνιαυτὸν ἐπίσημον ἄγουσι πάντες οἱ
τὴν Ῥώμην κατοικοῦντες καὶ οἱ ἐνεπιδημοῦντες τῇ
πόλει. ὁ οὖν Οὐλπιανός, ἄνδρες, ἔφη, τί τοῦτο; ||

362   εἰλαπίνη ἠὲ γάμος; ἐπεὶ οὐκ ἔρανος τάδε γ'
ἐστίν.

καί τινος εἰπόντος ὅτι βαλλίζουσιν οἱ κατὰ τὴν πόλιν
ἅπαντες τῇ θεῷ, ὦ λῷστε, ὁ Οὐλπιανὸς γελάσας ἔφη,
καὶ τίς Ἑλλήνων τοῦτο βαλλισμὸν ἐκάλεσεν, δέον
εἰρηκέναι κωμάζουσιν ἢ χορεύουσιν ἤ τι ἄλλο τῶν
εἰρημένων; σὺ δὲ ἡμῖν ἐκ τῆς Συβούρας ὄνομα πριάμενος

ἀπώλεσας τὸν οἶνον ἐπιχέας ὕδωρ.

καὶ ὁ Μυρτίλος ἔφη· ἀλλὰ μὴν καὶ Ἑλληνικώτερον
b   ἀποδείξω | σοι τὸ ὄνομα, ὦ φίλε Ἐπιτίμαιε. πάντας

---

[24] Παράλια ACE: corr. Palmer

230 Celebrated on April 21. The temple referred to below is
that of Venus and Rome. For the outspoken praise of Hadrian
(reigned 117–138 CE), cf. 3.115b; 13.574f.
231 Quoted again at 8.362d, along with the verse that precedes
it.
232 A commercial section of Rome with a dubious reputation.

became audible throughout the entire city. It happened
to be the festival referred to long ago as the Parilia, but
known today as the Romaia,[230] the associated temple in
honor of the city's Fortune having been established by the
universally excellent and immensely cultivated emperor
Hadrian. All the inhabitants of Rome, along with any visitors to the city, celebrate that day every year as an important occasion. Ulpian accordingly said: What is this,
gentlemen?

> A banquet or a wedding feast? Since this is not a
>   meal to which the guests contribute. (*Od*.
>   1.226)[231]

When someone replied: Everyone in the city is singing
and dancing (*ballizousin*) in honor of the goddess, Ulpian
laughed and said: My good sir, what Greek ever referred
to this as *ballismos*? You ought to have said *kōmazousin*
("they are celebrating, revelling") or *chōreuousin* ("they
are singing and dancing"), or have used some other conventional expression. By buying us a word in the Subura[232]
(Aristias *TrGF* 9 F 4)[233]

> you ruined our wine[234] by pouring water into it.

But Myrtilus responded: I will show you that the term is
in fact quite acceptable Greek, my dear Epitimaeus[235].

For Ulpian's fussy refusal to use Latin (or Latinate) vocabulary, cf.
9.376e with n.
  233 Identified by Apostolius as coming from the satyr play *Cyclops*, making it likely that the speaker is Polyphemus.
  234 I.e. in context "our pure Greek"; cf. Ulpian's angrier out-
burst at Cynulcus at 3.121e–f.   235 "Fault-finder"; cf. 6.272b.

γὰρ ἐπιστομίζειν πειρώμενος οὐδενὸς μὲν ἀμαθίαν
κατέγνως, σαυτὸν δ᾽ ἀποφαίνεις κενότερον λεβηρίδος.
Ἐπίχαρμος, ὦ θαυμασιώτατε, ἐν τοῖς Θεαροῖς μέμνηται τοῦ βαλλισμοῦ, καὶ οὐ μακράν ἐστι τῆς Σικελίας
ἡ Ἰταλία. ἐν οὖν τῷ δράματι οἱ θεωροὶ καθορῶντες τὰ
ἐν Πυθοῖ ἀναθήματα καὶ περὶ ἑκάστου λέγοντές φασι
καὶ τάδε·

> λέβητες χάλκιοι,
> κρατῆρες, ὀδελοί. τοῖς γα μὰν ὑπωδέλοις
> † καιλωτε † βαλλίζοντες † σιοσσον χρῆμα |

c
> εἴη †.

καὶ Σώφρων δ᾽ ἐν τῇ ἐπιγραφομένῃ Νυμφοπόνῳ φη-
σίν· κἤπειτα λαβὼν προῆχε, τοὶ δ᾽ ἐβάλλιζον. καὶ
πάλιν· βαλλίζοντες τὸν θάλαμον σκάτους ἐνέπλησαν.
ἀλλὰ μὴν καὶ Ἄλεξις ἐν Κουρίδι φησί·

> καὶ γὰρ ἐπικώμων < . . . > ἀνθρώπων ὁρῶ
> πλῆθος προσιὸν ὡς τῶν καλῶν τε κἀγαθῶν
> ἐνθάδε συνόντων. μὴ γένοιτό μοι μόνῳ
> νύκτωρ ἀπαντῆσαι καλῶς πεπραγόσιν
> ὑμῖν περὶ τὸν βαλλισμόν· οὐ γὰρ ἄν ποτε |

d
> θοἰμάτιον ἀπενέγκαιμι μὴ φύσας πτερά.

---

236 Doubtless proverbial; cf. Stratt. fr. 52; Diogen. 3.73.

237 Meaning that a term used by a Greek-speaker like
Epicharmus in Syracuse could reasonably be used in Rome as
well.

238 The first two verses of the fragment are quoted at 9.408d.

For despite your efforts to muzzle us all, you have convicted no one of ignorance, but are merely demonstrating that you yourself are emptier than a discarded snake-skin.[236] Epicharmus uses the term *ballismos* in his *Sacred Envoys*, marvelous sir—and Italy is not far from Sicily.[237] In the play, at any rate, the envoys are examining the dedications at Delphi and discussing them individually, and they say the following (fr. 68.2–4):[238]

> bronze basins,
> mixing-bowls, and spits. On the spit-supports, in fact,
> [corrupt] dancing (*ballizontes*) [corrupt] † a matter
>   might be. †

Sophron as well says in his mime entitled *The Bridesmaid* (fr. 11, encompassing both quotations): And then he took it and led the way, and they started to dance (*eballizon*). Again: As they danced (*ballizontes*)[239], they filled the room with shit. Alexis, moreover, says in *The Female Barber* (fr. 112):

> In fact, I see a crowd of wild
> drunks approaching; it looks like the nobility's
> assembled here. I hope I never come face-to-face
> with you at night when I'm alone and you're enjoying
> yourselves *peri ton ballismon*[240]. Because if I did, I'd
>   never
> get away with my robe, unless I sprouted wings.

[239] In both passages the verb could just as easily refer to throwing something (a more normal sense of the word).

[240] Probably to be taken "roughing people up" rather than "dancing", as Athenaeus (or his source) would have it.

οἶδα δὲ καὶ ἀλλαχόθι τοὖνομα καὶ ἀναπεμπασάμενος
ἐξοίσω. σὺ δὲ ἡμῖν δίκαιος εἶ λέγειν, ὁ καὶ τῶν
Ὁμηρικῶν μεμνημένος τούτων·

τίς δαίς, τίς δαὶ ὅμιλος ὅδ᾽ ἔπλετο; τίπτε δέ σε
    χρεώ;
εἰλαπίνη ἠὲ γάμος; ἐπεὶ οὐκ ἔρανος τάδε γ᾽
    ἐστίν,

τίνι διαφέρει ἀλλήλων. ἐπεὶ δὲ σιγᾷς, ἐγὼ ἐρῶ. κατὰ
γὰρ τὸν Συρακόσιον ποιητήν·

τὰ πρὸ τοῦ δύ᾽ ἄνδρες ἔλεγον, εἷς ἐγὼν
    ἀποχρέω.[25]

e τὰς | θυσίας καὶ τὰς λαμπροτέρας παρασκευὰς ἐκά-
λουν οἱ παλαιοὶ εἰλαπίνας καὶ τοὺς τούτων μετέχοντας
εἰλαπιναστάς. ἔρανοι δέ εἰσιν αἱ ἀπὸ τῶν συμβαλλο-
μένων συναγωγαί, ἀπὸ τοῦ συνερᾶν καὶ συμφέρειν
ἕκαστον. καλεῖται δ᾽ ὁ αὐτὸς καὶ ἔρανος καὶ θίασος
καὶ οἱ συνιόντες ἐρανισταὶ καὶ θιασῶται. καλεῖται δὲ
καὶ ὁ τῷ Διονύσῳ παρεπόμενος ὄχλος θίασος, ὡς
Εὐριπίδης φησίν·

ὁρῶ δὲ θιάσους τρεῖς γυναικείων χορῶν.

[25] Better punctuated as a question, as in *PCG*.

---

[241] The promise is never fulfilled.
[242] Also quoted at 7.308c, in a similar context.

160

I am aware that the word appears elsewhere as well; after I think the matter through, I will quote the passages.[241] But since you have cited (8.362a) the following Homeric lines (*Od*. 1.225–6):

> What is this feast, this crowd? How does this involve
> you?
> (Is this) a banquet (*eilapinē*) or a wedding feast?
>> Since this is not a meal to which the guests
>> contribute (*eranos*),

you are the right person to tell us: How do these occasions differ? And since you have nothing to say, I will tell you. For to quote the Syracusan poet (Epich. fr. 161)[242],

> I will suffice by myself for things two men said
> previously.

The ancients referred to sacrifices and particularly lavish parties as *eilapinai*, and to the individuals who participated in them as *eilapinastai*.[243] Gatherings made up of people who contribute to the cost of the event are *eranoi*, from the fact that they form a group (*suneran*) and everyone brings something. The terms *eranos* and *thiasos* ("band, company") can be used to describe the same occasion, and the members of the group are *eranistai* or *thiasōtai*. The crowd that accompanies Dionysus is also referred to as a *thiasos*, as Euripides says (*Ba*. 680):

> And I saw three *thiasoi* of dancing women.[244]

---

[243] Cf. Ar. Byz. frr. 285–6 Slater.
[244] Describing the Theban maenads on Mt. Cithaeron.

τοὺς μὲν οὖν θιάσους ἀπὸ τοῦ θεοῦ προσηγόρευον· |

f καὶ γὰρ αὐτοὺς τοὺς θεοὺς οἱ Λάκωνες σιούς φασι·
τὰς δ᾽ εἰλαπίνας ἀπὸ τῆς ἐν αὐταῖς παρασκευῆς γινομένης καὶ δαπάνης. λαφύττειν γὰρ καὶ λαπάζειν τὸ
ἐκκενοῦν καὶ ἀναλίσκειν, ὅθεν καὶ ἐπὶ τοῦ πορθεῖν τὸ
ἀλαπάζειν οἱ ποιηταὶ τάττουσι, καὶ τὰ διαρπαζόμενα
κατὰ τὴν λάφυξιν λάφυρα. τὰς δὲ τοιαύτας εὐωχίας
Αἰσχύλος καὶ Εὐριπίδης εἰλαπίνας ἀπὸ τοῦ λελα-

363 πάχθαι. ‖ λάπτειν δὲ τὸ τὴν τροφὴν ἐκπέττειν καὶ
κενούμενον λαγαρὸν γίγνεσθαι· ὅθεν ἀπὸ μὲν τοῦ
λαγαροῦ ἡ λαγών, ὥσπερ καὶ λάγανον, ἀπὸ δὲ τοῦ
λαπάττειν λαπάρα. λαφύττειν δέ ἐστι τὸ δαψιλῶς καὶ
ἐπὶ πολὺ λαπάττειν καὶ ἐκκενοῦν. τὸ δὲ δαπανᾶν ἀπὸ
τοῦ δάπτειν λέγεται· καὶ τοῦτο δὲ τοῦ δαψιλοῦς ἔχεται·
διόπερ ἐπὶ τῶν ἀπλήστως καὶ θηριωδῶς ἐσθιόντων τὸ
δάψαι καὶ δαρδάψαι. Ὅμηρος·

τὸν δ᾽ ἄρα ἀλλὰ κύνες τε καὶ οἰωνοὶ
κατέδαψαν.[26] |

b τὰς δ᾽ εὐωχίας ἐκάλουν οὐκ ἀπὸ τῆς ὀχῆς, ἥ ἐστι
τροφή, ἀλλ᾽ ἀπὸ τοῦ κατὰ ταῦτα εὖ ἔχειν. εἰς ἃς δὴ
συνιόντες οἱ τὸ θεῖον τιμῶντες καὶ εἰς εὐφροσύνην καὶ

[26] Thus Athenaeus; the traditional text of Homer has ἀλλ᾽
ἄρα τόν γε κύνες κτλ.

[245] Apparently an attempt to make the etymology more convincing.

They derived the word *thiasos* from *theos* ("god")—the Spartans in fact refer to the gods themselves as *sioi*[245]— and they called them *eilapinai* because of the planning and expense involved,[246] since *laphuttein* and *lapazein* mean "to waste one's resources" and "to spend money". The poets accordingly use the verb *alapazein* to mean "to plunder" (e.g. *Il.* 9.328), while goods that are stolen and gluttonously consumed are *laphura*. Aeschylus (fr. 424) and Euripides (e.g. *Med.* 193) refer to feasts of this sort as *eilapinai*, deriving the word from *lelapachthai* ("to have been emptied, sacked"). To digest one's food is *laptein*, and an object that is emptied becomes *lagaros*; the word *lagōn* ("hollow, flank") thus comes from *lagaros*, as does *laganon*,[247] while *lapara* ("flank") is derived from *lapattein* ("to empty"). To empty and clear out something systematically and carefully is *laphuttein*. *Dapanân* ("to spend money") comes from *daptein* ("to devour"), and is also connected to *dapsilēs* ("abundant, plentiful");[248] as a result, the verbs *daptō* and *dardaptō* (both "to devour, consume") are applied to people who eat gluttonously, like wild animals. Homer (*Od.* 3.259):

but dogs and birds devoured (*katedapsan*) him.

They got the word *euōchia* ("feast") not from *ochē*, which means "nourishment", but from being well-off (*eu echein*) in this regard.[249] When people gathered to honor the gods

---

[246] The actual origin of the word is unknown, and the discussion that follows is (from a modern linguistic perspective) largely misguided.   [247] "wafer-bread"; see 3.110a.

[248] This is probably correct.

[249] This is probably correct.

ἄνεσιν αὐτοὺς μεθιέντες τὸ μὲν ποτὸν μέθυ, τὸν δὲ
τοῦτο δωρησάμενον θεὸν Μεθυμναῖον καὶ Λυαῖον καὶ
Εὔιον καὶ Ἰήιον προσηγόρευον, ὥσπερ καὶ τὸν μὴ
σκυθρωπὸν καὶ σύννουν ἱλαρόν· διὸ καὶ τὸ δαιμόνιον
ἵλεων ἠξίουν γίνεσθαι ἐπιφωνοῦντες ἰὴ ἰή. ὅθεν καὶ
τὸν τόπον ἐν ᾧ τοῦτο ἔπραττον ἱερὸν ὠνόμαζον. ὅτι δὲ

c τὸν αὐτὸν | ἵλεων καὶ ἱλαρὸν ἔλεγον δηλοῖ Ἔφιππος
ἐν τῷ ἐπιγραφομένῳ δράματι Ἐμπολή· περὶ ἑταίρας
δέ τινος λέγει·

ἔπειτά γ᾽ εἰσιόντ᾽, ἐὰν λυπούμενος
τύχῃ τις ἡμῶν, ἐκολάκευσεν ἡδέως·
ἐφίλησεν οὐχὶ συμπιέσασα τὸ στόμα
ὥσπερ πολέμιον, ἀλλὰ τοῖσιν στρουθίοις
χανοῦσ᾽ ὁμοίως † ἤ σε † παρεμυθήσατο
ἐποίησέ θ᾽ ἱλαρὸν εὐθέως τ᾽ ἀφεῖλε πᾶν
αὐτοῦ τὸ λυποῦν κἀπέδειξεν ἵλεων. |

d Οἱ δ᾽ ἀρχαῖοι καὶ τοὺς θεοὺς ἀνθρωποειδεῖς ὑποστησάμενοι καὶ τὰ περὶ τὰς ἑορτὰς διέταξαν. ὁρῶντες
γὰρ ὡς τῆς μὲν ἐπὶ τὰς ἀπολαύσεις ὁρμῆς οὐχ οἷόν τε
τοὺς ἀνθρώπους ἀποστῆσαι, χρήσιμον δὲ καὶ συμ-
φέρον τοῖς τοιούτοις εὐτάκτως καὶ κοσμίως ἐθίζειν
χρῆσθαι, χρόνον ἀφορίσαντες καὶ τοῖς θεοῖς προ-
θύσαντες οὕτω μεθῆκαν αὐτοὺς εἰς ἄνεσιν, ἵν᾽ ἕκαστος

---

[250] In fact, *methu* is the Greek form of an Indo-European
word that means "honey, mead".

[251] All epithets of Dionysus.   [252] The words are in fact
related.   [253] Quoted again at 13.571e–f.

at this type of feast and allowed (*methientes*) themselves to be happy and relax, they began to refer to what they drank as *methu* ("wine"),[250] and to the god who had given it to them as *Methumnaios*, *Luaios*, *Euios*, or *Iâios*,[251] and likewise to anyone who did not scowl or act gloomy as *hilaros* ("cheerful"); they accordingly expected the deity to be well-disposed (*hileōs*) to them if they addressed him with the cry *iē iē*. As a consequence, they began to call the place where they did all this *hieron* ("holy"). That they referred to the same individual as *hileōs* and *hilaros*[252] is made clear by Ephippus in his play entitled *Merchandise* (fr. 6).[253] He says about a certain courtesan:

Then, if one of us happens to be unhappy
when he goes into her house, she's sweet and
    flattering.
She doesn't kiss him with his lips squeezed together,
as if he was an enemy; instead, she opens her mouth
    wide,
just like baby swallows do † she who you † and coaxes
    him
and makes him cheerful (*hilaros*); and in a flash she
    makes whatever's
upsetting him disappear, and puts him in a good
    mood (*hileōs*).

The ancients assumed that the gods resembled human beings, and they arranged their festivals accordingly. Because they saw that people are incapable of resisting the urge to enjoy themselves, and that it is useful and expedient to accustom them to doing so in an organized and orderly fashion, they set time aside and began with an offering to the gods, allowing themselves to relax in this setting,

ἡγούμενος ἥκειν τοὺς θεοὺς ἐπὶ τὰς ἀπαρχὰς καὶ τὰς
σπονδὰς μετὰ αἰδοῦς τὴν συνουσίαν ποιῆται. Ὅμη-
e ρος γοῦν | φησιν·

ἦλθε δ' Ἀθήνη

ἱρῶν ἀντιόωσα.

καὶ ὁ Ποσειδῶν

Αἰθίοπας μετεκίαθε τηλόθ' ἐόντας,
ἀντιόων ταύρων τε καὶ ἀρνειῶν ἑκατόμβης.

καὶ ὁ Ζεὺς

χθιζὸς ἔβη κατὰ δαῖτα, θεοὶ δ' ἅμα πάντες
ἕποντο.

κἂν ἄνθρωπος δέ που παρῇ πρεσβύτερος καὶ τῇ προ-
αιρέσει σπουδαῖος, αἰδοῦνται λέγειν τι τῶν ἀσχημό-
f νων ἢ καὶ πράττειν, ὡς καὶ Ἐπίχαρμός πού | φησιν·

ἀλλὰ καὶ σιγὴν ἀγαθόν, ὅκκα παρέωντι
κάρρονες.

ὑπολαμβάνοντες οὖν τοὺς θεοὺς πλησίον αὑτῶν εἶναι
τὰς ἑορτὰς κοσμίως καὶ σωφρόνως διῆγον. ὅθεν οὔτε
κατακλίνεσθαι παρὰ τοῖς ἀρχαίοις ἔθος, ἀλλὰ

δαίννυνθ' ἑζόμενοι,

οὔτ' εἰς μέθην πίνειν, ἀλλ'

166

so that everyone would imagine that the gods had come for the preliminary offerings and the libations, and would behave decently while they were together. Homer says, for example (*Od*. 3.435–6):

> Athena came
> and attended the sacrifice.

So too Poseidon (*Od*. 1.22, 25)

> went off to visit the distant Ethiopians
> and attended a massive sacrifice of bulls and sheep.

And Zeus (*Il*. 1.424)

> left yesterday for a feast, and all the gods
> accompanied him.

If an older person of a serious character, moreover, happens to be there, their sense of respect and shame keeps them from saying or doing anything inappropriate, as Epicharmus (fr. 163) says somewhere:

> But it's good to keep quiet, when people better than
> you are present.

Because they felt that the gods were near them, therefore, they conducted their festivals in an orderly, thoughtful way. As a consequence, it was not the ancients' practice to lie down, but instead (e.g. *Od*. 3.471)

> they feasted sitting.

Nor they did drink until they got drunk, but instead (e.g. *Od*. 3.395–6)

< . . . > ἐπεὶ σπεῖσάν τ᾽ ἔπιόν θ᾽ ὅσον ἤθελε
  θυμός,

<   . . .   > ἔβαν οἰκόνδε ἕκαστος.

οἱ δὲ νῦν προσποιούμενοι θεοῖς θύειν καὶ συγκα-
λοῦντες ἐπὶ τὴν θυσίαν τοὺς φίλους καὶ τοὺς οἰκειο-
364 τάτους ‖ καταρῶνται μὲν τοῖς τέκνοις, λοιδοροῦνται δὲ
ταῖς γυναιξί, κλαυθμυρίζουσιν τοὺς οἰκέτας, ἀπειλοῦ-
σι τοῖς πολλοῖς, μονονουχὶ τὸ τοῦ Ὁμήρου λέγοντες·

  νῦν δ᾽ ἔρχεσθ᾽ ἐπὶ δεῖπνον, ἵνα ξυνάγωμεν ἄρηα,

ἐπὶ νοῦν λαμβάνοντες τὰ εἰρημένα ὑπὸ τοῦ τὸν Χείρωνα πεποιηκότος, εἴτε Φερεκράτης ἐστὶν εἴτε Νικόμα-
χος ὁ ῥυθμικὸς ἢ ὅστις δή ποτε·

  μηδὲ σύ γ᾽ ἄνδρα φίλον καλέσας ἐπὶ δαῖτα
    θάλειαν ǀ
b ἄχθου ὁρῶν παρεόντα· κακὸς γὰρ ἀνὴρ τόδε
    ῥέζει·
  ἀλλὰ μάλ᾽ εὔκηλος τέρπου φρένα τέρπε τ᾽
    ἐκεῖνον.

νῦν δὲ τούτων μὲν οὐδ᾽ ὅλως μέμνηνται, τὰ δὲ ἐξῆς
αὐτῶν ἐκμανθάνουσιν, ἅπερ πάντα ἐκ τῶν εἰς Ἡσίο-
δον ἀναφερομένων Μεγάλων Ἠοίων[27] πεπαρῴδηται·

---

[27] Μεγάλων Ἠοίων καὶ Μεγάλων Ἔργων A: καὶ Μεγάλων Ἔργων del. Dindorf

After they poured a libation and drank as much as
    their heart desired,
          . . .   they all went home.

People today, on the other hand, make a pretence of sacrificing to the gods and inviting their friends and family to
the event, but then swear at their children, speak rudely to
their wives, reduce their slaves to tears, threaten the group
as a whole, and do everything but quote the Homeric line
(*Il.* 2.381):

But now go to your dinner, so that we can join battle,

not keeping in mind the words of the author of the
Cheiron—whether this is Pherecrates (fr. 162, including
the ten verses allegedly adapted from Hesiod that follow),
or the rhythmician Nicomachus, or whoever it may be:[254]

If you invite a friend to a large meal, don't
be upset when you see him there; this is how a bad
    man behaves.
Instead, enjoy yourself, entirely at your ease, and
    make him happy.

Whereas nowadays they forget these lines entirely, and
memorize those that come immediately after them, all of
which are adapted from the *Great Ehoiai* attributed to
Hesiod:[255]

[254] For doubts about the authorship of *Cheiron* (shared by
other ancient authorities), cf. 9.368a–b, 388f; 14.653e–f.
[255] In fact, the first three verses of this fragment (quoted
above) appear to be Hesiodic, while those that follow do not; most
likely Athenaeus (or his source) has got the situation backward.

ἡμῶν δ᾽ ἤν τινά τις καλέσῃ θύων ἐπὶ δεῖπνον,
ἀχθόμεθ᾽, ἢν ἔλθῃ, καὶ ὑποβλέπομεν παρεόντα,
χὤττι τάχιστα θύραζ᾽ ἐξελθεῖν βουλόμεθ᾽
    αὐτόν. |

c εἶτα γνούς πως τοῦθ᾽ ὑποδεῖται· κᾆτά τις εἶπε
τῶν ξυμπινόντων· "ἤδη σύ; τί οὐχ ὑποπίνεις;
οὐχ ὑπολύσεις αὐτόν;" ὁ δ᾽ ἄχθεται αὐτὸς ὁ θύων
τῷ κατακωλύοντι καὶ εὐθὺς ἔλεξ᾽ ἐλεγεῖα·
"μηδένα μήτ᾽ ἀέκοντα μένειν κατέρυκε παρ᾽ ἡμῖν,
μήδ᾽ εὕδοντ᾽ ἐπέγειρε, Σιμωνίδη." οὐ γὰρ ἐπ᾽
    οἴνοις
τοιαυτὶ λέγομεν δειπνίζοντες φίλον ἄνδρα;

ἔτι δὲ καὶ ταῦτα προστίθεμεν· |

d μηδὲ πολυξείνου δαιτὸς δυσπέμφελος εἶναι·
ἐκ κοινοῦ πλείστη τε χάρις δαπάνη τ᾽ ὀλιγίστη.

καὶ θύοντες μὲν τοῖς θεοῖς ὀλίγιστα εἰς τὰς θυσίας καὶ
τὰ τυχόντα δαπανῶμεν, ὥσπερ ὁ καλὸς Μένανδρος ἐν
τῇ Μέθῃ παρίστησιν·

εἶτ᾽ οὐχ ὅμοια πράττομεν καὶ θύομεν;
ὅπου γε τοῖς θεοῖς μὲν ἠγορασμένον
δραχμῶν ἄγω προβάτιον ἀγαπητὸν δέκα,

---

[256] Adapted from Thgn. 467, 469.
[257] The first six verses of the fragment are quoted also at
4.146d–e.

If one of us invites a guest to dinner when he's
> making a sacrifice,
we're upset if the fellow comes, and we give him
> dirty looks while he's there,
and want him to leave as soon as possible.
Then somehow he recognizes this and puts on his
> shoes; but one of the other guests
says "Are you leaving already? Why don't you drink a
> bit?
Take off his shoes!" And the man making the sacrifice
> gets upset
at the one doing the detaining, and immediately
> quotes the elegiac lines:
"Neither hold back anyone who is unwilling to
> remain with us,
nor wake the man who is asleep, Simonides."[256] Don't
> we say things like this
over our wine, when we have a friend to dinner?

I also add the following passage (Hes. *Op*. 722–3):

Don't act put out if there are many guests at a feast;
when everyone contributes, there's more pleasure
> and considerably less expense.

When we sacrifice to the gods, we spend as little as we can
on the meal and the incidentals, as the noble Menander
establishes in his *Drunkenness* (fr. 224):[257]

So doesn't how we do in life match the way we
> sacrifice?
Since I'm bringing the gods a nice little
goat purchased for ten drachmas,

αὐλητρίδας δὲ καὶ μύρον καὶ ψαλτρίας,
† Μενδαῖον † Θάσιον, ἐγχέλεις, τυρόν, μέλι, |
e   μικροῦ τάλαντον, γίνεταί τε κατὰ λόγον
δραχμῶν μὲν ἀγαθὸν ἄξιον λαβεῖν δέκα
ἡμᾶς, ἐὰν καὶ καλλιερηθῇ τοῖς θεοῖς·
τούτων δὲ πρὸς ταῦτ᾽ ἀντανελεῖν τὴν ζημίαν,
πῶς οὐχὶ τὸ κακὸν τῶν ἱερῶν διπλάζεται;
ἐγὼ μὲν οὖν ὤν γε θεὸς οὐκ εἴασα τὴν
ὀσφὺν ἂν ἐπὶ τὸν βωμὸν ἐπιθεῖναί ποτε,
εἰ μὴ καθήγιζέν τις ἅμα τὴν ἔγχελυν,
ἵνα Καλλιμέδων ἀπέθανεν εἷς τῶν συγγενῶν. |

f   ὀνομάζουσι δ᾽ οἱ ἀρχαῖοι καὶ ἐπιδόσιμά τινα δεῖπνα,
ἅπερ Ἀλεξανδρεῖς λέγουσιν ἐξ ἐπιδομάτων. Ἄλεξις
γοῦν ἐν Τῇ Εἰς τὸ Φρέαρ φησί·

(A.) νυνί τε μοι
ὁ δεσπότης προὔπεμψεν οἴνου κεράμιον
τῶν ἔνδοθεν κομιοῦντ᾽ ἐκεῖθεν. (B.) μανθάνω·
ἐπιδόσιμον παρὰ τἆλλα τοῦτ᾽ ἔσται. (A.) φιλῶ
αἰσθητικὴν γραῦν.

καὶ Κρώβυλος ἐν Ψευδυποβολιμαίῳ· ||

---

258 Actually an immense amount of money (6000 drachmas).
259 A standard part of sacrificial procedure; how the tailbone
burned was taken to indicate the god's attitude toward the offering
and thus the request that accompanied it.

whereas the cost of the dancing-girls, perfume, harp-
    girls,
† Mendaean and † Thasian wine, eels, cheese, and
    honey
is minimal—a talent.[258] And it's reasonable for
us to get ten drachmas worth of blessings—
assuming the gods take pleasure in the sacrifice!
But if we have to match what we spend on them with
    what we spend on ourselves,
isn't the trouble sacrifices put us to doubled?
If I were a god, I'd never let anyone
put the tailbone on the altar[259]
unless he simultaneously offered his eel—
which would be the death of its relative
    Callimedon![260]

The ancients also refer to certain dinners as *epidosima*,
which are what the Alexandrians call dinners "via contri-
butions". Alexis, for example, says in *The Woman Who Fell
into the Well* (fr. 85):

             (A.) But as it is, my
master sent me off to fetch a jar of wine
from the people who live inside that house there. (B.)
    I get it;
this is going to be a contribution (*epidosimon*) on top
    of everything else. (A.) I love
a perceptive old woman.

Also Crobylus in *Falsely Supposititious* (fr. 5):

[260] For the seafood-lover Callimedon "the Crayfish", see
8.338f n.

173

365   (Α.) Λάχης. (Λα.) ἐγὼ δὲ πρὸς σέ. (Α.)
        πρόαγε. (Λα.) ποῖ;
       (Α.) ὅποι μ' ἐρωτᾷς; ὡς Φιλουμένην, παρ' ᾗ
       τἀπιδόσιμ' ἡμῖν ἐστιν· ἧς ἐχθὲς πιεῖν
       κυάθους ἕκαστον ἐβιάσω σὺ δώδεκα.

οἴδασι δὲ οἱ ἀρχαῖοι καὶ τὰ νῦν καλούμενα ἀπὸ
σπυρίδος δεῖπνα. ἐμφανίζει δὲ Φερεκράτης περὶ τούτων ἐν Ἐπιλήσμονι ἢ Θαλάττῃ οὕτως·

    συσκευασάμενος δεῖπνον ἐς τὸ σπυρίδιον
    ἐβάδιζεν ὡς † πρὸς ωφελην †.

τοῦτο δὲ σαφῶς δηλοῖ τὸ ἀπὸ σπυρίδος δεῖπνον, ὅταν
b τις αὐτὸς | αὑτῷ σκευάσας δεῖπνον καὶ συνθεὶς εἰς
σπυρίδα παρά τινα δειπνήσων ἴῃ. σύνδειπνον εἴρηκεν
ἐπὶ συμποσίου Λυσίας ἐν τῷ Κατὰ Μικίνου Φόνου.
φησὶν γάρ· ἐκεῖνον ἐπὶ τὸ σύνδειπνον κεκλημένον. καὶ
Πλάτων δ' ἔφη· τοῖς τὸ σύνδειπνον ποιησαμένοις. καὶ
Ἀριστοφάνης Γηρυτάδῃ·

    ἐν τοῖσι συνδείπνοις ἐπαινῶν Αἰσχύλον.

διόπερ τινὲς καὶ τὸ Σοφοκλέους δρᾶμα κατὰ τὸ οὐδέτερον ἐπιγράφειν ἀξιοῦσιν Σύνδειπνον. καλοῦσι δέ τινα
καὶ συναγώγιμα δεῖπνα, ὡς Ἄλεξις ἐν Φιλοκάλῳ ἢ
Νύμφαις· |

(A.) Laches! (B.) *I'm* coming to *you*. (A.) Lead the
    way. (B.) To where?
(A.) You're asking me where? To visit Philoumene;
    our
epidosima are at her house. Yesterday you forced
us all to drink a dozen ladles in her honor.

The ancients were also familiar with what are today referred to as "dinners from a basket". Pherecrates in *The
Forgetful Man or The Sea* (fr. 57) has the following to say
about them:

He arranged his dinner in the basket
and went to [corrupt].

What leaves no doubt that a "dinner from a basket" is involved, is when an individual prepares dinner for himself,
puts it in a basket, and goes off to another person's house to
eat. Lysias uses the word *sundeipnon* for a drinking party
(*sumposion*) in his *Against Micinus for Murder* (fr. 233
Carey). He says: he had been invited to the *sundeipnon*.
Plato as well said (cf. *Smp.* 172b): to those who prepared
the *sundeipnon*. Also Aristophanes in *Gerytades* (fr. 161):

praising Aeschylus at the *sundeipna*.

This is why some authorities believe that Sophocles' play
should have the title *Sundeipnon*, in the neuter.[261] The
ancients also refer to certain dinners as *sunagōgima* ("col-
lective"), as for example Alexis in *The Man Who Loved
Elegance or Nymphs* (fr. 253):

261 Sc. rather than the masculine plural *Sundeipnoi*, as at
15.678f, 685f; cf. 1.17d.

c   (Α.) κατάκεισο κἀκείνας κάλει.
συναγώγιμον ποιῶμεν. (Β.) ἀλλ᾽ εὖ οἶδ᾽ ὅτι
κυμινοπρίστης ὁ τρόπος ἐστί σου πάλαι.

καὶ Ἔφιππος ἐν Γηρυόνῃ·

             καὶ συναγώγιμον
συμπόσιον ἐπιπληροῦσιν.

ἔλεγον δὲ συνάγειν καὶ τὸ μετ᾽ ἀλλήλων πίνειν καὶ
συναγώγιον τὸ συμπόσιον. Μένανδρος Ἐμπιμπρα-
μένῃ·

   καὶ νῦν ὑπὲρ τούτων συνάγουσι κατὰ μόνας.

εἶθ᾽ ἑξῆς ἔφη·

   < . . . > ἐπλήρωσέν τε τὸ συναγώγιον.

d μήποτε δὲ | τοῦτ᾽ ἐστὶ τὸ ἀπὸ συμβολῶν καλούμενον.
τίνες δ᾽ εἰσὶν αἱ συμβολαὶ <ὁ> αὐτὸς Ἄλεξις ἐν
Μανδραγοριζομένῃ σημαίνει διὰ τούτων·

   (Α.) ἥξω φέρουσα συμβολὰς τοίνυν ἅμα.
   (Β.) πῶς συμβολάς; (Α.) τὰς ταινίας οἱ
           Χαλκιδεῖς
   καὶ τοὺς ἀλαβάστους συμβολὰς καλοῦσι, γραῦ.

Ἀργεῖοι δ᾽, ὡς ἐν τοῖς Ὑπομνήμασί φησιν Ἡγήσαν-

       (A.) Lie down and invite the women in!
Let's have a *sunagōgimon*! (B.) But I know perfectly
      well that
you've been a cheapskate forever.

Also Ephippus in *Geryon* (fr. 4):

         And they fill up
a *sunagōgimon* drinking party.

They used the verb *sunagein* ("to assemble") to refer to
drinking with one another, and *sunagōgion* to refer to a
drinking party. Menander in *The Girl Who Was on Fire* (fr.
123, encompassing both quotations):

And now as a result they're getting together
      (*sunagousi*) separately.

Then immediately after this he said:

and he filled up the *sunagōgion*.

Perhaps this is what is referred to as (drinking) *apo sum-
bolōn* ("from tokens"). What *sumbolai* are is shown by the
same Alexis in *The Woman Who Ate Mandrake* (fr. 147), in
the following passage:

(A.) Well then, I'll come, and I'll bring the *sumbolai*
      with me.
(B.) What do you mean by "*sumbolai*"? (A.) The
      Chalcidians refer
to ribbons and perfume-flasks as *sumbolai*, old
      woman.

But the Argives (do things differently), according to Hegesander in his *Commentaries* (fr. 31, *FHG* iv.419). He

177

δρος· γράφει δ᾽ οὕτως· τὴν συμβολὴν τὴν εἰς τὰ συμπόσια ὑπὸ τῶν πινόντων εἰσφερομένην Ἀργεῖοι χῶν καλοῦσι, τὴν δὲ μερίδα αἶσαν.

e   Οὐκ | ἀνάρμοστον δὲ καὶ τούτου τοῦ συγγράμματος τέλος εἰληφότος, ἑταῖρε Τιμόκρατες, αὐτοῦ καταπαύσω τὸν λόγον, μὴ καὶ ἡμᾶς τις οἰηθῇ κατὰ τὸν Ἐμπεδοκλέα ἰχθῦς ποτε γεγονέναι. φησὶ γὰρ ὁ φυσικός·

ἤδη γάρ ποτ᾽ ἐγὼ γενόμην κοῦρός τε κόρη τε
θάμνος τ᾽ οἰωνός τε καὶ ἔξαλος ἔλλοπος ἰχθύς.

writes as follows: The Argives refer to the *sumbolē* the
members of the group bring to their drinking parties as a
chōs, and to an individual share[262] as an *aisa*.

Since this treatise too has come to an end, my friend
Timocrates, it is appropriate for me to conclude my speech
at this point, so that no one believes that I was ever a fish,[263]
as Empedocles was. For the scientist says (31 B 117 D–K):

Because before this I was a boy, a girl,
a bush, a bird, and an *ellopos* fish leaping out of the
     sea.

[262] Sc. of the cost of the party.
[263] Sc. "and am thus overly interested in them".

Θ

366   Δόρπου δ' ἐξαῦτις μνησώμεθα, χερσὶ δ' ἐφ' ὕδωρ
χευάντων· μῦθοι δὲ καὶ ἠῶθέν περ ἔσονται

ἐμοί τε καὶ σοί, ὦ Τιμόκρατες. περιενεχθέντων γὰρ
κωλήνων καί τινος εἰπόντος εἰ τακεραί εἰσι, παρὰ τίνι
κεῖται τὸ τακερόν;, ὁ Οὐλπιανὸς ἔφη. καὶ σίναπυ δὲ
τίς εἴρηκε τὸ νᾶπυ; ὁρῶ γὰρ ἐν παροψίσι περιφερόμενον μετὰ τῶν κωλεῶν. οἶδα γὰρ καὶ οὕτως λεγόμενον κωλεὸν ἀρσενικῶς καὶ οὐχ, ὡς οἱ ἡμεδαποὶ Ἀθη-
b   ναῖοι, μόνως θηλυκῶς. Ἐπίχαρμος | γοῦν ἐν Μεγαρίδι
φησίν·

    † ορεατηρηδιον † κωλεοί, σφόνδυλοι, τῶν δὲ
      βρωμάτων οὐδὲ ἕν.

καὶ ἐν Κύκλωπι·

    χορδαί τε ἁδύ, ναὶ μὰ Δία, χὠ κωλεός.

μάθετε δὲ καὶ τοῦτο παρ' ἐμοῦ, ὦ σοφώτατοι, ὅτι νῦν ὁ
Ἐπίχαρμος καὶ χορδὴν ὠνόμασεν, ἀεί ποτε ὀρύαν

BOOK IX

Let us think once again of our dinner, and let them
     pour water
over our hands; and beginning at dawn there will be
     stories (*Od.* 4.213–14)

for you and me, Timocrates. Because when hams (*kōlēnai*)
were served, someone asked if they were tender (*takerai*),
and Ulpian said: In what author is the word *takeros* attested? And who refers to mustard (*napu*) as *sinapu*?;
because I see that it is being served in sauce-dishes along
with the hams (*kōleōn*). For I know that the word is also
pronounced this way, as masculine *kōleon*, and is not exclusively feminine, as our Athenians would have it. Epicharmus, for example, says in *The Woman from Megara*
(fr. 81):

> [corrupt] hams (*kōleoi*), vertebrae—but nothing
>   edible.

And in *Cyclops* (fr. 71):

> Sausages (*chordai*) are delicious food, by Zeus, as is
>   the ham (*kōleos*)!

Here is something else you can learn from me, my brilliant
friends: Epicharmus used the word *chordē* here, but else-

181

καλῶν. καὶ ἅλας δὲ ἡδυσμένους ὁρῶ ἐν ἄλλαις παρ-
οψίσιν. ἀνηδύντων δὲ ἁλῶν πλήρεις οἱ κυνικοί, παρ᾽
οἷς κατὰ τὸν Ἀντιφάνην, λέγει δ᾽ ἐν Κωρύκῳ τις
ἄλλος κύων·

    (Α.) τῶν θαλαττίων δ᾽ ἀεὶ |
c ὄψων ἓν ἔχομεν, διὰ τέλους δὲ τοῦθ᾽, ἅλα.
    < . . . > ἐπὶ δὲ τούτοις πίνομεν
    οἰνάριον. (Β.) ἡδός, νὴ Δί᾽, οἰκίας τρόπον.
    (Α.) πῶς ἡδός; οἷον τοῖς παροῦσι συμφέρει
    ἀπαξάπασιν ὀξυβάφῳ ποτηρίῳ.

ὁρῶ δὲ καὶ μετὰ ὄξους ἀναμεμιγμένον γάρον· οἶδα δὲ
ὅτι νῦν τινες τῶν Ποντικῶν ἰδίᾳ καθ᾽ αὑτὸ κατασκευ-
άζονται ὀξύγαρον.

    Πρὸς ταῦτα ἀπαντήσας ὁ Ζωίλος ἔφη· Ἀριστο-
φάνης, ὦ οὗτος, ἐν Λημνίαις τὸ τακερὸν ἔταξεν ἐπὶ τοῦ
τρυφεροῦ λέγων οὕτως· |

d Λῆμνος κυάμους τρέφουσα τακεροὺς καὶ καλούς.

καὶ Φερεκράτης Κραπατάλλοις·

    τακεροὺς ποῆσαι τοὺς ἐρεβίνθους αὐτόθι.

---

[1] Cf. 3.94f, where Athenaeus claims that Epicharmus composed an (otherwise unattested) play entitled *Orua*. The word is
not attested elsewhere in what we have of his plays, but is perhaps
to be restored in fr. 81 (above), where the manuscripts offer the
corrupt *oreatērēdion*.

where always refers to this as *orua*.[1] I also see seasoned salt in other sauce-dishes. Whereas the Cynics are full of unseasoned salt; according to Antiphanes in *The Beggar's Bag* (fr. 132), another dog (*kuōn*) in their pack says:

> (A. We always have one type of
> seafood, and we have it constantly: salt.
> . . . And to go with these items, we drink
> a little wine. (B.) It's nice (*hēdos*),[2] by Zeus—in the
>   house-style!
> (A.) What do you mean, "nice"? It's the kind that's
>   good for everyone
> who's there, provided you use a vinegar-cruet as a
>   cup.

I see that fermented fish-sauce has been mixed with the vinegar, and I know that nowadays some residents of the Black Sea region manufacture a vinegar-and-fermented-fish sauce specifically as such.

In response to these remarks, Zoilus said: Aristophanes in *Lemnian Women* (fr. 372), sir, used the adjective *takeros* to describe dainty food, saying the following:

> Lemnos, which produces fine, dainty (*takeroi*) beans.

Also Pherecrates in *Small Change* (fr. 89):

> to make the chickpeas dainty then and there.

[2] Or perhaps "It's vinegar" (if the word is given a smooth breathing); but the humor is in any case obscure.

σίνηπυ δ᾽ ὠνόμασε Νίκανδρος ὁ Κολοφώνιος ἐν μὲν Θηριακοῖς οὕτως·

ἦ μὴν καὶ σικύην χαλκήρεα ἠὲ σίνηπυ.[1]

ἐν δὲ τοῖς Γεωργικοῖς·

σπέρματά τ᾽ ἐνδάκνοντα σινήπυος.

καὶ πάλιν·

κάρδαμ᾽ ἀνάρρινόν τε μελάμφυλλόν τε σίνηπυ.

Κράτης δ᾽ ἐν τοῖς Περὶ τῆς Ἀττικῆς Λέξεως Ἀριστο-
φάνη παριστᾷ λέγοντα· ‖

367   κἄβλεπε σίναπυ καὶ τὰ πρόσωπ᾽ ἀνέσπασε,

καθά φησι Σέλευκος ἐν τοῖς Περὶ Ἑλληνισμοῦ· ἐστὶ δ᾽
ὁ στίχος ἐξ Ἱππέων καὶ ἔχει οὕτως·

κἄβλεψε νᾶπυ.

οὐδεὶς δ᾽ Ἀττικῶν σίναπυ ἔφη· ἔχει δὲ ἑκάτερον λόγον.
νᾶπυ μὲν γὰρ οἷον νᾶφυ, ὅτι ἐστέρηται φύσεως· ἀφυὲς
γὰρ καὶ μικρόν, ὥσπερ καὶ ἡ ἀφύη. σίναπυ δὲ ὅτι
σίνεται τοὺς ὦπας ἐν τῇ ὀδμῇ, ὡς καὶ τὸ κρόμμυον ὅτι

---

[1] The traditional text of Nicander is very different: ναὶ μὴν
καὶ σικύην χαλκήρεα λοιγέϊ τύψει.

[3] Part of a much longer fragment, overlapping portions of
which are quoted at 4.133d–e; 9.369b–c.

184

Nicander of Colophon used the word *sinēpu* in the *Theriaca* (921), as follows:

assuredly a bronze cupping-glass or *sinēpu*.

And in his *Georgics* (fr. 70.16 Schneider):[3]

and pungent mustard (*sinēpu*)-seed.

Again (fr. 84 Schneider):

nose-smart and pepper-grass and black-leaved *sinēpu*.

Crates in his *On the Attic Dialect* (*FGrH* 362 F 11 = fr. 111 Broggiato) cites Aristophanes, who says:

and he was giving me a mustard (*sinapu*) look and
    arching his eyebrows,

according to Seleucus in his *On Hellenism* (fr. 69 Müller). But the line comes from *Knights* (631) and actually runs as follows:

and he was giving me a mustard (*napu*) look.[4]

No Attic author used *sinapu*; but either form makes sense. *Napu* is, as it were, *naphu*, because it has not been allowed to grow,[5] since it is stunted (*aphues*) and small, like small-fry (*aphuē*).[6] Whereas it might be *sinapu* because the smell hurts our eyes (*sinetai . . . ōpes*), just as we say *krommuon* ("onion") because we squeeze our eyes shut (*koras*

---

[4] Thus in fact the manuscripts of Aristophanes.

[5] As if *naphu* were constructed out of an initial privative combined with a word cognate with *phuō* ("to grow").

[6] For this (false) etymology, cf. 7.324d.

τὰς κόρας μύομεν. Ξέναρχος δὲ ὁ κωμῳδιοποιὸς ἐν
Σκύθαις ἔφη·

τουτὶ τὸ κακὸν οὐκ ἔστ᾽ ἔτι
b   κακόν, τὸ θυγάτριόν τε μου | σεσινάπικεν
διὰ τῆς ξένης.

ἁλῶν δὲ καὶ ὄξους μέμνηται ὁ καλὸς Ἀριστοφάνης ἐν
τοῖς περὶ Σθενέλου τοῦ τραγικοῦ λέγων·

(Α.) καὶ πῶς ἐγὼ Σθενέλου φάγοιμ᾽ ἂν ῥήματα;
(Β.) εἰς ὄξος ἐμβαπτόμενος ἢ ξηροὺς ἅλας.

ἡμεῖς μὲν οὖν σοι ταῦτα, καλὲ ἄνθρωπε, ζητοῦντι
συνεισευπορήσαμεν· σὺ δ᾽ ἡμῖν ἀποκρίνασθαι δίκαιος εἶ παρὰ τίνι ἐπὶ τοῦ ἀγγείου ἡ παροψὶς κεῖται. ἐπὶ
c   μὲν γὰρ ὄψου παρεσκευασμένου ποικίλου | καὶ εἴδους
τινὸς τοιούτου Πλάτωνα οἶδα εἰρηκότα ἐν Ἑορταῖς
οὕτως·

ὁπόθεν ἔσοιτο μᾶζα καὶ παροψίδες.

ἐν δὲ Εὐρώπῃ πάλιν ἐπὶ παροψήματος διὰ πλειόνων
εἴρηκεν, ἐν οἷς ἐστι καὶ τάδε·

(Α.) γυνὴ καθεύδουσ᾽ ἐστὶν ἀργόν. (Β.) μανθάνω.

---

7 Sc. when we eat it, because of its smell.
8 *TrGF* 32. The fragment is identified by Σ^RVΓ Ar. *V.* 1312 as
coming from *Gerytades* (probably 408 or 407 BCE).
9 At 9.366a.

186

muomen).[7] The comic poet Xenarchus said in *Scythians* (fr. 12):

> This problem's no longer
> a problem; my daughter's applied a mustard-plaster
>   (*sesinapiken*)
> with the foreign woman's help.

The noble Aristophanes mentions salt and vinegar in the passage about the tragic poet Sthenelus,[8] where he says (fr. 158):

> (A.) And how could I stomach Sthenelus' speeches?
> (B.) By dipping them in vinegar or dry salt.

I furnished you, my good sir, with these responses to the questions you posed.[9] But you are the right person to tell us in what author *paropsis* is attested as referring to a vessel.[10] For I am aware that Plato in *Festivals* (fr. 32)[11] uses the word of an elaborately-prepared dish of some such type, as follows:

> from which a barley-cake and *paropsides* might
>   come.

Again, in his *Europa* (fr. 43) he uses it repeatedly to refer to a side-dish (*paropsēma*), including in the following passage:

> (A.) A woman who's asleep doesn't get you anywhere.
>   (B.) I understand.

10 The word more often means "side-dish" (see below), but Ulpian used it twice to refer to a vessel at 9.366a–b.

11 Quoted again at 9.368c, presumably from a different source-document. Cf. 9.368d n.

(A.) ἐγρηγορυίας δ᾽ εἰσὶν αἱ παροψίδες
αὐταὶ μόνον κρεῖττον πολὺ χρῆμ᾽ εἰς ἡδονὴν
ἢ τἆλλα. (B.) βίνου γάρ τινες παροψίδες |
d   εἰσ᾽, ἀντιβολῶ σ᾽;

κἂν τοῖς δ᾽ ἑξῆς δίεισιν ὥσπερ ἐπὶ παροψήματος
λέγων τῶν παροψίδων. ἐν δὲ Φάωνι·

τὰ δ᾽ ἀλλότρι᾽ ἔσθ᾽ ὅμοια ταῖς παροψίσι·
βραχὺ γάρ ⟨τι⟩ τέρψαντ᾽ ἐξανήλωται ταχύ.

Ἀριστοφάνης Δαιδάλῳ·

πάσαις γυναιξὶν ἐξ ἑνός γε του ⟨τρόπου⟩
ὥσπερ παροψὶς μοιχὸς ἐσκευασμένος.

Σιωπῶντος οὖν τοῦ Οὐλπιανοῦ, ἀλλ᾽ ἐγώ, φησὶν ὁ
Λεωνίδης, εἰπεῖν εἰμι δίκαιος πολλὰ ἤδη σιωπήσας· |

e   πολλοῖς δ᾽ ἀντιλέγειν

κατὰ τὸν Πάριον Εὔηνον

ἔθος περὶ παντὸς ὁμοίως,
ὀρθῶς δ᾽ ἀντιλέγειν, οὐκέτι τοῦτ᾽ ἐν ἔθει.
καὶ πρὸς μὲν τούτους ἀρκεῖ λόγος εἷς ὁ παλαιός·
σοὶ μὲν ταῦτα δοκοῦντ᾽ ἔστω, ἐμοὶ δὲ τάδε.

---

[12] Quoted again at 9.368b–c, presumably from a different
source-document.

[13] The fourth verse is quoted again in a similar context at
10.429f.

(A.) But once she's awake, her side-dishes
        (*paropsides*)
all by themselves are a much greater contribution to
        pleasure
than the rest is. (B.) But are there any side-dishes
        (*paropsides*) to
fucking, I'd like to know?

And in what follows he goes through the "*paropsides*" as if
he were actually discussing side-dishes. Also in *Phaon* (fr.
190):

Other people's stuff is like side-dishes (*paropsides*);
it makes you happy for a little while, but it's quickly
        used up.

Aristophanes in *Daedalus* (fr. 191):[12]

For all women, one way or another,
a seducer's ready, like a side-dish (*paropsis*).

When Ulpian remained silent, Leonides said: Well, I
am the right person to speak, given that I have kept quiet
for a long time.

Many people are in the habit—

to quote Evenus of Paros (fr. 1 West²)[13]—

        of arguing about absolutely everything;
    but as for arguing correctly, that's not what they
        do.
To answer them, a single ancient saying's enough:
    "You can think that, but I think something else!"

τοὺς ξυνετοὺς δ' ἄν τις πείσειε τάχιστα
   λέγων εὖ,
οἵπερ καὶ ῥήστης εἰσὶ διδασκαλίης.

ἐπὶ τοῦ σκεύους οὖν εἴρηκεν, ὦ φιλότης Μυρτίλε

f   (προήρπασα | γάρ σου τὸν λόγον), Ἀντιφάνης Βοι-
ωτίῳ·

   καλέσας τε παρατίθησιν ἐν παροψίδι.

καὶ Ἄλεξις ἐν Ἡσιόνῃ·

   ὡς εἶδε τὴν τράπεζαν ἀνθρώπους δύο
   φέροντας εἴσω ποικίλων παροψίδων
   κόσμου βρύουσαν, οὐκέτ' εἰς ἔμ' ἔβλεπεν.

καὶ ὁ τὰ εἰς Μάγνητα ἀναφερόμενα ποιήσας ἐν Διονύσῳ πρώτῳ·

   καὶ ταῦτα μέν μοι τῶν κακῶν παροψίδες. ‖

368   Ἀχαιὸς δ' ἐν Αἴθωνι σατυρικῷ·

   κεκερματίσθω δ' ἄλλα μοι παροψίδων
   κάθεφθα καὶ κνισηρὰ παραφλογίσματα.

Σωτάδης δ' ὁ κωμικὸς Παραλυτρουμένῳ·

---

[14] Pollux 10.88 quotes the next word ("hyacinth-bulbs"; simple, bitter food) as well, supplying a direct object for the verb.

Whereas if you make a good case, you could easily
      convince intelligent people,
because they're easy to teach.

Antiphanes in *The Boeotian* (fr. 61.1), my good friend
Myrtilus—I know I snatched the words out of your
mouth—applies the term to a vessel:

and if he invites anyone, he serves him (food) in
      paropsides.[14]

Also Alexis in *Hesione* (fr. 89):

When he saw two people carrying
the table inside, loaded with an array of all sorts
of side-dishes (*paropsides*), he stopped paying
      attention to me.

And the author of the lines attributed to Magnes (fr. 1) in
Dionysus I:[15]

And these are side-dishes (*paropsides*) to my
      troubles.

Achaeus in the satyr play *Aethon* (*TrGF* 20 F 7):

Let other stewed-down, flame-roasted
side-dishes (*paropsides*) smelling of fat be chopped
      up for me!

The comic author Sotades in *The Man Who Was Being
Ransomed* (fr. 3):

15 For reservations about the authorship of the play, cf.
14.646e.

191

παροψὶς εἶναι φαίνομαι τῷ Κρωβύλῳ·
τοῦτον μασᾶται, παρακατεσθίει δ᾽ ἐμέ.

ἀμφιβόλως δ᾽ εἴρηται τὸ παρὰ τῷ Ξενοφῶντι ἐν πρώτῳ Παιδείας. φησὶ γὰρ ὁ φιλόσοφος· προσῆγεν αὐτῷ
παροψίδας καὶ παντοδαπὰ ἐμβάμματα καὶ βρώματα.
καὶ παρὰ τῷ τὸν Χείρωνα δὲ πεποιηκότι τὸν εἰς
b Φερεκράτην ἀναφερόμενον ἐπὶ ἡδύσματος | ἡ παροψὶς
κεῖται καὶ οὐχ, ὡς Δίδυμος ἐν τῷ Περὶ Παρεφθορυίας
Λέξεως, ἐπὶ τοῦ ἀγγείου. φησὶ γάρ·

νὴ τὸν Δί᾽ ὥσπερ αἱ παροψίδες
τὴν αἰτίαν ἔχουσ᾽ ἀπὸ τῶν ἡδυσμάτων,
† οὓς ὁ καλετας † ἀξιοῖ τοῦ μηδενός.

Νικοφῶν Σειρῆσιν·

ἀλλᾶς μαχέσθω περὶ ἕδρας παροψίδι.

Ἀριστοφάνης Δαιδάλῳ· |

c πάσαις γυναιξὶν ἐξ ἑνός γε του ⟨τρόπου⟩
ὥσπερ παροψὶς μοιχὸς ἐσκευασμένος.

Πλάτων Ἑορταῖς·

ὁπόθεν ἔσοιτο μᾶζα καὶ παροψίδες.

Apparently I'm a side-dish (*paropsis*) to Crobylus:
she's chewing on him, but eating me on the side.

The sense of the word is ambiguous in Book I of Xenophon's *Education* (*Cyr.* 1.3.4), because the philosopher says: He brought him *paropsides* and dipping-sauces and other foods of all types. The word *paropsis* is also attested in the author of the *Cheiron* attributed to Pherecrates,[16] referring to a sauce and not, as Didymus claims in his *On Corrupt Vocabulary* (p. 19 Schmidt), to the vessel. Because he says (Pherecr. fr. 157):

By Zeus, they're just like side-dishes (*paropsides*)—
they're held responsible for the sauce they're in!
† which the one who [corrupt] † thinks are worthless!

Nicopho in *Sirens* (fr. 22):[17]

Let a sausage fight against side-dishes (*paropsides*)
for a seat!

Aristophanes in *Daedalus* (fr. 191):[18]

For all women, one way or another,
a seducer's ready, like a side-dish (*paropsis*).

Plato in *Festivals* (fr. 32):[19]

from which a barley-cake and *paropsides* might
come.

[16] For the disputed authorship of the play, see 8.363f n.
[17] Probably from the same passage as fr. 21 (quoted at 6.269e–f).
[18] Quoted also at 9.367d, where see n.
[19] Quoted also at 9.367c, where see n.

περὶ βολβῶν δ' ἀρτύσεως καὶ σκευασίας τὸν λόγον ποιεῖται. οἱ δ' Ἀττικοί, ὦ Συραττικὲ Οὐλπιανέ, καὶ ἔμβαμμα λέγουσιν, ὡς Θεόπομπος ἐν Εἰρήνῃ·

ὁ μὲν ἄρτος ἡδύ, τὸ δὲ φενακίζειν προσὸν |

d   ἔμβαμμα τοῖς ἄρτοις πονηρὸν γίγνεται.

Καὶ κωλῆνα δὲ λέγουσι καὶ κωλῆν. Εὔπολις Αὐτολύκῳ·

σκέλη δὲ καὶ κωλῆνες εὐθὺ τοὐρόφου.

Εὐριπίδης Σκίρωνι·

< . . . > οὐδὲ κωλῆνες νεβρῶν.

ἀπὸ δὲ τοῦ κωλέα συνηρημένον ἐστὶν ὡς συκέα συκῆ, λεοντέα λεοντῆ, κωλέα κωλῆ. Ἀριστοφάνης Πλούτῳ δευτέρῳ·

οἴμοι δὲ κωλῆς ἣν ἐγὼ κατήσθιον.

καὶ ἐν Δαιταλεῦσι· |

e   καὶ δελφακίων ἁπαλῶν κωλαῖ καὶ χναυμάτια
        πτερόεντα.

ἐν δὲ Πελαργοῖς·

κεφαλάς τ' ἀρνῶν κωλᾶς <τ'> ἐρίφων.

He then discusses how hyacinth-bulbs are seasoned and prepared. Attic authors, my Syrian friend Ulpian, use the term *embamma* ("dipping-sauce"), for example Theopompus in *Peace* (fr. 9):

> The bread's delicious; but the cheating, which is
>   there
> as a dipping-sauce (*embamma*) for the bread, is nasty.

They say both *kōlē* and *kōlēn*.[20] Eupolis in *Autolycus* (fr. 54):

> legs and hams (*kōlēnes*) hanging from the roof.

Euripides in *Sciron* (fr. 677):

> and no fawns' hams (*kōlēnes*).

The form is contracted from *kōlea*, like *sukē* ("fig") from *sukea*, and *leontē* ("lion's skin") from *leontea*; so *kōlē* from *kōlea*. Aristophanes in *Wealth II*[21] (1128):

> Alas! the ham (*kōlē*) I used to gobble down!

Also in *Banqueters* (fr. 236):

> and hams (*kōlai*) of tender piglets, and winged
>   tidbits.

And in *Storks* (fr. 449):

> and lambs' heads and kids' hams (*kōlai*).

---

[20] Sc. to mean "ham"; responding to Ulpian's points about various forms of the word at 9.366a–b.

[21] I.e. the preserved version of the play.

Πλάτων Γρυψίν·

< . . . > ἰχθῦς, κωλᾶς, φύσκας.

Ἀμειψίας Κόννῳ·

δίδοται μάλισθ᾽ ἱερώσυνα,
κωλῆ, τὸ πλευρόν, ἡμίκραιρ᾽ ἀριστερά.

Ξενοφῶν Κυνηγετικῷ· κωλῆν σαρκώδη, λαγόνας
ὑγράς. καὶ Ξενοφάνης δ᾽ ὁ Κολοφώνιος ἐν τοῖς Ἐλε-
γείοις φησί· |

f   πέμψας γὰρ κωλῆν ἐρίφου σκέλος ἤραο πῖον
        ταύρου λαρινοῦ, τίμιον ἀνδρὶ λαχεῖν
    τοῦ κλέος Ἑλλάδα πᾶσαν ἀφίξεται, οὐδ᾽
        ἀπολήξει,
    ἔστ᾽ ἂν ἀοιδάων ᾖ γένος Ἑλλαδικόν.

Ἐξῆς δὲ τούτων πολλῶν καὶ παντοδαπῶν ἐπιφερο-
μένων ἡμεῖς ἐπισημανούμεθα τὰ μνήμης ἄξια. καὶ
γὰρ ὀρνίθων πλῆθος ἦν αἰεὶ καὶ χηνῶν, ἔτι δὲ τῶν
369 νεοσσῶν ὀρνίθων, οὓς πίπους[2] τινὲς καλοῦσι, ‖ καὶ
χοίρων καὶ τῶν περισπουδάστων φασιανικῶν ὀρνίθων. περὶ λαχάνων οὖν πρότερον ἐκθέμενός σοι καὶ
περὶ τῶν ἄλλων μετὰ ταῦτα διηγήσομαι.

____

[2] πίπους Casaubon: ἴππους ACE

196

Plato in *Griffins* (fr. 17):

fish, hams (*kōlai*), stuffed large intestines.

Amipsias in *Connus* (fr. 7.1–2):

The priest's share is certainly being offered:
a ham (*kōlē*), a side of ribs, and the left half of the
head.

Xenophon in the *Art of Hunting* (5.30): an upper leg (*kōlē*)
with plenty of flesh, loose flanks.[22] Xenophanes of Colophon too says in his *Elegies* (fr. B 6 West[2]):

Because although you sent only a kid's ham (*kōlē*),
you took home a meaty leg
of a fatted bull, a mark of honor for the man to
whom it falls,
whose fame will spread throughout Greece and will
never fail,
so long as the Greek tribe of bards endures.

Immediately after this, many different types of food
were served; I will describe only those that deserve special
mention. There was, in fact, always a substantial supply
of birds, including geese, as well as the young birds some
authorities refer to as *pipoi* ("cheepers"), and also pigs and
pheasants, which are much sought-after. After first describing the vegetables, therefore, I will offer you an account of these items afterward.[23]

[22] Referring to a hare.
[23] Beginning at 9.373a. The fiction of offering an account of a
conversation among a number of different parties is abandoned
until 9.373a.

Γογγυλίδες. ταύτας Ἀπολλᾶς ἐν τῷ Περὶ τῶν ἐν
Πελοποννήσῳ Πόλεων ὑπὸ Λακεδαιμονίων γάστρας
φησὶ καλεῖσθαι. Νίκανδρος δ᾽ ὁ Κολοφώνιος ἐν ταῖς
Γλώσσαις παρὰ Βοιωτοῖς γάστρας ὀνομάζεσθαι τὰς
κράμβας, τὰς δὲ γογγυλίδας ζεκελτίδας· Ἀμερίας δὲ
καὶ Τιμαχίδας τὰς κολοκύντας ζεκελτίδας καλεῖ-
b σθαι. | Σπεύσιππος δ᾽ ἐν δευτέρῳ Ὁμοίων, ῥαφανίς,
φησί, γογγυλίς, ῥάφυς, ἀνάρρινον ὅμοια. τὴν δὲ
ῥάφυν Γλαῦκος ἐν τῷ Ὀψαρτυτικῷ διὰ τοῦ -π ψιλῶς
καλεῖ ῥάπυν. τούτοις δ᾽ οὐδὲν ἄλλο ἐστὶν ὅμοιον εἰ μὴ
ἡ νῦν προσαγορευομένη βουνιάς. Θεόφραστος δὲ
βουνιάδα μὲν οὐκ ὀνομάζει, ἄρρενα δὲ καλεῖ τινα
γογγυλίδα, καὶ ἴσως αὕτη ἐστὶν ἡ βουνιάς. Νίκανδρος δ᾽ ἐν τοῖς Γεωργικοῖς τῆς βουνιάδος μνημονεύει·

γογγυλίδας σπείροις δὲ κυλινδρωτῆς ἐφ᾽ ἅλωος |
c   ὄφρ᾽ ἂν ἴσαι πλαθάνοισι χαμηλοτέροις
        θαλέθωσι·
βουνιὰς † ἀλλ᾽ εἴσω ῥαφάνοις εἴσω
        λαθαρωκοί †.
γογγυλίδος δισσὴ γὰρ ἰδ᾽ ἐκ ῥαφάνοιο γενέθλη
μακρή τε στιφρή τε φαείνεται ἐν πρασιῇσι.

Κηφισιακῶν δὲ γογγυλίδων μνημονεύει Κράτης ἐν
Ῥήτορσιν οὕτως·

Κηφισιακαῖσι γογγυλίσιν ὅμοια πάνυ.

Turnips. Apollas in his *On the Cities in the Peloponnese*
(fr. 3, *FHG* iv.307) reports that the Spartans refer to these
as *gastrai*. Nicander of Colophon in his *Glossary* (fr. 132
Schneider) claims that the Boeotians call cabbages *gastrai*,
and turnips *zekeltides*; but Amerias (p. 8 Hoffmann) and
Timachidas (fr. 27 Blinkenberg) say that gourds are referred to as *zekeltides*.[24] Speusippus says in Book II of
Similar Things (fr. 24 Tarán): Radish, turnip, *raphus*, and
pepper-grass are similar. Glaucus in his *Art of Cooking* refers to *raphus* as *rapus*, with an unaspirated *pi*. No other
vegetable resembles these, except what is known today
as *bounias*. Theophrastus does not mention *bounias*, but
does refer (*HP* 7.4.3) to a male turnip, which is perhaps to
be identified with *bounias*. Nicander in his *Georgics* (fr.
70) mentions the *bounias*:[25]

You might sow turnips on garden-land leveled with a
    roller,
so that they grow in the shape of bread-pans set in
    the ground;
bounias † but within cabbages within [obscure] †.
For two varieties of turnip and cabbage[26],
both large and firm, are seen in our garden-beds.

Crates in *Orators* (fr. 30) mentions Cephisian turnips, as
follows:

closely resembling Cephisian turnips.

[24] Cf. Hsch. ζ 108 "*zelkia*: vegetables".
[25] A considerably longer fragment of the poem that overlaps
with this one is quoted at 4.133d–e.
[26] But see 4.133d n.

Θεόφραστος δε γογγυλίδων φησὶν εἶναι γένη δύο,
ἄρρεν καὶ θῆλυ· γίνεσθαι δ' ἄμφω ἐκ τοῦ αὐτοῦ
d σπέρματος. Ποσειδώνιος δ' ὁ ἀπὸ τῆς | στοᾶς ἐν τῇ
ἑβδόμῃ καὶ εἰκοστῇ τῶν Ἱστοριῶν περὶ τὴν Δαλμα-
τίαν φησὶ γίγνεσθαι γογγυλίδας ἀκηπεύτους καὶ
ἀγρίους σταφυλίνους. Δίφιλος δ' ὁ Σίφνιος ἰατρός, ἡ
γογγυλίς, φησί, λεπτυντική ἐστι καὶ δριμεῖα καὶ
δύσπεπτος, ἔτι δὲ πνευματωτική. κρείττων δέ, φησίν,
ἡ βουνιὰς καθέστηκεν· γλυκυτέρα γάρ ἐστι καὶ πεπτι-
κωτέρα πρὸς τῷ εὐστόμαχος εἶναι καὶ τρόφιμος. ἡ δὲ
ὀπτωμένη, φησί, γογγυλὶς μᾶλλον πέττεται, περιττό-
τερον δὲ λεπτύνει. ταύτης μνημονεύει Εὔβουλος ἐν
Ἀγκυλίωνι οὕτως· |

e   ὀπτήσιμον γογγυλίδα ταυτηνὶ φέρω.

καὶ Ἄλεξις ἐν Θεοφορήτῳ·

        λαλῶ Πτολεμαίῳ γογγυλίδος ὀπτῶν τόμους.

ἡ δὲ ταριχευομένη γογγυλὶς λεπτυντικωτέρα ἐστὶ τῆς
ἑφθῆς καὶ μάλιστα ἡ διὰ νάπυος γινομένη, ὥς φησιν
ὁ Δίφιλος.

     Κράμβη. Εὔδημος ὁ Ἀθηναῖος ἐν τῷ Περὶ Λαχά-
νων κράμβης φησὶν εἶναι γένη τρία, τῆς τε καλουμένης ἁλμυρίδος καὶ λειοφύλλου καὶ σελινούσσης· τῇ
f δ' ἡδονῇ πρώτην κεκρίσθαι τὴν ἁλμυρίδα. φύεται | δ'
ἐν Ἐρετρίᾳ καὶ Κύμῃ καὶ Ῥόδῳ, ἔτι δὲ Κνίδῳ καὶ
Ἐφέσῳ· ἡ δὲ λειόφυλλος ἀνὰ πᾶσαν, φησί, χώραν
γίγνεται. ἡ δὲ σελινοῦσσα τὴν ὀνομασίαν ἔχει διὰ

Theophrastus (*HP* 7.4.3) claims that there are two varieties of turnip, a male and a female, but that both grow from the same seed. Posidonius the Stoic in Book XXVII of his *History* (*FGrH* 87 F 19 = fr. 70 Edelstein–Kidd) reports that uncultivated turnips and wild carrots grow in Dalmatia. The physician Diphilus of Siphnos says: The turnip promotes weight-loss; is acrid and difficult to digest; and also tends to produce gas. But the *bounias*, he reports, is better, because it is sweeter, more digestible and thus easier on the stomach, and nourishing. Roasted turnip, he claims, is more easily digested and is particularly effective for promoting weight-loss. Eubulus in *Ancylion* (fr. 3) mentions roasted turnip, as follows:

I'm bringing this roasted turnip here.

Also Alexis in *The Man Who Was Possessed by a God* (fr. 92):

I'm talking while roasting slices of turnip for Ptolemy.

Pickled turnip promotes weight-loss more effectively than stewed turnip, especially when prepared with mustard, according to Diphilus.

Cabbage. Eudemus of Athens in his *On Vegetables* reports that there are three varieties of cabbage: the type known as *halmuris* ("salty"), as well as smooth-leaved and celery-leaved varieties; but the *halmuris* is thought to be the tastiest. It grows in Eretria, Cumae, and Rhodes, as well as in Cnidus and Ephesus, whereas the smooth-leaved variety, he says, is found everywhere. The celery-leaved

τὴν οὐλότητα· ἐμφερὴς γάρ ἐστι σελίνῳ καὶ κατὰ τὴν
ἄλλην πύκνωσιν. Θεόφραστος δὲ οὕτως γράφει· τῆς
δὲ ῥαφάνου (λέγω δὲ τὴν κράμβην) ἡ μέν ἐστιν
οὐλόφυλλος, ἡ δὲ ἀγρία. Δίφιλος δ᾽ ὁ Σίφνιός φησι·
κράμβη δὲ καλλίστη γίνεται καὶ γλυκεῖα ἐν Κύμῃ, ἐν
δὲ Ἀλεξανδρείᾳ πικρά. τὸ δ᾽ ἐκ Ῥόδου φερόμενον
σπέρμα εἰς Ἀλεξάνδρειαν ἐπὶ ἐνιαυτὸν γλυκεῖαν ποιεῖ
τὴν κράμβην, μεθ᾽ ὃν χρόνον πάλιν ἐπιχωριάζει. Νίκανδρος δ᾽ ἐν Γεωργικοῖς· ‖

370   λείη μὲν κράμβη, ὁτὲ δ᾽ ἀγριὰς ἐμπίπτουσα
       σπειρομέναις πολύφυλλος ἐνηβῆσαι πρασιῇσιν
       ἢ οὔλη † καὶ τύριος ὀθάμνιτις † πετάλοισιν
       ἢ ἐπιφοινίσσουσα καὶ αὐχμηρῇσιν ὁμοίη
       βατραχέη Κύμῃ τε κακόχροος ἢ μὲν ἔοικε
       πέλμασιν οἷσι πέδιλα παλίμβολα κασσύουσιν,
       ἣν μάντιν λαχάνοισι παλαιόγονοι ἐνέπουσιν.

       μήποτε δὲ ὁ Νίκανδρος μάντιν κέκληκε τὴν κράμβην
b   ἱερὰν οὖσαν, ἐπεὶ καὶ παρ᾽ Ἱππώνακτι | ἐν τοῖς Ἰάμ-
       βοις ἐστί τι λεγόμενον τοιοῦτον·

           ὁ δ᾽ ἐξολισθὼν ἱκέτευε τὴν κράμβην
           τὴν ἑπτάφυλλον, ᾗ θύεσκε Πανδώρη
           Ταργηλίοισιν ἔγχυτον πρὸ φαρμακοῦ.

---

[27] For the problem of terminology, cf. 1.34d–e; 9.370f.
[28] Literally "sandals that have been turned inside-out", sc. to
be refurbished for sale.

variety gets its name from its curliness; it also resembles celery in its general density. Theophrastus (*HP* 7.4.4, adapted) writes as follows: One type of *rhaphanos*—I am referring to cabbage (*krambē*)[27]—has curly leaves, while the other grows wild. Diphilus of Siphnos says: The best cabbage grows in Cumae and is sweet there, whereas in Alexandria it is bitter. Seed brought to Alexandria from Rhodes produces sweet cabbage for a year, but afterward reverts to its local character. Nicander in the *Georgics* (fr. 85 Schneider):

> Cabbage is smooth-leaved. But sometimes a wild
>   variety invades
> sown garden-beds and flourishes there with many
>   leaves,
> either the curly variety † and Tyrian [corrupt] † with
>   foliage,
> or the green variety that has a purple tinge and looks
>   like
> unkempt hair, and the Cumaean type with its
>   unattractive color, which resembles
> the soles used to mend second-hand sandals;[28]
> the ancients refer to this variety as a prophet among
>   vegetables.

Perhaps Nicander calls the cabbage a prophet because it is sacred, since Hipponax says something along the following lines in his *Iambs* (fr. 107.47–9 Degani):

> He slipped away and supplicated the seven-leaved
> cabbage, to which Pandora used to sacrifice
> a moulded cake as a scapegoat-offering at the
>   Targelia festival.

καὶ Ἀνάνιος δέ φησι·

καὶ σὲ πολλὸν ἀνθρώπων
ἐγὼ φιλέω μάλιστα, ναὶ μὰ τὴν κράμβην.

καὶ Τηλεκλείδης Πρυτάνεσιν

< . . . > ναὶ μὰ τὰς κράμβας

ἔφη. καὶ Ἐπίχαρμος ἐν Γᾷ καὶ Θαλάσσα·

< . . . > ναὶ μὰ τὰν κράμβαν.

Εὔπολις Βάπταις·

< . . . > ναὶ μὰ τὰς κράμβας.

c   ἐδόκει δὲ Ἰωνικὸς εἶναι ὁ ὅρκος· καὶ οὐ | παράδοξον εἰ
κατὰ τῆς κράμβης τινὲς ὤμνυον, ὁπότε καὶ Ζήνων ὁ
Κιτιεὺς ὁ τῆς στοᾶς κτίστωρ μιμούμενος τὸν κατὰ τῆς
κυνὸς ὅρκον Σωκράτους καὶ αὐτὸς ὤμνυε τὴν κάππαριν, ὡς Ἔμπεδός φησιν ἐν Ἀπομνημονεύμασιν. Ἀθήνησι δὲ καὶ ταῖς τετοκυίαις κράμβη παρεσκευάζετο ὥς
τι ἀντιφάρμακον εἰς τροφήν. Ἔφιππος γοῦν ἐν Γηρυόνῃ φησίν·

ἔπειτα πῶς
οὐ στέφανος οὐδείς ἐστι πρόσθε τῶν θυρῶν, |
d   οὐ κνῖσα κρούει ῥινὸς ὑπεροχὰς ἄκρας

---

[29] But Epicharmus is a Doric poet, suggesting that the quotation of his fr. 22, at least, has been clumsily inserted by Athenaeus
into his source-document.

Ananius (fr. 4 West²) as well says:

> And I love you more
> than anyone else, by the cabbage!

Teleclides in *Prytaneis* (fr. 29) also said:

> Yes, by the cabbages!

Epicharmus in *Earth and Sea* (fr. 22) as well:

> Yes, by the cabbage!

Eupolis in *Dyers* (fr. 84.2):

> Yes, by the cabbages!

This was apparently an Ionian oath.[29] Nor is it surprising that some people swore by the cabbage, given that Zeno of Citium, the founder of the Stoa, imitated Socrates' oath "by the dog" (cf. Pl. *Ap*. 22a; *Grg*. 482b; *R*. 399e) and swore for his part by the caper, according to Empedus in the *Memoirs* (*FHG* iv.403–4 = Zeno fr. 32a, *SVF* i.12). In Athens, cabbage was prepared for women who had just given birth, as a sort of antidote intended to nourish them. Ephippus in *Geryon* (fr. 3),[30] for example, says:

> How is it, then,
> that there's no wreath in front of the doors,
> and the smell of roasting meat doesn't assault the tip
>   of one's nose,

---

[30] At 2.65c–d (where see n.) verses identical to Ephipp. fr. 3.4–11 are assigned to Eubulus (= fr. dub. 148).

Ἀμφιδρομίων ὄντων; ἐν οἷς νομίζεται
ὀπτᾶν τε τυροῦ Χερρονησίτου τόμους
ἕψειν τ᾽ ἐλαίῳ ῥάφανον ἠγλαϊσμένην
πνίγειν τε παχέων ἀρνίων στηθύνια
τίλλειν τε φάττας καὶ κίχλας ὁμοῦ σπίνοις
κοινῇ τε χνάειν τευθίσιν σηπίδια
πιλεῖν τε πολλὰς πλεκτάνας ἐπιστρόφως
πίνειν τε πολλὰς κύλικας εὐζωρεστέρας.

Ἀντιφάνης δ᾽ ἐν Παρασίτῳ ὡς εὐτελοῦς βρώματος |
e τῆς κράμβης μέμνηται ἐν τούτοις·

οἷα δ᾽ ἐστὶν οἶσθας, ὦ γύναι·
ἄρτοι, σκόροδα, τυρός, πλακοῦντες, πράγματα
ἐλευθέρι᾽, οὐ τάριχος οὐδ᾽ ἡδύσμασιν
ἄρνεια καταπεπασμέν᾽ οὐδὲ θρυμματὶς
τεταραγμένη, καὶ λοπάδες ἀνθρώπων φθοραί.
καὶ μὴν ῥαφάνους γ᾽ ἕψουσι λιπαράς, ὦ θεοί,
ἔτνος θ᾽ ἅμ᾽ αὐταῖς πίσινον.

Δίφιλος δ᾽ ἐν Ἀπλήστῳ·

ἥκει φερόμεν᾽ αὐτόματα πάντα τἀγαθά, |
f ῥάφανος λιπαρά, σπλαγχνίδια πολλά, σαρκία
ἁπαλώτατ᾽, οὐδὲν μὰ Δία τοῖς ἐμοῖς βλίτοις
ὅμοια πράγματ᾽ οὐδὲ ταῖς ⟨ . . . ⟩
θλασταῖς ἐλάαις.

206

given that the Amphidromia is going on, where it's
      the custom
to roast slices of Chersonesian cheese,
stew cabbage shimmering with oil,
bake fat lambs' breasts,
pluck ringdoves and thrushes, as well as finches,
nibble on cuttlefish and small-fry together,
vigorously pound numerous octopus tentacles,
and drink many cups of strong wine?

Antiphanes in *The Parasite* (fr. 181) refers to cabbage as
inexpensive food, in the following passage:

      You understand the sort of food this is, woman:
loaves of bread, garlic, cheese, unbaked cakes—what
      free
men eat, rather than saltfish, or lamb
sprinkled with spices, or a pastry stuffed
with a jumble of ingredients, and casserole-dishes
      that ruin people's lives!
In fact, they're stewing cabbages covered with oil, by
      the gods;
and there's bean-soup to go with them.

Diphilus in *The Greedy Man* (fr. 14):

Good food of every sort has arrived, transported
      under its own power:
a cabbage covered with oil, lots of bits of entrails,
      extremely tender
little chunks of meat—nothing the least bit like my
blite, by Zeus, or the . . .
bruised olives!

207

Ἀλκαῖος Παλαίστρᾳ·

ἤδη δ᾽ ἧψε χύτραν ῥαφάνων.

Πολύζηλος δ᾽ ἐν Μουσῶν Γοναῖς κράμβας αὐτὰς ὀνομάζων φησί·

ὑψιπέταλοί τε κράμβαι συχναί.

Σεῦτλα. τούτων φησὶν ὁ Θεόφραστος εὐχυλότερον
371 εἶναι τὸ λευκὸν ‖ τοῦ μέλανος καὶ ὀλιγοσπερμότερον
καὶ καλεῖσθαι Σικελικόν. ἡ δὲ σευτλὶς ἕτερον, φησί,
τοῦ τεύτλου ἐστί. διὸ καὶ Δίφιλος ὁ κωμῳδιοποιὸς ἐν
Ἥρωι δράματι ἐπιτιμᾷ τινι ὡς κακῶς λέγοντι καὶ τὰ
τεῦτλα τευτλίδας καλῶν. Εὔδημος δ᾽ ἐν τῷ Περὶ Λαχάνων τέτταρα γένη φησὶν εἶναι τεύτλων, σπαστόν,
καυλωτόν, λευκόν, πάνδημον· τοῦτο δ᾽ εἶναι τῇ χρόᾳ
φαιόν. Δίφιλος δ᾽ ὁ Σίφνιος τὸ σευτλίον φησὶν εὐχυλότερον εἶναι τῆς κράμβης καὶ θρεπτικώτερον με-
τρίως· ἐκζεστὸν δὲ καὶ λαμβανόμενον μετὰ νάπυος
b λεπτυντικώτερον | εἶναι καὶ ἑλμίνθων φθαρτικόν. εὐ-
κοιλιώτερον δὲ τὸ λευκόν, τὸ δὲ μέλαν οὐρητικώτερον.
ὑπάρχειν δ᾽ αὐτῶν καὶ τὰς ῥίζας εὐστομωτέρας καὶ
πολυτροφωτέρας.

Σταφυλῖνος. οὗτος δριμύς ἐστι, φησὶν ὁ Δίφιλος,
ἱκανῶς δὲ θρεπτικὸς καὶ εὐστόμαχος μέσως διαχωρη-

---

31 I.e. cabbages (normally *rhaphanoi*; cf. 9.369f n.).

32 *Seutlos* (Attic *teutlos*) is the normal word for a beet. The observation recorded here is not found in Theophrastus, and the

Alcaeus in *The Wrestling-School* (fr. 24):

> She just now stewed a pot of cabbages.

But Polyzelus in *The Birth of the Muses* (fr. 10) refers to them[31] as *krambai*, when he says:

> and many cabbages (*krambai*) with lofty leaves.

Beets (*seutla*). Theophrastus (*HP* 7.4.4) reports that the white variety of these is juicier than the black variety; has fewer seeds; and is referred to as Sicilian. The *seutlis*, he claims, is different from the *teutlos*.[32] This is why the comic poet Diphilus in his play *The Hero* (fr. 46) criticizes someone for speaking bad Greek, referring to *teutla* as *teutlides*.[33] Eudemus in his *On Vegetables* says that there are four varieties of beet: *spaston* ("drawn", i.e. "long"), stalked, white, and common. Also that the latter is a grayish color. Diphilus of Siphnos claims that the beet (*seutlion*) is juicier than the cabbage and moderately more nourishing; when stewed and eaten with mustard, it is better at promoting weight-loss and helps eliminate worms. The white variety is easier on the intestines, whereas the black variety is more effective at promoting urination. Their roots have a better flavor and are more nourishing.

Carrot. According to Diphilus, this has a sharp flavor; is quite nourishing and moderately easy on the stomach;

---

subject of the verb must be the author of a grammatical treatise on which Athenaeus is drawing.

[33] Thus Athenaeus; but it must in fact have been the character whose Greek was criticized who used *teutlides* rather than the standard Attic *teutla*.

τικός τε καὶ πνευματώδης, δύσπεπτος, οὐρητικὸς ἱκανῶς, διεγερτικὸς πρὸς ἀφροδίσια· διὸ καὶ ὑπ᾽ ἐνίων
φίλτρον καλεῖται. Νουμήνιος δ᾽ ἐν τῷ Ἁλιευτικῷ
φησι·

> φύλλων δ᾽ ὅσσ᾽ ἄσπαρτα τά τ᾽ ἐρρίζωται
> ἀρούραις |
>
> c χείματος ἠδ᾽ ὁπόταν πολυάνθεμον εἶαρ ἵκηται,
> αὐχμηρὴν σκόλυμόν τε καὶ ἀγριάδα σταφυλῖνον,
> † ῥάφιν τ᾽ ἔμπεδον † καὶ καυ<κα>λίδ᾽ ἀγροιῶτιν.

Νίκανδρος δ᾽ ἐν δευτέρῳ Γεωργικῶν φησιν·

> ἐν δέ τε καὶ μαράθου καυλὸς βαθύς, ἐν δέ τε
> ῥίζαι
> πετραίου, σὺν δ᾽ αὐτὸς ἐπαυχμήεις σταφυλῖνος,
> σμυρνεῖον σόγκος τε κυνόγλωσσός τε σέρις τε·
> σὺν καὶ ἄρου δριμεῖα καταψήχοιο πέτηλα
> ἠδ᾽ ὅπερ ὄρνιθος κλέεται γάλα.

μνημονεύει τοῦ σταφυλίνου καὶ Θεόφραστος. Φαινίας
d δ᾽ ἐν | πέμπτῳ Περὶ Φυτῶν γράφει οὕτως· κατὰ δὲ τὴν
αὐτοῦ τοῦ σπέρματος φύσιν ὁ καλούμενος σὴψ καὶ τὸ
τοῦ σταφυλίνου σπέρμα. κἀν τῷ πρώτῳ δέ φησι·
πετασώδη τὴν τῶν σπερμάτων ἀπείληφε φύσιν ἄννη-
σον, μάραθον, σταφυλῖνος, καυκαλίς, κώνειον, κόριον,

---

[34] It is difficult to see how this passage could possibly come
from the *Art of Fishing*, and the quotation from Numenius and
the lemma that followed it may have fallen out of the text.

promotes bowel movements and the production of gas; is difficult to digest; substantially encourages urination; and stirs up sexual desire. This is why some authorities refer to it as a love-charm. Numenius says in his *Art of Fishing* (*SH* 582):[34]

> whatever herbs are not sown, but take root in the
>   fields
> during the winter or when the spring rich in flowers
>   arrives:
> shaggy thistle and wild carrot,
> † and deep-rooted *raphis* † and rustic *kaukalis*.

Nicander says in Book II of the *Georgics* (fr. 71 Schneider):

> and among them high fennel-stalk, and among them
>   also roots
> of stone sperage, and with them the shaggy carrot
>   itself,
> Cretan alexander, and sow-thistle, and dog's-tongue,
>   and endive;
> you might also grind up the pungent leaves of
>   cuckoo-pint along with them,
> or what is referred to as bird's-milk.

Theophrastus (fr. 407 Fortenbaugh) also mentions the carrot. Phaenias in Book V of *On Plants* (fr. 39 Wehrli, encompassing all three quotations) writes as follows: as for the character of the seed itself, the so-called *sēps* and carrot-seed. And in Book I he says: Plants with unbelliferous seed-pods are anise, fennel, carrot, *kaukalis*, hemlock,

σκίλλα, ἣν ἔνιοι μυηφόνον. ἐπεὶ δὲ ἄρου ἐμνημόνευ-
σεν ὁ Νίκανδρος, προσαποδοτέον ὅτι καὶ Φαινίας ἐν
τῷ προειρημένῳ βιβλίῳ γράφει οὕτως· δρακόντιον, ὃ
ἔνιοι ἄρον[3]. τὸν δὲ σταφυλῖνον Διοκλῆς ἐν πρώτῳ
e Ὑγιεινῶν ἀσταφυλῖνον καλεῖ. | τὸ δὲ καρτὸν καλού-
μενον (μέγας δ᾽ ἐστὶν καὶ εὐαυξὴς σταφυλῖνος) εὐχυ-
λότερόν ἐστι τοῦ σταφυλίνου καὶ μᾶλλον θερμαντι-
κώτερον, οὐρητικώτερον, εὐστόμαχον, εὐοικονόμητον,
ὡς ὁ Δίφιλος ἱστορεῖ.

Κεφαλωτόν. τοῦτο καὶ πράσιον καλεῖσθαί φησιν ὁ
αὐτὸς Δίφιλος καὶ εὐχυλότερον εἶναι τοῦ καρτοῦ. εἶναι
δὲ καὶ αὐτὸ μέσως λεπτυντικόν, θρεπτικόν τε καὶ
πνευματῶδες. Ἐπαίνετος δ᾽ ἐν Ὀψαρτυτικῷ τὰ κεφα-
λωτὰ καλεῖσθαί φησι γηθυλλίδας. τοῦτο δὲ τὸ ὄνομα
f μνήμης εὑρίσκω | τετυχηκὸς παρὰ μὲν Εὐβούλῳ ἐν
Πορνοβοσκῷ οὕτως·

 οὐκ ἂν δυναίμην ἐμφαγεῖν ἄρτον τινά·
παρὰ Γναθαινίῳ γὰρ ἄρτι κατέφαγον
ἔψουσαν αὐτὴν καταλαβὼν γηθυλλίδας.

οἱ δὲ τὸ γήθυον καλούμενον τοῦτό φασιν εἶναι, οὗ
μνημονεύει Φρύνιχος ἐν Κρόνῳ· ὅπερ ἐξηγούμενος
δρᾶμα Δίδυμος ὅμοιά φησιν εἶναι τὰ γήθυα τοῖς
λεγομένοις ἀμπελοπράσοις, τὰ δ᾽ αὐτὰ καὶ γηθυλ-

---

[3] ἄρον ἀρωνια A

coriander, and squill (referred to by some authorities as mousebane). Given that Nicander mentioned cuckoo-pint (fr. 71.4 Schneider, quoted above), I should also acknowledge that Phaenias writes as follows in the book quoted above: *drakontion*, referred to by some authorities as cuckoo-pint. Diocles in Book I of *Matters of Health* (fr. 199 van der Eijk) calls the carrot (*staphulinos*) an *astaphulinos*. What is referred to as a *kartos*—this is a large, long carrot—produces better *chulē* than the carrot (*staphulinos*) and is more warming; promotes urination more effectively; and is easy on the stomach and easily assimilated, according to Diphilus.

Leek (*kephalōton*). The same Diphilus reports that this is also referred to as *prasion* and produces more *chulē* than the *kartos*; it is also moderately effective in promoting weight-loss, and is nourishing and produces gas. Epaenetus in the *Art of Cooking* reports that leeks are referred to as *gēthullides*. I find that this word has been used by Eubulus in *The Pimp* (fr. 88), as follows:

> I couldn't eat any bread;
> because I had something just now at Gnathaena's[35]
>   house,
> when I caught her stewing *gēthullides*.

But other authorities claim that this is what is referred to as *gēthuon*, which Phrynichus mentions in *Cronus* (fr. 12). In his explication of the play, Didymus (pp. 306–7 Schmidt) says that *gēthua* resemble what are called *ampeloprasoi* (literally "grapevine-leeks"), and that the same vegeta-

---

[35] Presumably a reference to the well-known Athenian courtesan (*PAA* 278790); cf. 9.384e–f with n.

λίδας λέγεσθαι. μνημονεύει τῶν γηθυλλίδων καὶ Ἐπίχαρμος ἐν Φιλοκτήτῃ οὕτως· ‖

372   ἐν δὲ σκόροδα † δύο καὶ γαθυλλίδες δύο.

Ἀριστοφάνης Αἰολοσίκωνι δευτέρῳ·

                              τῶν δὲ γηθύων
ρίζας ἐχούσας σκοροδομίμητον φύσιν.

Πολέμων δ᾽ ὁ περιηγητὴς ἐν τῷ Περὶ Σαμοθρᾴκης καὶ
κιττῆσαί φησι τῆς γηθυλλίδος τὴν Λητώ, γράφων
οὕτως· διατέτακται παρὰ Δελφοῖς τῇ θυσίᾳ τῶν Θεο-
ξενίων, ὃς ἂν κομίσῃ γηθυλλίδα μεγίστην τῇ Λητοῖ,
λαμβάνειν μοῖραν ἀπὸ τῆς τραπέζης. ἑώρακα δὲ καὶ
αὐτὸς οὐκ ἐλάττω γηθυλλίδα γογγυλίδος καὶ τῆς
στρογγύλης ῥαφανίδος. ἱστοροῦσι δὲ τὴν Λητὼ κύου-
b   σαν τὸν Ἀπόλλωνα | κιττῆσαι γηθυλλίδος· διὸ δὴ τῆς
τιμῆς τετυχηκέναι ταύτης.

    Κολοκύντη. χειμῶνος δὲ ὥρᾳ ποτὲ κολοκυντῶν
ἡμῖν περιενεχθεισῶν πάντες ἐθαυμάζομεν νεαρὰς εἶναι νομίζοντες, καὶ ὑπεμιμνησκόμεθα ὧν ἐν Ὥραις ὁ
χαρίεις Ἀριστοφάνης εἶπεν ἐπαινῶν τὰς καλὰς Ἀθήνας ἐν τούτοις·

    (Α.) ὄψει δὲ χειμῶνος μέσου σικυούς, βότρυς,
        ὀπώραν,

bles are also referred to as *gēthullides*. Epicharmus in
Philoctetes (fr. 132) mentions *gēthullides*, as follows:

> In it were two † heads of garlic and two *gathullides*.

Aristophanes in *Aeolosicon II* (fr. 5):

> *gēthua*
> roots, which look a lot like garlic.

The travel-writer Polemon in his *On Samothrace* (fr. 36
Preller) claims that Leto craved leeks (*gēthullis*), writing as
follows: The people of Delphi have a custom associated
with the sacrifice at the Theoxenia festival,[36] which is that
whoever brings Leto the largest leek (*gēthullis*) is given a
share of the food from the table. I personally have seen a
leek (*gēthullis*) that was at least as large as a turnip or the
round variety of radish.[37] The story is that when Leto was
pregnant with Apollo, she craved leeks (*gēthullis*), which is
why she is accorded this honor.

Gourd. At one point we were served gourds during
the winter, and we all expressed amazement, because we
thought that they were fresh, and were reminded of what
the witty Aristophanes said in *Seasons* (fr. 581), where he
praises the lovely city of Athens in the following passage:

> (A.) In mid-winter you'll see cucumbers, grapes, fruit
>   of all kinds,

[36] A generic term for a festival at which a god or gods (here
Leto) were imagined as dining with human celebrants.

[37] This sentence appears to interrupt the quotation from
Polemon.

στεφάνους ἴων ⟨(Β.) οἶμαι δὲ καὶ⟩ κονιορτὸν
    ἐκτυφλοῦντα.
(Α.) αὐτὸς δ᾽ ἀνὴρ πωλεῖ κίχλας, ἀπίους,
    σχαδόνας, ἐλάας,

c   πυόν, χόρια, | χελιδόνας, τέττιγας, ἐμβρύεια.
ὑρίσους δ᾽ ἴδοις ἂν νειφομένους σύκων ὁμοῦ τε
    μύρτων.
(Β.) ἔπειτα κολοκύντας ὁμοῦ ταῖς γογγυλίσιν
    ἀροῦσιν,
ὥστ᾽ οὐκέτ᾽ οὐδεὶς οἶδ᾽ ὁπηνίκ᾽ ἐστὶ τοὐνιαυτοῦ;
(Α.) ⟨ἆρ᾽ οὐ⟩ μέγιστον ἀγαθόν, εἴπερ ἔστι δι᾽
    ἐνιαυτοῦ
ὅτου τις ἐπιθυμεῖ λαβεῖν; (Β.) κακὸν μὲν οὖν
    μέγιστον·
εἰ μὴ γὰρ ἦν, οὐκ ἂν ἐπεθύμουν οὐδ᾽ ἂν
    ἐδαπανῶντο.
ἐγὼ δὲ τοῦτ᾽ ὀλίγον χρόνον χρήσας ἀφειλόμην
    ἄν.
(Α.) κἄγωγε ταῖς ἄλλαις πόλεσι δρῶ ταῦτα πλὴν
    Ἀθηνῶν·

d   τούτοις δ᾽ ὑπάρχει ταῦτ᾽, ἐπειδὴ τοὺς | θεοὺς
    σέβουσιν.
(Β.) ἀπέλαυσαν ἄρα σέβοντες ὑμᾶς, ὡς σὺ φής.
    (Α.) τιὴ τί;
(Β.) Αἴγυπτον αὐτῶν τὴν πόλιν πεπόηκας ἀντ᾽
    Ἀθηνῶν.

ἐθαυμάζομεν οὖν τὰς κολοκύντας μηνὶ Ἰανουαρίῳ

garlands of violets—(B.) Also a blinding duststorm, I
    expect!
(A.) The same man will be selling thrushes, pears,
    honey-comb, olives,
beestings, after-birth pudding, swallow-figs, cicadas,
    still-born kids;
and you'd see harvest-baskets pouring out a mix of
    figs and myrtle-berries as thick as snow.
(B.) So they're going to sow gourds along with their
    turnips,
with the result that no one knows what time of year it
    is any more?
(A.) Isn't this the best possible situation—if a person
    can buy
whatever he wants anytime of year? (B.) No—it's the
    greatest disaster possible!
Because otherwise they wouldn't desire things or
    spend their money.
I would lend them this for a little while, and then
    take it away.
(A.) I do this too, for the other cities except for
    Athens;
but *they* have these advantages, because they respect
    the gods.
(B.) A lot of good they've got from showing you
    respect, according to you! (A.) What do you
    mean?
(B.) You've turned their city into Egypt instead of
    Athens.

So we were astonished to be eating gourds in January, be-

ATHENAEUS

ἐσθίοντες· χλωραί τε γὰρ ἦσαν καὶ τὸ ἴδιον ἀπεδί-
δοσαν τοῦ χυμοῦ. ἐτύγχανον δ᾽ οὖσαι τῶν συντεθει-
μένων ὑπὸ τῶν τὰ τοιαῦτα μαγγανεύειν εἰδότων ὀψαρ-
τυτῶν. ἐζήτει οὖν ὁ Λαρήνσιος εἰ καὶ τὴν χρῆσιν
ταύτην ἠπίσταντο οἱ ἀρχαῖοι. καὶ ὁ Οὐλπιανὸς ἔφη·
e   Νίκανδρος ὁ Κολοφώνιος ἐν τῷ δευτέρῳ | τῶν Γεωρ-
γικῶν μνημονεύει ταύτης τῆς χρήσεως σικύας ὀνομάζων τὰς κολοκύντας· οὕτως γὰρ ἐκαλοῦντο, ὡς πρότερον εἰρήκαμεν· λέγει δ᾽ οὕτως·

αὐτὰς μὴν σικύας τμήγων ἀνὰ κλώσμασι πείραις
ἠέρι δὲ ξήρανον· ἐπεγκρεμάσαιο δὲ καπνῷ,
χείμασιν ὄφρ᾽ ἂν δμῶες ἅλις περιχανδέα
     χύτρον |
f   πλήσαντες ῥοφέωσιν ἀεργέες, † ἔνθα τε μέτρια †
ὄσπρια πανσπερμηδὸν ἐπεγχεύησιν ἀλετρίς.
τῇ ἔνι μὲν σικύης ὅρμους βάλον ἐκπλύναντες,
ἐν δὲ μύκην σειράς τε πάλαι λαχάνοισι
     πλακείσας
αὐτοτέροις † καυλοῖς τε μιγήμεναι εὐφαορίζῃ †. ||

373   Ὄρνεις. ἐπεὶ δὲ καὶ ὄρνεις ἐπῆσαν ταῖς κολοκύν-
ταις καὶ ἄλλοις κνιστοῖς λαχάνοις (οὕτως δ᾽ εἴρηκεν †
Ἀριστοφάνης † ἐν Δηλίᾳ τὰ σύγκοπτα λάχανα, κνι-
στὰ ἢ στέμφυλα), ὁ Μυρτίλος ἔφη· ἀλλὰ μὴν καὶ
ὄρνιθας καὶ ὀρνίθια νῦν μόνως ἡ συνήθεια καλεῖ τὰς

218

cause they were fresh and juicy. But they were actually an example of the type of food produced by chefs who know how to pull off tricks of this kind. Larensius accordingly posed the question of whether the ancients were familiar with this way of preparing them, and Ulpian said: Nicander of Colophon in Book II of his *Georgics* (fr. 72 Schneider) mentions this way of preparing gourds, which he refers to as *sikuai*. Because this is what they used to call them, as I noted earlier (2.58f–9a). He says the following:

> You might slice up the gourds (*sikuai*) themselves,
>   string them on threads,
> and dry them in the air. And you might hang them
>   over the fire,
> so that during the winter your slaves could fill a quite
>   capacious
> cookpot and gulp them down at their ease, † and then
>   moderate †
> a woman who grinds grain can dump in peas and
>   beans of all sorts.
> Then they wash the gourd-braids and throw them
>   into the mess,
> along with mushrooms, and strings tied long ago
>   around dried
> vegetables † and with stems to mix together
>   [corrupt] †.

Chickens. Since chickens followed the gourds and the other grated vegetables—this is how † Aristophanes † refers to minced vegetables in *The Girl from Delos* (Ar. fr. dub. 938 = Antiph. fr. dub. 323), as grated or pressed into cakes—Myrtilus said: It is in fact the modern practice to use the terms *ornithes* and *ornithia* to refer exclusively to

219

θηλείας, ὧν ὁρῶ περιφερόμενον πλῆθος (καὶ Χρύσιππος δ᾽ ὁ φιλόσοφος ἐν τῷ πέμπτῳ Περὶ τοῦ Καλοῦ
καὶ τῆς Ἡδονῆς γράφει οὕτως· καθάπερ τινὲς τὰς
λευκὰς ὄρνιθας τῶν μελαινῶν ἡδίους εἶναι μᾶλλον),
b ἀλεκτρυόνας | δὲ καὶ ἀλεκτοριδέας τοὺς ἄρρενας· τῶν
ἀρχαίων δὲ τὸ ὄρνις καὶ ἀρσενικῶς καὶ θηλυκῶς
λεγόντων ἐπ᾽ ἄλλων ὀρνέων, οὐ περὶ τούτου τοῦ
εἰδικοῦ, περὶ οὗ φησιν ἡ συνήθεια "ὄρνιθας ὠνή-
σασθαι". Ὅμηρος μὲν οὖν φησι·

ὄρνιθες δέ τε πολλοὶ ὑπ᾽ αὐγὰς ἠελίοιο.

καὶ ἀλλαχόθι θηλυκῶς·

ὄρνιθι λιγυρῇ.

καί·

ὡς δ᾽ ὄρνις ἀπτῆσι νεοσσοῖσι προφέρῃσι
μάστακ᾽, ἐπεί κε λάβῃσι, κακῶς δ᾽ ἄρα οἱ πέλει
αὐτῇ. |

c Μένανδρος δ᾽ ἐν Ἐπικλήρῳ πρώτῃ σαφῶς τὸ ἐπὶ τῆς
συνηθείας φησὶν ἐμφανίζων οὕτως·

ἀλεκτρυών τις ἐκεκράγει μέγα.
< . . . > "οὐ σοβήσετ᾽ ἔξω", φησί, "τὰς
ὄρνις ἀφ᾽ ἡμῶν;"

καὶ πάλιν·

αὕτη ποτ᾽ ἐξεσόβησε τὰς ὄρνις μόλις.

220

hens (a large number of which, I see, are being served)—
the philosopher Chrysippus in Book V of *On the Good and
Pleasure* (xxviii fr. 4, *SVF* iii.199) also writes as follows: Just
as some people regard white hens (*ornithes,* fem.) as tastier than black ones—and to use the terms *alektruones* and
alektorideis to refer to roosters. The ancients, on the other
hand, applied the word *ornis* in both the masculine and the
feminine to other birds, and not specifically to this variety,
to which conventional usage refers by saying simply "to
buy *ornithes*". Thus Homer (*Od.* 2.181) says:

> and many birds (*ornithes*, masc.) beneath the rays of
> the sun.

And elsewhere in the feminine (*Il.* 14.290):

> to a shrill (fem.) bird (*ornis*).

And (*Il.* 9.323–4):

> Just as a bird (*ornis*) offers a morsel to her unfledged
> nestlings, when she gets one, but her life is hard.

Menander in *The Heiress I* (fr. 132, encompassing both
quotations) brings out colloquial usage clearly when he
says the following:

> A rooster crowed loudly.
> "Shove the hens (*ornis*, fem.) outside,"
> he says, "away from us!"

And again:

> At one time she had trouble shooing out the hens
> (*ornis*, fem.).

ὀρνίθια δ᾽ εἴρηκε Κρατῖνος ἐν Νεμέσει οὕτως·

< . . . > τἆλλα πάντ᾽ ὀρνίθια.

ἐπὶ δὲ τοῦ ἀρσενικοῦ οὐ μόνον ὄρνιν ἀλλὰ καὶ ὄρνιθα.
d ὁ αὐτὸς Κρατῖνος | ἐν τῷ αὐτῷ δράματι·

ὄρνιθα φοινικόπτερον.

καὶ πάλιν·

ὄρνιθα τοίνυν δεῖ σε γίγνεσθαι μέγαν.

καὶ Σοφοκλῆς Ἀντηνορίδαις·

ὄρνιθα καὶ κήρυκα καὶ διάκονον.

Αἰσχύλος Καβείροις·

ὄρνιθα δ᾽ οὐ ποιῶ σε τῆς ἐμῆς ὁδοῦ.

Ξενοφῶν δ᾽ ἐν δευτέρῳ Παιδείας· ἐπὶ μὲν τοὺς ὄρνιθας
τῷ ἰσχυροτάτῳ χειμῶνι. Μένανδρος Διδύμαις·

ὄρνεις φέρων ἐλήλυθα.

καὶ ἑξῆς

ὄρνιθας ἀποστέλλει

φησίν. ὅτι δὲ καὶ ἐπὶ τοῦ πληθυντικοῦ ὄρνις λέγουσι
e πρόκειται τὸ Μενάνδρειον μαρτύριον· | ἀλλὰ καὶ
Ἀλκμάν πού φησι·

Cratinus in *Nemesis* (fr. 120) uses the diminutive *ornithia*, as follows:

all the other *ornithia*.

In the masculine one finds not just accusative *ornin*, but *ornitha* as well. The same Cratinus (fr. 121) in the same play:

a scarlet-plumed bird (*ornitha*).

And again (Cratin. fr. 114):

You need to turn into a large bird (*ornitha*), then!

Also Sophocles in *The Sons of Antenor* (fr. 137):

a bird (*ornitha*), a herald, and a servant.

Aeschylus in *Cabeiri* (fr. 95):

I am not making you a bird[38] (*ornitha*) of my journey.

Xenophon in Book II of the *Education* (*Cyr.* 1.6.39): after the birds (*ornithas*) in the coldest weather. Menander in *Twin Girls* (fr. 115, encompassing both quotations):

I've come, bringing birds (*orneis*).

And immediately after this he says:

He's sending birds (*ornithas*).

The evidence from Menander cited above (fr. 132.3, cited at 9.373c) shows that they also use *ornis* as a plural. Alcman as well says somewhere (*PMG* 82):

---

38 I.e. "an omen".

λῦσαν δ᾽ ἄπρακτα νεάνιδες ὥ-
τ᾽ ὄρνις Ϝιέρακος ὑπερπταμένω.

καὶ Εὔπολις ἐν Δήμοις·

οὐ δεινὸν οὖν κριοὺς μὲν ἐκγεννᾶν τέκνα
ὄρνις θ᾽ ὁμοίους τοὺς νεοττοὺς τῷ πατρί;

τὸν δ᾽ ἀλεκτρυόνα ἐκ τῶν ἐναντίων οἱ ἀρχαῖοι καὶ
θηλυκῶς εἰρήκασι. Κρατῖνος Νεμέσει·

Λήδα, σὸν ἔργον· δεῖ σ᾽ ὅπως εὐσχημόνως
ἀλεκτρυόνος μηδὲν διοίσεις τοὺς τρόπους,
ἐπὶ τῷδ᾽ ἐπῴζουσ᾽, ὡς ἂν ἐκλέψῃς καλὸν |
f   ἡμῖν τι καὶ θαυμαστὸν ἐκ τοῦδ᾽ ὄρνεον.

Στράττις Ψυχασταῖς·

αἱ δ᾽ ἀλεκτρυόνες ἅπασαι
καὶ τὰ χοιρίδια τέθνηκε
καὶ τὰ μίκρ᾽ ὀρνίθια.

Ἀναξανδρίδης Τηρεῖ·

ὀχευομένους δὲ τοὺς κάπρους
καὶ τὰς ἀλεκτρυόνας θεωροῦσ᾽ ἄσμενοι.

ἐπεὶ δὲ τοῦ κωμικοῦ τούτου ἐμνήσθην καὶ οἶδα τὸ
374   δρᾶμα τὸν Τηρέα αὐτοῦ μὴ κεκριμένον ‖ ἐν τοῖς
πρώτοις, ἐκθήσομαι ὑμῖν, ἄνδρες φίλοι, εἰς κρίσιν ἃ

The girls separated, their business undone, like
birds (*ornis*) when a hawk flies overhead.

Also Eupolis in *Demes* (fr. 111):

Isn't it terrible, then, that rams produce kids
and birds (*ornis*) produce nestlings that resemble
    their fathers?

On the other hand, the ancients use *alektruōn*[39] as a feminine form. Cratinus in *Nemesis* (fr. 115):

Leda, it's up to you. You've got to act
exactly like a lovely *alektruōn*
and cluck over this, so that you hatch us
a nice, wonderful bird out of it.

Strattis in *Men Who Keep Cool* (fr. 61):

All the *alektruones* (fem.)
and piglets are dead,
    along with the little birdies.

Anaxandrides in *Tereus* (fr. 48):

They enjoy watching the boars
and the *alektruones* (fem.) being mounted.

Since I mentioned this comic author and am aware that his
play *Tereus* is not considered one of his best,[40] I am going
to offer for your consideration, my friends, the remarks

[39] Generally "rooster".
[40] Or perhaps "did not take first place". The quotation from
Chamaeleon momentarily interrupts the grammatical discussion
of the word *alektruōn*, which resumes again below.

εἴρηκε περὶ αὐτοῦ Χαμαιλέων ὁ Ἡρακλεώτης ἐν ἕκτῳ
Περὶ Κωμῳδίας γράφων ὧδε· Ἀναξανδρίδης διδάσκων ποτὲ διθύραμβον Ἀθήνησιν εἰσῆλθεν ἐφ᾽ ἵππου
καὶ ἀπήγγειλέν τι τῶν ἐκ τοῦ ᾄσματος. ἦν δὲ τὴν ὄψιν
καλὸς καὶ μέγας καὶ κόμην ἔτρεφε καὶ ἐφόρει ἁλουρ-
γίδα καὶ κράσπεδα χρυσᾶ. πικρὸς δ᾽ ὢν τὸ ἦθος ἐποίει
τι τοιοῦτο περὶ τὰς κωμῳδίας· ὅτε γὰρ μὴ νικῴη,
b λαμβάνων ἔδωκεν εἰς | τὸν λιβανωτὸν κατατεμεῖν καὶ
οὐ μετεσκεύαζεν ὥσπερ οἱ πολλοί. καὶ πολλὰ ἔχοντα
κομψῶς τῶν δραμάτων ἠφάνιζε, δυσκολαίνων τοῖς
θεαταῖς διὰ τὸ γῆρας. λέγεται δ᾽ εἶναι τὸ γένος Ῥόδιος ἐκ Καμίρου. θαυμάζω οὖν πῶς καὶ ὁ Τηρεὺς
περιεσώθη μὴ τυχὼν νίκης καὶ ἄλλα δράματα τῶν
ὁμοίων τοῦ αὐτοῦ. καὶ Θεόπομπος δὲ ἐν Εἰρήνῃ ἐπὶ
τῆς θηλείας ἔταξε τὸν ἀλεκτρυόνα λέγων οὕτως·

> ἄχθομαι δ᾽ ἀπολωλεκὼς
> ἀλεκτρυόνα τίκτουσαν ᾠὰ πάγκαλα.

c καὶ Ἀριστοφάνης | Δαιδάλῳ·

> ᾠὸν μέγιστον τέτοκεν, ὡς ἀλεκτρυών.

καὶ πάλιν·

> πολλαὶ τῶν ἀλεκτρυόνων βίᾳ
> ὑπηνέμια τίκτουσιν ᾠὰ πολλάκις.

Chamaeleon of Heracleia made about him in Book VI of
On Comedy (fr. 43 Wehrli), where he writes as follows:
Once when Anaxandrides (test. 2) was producing a dithy-
ramb in Athens, he entered (the Theater) on horseback
and recited part of the song. He was tall and good-looking;
had long hair; and wore a purple robe with a gold border.
But because he was an unpleasant person, he would do
something along the following lines with his comedies.
When he failed to win the prize, he took them and turned
them over to the incense-dealers to cut up,[41] rather than
revising them, as most authors did; he did away with many
clever plays, since his advanced age made him peevish toward his audience. His family is said to have been from
Camirus on Rhodes. I am therefore surprised that the
Tereus survived (along with other plays of his, which got a
similar reception), given that it failed to take the prize.
Theopompus in *Peace* (fr. 10) also used *alektruōn* in the
feminine, saying the following:

> I'm upset at losing
> an *alektruōn* that lays (fem.) lovely eggs.

Also Aristophanes in *Daedalus* (fr. 193):

> She's laid an enormous egg, as if she were an
> *alektruōn*.

And again (fr. 194.1–2):

> Many (fem.) *alektruones* are
> repeatedly forced to lay wind-eggs[42].

---

[41] Sc. as wrapping-material for their goods.
[42] I.e. infertilized eggs; cf. 2.57d–e with 2.57e n.; 9.397b.

227

ἐν δὲ Νεφέλαις διδάσκων τὸν πρεσβύτην περὶ ὀνόματος διαφορᾶς φησι·

(Στ.) νῦν δὲ πῶς με χρὴ καλεῖν;
(Σω.) ἀλεκτρύαιναν, τὸν δ᾽ ἕτερον ἀλέκτορα.

λέγεται δὲ καὶ ἀλεκτορὶς καὶ ἀλέκτωρ. Σιμωνίδης |

d   ἱμερόφων᾽ ἀλέκτωρ

ἔφη. Κρατῖνος Ὥραις·

ὥσπερ ὁ Περσικὸς ὥραν πᾶσαν καναχῶν
ὁλόφωνος ἀλέκτωρ.

εἴρηται δ᾽ οὕτως ἐπειδὴ καὶ ἐκ τοῦ λέκτρου ἡμᾶς διεγείρει. οἱ δὲ Δωριεῖς λέγοντες ὄρνιξ τὴν γενικὴν διὰ τοῦ χ̄ λέγουσιν ὄρνιχος. Ἀλκμὰν δὲ διὰ τοῦ σ̄ τὴν εὐθεῖαν ἐκφέρει·

< . . . > ἁλιπόρφυρος ἱαρὸς ὄρνις.

καὶ τὴν γενικήν·

Ϝοῖδα δ᾽ ὀρνίχων νόμως
παντῶν.

Δέλφαξ. Ἐπίχαρμος τὸν ἄρρενα χοῖρον οὕτως καλεῖ ἐν Ὀδυσσεῖ Αὐτομόλῳ· |

---

43 A comic feminine ("roosteress") invented to match masculine *alektōr*.

In *Clouds* (665–6), when he is teaching the old man to distinguish among words, he says:

> (Strepsiades) So how should I refer to it now?
> (Socrates) As an *alektruaina*[43], and to the male as an *alektōr*.

Alektoris and *alektōr* are both used. Simonides said (*PMG* 583):

> an *alektōr* with a lovely voice.

Cratinus in *Seasons* (fr. 279):

> like the full-voiced Persian *alektōr* that crows at any hour.

It has this name because it rouses us from bed (*lektron*).[44] The Dorians say *ornix*[45] and accordingly pronounce the genitive with a *chi*, *ornichos*. But Alcman[46] (*PMG* 26.4) offers the nominative in *sigma*:

> a sacred sea-purple bird (*ornis*).

Also the genitive (Alcm. *PMG* 40):

> I know the songs of all
> the birds (*ornichōn*).

Pig (*delphax*). Epicharmus uses this term for a male piglet (*choiros*) in *Odysseus the Deserter* (fr. 99):

---

[44] As if the word were a combination of this word and an initial privative.

[45] Sc. rather than common *ornis* ("bird, chicken"; genitive *ornithos*).

[46] A Doric poet, who ought therefore to use *ornix*.

e   δέλφακά τε τῶν γειτόνων
τοῖς Ἐλευσινίοις φυλάσσων δαιμονίως ἀπώλεσα
οὐχ ἑκών· καὶ ταῦτα δή με συμβολατεύειν μ' ἔφα
τοῖς Ἀχαιοῖσιν προδιδόμειν τ' ὤμνυέ με τὸν
     δέλφακα.

καὶ Ἀναξίλας δ' ἐν Κίρκῃ καὶ ἀρσενικῶς εἴρηκε τὸν
δέλφακα καὶ ἐπὶ τοῦ τελείου τέθεικε τοὔνομα εἰπών·

    τοὺς μὲν ὀρεινόμους ὑμῶν ποιήσει δέλφακας
      ὑλιβάτας,
f   τοὺς δὲ πάνθηρας, | ἄλλους ἀγρώστας λύκους,
    λέοντας.

ἐπὶ δὲ τῶν θηλειῶν τοὔνομα τάττει Ἀριστοφάνης Τα-
γηνισταῖς

              ἢ δέλφακος ὀπωρινῆς
   ἠτριαῖον[4].

καὶ ἐν Ἀχαρνεῦσιν·

    νέα γάρ ἐστιν. ἀλλὰ δελφακουμένα
    ἐξεῖ μεγάλαν τε καὶ παχεῖαν κἠρυθράν. ||
375   ἀλλ' αἰ τράφειν λῇς, ἅδε τοι χοῖρος καλά.

---

[4] ἠτριεα 3.96c–d: ἠτριαίαν 3.110f

[47] A more substantial version of the fragment is quoted, with
minor variants, at 3.96c–d, cf. 3.110f.

230

            And when I was keeping my neighbors'
delphax safe for the Eleusinia festival, I lost it by
        some god's will,
not my own. As a result, he claimed I was engaged in
        barter
with the Achaeans, and swore I was betraying the
        delphax.

So too Anaxilas in *Circe* (fr. 12) both uses *delphax* in the masculine and applies the word to a full-grown animal, saying:

She'll turn some of you into mountain-ranging, mud-
        trodding *delphakes*,
some into wildcats, others into savage wolves
or lions.

Aristophanes in *Frying-Pan Men* (fr. 520.6–7),[47] on the other hand, uses the word of sows:

                         or a paunch of a *delphax*
butchered (fem.) in the fall.

And in *Acharnians* (786–8):

Because she's young! But once she turns into a
        delphax,
she'll have a big, fat, pink (tail)!
If you're willing to raise her, this is a nice piglet
        (*choiros*)[48] for you.

[48] An obscene double-entendre (since *choiros* also had the colloquial sense "cunt", and the tail referred to in the preceding line is a penis), as perhaps again in Cratin. fr. 4 (quoted below).

καὶ Εὔπολις ἐν Χρυσᾷ Γένει. καὶ Ἱππῶναξ δ' ἔφη·

† ὡς † Ἐφεσίη δέλφαξ.

κυρίως δ' αἱ θήλειαι οὕτως λεχθεῖεν ἂν αἱ δελφύας ἔχουσαι· οὕτως δὲ αἱ μῆτραι καλοῦνται καὶ οἱ ἀδελφοὶ ἔνθεν ἐτυμολογοῦνται. περὶ δὲ τῆς ἡλικίας τοῦ ζῴου Κρατῖνός φησιν ἐν Ἀρχιλόχοις·

< . . . > ἤδη δέλφακες, χοῖροι δὲ τοῖσιν ἄλλοις.

Ἀριστοφάνης δ' ὁ γραμματικὸς ἐν τᾷ Περὶ Ἡλικιῶν φησι· τῶν δὲ συῶν τὰ μὲν ἤδη συμπεπηγότα δέλφα-
b κες, τὰ δ' ἁπαλὰ | καὶ ἔνικμα χοῖροι. ἔνθεν τὸ Ὁμηρι-κὸν σαφὲς γίνεται·

τά τε δμώεσσι πάρεστι
χοῖρε', ἀτὰρ σιάλους γε σύας μνηστῆρες ἔδουσι.

Πλάτων δ' ὁ κωμῳδιοποιὸς ἐν Ποιητῇ ἀρρενικῶς ἔφη·

τὸν δέλφακα
ἀπῆγε σιγῇ.

ἦν δὲ καὶ παλαιὸς νόμος, ὥς φησιν Ἀνδροτίων, τῆς ἐπιγονῆς ἕνεκα τῶν θρεμμάτων μὴ σφάττειν πρόβα-

---

[49] A quotation has probably dropped out of the text; the passage referred to is preserved at 14.657a.

[50] Apparently the correct etymology.

[51] Cf. 9.374f–5a n. on Ar. *Ach.* 786–8 (quoted above).

Also Eupolis in *The Golden Age* (fr. 301.1).[49] Hipponax (fr. 136 Degani) too said:

† like † an Ephesian (fem.) *delphax*.

Properly only sows would be referred to this way, because they have *delphuai*, which is a term for the womb and the source of the word *adelphos* ("womb-mate", i.e. "brother").[50] As for the age of the animal, Cratinus says in *Archilochuses* (fr. 4):

At the moment, they're *delphakes*; but they're *choiroi* in other respects.[51]

The grammarian Aristophanes says in his *On Ages* (fr. 170 Slater): Hogs whose flesh has become firm are *delphakes*, whereas those that are soft and moist are *choiroi*. This explains the Homeric passage (*Od*. 14.80–1):

what slaves have at their disposal—
the flesh of *choiroi*—whereas the suitors eat fattened
hogs.

The comic poet Plato in *The Poet* (fr. 118) used the word as a masculine:

Quietly lead
the *delphax*[52] away!

Accordingly to Androtion (*FGrH* 324 F 55), there was an ancient law, intended to increase the number of domestic animals, forbidding anyone to slaughter a lamb or kid that

[52] The definite article is masculine, but could easily be emended to feminine.

c   τον ἄπεκτον ἢ ἄτοκον· διὸ τὰ ἤδη τέλεια | ἤσθιον·

   ⟨ . . . ⟩ ἀτὰρ σιάλους γε σύας μνηστῆρες
   ἔδουσι.

καὶ νῦν δὲ τὴν τῆς Ἀθηνᾶς ἱέρειαν οὐ θύειν ἀμνὴν
οὐδὲ τυροῦ γεύεσθαι. καὶ κατὰ χρόνον δέ τινα ἐκλι-
πόντων τῶν βοῶν, φησὶν ὁ Φιλόχορος, νομοθετηθῆναι
διὰ τὴν σπάνιν ἀπέχεσθαι αὐτοὺς τῶν ζῴων, συνάγειν
βουλομένους καὶ πληθῦσαι τὰ μὴ καταθύεσθαι. χοῖρον δ᾽ οἱ Ἴωνες καλοῦσι τὴν θήλειαν, ὡς Ἱππῶναξ·

   σπονδῇ τε καὶ σπλάγχνοισιν ἀγρίης χοίρου.

d   καὶ Σοφοκλῆς | Ἐπιταιναρίοις·

   τοιγὰρ † ἰωδὴ † φυλάξαι χοῖρον ὥστε δεσμίαν.

Πτολεμαῖος δ᾽ ὁ τῆς Αἰγύπτου βασιλεὺς ἐν τᾷ ἐνάτῳ
τῶν Ἀπομνημονευμάτων[5], εἰς Ἄσσον, φησίν, ἐπιδη-
μήσαντί μοι οἱ Ἄσσιοι παρέστησαν χοῖρον[6] ἔχοντα
τὸ μὲν ὕψος δύο καὶ ἡμίσους πήχεων, ὅλον δ᾽ ἄρτιον
πρὸς τὸ μῆκος, τῇ χροιᾷ χιόνινον. ἔφασάν τε τὸν
βασιλέα Εὐμένη τὰ τοιαῦτα ἐπιμελῶς ὠνεῖσθαι παρ᾽

---

[5] Ὑπομνημονευμάτων Olson: Ἀπομνημονευμάτων A
[6] χοῖρον tantum CE: χοῖρον υἱὸν A

had not given birth or been sheared.[53] This is why they ate full-grown animals (*Od.* 14.81):

> whereas the suitors eat fatted hogs.

Even today Athena's priestess is not allowed to sacrifice a lamb or to taste cheese. And at one time, according to Philochorus (*FGrH* 328 F 169b), when there were not enough cows, a law was passed in response to the shortage, that they were not to consume the animals, since they wanted to accumulate them and increase their number by not sacrificing them. The Ionians refer to a sow as a *choiros*, for example Hipponax (fr. 105.9 Degani):

> with both a libation and the entrails of a wild (fem.)
>   *choiros*.

Also Sophocles in *Epitainarioi* (fr. 198a):

> So [corrupt] guard like a *choiros* (fem.) tied to a rope
>   (fem.)!

Ptolemy the king of Egypt says in Book IX of his *Commentaries* (*FGrH* 234 F 10): When I visited Assos, the local people presented me with a *choiros*[54] that was four feet[55] tall, proportionately wide across, and the color of snow. They claimed that King Eumenes had been eager to pur-

---

[53] Cf. Philoch. *FGrH* 328 F 169a (cited at 1.9c–d).

[54] Here, as in the three poetic quotations that follows, the noun is masculine.

[55] Literally "two-and-a-half cubits".

αὐτῶν, διδόντα τοῦ ἑνὸς δραχμὰς τετρακισχιλίας.
Αἰσχύλος δέ φησιν· |

e   ἐγὼ δὲ χοῖρον καὶ μάλ' εὐθηλούμενον
    τόνδ' ἐν νοτοῦντι κριβάνῳ θήσω. τί γὰρ
    ὄψον γένοιτ' ἂν ἀνδρὶ τοῦδε βέλτιον;

καὶ πάλιν·

    λευκός—τί δ' οὐχί;—καὶ καλῶς ἠφευμένος
    ὁ χοῖρος· ἕψου μηδὲ λυπηθῇς πυρί.

καὶ ἔτι·

    θύσας δὲ χοῖρον τόνδε τῆς αὐτῆς ὑός,
    ἣ πολλά μ' ἐν δόμοισιν εἴργασται κακά,
    δονοῦσα καὶ τρέπουσα τύρβ' ἄνω κάτω. |

f ταῦτα δὲ παρέθετο Χαμαιλέων ἐν τᾷ Περὶ Αἰσχύλου.

    Περὶ δὲ ὑῶν ὅτι ἱερόν ἐστι τὸ ζᾷον παρὰ Κρησὶν
Ἀγαθοκλῆς ὁ Βαβυλώνιος ἐν πρώτῳ Περὶ Κυζίκου
φησὶν οὕτως· μυθεύουσιν ἐν Κρήτῃ γενέσθαι τὴν Διὸς
τέκνωσιν ἐπὶ τῆς Δίκτης, ἐν ᾗ καὶ ἀπόρρητος γίνεται
376 θυσία. || λέγεται γὰρ ὡς ἄρα Διὶ θηλὴν ὑπέσχεν ὗς
καὶ τᾷ σφετέρῳ γρυσμᾷ περιοιχνεῦσα τὸν κνυζηθμὸν
τοῦ βρέφεος ἀνεπάιστον τοῖς παριοῦσιν ἐτίθει. διὸ

---

56 The Ptolemy in question is Ptolemy VIII Euergetes II
(reigned 170–116 BCE), and Eumenes must therefore be
Eumenes II of Pergamum (reigned 197–158). One would like to
know whether the Assians' ploy convinced Ptolemy to pay a similar
sum (or more) for the pig.

chase animals like these from them and had paid 4000 drachmas apiece.[56] Aeschylus (fr. 309)[57] says:

> But I'm going to put this enormously fat
> *choiros* in a moist baking-shell. Because what
> dish could a man have that's better than this?

And again (A. fr. 310):

> The *choiros* is white—why not?—and nicely
> singed. Get cooked, and don't worry about the fire!

Furthermore (A. fr. 311):

> sacrificing this *choiros* produced by the same sow
> who's done a lot of damage in my house
> by galloping around and turning everything upside-
>   down, making a mess.

Chamaeleon cited these passages in his *On Aeschylus* (fr. 39 Wehrli).

As for the fact that the Cretans regard the pig as a sacred animal, Agathocles of Babylon says the following in Book I of *On Cyzicus* (*FGrH* 472 F 1): According to a story told on Crete, Zeus was born on Mt. Dicte, where a secret sacrificial ritual is carried out. They say that a sow offered a teat to Zeus, and her grunting as she ran around kept passers-by from hearing the baby's whimpering.[58] This is

---

[57] A. frr. 309–11 are most likely all from a single satyr play and refer to the same set of events.

[58] A crucial detail, because Cronus was eager to find his son and swallow him; cf. E. *Ba.* 120–34 (where the Corybantes protect the child in much the same way as the sow does here).

πάντες τὸ ζῷον τοῦτο περίσεπτον ἡγοῦνται καὶ οὐκ ἄν,
φησί, τῶν κρεῶν δαίσαιντο. Πραίσιοι δὲ καὶ ἱερὰ
ῥέζουσιν ὗί, καὶ αὕτη προτελὴς αὐτοῖς ἡ θυσία νε-
νόμισται. τὰ παραπλήσια ἱστορεῖ καὶ Νεάνθης ὁ
Κυζικηνὸς ἐν δευτέρῳ Περὶ Τελετῆς. πεταλίδων συῶν
μνημονεύει Ἀχαιὸς ὁ Ἐρετριεὺς ἐν Αἴθωνι σατυρικᾷ
λέγων οὕτως·

b   πεταλίδων δέ τοι | συῶν
     < . . . > † μορφαῖς ταῖσδε πόλλ' ἐπάιον.

πεταλίδας δ' αὐτὰς εἴρηκε μεταφέρων ἀπὸ τῶν
μόσχων· οὗτοι γὰρ πέτηλοι λέγονται ἀπὸ τῶν κερά-
των, ὅταν αὐτὰ ἐκπέταλα ἔχωσι. παραπλησίως δὲ τᾷ
Ἀχαιᾷ καὶ Ἐρατοσθένης ἐν Ἀντερινύι τοὺς σύας
λαρινοὺς προσηγόρευσε μεταγαγὼν καὶ αὐτὸς ἀπὸ
τῶν λαρινῶν βοῶν· οἳ οὕτως ἐκλήθησαν ἤτοι ἀπὸ τοῦ
λαρινεύεσθαι, ὅπερ ἐστὶ σιτίζεσθαι (Σώφρων· βόες δὲ
λαρινεύονται), ἢ ἀπό τινος κώμης Ἠπειρωτικῆς Λαρί-
c   νης ἢ ἀπὸ τοῦ βουκολοῦντος | αὐτάς· Λαρῖνος δ' οὗτος
ἐκαλεῖτο.

     Εἰσαχθέντος δὲ ἡμῖν ποτε καὶ δέλφακος, οὗ τὸ μὲν
ἥμισυ κραμβαλέον ἦν ἐπιμελῶς πεποιημένον, τὸ δὲ
ἥμισυ ὡς ἂν ἐξ ὕδατος ἡψημένον τακερῶς, καὶ πάντων
θαυμαζόντων τοῦ μαγείρου τὴν σοφίαν, μέγα φρονῶν
ἐκεῖνος ἐπὶ τῇ τέχνῃ ἔφη· ἀλλὰ μὴν οὐδὲ τὴν σφαγὴν
ἔχει τις ὑμῶν ἐπιδεῖξαι ὅπου ἐγένετο ἢ πῶς αὐτοῦ ἡ
γαστὴρ πεπλήρωται παντοίων ἀγαθῶν. καὶ γὰρ κίχλας ἐν ἑαυτᾷ ἔχει καὶ ἄλλα ὀρνίθια ὑπογαστρίων τε

why they universally regard this animal as deserving considerable respect and, he claims, refuse to eat its flesh. The inhabitants of Praesus actually make sacrifices to a pig, and this is their standard preliminary sacrifice. Neanthes of Cyzicus in Book II of *On Initiation* (*FGrH* 84 F 15) offers similar information. Achaeus of Eretria in the satyr play *Aethon* (*TrGF* 20 F 8) mentions *petalides* ("full-grown") pigs, saying the following:

> In fact I often heard *petalides*
> pigs . . . † with these shapes.

When he refers to them as *petalides*, he is transferring to them a term normally used of calves, which are called *petēloi* when they have outspread (*ekpetala*) horns. Eratosthenes in *The Anti-Fury* (fr. 20, p. 64 Powell) did something like what Achaeus did, when he referred to pigs as *larinoi* ("fatted"), in his case importing the term from "fatted (*larinoi*) cows". Cows were described thus either from the verb *larineuesthai*, which means "to be fed" (Sophron [fr. 99]: cows are being fed [*larineuontai*]); or from a village in Epirus called Larinē; or from the cowherd who cared for them, who was named Larinus.

At one point we were served a pig (*delphax*), half of which had been carefully roasted, while the other half was as tender as if it had been stewed in water. We all expressed astonishment at the cook's artistry, and as he was proud of his abilities, he said: Yes, indeed; none of you can identify the wound that killed it, or explain how its belly came to be stuffed with delicious food of all kinds. Because there are thrushes inside it, as well as various other birds, bits of ba-

d μέρη χοιρείων καὶ | μήτρας τόμους καὶ τῶν ᾠῶν τὰ
χρυσᾶ, ἔτι δὲ ὀρνίθων

γαστέρας
αὐταῖσι μήτραις καὶ καλῶν ζωμῶν πλέας,

καὶ τὰ ἐκ τῶν σαρκῶν εἰς λεπτὰ κατακνιζόμενα καὶ
μετὰ πεπερίδων συμπλαττόμενα· ἰσίκια γὰρ

< . . . > ὀνομάζειν < . . . > αἰδοῦμαι

τὸν Οὐλπιανόν, καίπερ αὐτὸν εἰδὼς ἡδέως αὐτοῖς χρώμενον. πλὴν ὁ ἐμός γε συγγραφεὺς Πάξαμος τῶν
ἰσικίων μέμνηται· καὶ οὔ μοι φροντὶς Ἀττικῶν χρή-
σεων. ὑμεῖς οὖν ἐπιδείξατε πῶς τε ὁ χοῖρος ἐσφάγη
e καὶ πῶς ἐξ ἡμισείας μέν ἐστιν ὀπτός, ἑφθὸς | δὲ κατὰ
θάτερα. ἔτ᾽ οὖν ἡμῶν ἀναζητούντων ὁ μάγειρος ἔφη·
ἀλλ᾽ ἢ νομίζετέ με ἔλαττον πεπαιδεῦσθαι τῶν ἀρχαίων ἐκείνων μαγείρων περὶ ὧν οἱ κωμῳδιοποιοὶ λέγουσι; Ποσείδιππος μὲν ἐν Χορευούσαις· μάγειρος δ᾽
ἐστὶν ὁ λέγων πρὸς τοὺς μαθητὰς τάδε·

μαθητὰ Λεύκων οἵ τε συνδιάκονοι
ὑμεῖς (ἅπας γάρ ἐστιν οἰκεῖος τόπος
ὑπὲρ τέχνης λαλεῖν τι)· τῶν ἡδυσμάτων
πάντων κράτιστόν ἐστιν ἐν μαγειρικῇ |
f ἀλαζονεία· τὸ καθ᾽ ὅλου δὲ τῶν τεχνῶν
ὄψει σχεδόν τι < . . . > τοῦθ᾽ ἡγούμενον.

con, slices of womb, and egg-yolks, along with chickens'

bellies,
wombs and all, full of fine broths (adesp. com.
fr. *114),

and chunks of meat grated fine and worked into a paste
with pepper. For (E. *Or.* 37)

I am ashamed to mention

isikia[59] in Ulpian's presence—even though I know that he
likes to eat it! (This is true) despite the fact that Paxamus
(cf. *FHG* iv.472), a prose-author with whom I am familiar,
mentions *isikia*; nor am I much concerned with Attic usage. So let me know how the pig was butchered, and how it
is that half of it is roasted, while the other half is stewed!
While we were still mulling over the question, the cook
said: What—do you consider me less well-trained than the
famous cooks in the old days, whom the comic poets discuss? Posidippus in *Dancing-Girls* (fr. 28); the speaker is a
cook, who says the following to his students:

Leucon my student, and you his fellow-
servants—since anywhere's a good place
to have a chat about our profession!—in the cook-
business,
the most important spice of all is
the ability to bullshit. In general, in fact, you'll see
that this is pretty much the number-one skill.

[59] "Hash"; a Latin word (*insicium*), hence the cook's reluc-
tance to use it in the presence of the aggressive Atticist Ulpian. Cf.
3.121e–f; 8.362a; 15.701b n.

ξεναγὸς οὗτος, ὅστις ἂν θώρακ᾽ ἔχῃ
φολιδωτὸν ἢ δράκοντα σεσιδηρωμένον,
ἐφάνη Βριάρεως, ἂν τύχῃ δ᾽ ἐστὶν λαγώς.
ὁ μάγειρος ἂν μὲν ὑποδιακόνους ἔχων
πρὸς τὸν ἰδιώτην καὶ μαθητὰς εἰσίῃ, ||

377   κυμινοπρίστας πάντας ἢ λιμοὺς καλῶν,
ἔπτηξ᾽ ἕκαστος εὐθύς· ἂν δ᾽ ἀληθινὸν
σαυτὸν παραβάλλῃς, καὶ προσεκδαρεὶς ἄπει.
ὅπερ οὖν ὑπεθέμην, τᾶ κενᾶ χώραν δίδου
καὶ τὰ στόμια γίνωσκε τῶν κεκλημένων·
ὥσπερ γὰρ εἰς τἀμπόρια, τῆς τέχνης πέρας
τοῦτ᾽ ἔστιν, ἂν εὖ προσδράμῃς πρὸς τὸ στόμα.
διακονοῦμεν νῦν γάμους. τὸ θῦμα βοῦς, |

b   ὁ διδοὺς ἐπιφανής, ἐπιφανὴς ὁ λαμβάνων.
τούτων γυναῖκες ἱέρειαι † τῇ θεᾷ θεοί, †
κορύβαντες, αὐλοί, παννυχίδες, ἀναστροφή·
ἱππόδρομος οὗτός ἐστί σοι μαγειρικῆς.
μέμνησο καὶ σὺ τοῦτο.

καὶ περὶ ἑτέρου δὲ μαγείρου (ὄνομα δ᾽ ἐστὶ Σεύθης) ὁ
αὐτός φησιν ποιητὴς οὕτως·

---

60 The most prominent of the Hesiodic Hundred-Handers
(*Th*. 149) and a symbol of overwhelming physical might; cf.
Timocl. fr. 12, quoted at 6.224a–b.

This mercenary commander, if he's wearing a
      breastplate
of scale-armor or has an iron-plated dragon (on his
      shield),
he looks like Briareus[60]—but he may turn out to be a
      hare!
So if a cook enters a private house
accompanied by a bunch of underlings and students,
and calls everyone cheapskates, and accuses them of
      starving their guests,
they all cower in front of him instantly. But if you
      expose
your true self, they'll skin you alive before you get
      out of there.
My advice, therefore, is to give big talk an
      opportunity
and be aware of what the guests like to eat.
It's just like sailing into harbor: the most important
      part
of our trade is to aim straight for the mouth!
At the moment, we're working a wedding feast.
      They're sacrificing an ox;
the guy giving away the bride is distinguished, and
      so's the groom;
their women are priestesses † to the goddess gods, †;
corybants, pipes, all-night festivities, and a lot of
      hullabaloo.
Your cooking's in a horserace now;
remember that!

The same poet says the following about another cook,
whose name is Seuthes (Posidipp. fr. 29):

ἰδιώτης μέγας |

c   αὐτοῖς ὁ Σεύθης. οἶσθας, ὦ βέλτισθ᾽, ὅτι
ἀγαθοῦ στρατηγοῦ διαφέρειν οὐθὲν δοκεῖ.
οἱ πολέμιοι πάρεισιν· ὁ βαθὺς τῇ φύσει
στρατηγὸς ἔστη καὶ τὸ πρᾶγμ᾽ ἐδέξατο.
πολέμιός ἐστι πᾶς ὁ συμπίνων ὄχλος.
κινεῖ γὰρ ἁθρόος οὗτος· εἰσελήλυθεν,
ἐκ πεντεκαίδεχ᾽ ἡμερῶν προηλπικὼς
τὸ δεῖπνον, ὁρμῆς μεστός, ἐκκεκαυμένος,
τηρῶν πότ᾽ ἐπὶ τὰς χεῖρας οἴσει τις. νόει
ὄχλου τοιούτου ῥαχίαν ἠθροισμένην. |

d ὁ δ᾽ ἐν τοῖς Εὔφρονος Συνεφήβοις μάγειρος ἀκούσατε
οἷα παραινεῖ·

ὅταν ἐρανισταῖς, Καρίων, διακονῇς,
οὐκ ἔστι παίζειν οὐδ᾽ ἃ μεμάθηκας ποεῖν.
ἐχθὲς κεκινδύνευκας· οὐδεὶς εἶχέ σοι
κωβιὸς ὅλως γὰρ ἧπαρ, ἀλλ᾽ ἦσαν κενοί·
ἐγκέφαλος ἠλλοίωτο. δεῖ δέ, Καρίων,
ὅταν μὲν ἔλθῃς εἰς τοιοῦτον συρφετόν,
Δρόμωνα καὶ Κέρδωνα καὶ Σωτηρίδην,
μισθὸν διδόντας ὅσον ἂν αἰτήσῃς, ἁπλῶς |
e εἶναι δίκαιον, οἳ δὲ νῦν βαδίζομεν
εἰς τοὺς γάμους, ἀνδροφόνον. ἂν τοῦτ᾽ αἰσθάνῃ,

Seuthes is a big
nobody in their eyes. You're aware, sir, that
he's patently no different from a fine general.
The enemy's here; the profoundly ingenious
general stands his ground and endures their assault.
The whole mob at the party is a hostile force.
They move as a unit; and when they come in,
they've been anticipating the meal for two
weeks, and they're full of energy and fired-up,
and watching for when a slave will bring them
washing-water. Imagine
the roar a mob like that produces!

Listen to the sort of advice the cook in Euphro's *Fellow-Ephebes* (fr. 9) offers:

When you work for the members of an *eranos*[61],
Cario,
you can't fool around or just do what you've been
taught.
You took chances yesterday. Not a single one of your
gobies had a liver—their bellies were empty—
and their brains got stolen! When you go to work
for a bunch of bums like that, Cario—
people named Dromo and Cerdo and Soterides,
who pay you whatever you ask—you have to be
100% honest. But where we're going now,
to a wedding feast, you need to be ready to kill. If
you understand this,

[61] A group of men who assembled on an occasional basis to
have dinner and drink, talk politics, carry out religious rites, and
the like.

245

ἐμὸς εἶ μαθητὴς καὶ μάγειρος οὐ κακός.
ὁ καιρὸς εὐκτός· ὠφελοῦ. φιλάργυρος
ὁ γέρων, ὁ μισθὸς μικρός· εἴ σε λήψομαι
νῦν μὴ κατεσθίοντα καὶ τοὺς ἄνθρακας,
ἀπόλωλας. εἴσω πάραγε· καὶ γὰρ οὑτοσὶ
αὐτὸς προσέρχεθ'. ὡς δὲ καὶ γλίσχρον βλέπει. |

f μέγας δέ ἐστι σοφιστὴς καὶ οὐδὲν ⟨ἥττων⟩[7] τῶν
ἰατρῶν εἰς ἀλαζονείαν καὶ ὁ παρὰ Σωσιπάτρῳ μάγειρος ἐν Καταψευδομένῳ λέγων ὧδε·

(A.) οὐ παντελῶς εὐκαταφρόνητος ἡ τέχνη,
ἂν κατανοήσῃς, ἐστὶν ἡμῶν, Δημύλε,
ἀλλὰ πέπλυται τὸ πρᾶγμα, καὶ πάντες σχεδὸν
εἶναι μάγειροί φασιν οὐθὲν εἰδότες·
ὑπὸ τῶν τοιούτων δ' ἡ τέχνη λυμαίνεται. ||
378   ἐπεὶ μάγειρον ἂν λάβῃς ἀληθινόν,
ἐκ παιδὸς ὀρθῶς εἰς τὸ πρᾶγμ' εἰσηγμένον
καὶ τὰς δυνάμεις κατέχοντα καὶ τὰ μαθήματα
ἅπαντ' ἐφεξῆς εἰδόθ', ἕτερόν σοι τυχὸν
φανήσεται τὸ πρᾶγμα. τρεῖς ἡμεῖς ⟨ . . . ⟩
ἐσμὲν ἔτι λοιποί, Βοιδίων καὶ Χαριάδης
ἐγώ τε· τοῖς λοιποῖς δὲ προσπέρδου. (Δη.) τί
          φής;
ἐγώ; (A.) τὸ διδασκαλεῖον ἡμεῖς σῴζομεν |

[7] add. Casaubon

you're my student and quite a fine cook.
This is the opportunity we've been praying for; take
        advantage of it! The old man's
a miser, and the wages are low; so today, if I catch
you *not* gobbling everything down, including the
        coals,
you've had it! Lead the way in! But here comes
the man himself. What a stingy expression he's got on
        his face!

The cook in Sosipater's *False Accuser* (fr. 1) is a real intellectual and no less of a bullshitter than the physicians when
he says the following:

(A.) Our business doesn't deserve complete
contempt, if you think about it, Demylus.
But it's got a bad reputation, and most people
who claim to be cooks don't know anything;
guys like this damage the profession.
If you hire a real cook,
someone actually brought up in the business since he
        was a boy,
who understands what we can do, and who's learned
all his lessons from A to Z, the situation'll
look different to you. There are still
three of us left: Boedion, Chariades,[62]
and me; piss on[63] the others! (Demeas) What do you
        mean?
I'm supposed to do that? (A.) We're preserving
        Sicon's

---

62 Cf. Euphro fr. 1.7 (quoted at 9.379e).
63 Literally "fart on".

b τὸ Σίκωνος· οὗτος τῆς τέχνης ἀρχηγὸς ἦν.
 ἐδίδασκεν ἡμᾶς πρῶτον ἀστρολογεῖν ‹ . . . ›·
 ἔπειτα μετὰ ταῦτ᾽ εὐθὺς ἀρχιτεκτονεῖν.
 περὶ φύσεως κατεῖχε πάντας τοὺς λόγους·
 ἐπὶ πᾶσι τούτοις ἔλεγε τὰ στρατηγικά.
 πρὸ τῆς τέχνης ἔσπευδε ταῦθ᾽ ἡμᾶς μαθεῖν.
 (Δη.) ἆρα σύ με κόπτειν οἷος εἶ γε, φίλτατε;
 (Α.) οὐκ ἀλλ᾽ ἐν ὅσῳ προσέρχετ᾽ ἐξ ἀγορᾶς ὁ
  παῖς, |

c μικρὰ διακινήσω σε περὶ τοῦ πράγματος,
 ἵνα τἀ λαλεῖν λάβωμεν εὔκαιρον χρόνον.
 (Δη.) Ἄπολλον, ἐργῶδές ‹γ᾽›. (Α.) ἄκουσον,
  ὦγαθέ·
 δεῖ τὸν μάγειρον εἰδέναι πρώτιστα μὲν
 περὶ τῶν μετεώρων, τάς τε τῶν ἄστρων δύσεις
 καὶ τὰς ἐπιτολάς, καὶ τὸν ἥλιον πότε
 ἐπὶ τὴν μακράν τε καὶ βραχεῖαν ἡμέραν
 ἐπάνεισι, κἀν ποίοισίν ἐστι ζῳδίοις.

d τὰ γὰρ ὄψα πάντα καὶ τὰ βρώματα | σχεδὸν
 ἐν τῇ περιφορᾷ τῆς ὅλης συντάξεως
 ἑτέραν ἐν αὑτοῖς λαμβάνει τὴν ἡδονήν.
 ὁ μὲν οὖν κατέχων τὰ τοιαῦτα τὴν ὥραν ἰδὼν
 τούτων ἑκάστοις ὡς προσήκει χρήσεται,

---

[64] Cf. 9.386a n.

school; he pioneered our system of doing things.
He taught us, first of all, how to interpret the stars;
and then next, after that, how to supervise building
      projects.
He was in charge of all our conversations on the
      subject of Nature;
and on top of all that, he discussed military strategy.
He wanted us to master these subjects before we
      studied our own profession.
(Demeas) So you're qualified to drive me crazy, my
      friend?
(A.) No; but while my slave is on his way back from
      the market,
I'm going to raise some minor questions about my
      business for you,
so we have the opportunity for a conversation.
(Demeas) Apollo![64] What a bother! (A.) Listen up,
      my good sir!
The first thing a cook has to know about
are celestial phenomena: when the stars set
and when they rise, when the sun
reaches the longest and the shortest day
of the year, and what signs of the Zodiac it's in.
Because almost all fish, like other types of food,
vary in how good or bad they taste
as the whole system revolves.
Someone who's mastered this sort of information will
      see what season it is,
and use each of these ingredients at the appropriate
      time;

ATHENAEUS

ὁ δ᾽ ἀγνοῶν ταῦτ᾽ εἰκότως τυντλάζεται.
πάλιν τὸ περὶ τῆς ἀρχιτεκτονικῆς ἴσως
ἐθαύμασας τί τῇ τέχνῃ συμβάλλεται.
(Δη.) ἐγὼ δ᾽ ἐθαύμασ᾽; (Α.) ἀλλ᾽ ὅμως ἐγὼ
    φράσω· |

e   τοὐπτάνιον ὀρθῶς καταβαλέσθαι καὶ τὸ φῶς
λαβεῖν ὅσον δεῖ καὶ τὸ πνεῦμ᾽ ἰδεῖν πόθεν
ἐστίν, μεγάλην χρείαν τιν᾽ εἰς τὸ πρᾶγμ᾽ ἔχει.
ὁ καπνὸς φερόμενος δεῦρο κἀκεῖ διαφορὰν
εἴωθε τοῖς ὄψοισιν ἐμποιεῖν τινα.
† τοιοῦτον † ἔτι σοι δίειμι τὰ στρατηγικὰ

*   *   *

ἔχω γε τὸν μάγειρον. ἡ τάξις σοφὸν
ἁπανταχοῦ μέν ἐστι κἂν πάσῃ τέχνῃ, |
f   ἐν τῇ καθ᾽ ἡμᾶς δ᾽ ὥσπερ ἡγεῖται σχεδόν.
τὸ γὰρ παραθεῖναι κἀφελεῖν τεταγμένως
ἕκαστα καὶ τὸν καιρὸν ἐπὶ τούτοις ἰδεῖν,
πότε δεῖ πυκνότερον ἐπαγαγεῖν καὶ πότε βάδην,
καὶ πῶς ἔχουσι πρὸς τὸ δεῖπνον καὶ πότε
εὔκαιρον αὐτῶν ἐστι τῶν ὄψων τὰ μὲν
θερμὰ παραθεῖναι, τὰ δ᾽ ἐπανέντα, τὰ δὲ μέσως,
τὰ δ᾽ ὅλως ἀποψύξαντα, ταῦτα πάντα < . . . > ‖
379   ἐν τοῖς στρατηγικοῖσιν ἐξετάζεται

250

whereas someone who's ignorant about such
      matters—not surprisingly—gets stuck in the
      mud.
Moving on—perhaps you wondered what
architecture contributes to our profession.
(Demeas) *I* wondered about that? (A.) I'm going to
      tell you anyway.
Laying out the kitchen-area properly, capturing the
      right
amount of light, and checking where the wind is
coming from, are very important in our business.
Whether the smoke goes this way or that tends
to have an effect on the food.
† this sort † I'll also run through the matter of
      military strategy for you.

*   *   *

I've got the cook. Organization implies wisdom
everywhere, in every profession;
but in ours it's almost the most important quality
      there is.
Serving and removing the various dishes
in an organized way, and recognizing the proper
      moment for them—
when you need to bring them in closer together,
      when a more leisurely pace is necessary,
how they're reacting to the meal, and when's
the perfect moment to serve the hot
dishes, or the ones that are just starting to cool down,
      or are at room temperature,
or are really cold—all these questions
are subsumed in the study of

μαθήμασιν. (Δη.) † τίς δή τι † παραδείξας ἐμοὶ
τὰ δέοντ᾽ ἀπελθὼν αὐτὸς ἡσυχίαν ἄγε.

καὶ ὁ παρὰ τᾷ Ἀλέξιδι δὲ ἐν Μιλησίοις μάγειρος οὐ
μακρὰν τούτου ἐστὶ λέγων τοιάδε·

    (Α.) οὐκ ἴστε ταῖς πλείσταισι τῶν τεχνῶν ὅτι
    οὐχ ἀρχιτέκτων κύριος τῆς ἡδονῆς
    μόνος καθέστηκ᾽, ἀλλὰ καὶ τῶν χρωμένων
    συμβάλλεταί τις, ἂν καλῶς χρῶνται, μερίς; |
b   (Β.) ποῖόν τι; δεῖ γὰρ κἀμὲ τὸν ξένον μαθεῖν.
    (Α.) τὸν ὀψοποιὸν σκευάσαι χρηστῶς μόνον
    δεῖ τοὔψον, ἄλλο δ᾽ οὐδέν. ἂν μὲν οὖν τύχῃ
    ὁ ταῦτα μέλλων ἐσθίειν τε καὶ κρινεῖν
    εἰς καιρὸν ἐλθών, ὠφέλησε τὴν τέχνην·
    ἂν δ᾽ ὑστερίζῃ τῆς τεταγμένης ἀκμῆς,
    ὥστ᾽ ἢ προοπτήσαντα χλιαίνειν πάλιν,
    ἢ μὴ προοπτήσαντα συντελεῖν ταχύ,
    ἀπεστέρησε τῆς τέχνης τὴν ἡδονήν.
    (Β.) εἰς τοὺς σοφιστὰς τὸν μάγειρον ἐγγράφω. |
c   (Α.) ἐστήκαθ᾽ ὑμεῖς, κάεται δέ μοι τὸ πῦρ,
    ἤδη πυκνοὶ δ᾽ ᾄττουσιν Ἡφαίστου κύνες

---

[65] Referred to at 6.240c as *The Girl from Miletus*.
[66] I.e. the sparks from the cook-fire. Cf. Eub. fr. 75.7 (quoted at 3.108b).

strategy. (Demeas) † who in fact something † now
    that you explained what
you had to to me—get out of here and leave me
    alone!

The cook in Alexis' *Milesians*[65] (fr. 153) is not much different from him and makes remarks along the following lines:

(A.) Don't you realize that in most professions
the man in charge isn't the only one who's responsible
for the pleasure produced, but some of it's
    contributed
by the people who enjoy it—assuming they *do* enjoy
    it?
(B.) What's this? I'm a foreigner; I need an
    explanation.
(A.) All the chef has to do is prepare the dishes
properly, nothing else. If the person who's going
to consume the food and pass judgment on it
shows up on time, he's made a positive contribution
    to the profession.
But if he arrives after the designated moment,
so that the cook has to warm the food up a second
    time after he roasts it,
or has to finish it quickly because he didn't finish
    roasting it,
the guest has reduced the pleasure our profession
    produces.
(B.) I'm adding the cook to my list of intellectuals.
(A.) You people stand around, and meanwhile my
    fire's burning,
and Hephaestus' hounds[66] are already racing, one
    after another,

κούφως πρὸς αἴθραν, οἷς τὸ γίγνεσθαί θ' ἅμα
καὶ τὴν τελευτὴν τοῦ βίου συνῆψέ τις
μόνοις ἀνάγκης θεσμὸς οὐχ ὁρώμενος.

Εὔφρων δέ, οὗ καὶ πρὸ βραχέος ἐμνήσθην, ἄνδρες
δικασταί (δικαστὰς γὰρ ὑμᾶς οὐκ ὀκνήσαιμ' ἂν καλεῖν, ἀναμένων τὴν ὑμετέραν τῶν αἰσθητηρίων κρί-
d σιν), ἐν τοῖς Ἀδελφοῖς τῷ δράματι ποιήσας | τινὰ
μάγειρον πολυμαθῆ καὶ εὐπαίδευτον μνημονεύοντά τε
τῶν πρὸ αὐτοῦ τεχνιτῶν καὶ τίνα ἕκαστος εἶχεν ἰδίαν
ἀρετὴν καὶ ἐν τίνι ἐπλεονέκτει, ὅμως οὐδενὸς ἐμνήσθη
τοιούτου ὧν ἐγὼ ὑμῖν πολλάκις τυγχάνω παρασκευ-
άζων. λέγει δ' οὖν οὕτως·

πολλῶν μαθητῶν γενομένων ἐμοί, Λύκε,
διὰ τὸ νοεῖν ἀεί τι καὶ ψυχὴν ἔχειν
ἄπει γεγονὼς μάγειρος ἐκ τῆς οἰκίας
ἐν οὐχ ὅλοις δέκα μησί, πολὺ νεώτατος. |
e   Ἆγις Ῥόδιος ὤπτηκεν ἰχθὺν μόνος ἄκρως·
Νηρεὺς δ' ὁ Χῖος γόγγρον ἧψε τοῖς θεοῖς·
θρῖον τὸ λευκὸν οὐξ Ἀθηνῶν Χαριάδης·
ζωμὸς μέλας ἐγένετο πρώτῳ Λαμπρίᾳ·
ἀλλᾶντας Ἀφθόνητος, Εὔθυνος φακήν,
† ἀπὸ συμβολῶν συνάγουσιν ἀρίστων πόρους. †

---

67 Cf. 7.295e n.
68 Cf. Sosip. fr. 1.11 (quoted at 9.378a).
69 The name of a seventh brilliant cook and a description of his most striking achievement must be concealed in this corrupt line (or the lacuna that perhaps precedes it).

254

lightly into the air. Some invisible law
of necessity bound their birth, and no one else's,
together with the end of their life.

Euphro, to whom I referred a little earlier (9.377d–e), gentlemen of the jury—for I would not hesitate to refer to you
as jurors, as I await the judgment rendered by your taste-
buds—in his play *The Brothers* (fr. 1) created a learned
and well-educated cook, who mentions the artisans who
preceded him, as well as the particular gift each of them
had and what he was best at. But all the same, he mentioned no one capable of making anything like the food I
regularly prepare for you. At any rate, he says the following:

> Although I've had lots of pupils, Lycus,
> the fact that you're always thinking and are brave
> means you're leaving my house having become a cook
> in less than ten months, far and away the youngest of
>   them.
> Agis of Rhodes was the only one who could roast a
>   fish perfectly;
> Nereus of Chios[67] stewed a conger eel fit for the
>   gods;
> Chariades of Athens[68] was responsible for the white
>   fig-leaf pastry;
> black broth was pioneered by Lamprias;
> Apthonetus made sausages, Euthynus lentil-soup;
> † from the money contributed they assemble of
>   lunches pores.[69] †

οὗτοι μετ' ἐκείνους τοὺς σοφιστὰς τοὺς πάλαι
γεγόνασιν ἡμῶν ἑπτὰ δεύτεροι σοφοί. |

f   ἐγὼ δ' ὁρῶν τὰ πολλὰ προκατειλημμένα
εὗρον τὸ κλέπτειν πρῶτος, ὥστε μηδένα
μισεῖν με διὰ τοῦτ', ἀλλὰ πάντας λαμβάνειν.
ὑπ' ἐμοῦ δ' ὁρῶν σὺ τοῦτο προκατειλημμένον
ἴδιον ἐφεύρηκάς τι, καὶ τοῦτ' ἐστὶ σόν.
πέμπτην ἔθυον ἡμέραν † οιτινι οἱ †
πολλοὶ γέροντες πλοῦν πολὺν πεπλευκότες, ‖

380   λεπτὸν ἔριφον καὶ μικρόν. οὐκ ἦν ἐκφορὰ
Λύκῳ κρεῶν τότ' οὐδὲ τῷ διδασκάλῳ.
ἑτέρους πορίσασθαι δύ' ἐρίφους ἠνάγκασας·
τὸ γὰρ ἧπαρ αὐτῶν πολλάκις σκοπουμένων
καθεὶς κάτω τὴν χεῖρα τὴν μίαν λαθὼν
ἔρριψας εἰς τὸν λάκκον ἰταμῶς τὸν νεφρόν. |

b   πολὺν ἐπόησας θόρυβον. "οὐκ εἶχε νεφρόν,"
ἔλεγον. ἔκυπτον οἱ παρόντες ἀποβολῇ.
ἔθυσαν ἕτερον· τοῦ δὲ δευτέρου πάλιν
τὴν καρδίαν εἶδόν σε καταπίνοντ' ἐγώ.
πάλαι μέγας εἶ, γίνωσκε· τοῦ γὰρ μὴ χανεῖν

---

[70] Thales of Miletus, Bias of Priene, Cleobulus of Lindos,
Pittacus of Mitylene, Solon of Athens, Chilon of Sparta, and
Periander of Corinth (all early 6th century BCE).

After the famous seven ancient wise men,[70] these
    people
represent our generation's second group of seven
    sages.
As for me, when I saw that lots of specialties had
    already been taken,
I became the first man to figure out how to steal food
    in a way that kept anyone
from hating me for it, and instead made them all try
    to hire me.
And since you saw that I'd already claimed that
    specialty,
you came up with another original trick, which no
    one knows but you.
Four days ago, [corrupt] a bunch of old men
who'd completed a long sea-voyage were sacrificing
a scrawny little kid. At that point, there wasn't any
meat for Lycus or his teacher to take home.
But you made them come up with two more kids;
because while they were searching around for the
    liver,
you discreetly put a hand inside the animal
and quickly tossed a kidney into the cistern.
Then you made a big fuss, and they said: "It was
    missing
a kidney!" Everyone there stared at the ground,
    dismayed by the deficiency.
They sacrificed another one, and again I saw you
gobbling down the heart of victim number two.
You're a past master, you can be sure of that! You're
    the only one

λύκον διακενῆς σὺ μόνος εὕρηκας τέχνην.
χορδῆς ὀβελίσκους ἡμέρας ζητουμένους
δύ' ἐχθὲς ὠμοὺς εἰς τὸ πῦρ ἀποσβέσας |
c   καὶ πρὸς τὸ δίχορδον ἐτερέτιζες. ἠσθόμην·
ἐκεῖνο δρᾶμα, τοῦτο δ' ἐστὶ παίγνιον.

μή τις τούτων τῶν δευτέρων ἑπτὰ σοφῶν ὀνομασθέν-
των τοιοῦτόν τι ἐπενόησε περὶ τοῦ χοίρου, πῶς καὶ τὰ
ἐντὸς πεπλήρωται καὶ τὸ μὲν ὀπταλέον ἐστὶν αὐτοῦ τὸ
δὲ ἐφθόν, αὐτὸς δ' ἐστὶν ἄσφακτο; δεομένων οὖν ἡμῶν
καὶ λιπαρούντων δεικνύναι τὴν σοφίαν, οὐκ ἐρῶ, φησί, τῆτες μὰ τοὺς ἐν Μαραθῶνι κινδυνεύσαντας καὶ
πρὸς ἔτι τοὺς ἐν Σαλαμῖνι ναυμαχήσαντας. ἔδοξεν
d   οὖν πᾶσι | διὰ τὸν τηλικόνδε ὅρκον μὴ βιάζεσθαι τὸν
ἄνθρωπον, ἐπ' ἄλλο δέ τι τῶν παραφερομένων τὰς
χεῖρας ἐπιβάλλειν. καὶ ὁ Οὐλπιανὸς ἔφη· μὰ τοὺς ἐν
Ἀρτεμισίῳ κινδυνεύσαντας οὐδείς τινος γεύσεται πρὶν
λεχθῆναι ποῦ κεῖται τὸ παραφέρειν· τὰ γὰρ γεύματα
ἐγὼ οἶδα μόνος. καὶ ὁ Μάγνος ἔφη· Ἀριστοφάνης ἐν
Προάγωνι·

---

[71] "The wolf with his mouth open" was a proverb used of those
who hope to get something, but do not succeed (Ar. fr. 350 ap.
Phot. λ 452), and the name of the animal (*lukos*) simultaneously
puns on that of the individual being addressed.

[72] Cf. 9.376c–d. The question of how the pig was prepared is
finally answered at 9.381a–c.

[73] An echo of D. 18.208 (referring to the Greek victories
against the Persian invaders in 490 and 480 BCE, respectively).

who's figured out how not to be a wolf with his mouth
    dangling open![71]
Yesterday, during the day, they were looking for two
    spits
of sausage (*chordē*), and you dropped them raw into
    the fire and put it out,
singing along with your two-stringed (*dichordos*)
    instrument. I understood;
the former was a complete play, but this latest was
    just a skit!

Surely no one claims that any of the second set of seven
sages just mentioned devised anything like this with a
pig—I mean, how its interior has been stuffed, and half
of it has been roasted and the other half stewed, and there
is no sign of it having been butchered![72] We therefore
begged and implored him to show us his trick, and he said:
I will not tell you this this year, by the men who risked their
lives at Marathon, or by those who fought the naval battle
at Salamis.[73] Because of the magnitude of this oath, we
all felt it would be wrong to force him to speak, and instead reached for some of the other items being served
(*parapheromenōn*). And Ulpian said: By the men who
risked their lives at Artemisium,[74] no one is going to taste
anything until we are told where the verb *parapherein*
("to bring, fetch, serve") is attested. Because I am the
sole authority on snacks (*geumata*). Magnus replied:
Aristophanes in *The Proagon* (fr. 482):

[74] Another echo of D. 18.208 (referring to another Greek victory over the Persians in 480 BCE).

ATHENAEUS

τί οὐκ ἐκέλευσας παραφέρειν τὰ ποτήρια; |

e Σώφρων δ' ἐν Γυναικείοις κατακοινότερον κέχρηται
λέγων· πάρφερε, Κοικόα, τὸν σκύφον μεστόν. καὶ
Πλάτων δ' ἐν Λάκωσιν ἔφη·

πάσας παραφερέτω.

Ἄλεξις Παμφίλῃ·

παρέθηκε τὴν τράπεζαν, εἶτα παραφέρων
ἀγαθῶν ἁμάξας.

περὶ δὲ τῶν γευμάτων ἃ σαυτῶν προὔπιες ὥρα σοι
λέγειν, Οὐλπιανέ. τὸ γὰρ γεῦσαι ἔχομεν ἐν Εὐπόλιδι
ἐν Αἰξί·

< . . . > τοῦδε νῦν γεῦσαι λαβών.

καὶ ὁ Οὐλπιανός, Ἔφιππος, ἔφη, ἐν Πελταστῇ· † ἔνθ'
f ὄνων ἵππων | τε στάσεις καὶ γεύματα οἴνων. † Ἀντι-
φάνης δ' ἐν Διδύμοις·

οἰνογευστεῖ, περιπατεῖ
ἐν τοῖς στεφάνοις.

Ἐπὶ τούτοις ὁ μάγειρος ἔφη· λέξω τοίνυν κἀγὼ οὐκ
ἀρχαίαν ἐπίνοιαν, ἀλλ' εὕρεσιν ἐμήν (ἵνα μὴ ὁ αὐλητὴς πληγὰς λάβῃ· ὁ γὰρ Εὔβουλος ἐν Λάκωσιν ἢ
Λήδᾳ ἔφη· ||

Why didn't you order him to fetch (*parapherein*) the
    cups?

Sophron in the *Women's Mimes* (fr. 14) uses the word in a
more conventional sense when he says: Coicoa! Fill the
bowl and bring it (*parphere*) here! Plato as well said in
Spartans (fr. 73):

Let him bring (*paraphereto*) them all!

Alexis in *Pamphile* (fr. 176):

He set the table beside us and then brought
    (*parapheron*)
wagon-loads of good food.

But now it is time, Ulpian, for you to discuss these snacks
(*geumata*) of yours that you mentioned in your toast. For
we have the verb *geusai* ("to taste") in Eupolis' *Nanny-
Goats* (fr. 10):

Take some of this now, and taste (*geusai*) it!

And Ulpian said: Ephippus in *The Peltast* (fr. 18, unmetrical): † where there are stalls for donkeys and horses,
and samples (*geumata*) of wine. † Antiphanes in *The Twins*
(fr. 83):

he samples wine (*oinogeustei*), he walks around
in the garland-market.

The cook responded: Well, I will tell you about something that is not an old trick, but my own invention—to
keep the pipe-player from being beaten; because Eubulus
said in *Spartans or Leda* (fr. 60):

381

ἀλλ' ἠκούσαμεν
καὶ τοῦτο, νὴ τὴν Ἑστίαν, οἴκοι ποθ' ὡς
<ὅσ'> ἂν ὁ μάγειρος ἐξαμάρτῃ, τύπτεται,
ὥς φασιν, αὐλητὴς παρ' ὑμῖν.

Φιλύλλιός τε ἢ ὁ ποιήσας τὰς Πόλεις φησίν·

ὅ τι ἂν τύχῃ
<ὁ> μάγειρος ἀδικήσας, τὸν αὐλητὴν λαβεῖν
πληγάς)

περὶ ἡμιόπτου καὶ ἡμιέφθου καὶ ἀσφάκτου γεμιστοῦ
χοίρου. ὁ μὲν χοῖρος ἐσφάγη ὑπὸ τὸν ὦμον σφαγὴν
b βραχεῖαν (καὶ ἐπέδειξεν). | ἔπειτα ἀπορρεύσαντος τοῦ
πολλοῦ αἵματος πάντα τὰ ἐντοσθίδια μετὰ τῆς ἐξαι-
ρέσεως (εἴρηται γὰρ καὶ ἐξαίρεσις,

< . . . > ὦ στωμυλήθραι δαιταλεῖς)

διακλύσας ἐπιμελῶς οἴνῳ πολλάκις ἐκρέμασα ἐκ
ποδῶν. εἶτα πάλιν οἴνῳ διέβρεξα καὶ προεψήσας μετὰ
πολλοῦ πιπέρεως τὰ προειρημένα χναύματα ἔβυσα
διὰ τοῦ στόματος, πολλὸν ἐπιχέας ζωμὸν εὖ πάνυ
πεποιημένον. καὶ μετὰ ταῦτα περιέπλασα τοῦ χοίρου
τὴν ἡμίσειαν, ὡς ὁρᾶτε, ἀλφίτοις πολλοῖς κριθῆς
c ἀναδεύσας αὐτὰ | οἴνῳ καὶ ἐλαίῳ. ἔπειτ' ἐνέθηκα
κριβάνῳ ὑποθεὶς τράπεζαν χαλκῆν ἐστάθευσά τε τῷ

---

[75] Athenaeus (or his source) also expresses doubts about the
authorship of the play at 3.86e, 92e; 4.140a.

But we heard
this once upon a time at home, by Hestia:
if the cook makes mistakes, people say,
it's the pipe-player you beat!

And Philyllius (fr. 9), or whoever the author of *Cities* is,[75]
says:

Whatever the cook
does wrong, the pipe-player
gets beaten—

and that involves a half-roasted, half-stewed, seemingly
unslaughtered, stuffed pig. The pig was slaughtered by
means of a small incision beneath its shoulder (and he
showed it to us). Then, after most of the blood had drained
out, I carefully washed its entire interior, as well as the
offal (*exairesis*)—because the word *exairesis* is used,[76]

you babbling banqueters (adesp. com. fr. *115)—

repeatedly with wine, and hung it up by its feet.[77] Then I
soaked it in wine again; gave it a preliminary stewing with a
large amount of pepper; and crammed the tidbits I mentioned earlier (9.376c–e) in through its mouth, after pouring a great deal of carefully made broth over them. After
that, I plastered half the pig, as you can see, with a large
quantity of barley-groats, into which I had mixed wine and
olive oil. Then I put a bronze tray under it, set it inside a

---

[76] The question is taken up below, after the way the pig was
cooked has been described.

[77] Sc. to drain the remaining blood from its body. The description that follows is perhaps all borrowed from some lost comedy.

πυρί, ὡς μήτε κατακαῦσαι μήτ᾽ ὠμὸν ἀφελεῖν. καὶ τῆς
φορίνης ἤδη γενομένης κραμβαλέας εἴκασα καὶ τἄλ-
λο μέρος ἡψῆσθαι ἀποβαλών τ᾽ αὐτοῦ τὰ ἄλφιτα οὕτω
φέρων ὑμῖν παρέθηκα. τὴν δ᾽ ἐξαίρεσιν, ὦ καλέ μου
Οὐλπιανέ, Διονύσιος ὁ κωμῳδιοποιὸς ἐν τοῖς Ὁμω-
νύμοις τῷ δράματι οὕτως εἴρηκε ποιήσας τινὰ μάγει-
ρον πρὸς τοὺς μαθητὰς διαλεγόμενον· |

d   ἄγε δὴ Δρόμων νῦν, εἴ τι κομψὸν ἢ σοφὸν
    ἢ γλαφυρὸν οἶσθα τῶν σεαυτοῦ πραγμάτων,
    φανερὸν πόησον τοῦτο τῷ διδασκάλῳ.
    νῦν τὴν ἀπόδειξιν τῆς τέχνης αἰτῶ σ᾽ ἐγώ.
    εἰς πολεμίαν ἄγω σε· θαρρῶν κατάτρεχε.
    ἀριθμῷ διδόασι τὰ κρέα καὶ τηροῦσί σε·
    τακερὰ ποήσας ταῦτα καὶ ζέσας σφόδρα
    τὸν ἀριθμὸν αὐτῶν, ὡς λέγω σοι, σύγχεον.
    ἰχθὺς ἁδρὸς πάρεστι· τἀντός ἐστι σά.
    κἂν τέμαχος ἐκκλίνῃς τι, καὶ τοῦτ᾽ ἐστὶ σόν, |
e   ἕως ἂν ἔνδον ὦμεν· ὅταν ἔξω δ᾽, ἐμόν.
    ἐξαιρέσεις καὶ τἄλλα τἀκόλουθ᾽ ὅσα
    οὔτ᾽ ἀριθμὸν οὔτ᾽ ἔλεγχον ἐφ᾽ ἑαυτῶν ἔχει,
    περικόμματος δὲ τάξιν ἢ θέσιν φέρει,
    εἰς αὔριον σε κἀμὲ ταῦτ᾽ εὐφρανάτω.

---

[78] Sc. (unless Athenaeus or his source has garbled the recipe)
to the outside of the baking-shell, thus heating its interior, where
the pig was.

baking-shell, and roasted it by applying the fire,[78] aiming to neither burn it nor have it still be raw when I took it out. Once the skin was roasted, I guessed that the other half must be done as well; so I removed the barley-groats from it, and brought it and served it to you without further ado. But as for the word *exairesis* ("offal"), my good Ulpian, the comic poet Dionysius in his play *Men Who Shared a Name* (fr. 3) represents a cook having a conversation with his students, and says the following:

> Come on now, Dromo! If you've got any subtlety,
> cleverness, or elegance in you,
>   show it to your teacher;
> I'm asking you to demonstrate your technique.
> I'm leading you into enemy territory; boldly lay it
>   waste!
> Suppose they count the chunks of meat as they hand
>   them over, and keep an eye on you;
> make them tender by stewing them intensely,
> and confuse the count the way I've described for you!
> Suppose there's a big fish; its guts are yours!
> And if you swipe a slice of the meat, that's yours
>   too—
> as long as we're inside the house. Once we're outside,
>   it's mine!
> As for the offal (*exaireseis*) and the other parts that
>   go with them,
> which can't be counted or checked,
> and have the rank and station of trimmings,
> tomorrow they can make us both happy.

ATHENAEUS

λαφυροπώλῃ παντάπασι μεταδίδου,
τὴν πάροδον ἵν᾽ ἔχῃς τῶν θυρῶν εὐνουστέραν.
τί δεῖ λέγειν με πολλὰ πρὸς συνειδότα;
ἐμὸς εἶ μαθητής, σὸς δ᾽ ἐγὼ διδάσκαλος.
μέμνησο τῶνδε καὶ βάδιζε δεῦρ᾽ ἅμα. |

f Πάντων οὖν ἡμῶν ἐπαινεσάντων τὸν μάγειρον ἐπί
τε τῷ ἑτοίμῳ τῶν λεγομένων καὶ τῇ τῆς τέχνης περι-
εργίᾳ ὁ καλὸς ἡμῶν ἑστιάτωρ Λαρήνσιος, καὶ πόσῳ
κάλλιον, ἔφη, τὰ τοιαῦτα ἐκμανθάνειν τοὺς μαγείρους
ἢ ἅπερ παρά τινι τῶν πολιτῶν ἡμῶν, ὃς ὑπὸ πλούτου
καὶ τρυφῆς τοὺς τοῦ θαυμασιωτάτου Πλάτωνος δια-
λόγους ἠνάγκαζεν ἐκμανθάνοντας τοὺς μαγείρους φέ-
382 ροντάς τε τὰς λοπάδας ἅμα λέγειν, "εἷς, δύο, τρεῖς· ||
ὁ δὲ δὴ τέταρτος ἡμῖν, ὦ φίλε Τίμαιε, ποῦ τῶν χθὲς
μὲν δαιτυμόνων, τὰ νῦν δ᾽ ἑστιατόρων;" ἔπειτ᾽ ἄλλος
ἀπεκρίνατο, "ἀσθένειά τις αὐτῷ ξυνέπεσεν, ὦ Σώκρα-
τες." διεξήρχοντό τε τοῦ διαλόγου τὰ πολλὰ τὸν
τρόπον τοῦτον, ὡς ἄχθεσθαι μὲν τοὺς εὐωχουμένους,
ὑβρίζεσθαι δὲ τὸν πάνσοφον ἐκεῖνον ἄνθρωπον
ὁσημέραι, καὶ διὰ τοῦτο πολλοὺς τῶν καθαρείων
ἐξόμνυσθαι τὰς παρ᾽ ἐκείνῳ ἑστιάσεις. οἱ δὲ ἡμέτεροι
οὗτοι ἅμα ἴσως ταῦτ᾽ ἐκμανθάνοντες οὐκ ὀλίγην ὑμῖν
θυμηδίαν παρέχουσιν. καὶ ὁ παῖς ἐπὶ τῇ μαγειρικῇ |
b σοφίᾳ ἐπαινεθείς, τί τοιοῦτον εὑρήκασιν, ἔφη, ἢ
εἰρήκασιν οἱ πρὸ ἐμοῦ; ἢ ἐπὶ μετρίους ἐμαυτὸν ἄγω οὐ

[79] The slave whose job it was to guard the door (and who is

By all means give the dealer in plunder[79] a share,
so you can get through the door with less worry.
Why should I make a long speech to someone who
    knows what I'm thinking?
You're my pupil, and I'm your teacher.
Remember my advice, and come along here with me.

We all accordingly applauded the cook for the virtuos-
ity with which he spoke and for his technical brilliance, and
our noble host Larensius said: How much better it is
for cooks to learn material like this by heart than what went
on in the house of one of my fellow-citizens, who was so
rich and addicted to luxury that he used to force his cooks
to memorize the dialogues of the marvellous Plato! And
when they brought in the casserole-dishes, he would make
them say (*Ti.* 17a): "One, two, three—my good Timaeus,
where is our fourth dinner-guest from yesterday, these
men who are now our hosts?" And then another cook
would answer: "He got sick, Socrates." They made their
way through much of the dialogue this way, and the result
was that the people attending the feast got bored and the
brilliant individual responsible was insulted on a daily basis; as a consequence, many sophisticated people swore off
attending his banquets. But my servants here, I trust, supply you with a fair amount of enjoyment when they memorize this material. And the slave, having been applauded
for his culinary sophistication, remarked: What have my
predecessors invented or said that was like this? Or am I
comparing myself to average individuals by not bragging

here assumed to be engaged in systematically looting the house)?
or the dog?

μεγαλαυχούμενος ἐπ' ἐμαυτῷ; καίτοι καὶ ὁ πρῶτος
τῶν τὸν Ὀλυμπίασιν ἀγῶνα ἀναδησαμένων Κόροιβος
ὁ Ἠλεῖος μάγειρος ἦν καὶ οὐχ οὕτως ὠγκύλλετο ἐπὶ
τῇ τέχνῃ ὡς ὁ παρὰ Στράτωνι μάγειρος ἐν τῷ Φοινι-
κίδῃ, περὶ οὗ τοιαῦτα λέγει ὁ μεμισθωμένος·

   σφίγγ' ἄρρεν', οὐ μάγειρον, εἰς τὴν οἰκίαν |
c   εἴληφ'. ἁπλῶς γὰρ οὐδὲ ἕν, μὰ τοὺς θεούς,
   ὧν ἂν λέγῃ συνίημι· καινὰ ῥήματα
   πεπορισμένος πάρεστιν. ὡς εἰσῆλθε γάρ,
   εὐθύς μ' ἐπηρώτησε προσβλέψας μέγα·
   "πόσους κέκληκας μέροπας ἐπὶ δεῖπνον; λέγε."
   "ἐγὼ κέκληκα Μέροπας ἐπὶ δεῖπνον; χολᾷς.
   τοὺς δὲ Μέροπας τούτους με γινώσκειν δοκεῖς;
   οὐδεὶς παρέσται· τοῦτο γὰρ, νὴ τὸν Δία, |
d   ἔστι κατάλοιπον, Μέροπας ἐπὶ δεῖπνον καλεῖν."
   "οὐδ' ἄρα παρέσται δαιτυμὼν οὐδεὶς ὅλως;"
   "οὐκ οἴομαί γε. Δαιτυμών;" ἐλογιζόμην·
   "ἥξει Φιλῖνος, Μοσχίων, Νικήρατος,
   ὁ δεῖν', ὁ δεῖνα." κατ' ὄνομ' ἀνελογιζόμην·
   οὐκ ἦν ἐν αὐτοῖς οὐδὲ εἷς μοι Δαιτυμών.

---

80 The sense of the sentence is difficult, and something may be
missing from the text.

81 Moretti #1 (victorious in the foot-race in 776 BCE); cf. Call.
fr. 541 Pfeiffer; Paus. 5.8.6; 8.26.3–4.   82 A very early papyrus (P.Cair. 65445; 3rd century BCE) preserves portions of a considerably shorter version of this speech (lacking Athenaeus' verses
9–10, 12, 16, 22, 26–33, but offering six additional verses at the
end). The additional verses in Athenaeus are in general leadenly

about my accomplishments?[80] In fact the first person to
wear a victor's garland at the Olympic games, Coroebus of
Elis,[81] was a cook, and he did not get as high and mighty
about his profession as the cook in Strato's *Phoenicides* (fr.
1.1–47), whose employer says the following about him:[82]

> I've taken a male Sphinx into my house,
> not a cook! By the gods, I don't understand
> a single word he says. He's here with a full supply
> of strange vocabulary. The minute he entered the
>   house,
> he immediately looked me in the eye and asked in a
>   loud voice:
> "How many *meropes*[83] have you invited to dinner?
>   Tell me!"
> "I've invited the Meropes to dinner? You're crazy;
> do you think I know these Meropes?
> None of them'll be there. By Zeus, this is
> too much—inviting Meropes to dinner!"
> "So isn't a single *daitumōn*[84] going to be present?"
> "I don't think so. Daitumōn?" I did a count:
> "Philinus is coming, and Moschion, and Niceratus,
> and so-and-so, and so-and-so." I went through them,
>   name by name;
> I didn't have a single Daitumōn among them.

dull, and what he preserves is apparently an expansion of the text
by someone who liked the dialogue and wanted to make it longer.
Verses 1–4 are also preserved at 14.659b–c, where they are assigned to Philemo.   [83] An obscure poetic word generally
treated as meaning "people".

[84] Homeric vocabulary ("guest"), although always used in epic
in the plural.

"οὐδεὶς παρέσται," φημί. "τί λέγεις; οὐδὲ εἷς;"
σφόδρ' ἠγανάκτησ' ὥσπερ ἠδικηβημένος
εἰ μὴ κέκληκα Δαιτυμόνα. καινὸν πάνυ. |

e   "οὐδ' ἄρα θύεις ἐρυσίχθον';" "οὐκ," ἔφην, "ἐγώ."
"βοῦν δ' εὐρυμέτωπον;" "οὐ θύω βοῦν, ἄθλιε."
"μῆλα θυσιάζεις ἆρα;" "μὰ Δί', ἐγὼ μὲν οὔ,
οὐδέτερον αὐτῶν, προβάτιον δ'." "οὔκουν," ἔφη,
"τὰ μῆλα πρόβατα;" "<μῆλα πρόβατ';> οὐ
       μανθάνω,
<μάγειρε,> τούτων οὐδέν, οὐδὲ βούλομαι. |

f   ἀγροικότερός εἰμ', ὥσθ' ἁπλῶς μοι διαλέγου."
"Ὅμηρον οὐκ οἶσθας λέγοντα;" "καὶ μάλα
ἐξῆν ὃ βούλοιτ', ὦ μάγειρ', αὐτῷ λέγειν.
ἀλλὰ τί πρὸς ἡμᾶς τοῦτο, πρὸς τῆς Ἑστίας;"
"κατ' ἐκεῖνον ἤδη πρόσεχε καὶ τὰ λοιπά μοι."
"Ὁμηρικῶς γὰρ διανοεῖ μ' ἀπολλύναι;"
"οὕτω λαλεῖν εἴωθα." "μὴ τοίνυν λάλει
οὕτω παρ' ἔμοιγ' ὤν." "ἀλλὰ διὰ τὰς τέτταρας ‖

383   δραχμὰς ἀποβάλω," φησί, "τὴν προαίρεσιν;
τὰς οὐλοχύτας φέρε δεῦρο." "τοῦτο δ' ἐστὶ τί;"
"κριθαί." "τί οὖν, ἀπόπληκτε, περιπλοκὰς λέγεις;"
"πηγὸς πάρεστι;" "πηγός; οὐχὶ λαικάσει,

---

85 I.e. an ox.

86 "Sheep"; but the word can also mean "apples" (hence the confusion that follows).

87 A Homeric term for the barley-grains that were mixed with salt (see below) and thrown at the victim or the altar before a sacrifice was made.

"No Daitumōn'll be there," I said. "What do you
      mean? Not one?"
He got real irritated, as if I was treating him badly
because I hadn't invited Daitumōn. Very strange.
"Aren't you sacrificing an earthbreaker[85]?" "No, I'm
      not," I said.
"A cow with a wide forehead?" "I'm not sacrificing a
      cow, you bastard."
"So you're making a sacrifice of *mēla*[86]?" "No, by
      Zeus, I'm not.
Neither of these—just a little sheep." "Aren't *mēla*
      sheep?",
he said. "Apples are sheep? I don't understand
any of this, cook," I said, "and I don't want to.
I'm quite unsophisticated; so talk to me very simply."
"Don't you realize that Homer uses these terms?"
        "He could
talk however he wanted to, cook!
But what does that have to do with us, by Hestia?"
"In the future, if you don't mind, keep him in mind."
"Are you planning to Homer me to death?"
"That's how I'm used to talking." "Well, don't talk
that way when you're around *me*!" "For four
      drachmas",
he says, "I'm supposed to abandon my principles?
Bring the *oulochutai*[87] here!" "What's that?"
"Barley." "So why, you idiot, do you talk in riddles?"
"Is any *pēgos*[88] available?" "*Pēgos*? Suck me!

[88] A rare adjective meaning "solid", applied to the sea's wave at
Od. 5.388; 23.235, hence the cook's—extremely odd—use of the
word as a metonym for "salt".

ἐρεῖς σαφέστερόν θ' ὃ βούλει μοι λέγειν;"
"ἀτάσθαλός γ' εἶ, πρέσβυ," φησ'. "ἅλας φέρε·
τοῦτ' ἔστι πηγός. ἀλλὰ δεῖξον χέρνιβα."
παρῆν· ἔθνεν, ἔλεγεν ἄλλα ῥήματα
τοιαῦθ' ἅ, μὰ τὴν Γῆν, οὐδὲ εἷς ἤκουσεν ἄν, |
b   μίστυλλα, μοίρας, δίπτυχ', ὀβελούς· ὥστε με
τῶν τοῦ Φιλίτα λαμβάνοντα βυβλίων
σκοπεῖν ἕκαστα⁸ τί δύναται τῶν ῥημάτων.
πλὴν ἱκέτευον αὐτὸν ἤδη μεταβαλεῖν
ἀνθρωπίνως λαλεῖν τε. τὸν δ' οὐκ ἂν ταχὺ
ἔπεισεν ἡ Πειθώ, μὰ τὴν Γῆν, οἶδ' ὅτι.

περίεργον δ' ἐστὶν ὡς ἀληθῶς τὸ πολὺ τῶν μαγείρων
γένος περί τε τὰς ἱστορίας καὶ τὰ ὀνόματα. λέγουσι
c   γοῦν αὐτῶν οἱ λογιώτατοι "γόνυ κνήμης | ἔγγιον" καὶ
† "περιῆλθον Ἀσίαν καὶ Εὐρώπην" †. ἐπιτιμῶντες δέ
τινί φασιν μὴ δεῖν τὸν Οἰνέα Πηλέα ποιεῖν. ἐγὼ δὲ ἕνα
τῶν ἀρχαίων μαγείρων τεθαύμακα πείρᾳ τῆς τέχνης

---

⁸ The papyrus has ἕκαστον (printed by K–A).

---

⁸⁹ "Chunks of meat (for spitting), portions (of roasted meat),
double-folded (fat for burning the gods' share), spits"; all words
reminiscent of, if not necessarily restricted to Homeric scenes of
sacrifice and feasting.

⁹⁰ A reference to the *Miscellaneous Glosses* of the late 4th-
century BCE poet and scholar Philetas of Cos (= Philet. test. 15
Sbardella).

⁹¹ I.e. "Charity begins at home" *vel sim.*; cf. Gow on Theoc.
16.18.

Say what you want to say to me more clearly!"
"You're an ignoramus, old man," he says. "Bring me
     some salt;
that's what *pēgos* is. Let me see a basin."
I had one. He made the sacrifice and used countless
     other
words of a sort no one, by Earth, could have
     understood:
mistulla, moires, diptucha, obeloi.[89] The result was
     that
I would've had to get Philetas' books
to figure out what all the vocabulary he used meant.[90]
Except now I began to beg him to take a different
     tack
and talk like a human being. I doubt Persuasion
     herself would
ever have convinced him, by Earth; I'm sure of that.

It is striking how genuinely devoted to serious research
and matters of vocabulary the majority of cooks are. The
most learned ones, at any rate, say (Zenob. 3.2): "The knee
is closer than the shin"[91] and (Archestr. fr. 2 Olson–Sens;
unmetrical)[92] † "I made a tour of Asia and Europe." † And
when they criticize someone, they say that you shouldn't
make Oineus into Peleus (Strömberg p. 29).[93] I myself
gained respect for one of the ancient cooks by trying a
technique he pioneered and having success with it. Alexis

92 Cf. 3.116f; 7.278d, 326d.
93 For Oineus, see 2.35a–b with n.; Peleus was the father of
Achilleus. But the real point of the names is that they allow for a
pun on *oinos* ("wine") and *pēlos* ("mud").

ἧς εἰσηγήσατο ἀπολαύσας. παράγει δ᾿ αὐτὸν Ἄλεξις
ἐν Λέβητι λέγοντα τάδε·

(A.) ἧψέ μοι δοκεῖ
πνικτόν † τιν᾿ ὄψον † δελφάκειον. (Γλ.) ἡδύ γε.
(A.) ἔπειτα προσκέκαυκε. (Γλ.) μηδὲν φροντίσῃς·
ἰάσιμον γὰρ τὸ πάθος ἐστί. (A.) τῷ τρόπῳ; |
d (Γλ.) ὄξος λαβὼν ἦν εἰς λεκάνην τιν᾿ ἐγχέας
ψυχρόν (ξυνιεῖς;) εἶτα θερμὴν τὴν χύτραν
εἰς τοὖξος ἐνθῇς· διάπυρος γὰρ οὖσ᾿ ἔτι
ἕλξει δι᾿ αὑτῆς νοτίδα καὶ ζυμουμένη
ὥσπερ κίσηρις λήψεται διεξόδους
σομφάς, δι᾿ ὧν τὴν ὑγρασίαν ἐκδέξεται·
τὰ κρεάδι᾿ ἔσται τ᾿ οὐκ ἀπεξηραμμένα,
ἔγχυλα δ᾿ ἀτρεμεὶ καὶ δροσώδη τὴν σχέσιν.
(A.) Ἄπολλον, ὡς ἰατρικῶς. ὦ Γλαυκία, |
e ταυτὶ ποήσω. (Γλ.) καὶ παρατίθει γ᾿ αὐτά, παῖ,
ὅταν παρατιθῇς (μανθάνεις;) ἐψυγμένα.
ἀτμὶς γὰρ οὕτως οὐχὶ προσπηδήσεται
ταῖς ῥισίν, ἀλλ᾿ ἄνω μάλ᾿ εἶσι † καταφαγών †
(A.) πολλῷ γ᾿ ἀμείνων, ὡς ἔοικας, ἦσθ᾿ ἄρα
λογογράφος ἢ μάγειρος. (Γλ.) ὃ λέγεις οὐ
λέγεις,
τέχνην δ᾿ ὀνειδίζεις.

---

94 This may be not the second speaker's name, but a sarcastic
reference to him as if he were the famous physician (Berve i #228)
who failed to save the life of Alexander the Great's general
Hephaestion (Arr. *An.* 7.14.4; Plu. *Alex.* 72; thus Webster).

in *The Cauldron* (fr. 129) brings him onstage saying the following:

(A.) Apparently he was stewing
† some dish † casseroled pork. (Glaucias) Very nice.
(A.) Then he burned it. (Glaucias) Don't worry;
the problem's fixable. (A.) How?
(Glaucias) If you get some vinegar and pour it into a
          pan—
cold vinegar, understand!—and then put the cookpot
in the vinegar, while it's hot. Because if it's still red-
          hot,
it'll draw the moisture into its walls; and as it bubbles
          and hisses,
it'll develop porous outlets, like a
sieve; and the moisture will be absorbed through
          them.
Then the pieces of meat won't be dried out;
instead, they'll be perfectly juicy and in a moist
          condition.
(A.) Apollo! You sound like a doctor! That's what
I'll do, Glaucias![94] (Glaucias) And when you serve
          them,
slave, serve them cold, understand?
That way the steam won't attack
their nostrils; it'll go straight up † gobbling down. †
(A.) Well, you're apparently a much better
speech-writer than you are a cook. (Glaucias) You
          don't mean what you're saying;
you're disparaging my profession.

καὶ μαγείρων μὲν ἅλις, ἄνδρες δαιταλεῖς, μὴ καί τις
αὐτῶν τὰ ἐκ Δυσκόλου Μενάνδρου βρενθυόμενος |
f λαρυγγίσῃ τάδε·

οὐδὲ εἷς
μάγειρον ἀδικήσας ἀθῷος διέφυγεν.
ἱεροπρεπής πώς ἐστιν ἡμῶν ἡ τέχνη.

ἐγὼ δ᾽ ὑμῖν, κατὰ τὸν ἥδιστον Δίφιλον,

παρατίθημ᾽ ὁλοσχερῆ
ἄρν᾽ ἐς μέσον σύμπτυκτον, ὠνθυλευμένον,
χοιρίδια περιφόρινα κρομβώσας ὅλα·
δούρειον ἐπάγω χῆνα τῷ φυσήματι. ‖

384   Χήν. περιενεχθέντων δὲ τούτων καὶ ἄλλων[9] περιτ-
τῶς ἐσκευασμένων ἔφη τις, οἱ χῆνες σιτευτοί. καὶ ὁ
Οὐλπιανός, ὁ δὲ σιτευτὸς χὴν παρὰ τίνι; πρὸς ὃν ὁ
Πλούταρχος· Θεόπομπος μὲν ἔφη ὁ Χῖος ἐν ταῖς
Ἑλληνικαῖς κἂν τῇ τρισκαιδεκάτῃ δὲ τῶν Φιλιππικῶν
Ἀγησιλάῳ τῷ Λάκωνι εἰς Αἴγυπτον ἀφικομένῳ πέμ-
ψαι τοὺς Αἰγυπτίους χῆνας καὶ μόσχους σιτευτούς.
καὶ Ἐπιγένης δ᾽ ὁ κωμῳδιοποιὸς ἐν Βάκχαις φησίν·

ἀλλ᾽ εἴ τις ὥσπερ χῆνα † ἔτρεφέν μοι λαβὼν
σιτευτόν. |

[9] ἄλλων χηνῶν A: χηνῶν del. Olson: ἄλλων ὀρνίθων Gulick

[95] Further material of a similar sort is collected at 9.403e–6b.

But enough of cooks, banqueters![95] We don't want one of them to feel proud and shout the following lines from Menander's *The Difficult Man* (644–6):

> No one
> escapes unpunished when he injures a cook;
> our profession has a sort of sanctity to it.

But to quote the delightful Diphilus (fr. 90), I

> am serving you an entire
> sheep trussed to a skewer and stuffed;
> I roasted whole piglets with the skin still on them;
> and I'm adding a goose blown up as big as the
>   Wooden Horse.

Goose. After these had been served, along with other carefully prepared dishes, someone said: The geese were fattened. Ulpian responded: In what author is the phrase "a fattened goose" attested? Plutarch answered him: Theopompus of Chios in his *History of Greece* and in Book XIII of his *History of Philip* (*FGrH* 115 F 106a)[96] claimed that when Agesilaus of Sparta arrived in Egypt, the Egyptians sent him fattened geese and calves. The comic poet Epigenes as well says in *Bacchants* (fr. 2):

> But if someone took and † fed for me just like a
>   fattened
> goose.

96 Cf. 14.616d (another anecdote about Agesilaus in Egypt), 657a–b, 676c–d (two additional references to the same passage in Theopompus). Agesilaus II of Sparta (Poralla #9; *c*.445–359 BCE) came to Egypt to assist Nectanebis II ("Tachos") as a mercenary in 361, and died before returning home.

b καὶ Ἀρχέστρατος ἐν τῷ πολυθρυλήτῳ ποιήματι·

σιτευτὸν καὶ χηνὸς ὁμοῦ σκεύαζε νεοττόν,
ὀπτὸν ἁπλῶς καὶ τόνδε.

σὺ δὲ ἡμῖν, ὦ Οὐλπιανέ, δίκαιος εἶ λέγειν, ὁ περὶ
πάντων πάντας ἀπαιτῶν, ποῦ μνήμης ἠξίωται παρὰ
τοῖς ἀρχαίοις τὰ πολυτελῆ ταῦτα τῶν χηνῶν ἥπατα.
ὅτι γὰρ χηνοβοσκοὺς οἴδασι μάρτυς Κρατῖνος ἐν
Διονυσαλεξάνδρῳ λέγων·

< . . . > χηνοβοσκοί, βουκόλοι.

Ὅμηρος δὲ καὶ θηλυκῶς καὶ ἀρσενικῶς εἴρηκεν·

αἰετὸς ἀργὴν χῆνα φέρων.

καί· |

c ὡς ὅδε χῆν᾽ ἥρπαξ᾽ ἀτιταλλομένην ἐνὶ οἴκῳ.

καί·

χηνές μοι κατὰ οἶκον ἐείκοσι πυρὸν ἔδουσιν
ἐξ ὕδατος.

χηνείων δὲ ἡπάτων (περισπούδαστα δὲ ταῦτα κατὰ
τὴν Ῥώμην) μνημονεύει Εὔβουλος ἐν Στεφανοπώλισι
λέγων οὕτως·

Also Archestratus in his notorious poem (fr. 58 Olson–Sens = *SH* 189):

Along with that, prepare a fattened gosling,
which should also be simply roasted.

But since you are always asking us all questions on every subject, Ulpian, you are the right person to tell us where in the ancient authors these expensive goose-livers have been deemed worthy of mention. For Cratinus in *Dionysalexandros* (fr. 49) proves that they were familiar with goose-farmers, when he says:

goose-farmers, cowherds.

Homer uses the word as both masculine and feminine (*Od*. 15.161):

an eagle carrying a white (fem.) goose.

And (*Od*. 15.174):

As this (bird) snatched a goose that was being raised
(fem.) in our house.

And (*Od*. 19.536–7):[97]

I have 20 geese in my house that eat grain
away from the water.

Eubulus mentions goose-livers—they are much sought-after in Rome—in *Female Garland-Vendors* (fr. 99), saying the following:

[97] The gender of the word "goose" is not apparent in the verses quoted here; but the same birds are referred to with masculine forms at *Od*. 19.539–40, 552–3.

εἰ μὴ σὺ χηνὸς ἧπαρ ἢ ψυχὴν ἔχεις.

Ἦσαν δὲ καὶ ἡμίκραιραι πολλαὶ δελφάκων. μνη-
μονεύει δ᾽ αὐτῶν Κρώβυλος ἐν Ψευδυποβολιμαίῳ· |

d   εἰσῆλθεν ἡμίκραιρα τακερὰ δέλφακος.
ταύτης μὰ τὸν Δί᾽ οὐχὶ κατέλιπον, λέγω,
οὐδέν.

μετὰ δὲ ταῦτα ὁ καλούμενος κρεωκάκκαβος· κρέα δ᾽
ἐστὶ ταῦτα συγκεκομμένα μεθ᾽ αἵματος καὶ λίπους ἐν
ζωμῷ γεγλυκασμένῳ. λέγειν δὲ οὕτως Ἀριστοφάνης
ὁ γραμματικὸς Ἀχαιούς, ὁ Μυρτίλος ἔφη. Ἀντικλεί-
δης δ᾽ ἐν ὀγδόῳ Νόστων, ἐν δείπνῳ, φησίν, μελλόντων
Χίων ὑπ᾽ Ἐρυθραίων ἐξ ἐπιβουλῆς ἀναιρεῖσθαι μα-
θών τις τὸ μέλλον γίνεσθαι ἔφη· |

e   ὦ Χῖοι, πολλὴ γὰρ Ἐρυθραίους ἔχει ὕβρις·
φεύγετε δειπνήσαντες ὑὸς κρέα μηδὲ μένειν
βοῦν.

ἀναβράστων δὲ κρεῶν μνημονεύει Ἀριστομένης Γόη-
σιν οὕτως· < . . . > καὶ ὄρχεις ἤσθιον, οὓς καὶ νεφροὺς
ἐκάλουν. Φιλιππίδης ἐν τῇ Ἀνανεώσει Γναθαίνης τῆς
ἑταίρας τὸ γαστρίμαργον ἐμφανίζων λέγει·

ἔπειτ᾽ ἐπὶ τούτοις πᾶσιν ἧκ᾽ ὄρχεις φέρων |

---

98 The quotation has fallen out of the text.

unless you've got the liver or soul of a goose.

There were also many split pigs'-heads. Crobylus mentions these in *Falsely Supposititious* (fr. 6):

Tender split pigs'-heads came in.
By Zeus, I didn't leave a bit of that pig behind,
I'm telling you.

These were followed by the so-called *kreokakkabos*; this is chunks of meat that have been chopped up and combined with blood and fat in a sweetened broth. Myrtilus said: The grammarian Aristophanes (fr. 351 Slater) (claims) that the inhabitants of Achaea use this term. Anticleides says in Book VIII of the *Homecomings* (*FGrH* 140 F 5): When the Chians were about to be murdered treacherously by the Erythraeans at a dinner party, someone who learned what was going to happen said:

Chians! The Erythraeans are involved in something
    truly outrageous!
So flee after you eat the pork, and don't wait for the
    beef!

Aristomenes mentions boiled meat in *Religious Quacks* (fr. 8), as follows: . . . [98] They also ate testicles, which they referred to as kidneys.[99] Philippides in his *Rejuvenation* (fr. 5) brings out the gluttony of the courtesan Gnathaena[100] when he says:

Then, after all these dishes, (a slave) came carrying a
    large number

[99] A bad deduction from the quotation that follows. For eating testicles, cf. 9.395f.

f   πολλούς. τὰ μὲν οὖν γύναια τἆλλ᾽ ἠκκίζετο,
   ἡ δ᾽ ἀνδροφόνος Γνάθαινα γελάσασα < . . . >
   "καλοί γε", φησίν, "οἱ νεφροί, νὴ τὴν φίλην
   Δήμητρα." καὶ δύ᾽ ἁρπάσασα κατέπιεν,
   ὥσθ᾽ ὑπτίους ὑπὸ τοῦ γέλωτος καταπεσεῖν.

εἰπόντος δὲ καὶ ἄλλου ἥδιστα γεγονέναι καὶ τὸν μετὰ
385 ὀξυλιπάρου ἀλεκτρυόνα ‖ ὁ φιλεπιτιμητὴς Οὐλπιανὸς
κατακείμενος μόνος, ὀλίγα δ᾽ ἐσθίων καὶ τηρῶν τοὺς
λέγοντας ἔφη· ὀξυλίπαρον δὲ τί ἐστι; πλὴν εἰ μὴ καὶ
κόττανα ἡμῖν καὶ λέπιδιν, τὰ πάτριά μου νόμιμα
βρώματα, ὀνομάζειν μέλλετε. καὶ ὅς, Τιμοκλῆς, ἔφη, ὁ
κωμικὸς ἐν Δακτυλίῳ μέμνηται τοῦ ὀξυλιπάρου λέγων
οὕτως·

     γαλεοὺς καὶ βατίδας ὅσα τε τῶν γενῶν
  ἐν ὀξυλιπάρῳ τρίμματι σκευάζεται.

ἀκρολιπάρους δέ τινας ἀνθρώπους κέκληκεν Ἄλεξις ‖
b   ἐν Πονήρᾳ οὕτως·

    ἀκρολίπαροι, τὸ δ᾽ ἄλλο σῶμ᾽ ὑπόξυλον.

παρατεθέντος δέ ποτε καὶ ἰχθύος μεγάλου ἐν ὀξάλμῃ
καὶ εἰπόντος τινὸς ἥδιστον εἶναι ὀψάριον πᾶν τὸ ἐν

---

100 Cf. 9.371f n. A number of additional anecdotes about
Gnathaena are preserved in Book 13.
101 Syria; cf. 3.119a–b (where the mysterious foods in question
are referred to as *kotta* and *lepidi*).

of testicles. The other women pretended not to
    notice them,
but the bloodthirsty Gnathaena laughed
and said, "What nice kidneys, by the beloved
Demeter!" And she grabbed two and gobbled them
    down,
making everyone collapse on their backs in laughter.

Someone else observed that chicken is delicious when
served in vinegar-and-oil sauce (*oxuliparon*), and Ulpian,
who loved to criticize others and was lying on a couch all by
himself, not eating much and keeping an eye on the participants in the conversation, said: What is vinegar-and-oil
sauce? Unless perhaps you intend to identify this for us as
kottana and *lepidis*, which are the traditional foods of my
native country.[101] The other man replied: The comic author Timocles in *The Ring* (fr. 3)[102] mentions vinegar-and-
oil sauce, saying the following:

> dogfish and skate and whatever types
> are prepared in vinegar-and-oil sauce.

Alexis in *The Miserable Woman* (fr. 197) refers to certain
people as *akroliparoi*[103], as follows:

> *akroliparoi*; but the rest of their body has a wooden
>   core.

At one point a large fish was served in vinegar-brine
(*oxalmē*), and someone remarked that any little fish
(*opsarion*) served in vinegar-brine was delicious. Ulpian,

---

102 Quoted also at 7.295b.
103 Literally "oily on top".

ὀξάλμη παρατιθέμενον, συναγαγὼν τὰς ὀφρῦς ὁ τὰς
ἀκάνθας ἀγείρων Οὐλπιανός, ποῦ κεῖται, ἔφη, ὀξάλμη; ‹ . . . › ὀψάριον γὰρ παρ’ οὐδενὶ τῶν ζώντων
λεγόμενον οἶδα. οἱ μὲν οὖν πολλοὶ μακρὰ χαίρειν
εἰπόντες αὐτῷ ἐδείπνουν, τοῦ Κυνούλκου τὰ ἐξ Αὐρῶν
Μεταγένους ἀναφωνήσαντος· |

c   ἀλλ’, ὠγαθέ, δειπνῶμεν ‹ . . . › κἄπειτά με πάντ’
        ἐπερωτᾶν
    ὅ τι ἂν βούλῃ· νῦν γὰρ πεινῶν δεινῶς πώς εἰμ’
        ἐπιλήσμων.

καὶ ὁ Μυρτίλος ἡδέως πως συναπογραφόμενος αὐτῷ,
ἵνα μηδενὸς μεταλαμβάνῃ, ἀλλὰ πάντα λαλῇ, ἔφη·
Κρατῖνος ἐν Ὀδυσσεῦσιν εἴρηκε τὴν ὀξάλμην διὰ
τούτων·

    ἀνθ’ ὧν πάντας ἑλὼν ὑμᾶς ἐρίηρας ἑταίρους, |
d   φρύξας χἀψήσας κἀπανθρακίσας κὠπτήσας,
    εἰς ἅλμην τε καὶ ὀξάλμην κᾆτ’ ἐς σκοροδάλμην
    χλιαρὸν ἐμβάπτων, ὃς ἂν ὀπτότατός μοι
        ἁπάντων
    ὑμῶν φαίνηται, κατατρώξομαι, ὦ στρατιῶται.

καὶ Ἀριστοφάνης Σφηξίν·

                    ἀποφυσήσας
    εἰς ὀξάλμην ἔμβαλε θερμήν.

ὀψάριον δὲ τῶν μὲν ζώντων ἡμεῖς λέγομεν, ἀτὰρ καὶ
Πλάτων ἐπὶ τοῦ ἰχθύος ἐν Πεισάνδρῳ· |

who always picked out the thorniest problems,[104] scowled and said: Where is the word *oxalmē* attested? . . . Because I know that no one alive today uses the word *opsarion*. Most of the group told him to stop pestering them, and began to eat their dinner. But Cynulcus shouted out the passage from Metagenes' *Breezes* (fr. 2):

> Please, good sir; let's eat our dinner first, and then
>   ask me anything
> you like. Because at the moment I'm really hungry,
>   and thus rather forgetful.

Myrtilus happily lent him support, in order to keep Ulpian from enjoying any of the food and force him to do nothing but talk, and said: Cratinus in *Odysseuses* (fr. 150) uses the word *oxalmē*, in the following passage:[105]

> In return, I'll take all you noble companions;
> fry you, stew you, bake you on the coals, and roast
>   you;
> dip you in brine-sauce and vinegar-brine (*oxalmē*),
>   and then
> in warm garlic-brine; and whoever out of all of you
> looks the most well-cooked, soldiers—I'll eat him!

Also Aristophanes in *Wasps* (330–1):

>   Blow off the ash
> and dip me in hot vinegar-brine (*oxalmē*)!

I am a living person who uses the word *opsarion*. But so does Plato in *Peisander* (fr. 102), referring to a fish:

104 Cf. 3.97c–d with n.
105 The Cyclops is speaking.

e   (A.) ἤδη φαγών τι πώποθ᾽, οἷα γίγνεται,
ὀψάριον ἔκαμες, καὶ προσέστη τοῦτό σοι;
(B.) ἔγωγε, πέρυσι κάραβον φαγών.

Φερεκράτης Αὐτομόλοις·

< . . . > τοὐψάριον τουτὶ παρέθηκέ τις ἡμῖν.

Φιλήμων Θησαυρῷ·

οὐκ ἔστ᾽ ἀληθὲς † παραλογίσασθ᾽ οὐδ᾽ ἔχειν
ὀψάρια χρηστά.

Μένανδρος Καρχηδονίῳ·

ἐπιθυμιάσας τῷ Βορέᾳ <λιβαν>ίδιον
ὀψάριον οὐδὲν ἔλαβον· ἑψήσω φακῆν. |

f   καὶ ἐν Ἐφεσίῳ·

                  ἐπ᾽ ἀρίστῳ λαβὼν
ὀψάριον.

εἶτ᾽ ἐπιφέρει·

τῶν ἰχθυοπωλῶν ἀρτίως τις τεττάρων
δραχμῶν ἐτίμα κωβιούς.

Ἀναξίλας Ὑακίνθῳ Πορνοβοσκῷ·

ἐγὼ δ᾽ ἰὼν ὀψάριον ὑμῖν ἀγοράσω.

καὶ μετ᾽ ὀλίγα·

(A.) Did you ever eat a little fish (*opsarion*)—it
happens—and then get sick and have it turn on you?
(B.) Absolutely; last year, when I ate a crayfish.

Pherecrates in *Deserters* (fr. 32):

Someone served us this little fish (*opsarion*) here.

Philemon in *The Treasure* (fr. 32):

It isn't true † to cheat someone or to have
good little fish (*opsaria*).

Menander in *The Carthaginian* (fr. 226 Koerte–Thier-
felder):

Even though I burned some incense to the North
        Wind,
I didn't catch a single little fish (*opsarion*); I'll cook
    lentil-soup.

And in *The Ephesian* (fr. 151, encompassing both quotations):

                    after buying a little fish (*opsarion*)
for lunch.

Then he continues:

Just now one of the fish-sellers was offering
gobies for four drachmas.

Anaxilas in *Hyacinthus the Pimp* (fr. 28, encompassing
both quotations):

I'll go buy you a little fish (*opsarion*).

And shortly thereafter:

σκεύαζε, παῖ, τοὐψάριον ἡμῖν.

τὸ δὲ ἐν Ἀναγύρῳ Ἀριστοφάνους·

εἰ μὴ παραμυθῇ μ᾽ ὀψαρίοις ἑκάστοτε,

ἀντὶ τοῦ προσοψήμασιν ἀκούομεν. καὶ γὰρ Ἄλεξις ‖
386 ἐν Παννυχίδι περιθεὶς μαγείρῳ τὸν λόγον φησίν·

        (Α.) θερμοτέροις † χαιρεοις † αἰεὶ
τοῖς ὀψαρίοις ἢ τὸ μέσον ἢ κατωτέρω;
(Β.) κατωτέρω; τί λέγεις δέ; (Α.) ποταπὸς οὑτοσὶ
ἄνθρωπος; οὐκ ἐπίστασαι ζῆν. ψυχρά σοι
ἅπαντα παραθῶ; (Β.) μηδαμῶς. (Α.) ζέοντα δέ;
(Β.) Ἄπολλον. (Α.) οὐκοῦν τὸ μέσον ἔστω. (Β.)
        δηλαδή.
(Α.) τοῦθ᾽ ἕτερος οὐδεὶς τῶν ὁμοτέχνων μου
        ποεῖ. |
b (Β.) οὐκ οἴομ᾽ οὐδ᾽ ἄλλ᾽ οὐδὲν ὧν σὺ νῦν ποεῖς.
(Α.) ἐγὼ δ᾽ † ἐρῶ † τοῖς γὰρ ἑστιωμένοις
τὸν καιρὸν ἀποδίδωμι τῆς συγκράσεως.
(Β.) σὺ πρὸς θεῶν, ἔθυσας < . . . > τὸν ἔριφον,
μὴ κόπτ᾽ ἔμ᾽, ἀλλὰ τὰ κρέα. (Α.) παῖδες,
        παράγετε.
ὀπτάνιόν ἐστιν; (Β.) ἔστι. (Α.) καὶ κάπνην ἔχει;
(Β.) δῆλον ὅτι. (Α.) μή μοι "δῆλον"· ἀλλ᾽ ἔχει
        κάπνην; |

Slave! Fix the little fish (*opsarion*) for us!

In the line from Aristophanes' *Anagyrus* (fr. 45):

unless you constantly reassure me with *opsaria*,

I take the word to be used to mean "side-dishes". Alexis in *The All-Night Festival* (fr. 177), in fact, gives the word to a cook and says:

> (A.) † You'd prefer † always your *opsaria*
> on the hot side, or in the middle, or lower?
> (B.) Lower? What do you mean? (A.) Where's this guy
> from? You don't know how to live! Should I serve you
> everything cold? (B.) Absolutely not. (A.) Boiling hot?
> (B.) Apollo![106] (A.) So you want your food in the middle. (B.) Obviously.
> (A.) Nobody else in my business does that.
> (B.) That or anything else you're doing at the moment, I imagine!
> (A.) I'll † tell; † because I offer the guests
> the opportunity for some variety.
> (B.) By the gods, . . . you killed the kid;
> butcher the meat, not me! (A.) Slaves! Bring my equipment!
> Is an oven set up? (B.) It is. (A.) Does it have a smoke-hole?
> (B.) Of course. (A.) Don't give me this "Of course."
> Does it have a smoke-hole?

---

106 The oath is frequently used to express shock, horror, disbelief, or the like; cf. 9.378c; 10.417b.

c   (Β.) ἔχει. (Α.) κακόν, εἰ τύφουσαν. (Β.) ἀπολεῖ μ᾽
οὑτοσί.

ταῦτά σοι παρ᾽ ἡμῶν τῶν ζώντων, ὀλβιογάστορ Οὐλπιανέ, ἀπεμνημόνευσα. καὶ σὺ γάρ, ὡς ἔοικε, μετ᾽
ἐμοῦ κατὰ τὸν Ἄλεξιν οὐδενὸς ἐμψύχου μεταλαμ-
βάνεις, ὅς φησιν ἐν Ἀτθίδι τάδε·

ὁ πρῶτος εἰπὼν ὅτι σοφιστὴς οὐδὲ εἷς
ἔμψυχον οὐδὲν ἐσθίει, σοφός τις ἦν.
ἐγὼ γὰρ ἥκω νῦν ἀγοράσας οὐδὲ ἓν |
d   ἔμψυχον. ἰχθῦς ἐπριάμην τεθνηκότας
μεγάλους· κρεᾴδι᾽ ἀρνός ἐστι πίονος
οὐ ζῶντος· οὐχ οἷόν τε γάρ. τί ἄλλο; ναί,
ἡπάτιον ὀπτὸν προσέλαβον. τούτων ἐὰν
δείξῃ τις ἢ φωνήν τι ἢ ψυχὴν ἔχον,
ἀδικεῖν ὁμολογῶ καὶ παραβαίνειν τὸν νόμον.

ἐπὶ τούτοις οὖν ἔασον ἡμᾶς δειπνεῖν. ἰδοὺ γάρ, ἕως
πρὸς σὲ διαλέγομαι, καὶ οἱ φασιανικοὶ παραπεπλεύ-
e   κασιν ὑπεριδόντες ἡμᾶς διὰ τὴν ἄκαιρόν | σου γλωσ-
σαλγίαν. ἀλλ᾽ ἢν ἐμοὶ εἴπῃς, ἔφη ὁ Οὐλπιανός,
διδάσκαλε Μυρτίλε, ὁ ὀλβιογάστωρ σοι πόθεν καὶ εἰ
φασιανικῶν τις ὀρνίθων μέμνηται τῶν παλαιῶν, ἐγώ
σοι

ἦρι μάλ᾽ (οὐκ) Ἑλλήσποντον ‹ . . . › πλεούσας,

ἀλλ᾽ εἰς τὴν ἀγορὰν πορευθεὶς ὠνήσομαι φασιανικόν,
ὃν συγκατέδομαί σοι. καὶ ὁ Μυρτίλος, ἐπὶ ταύταις,

(B.) It does. (A.) It's no good, if it's full of smoke. (B.)
　　This guy's gonna be the death of me!

I recalled these passages for you, Ulpian of the blessed
belly (*olbiogastōr*), from "we the living". For you are apparently like me, in that you eat nothing that is alive—to
quote Alexis, who says the following in *Atthis* (fr. 27):

> The first person to say that no one with an education
> eats anything that's alive was a wise man indeed.
> I've come back now, and I didn't buy anything
> that was living. I did purchase some large dead
> fish. And there are some cuts of a fat lamb,
> although it wasn't alive; because that's impossible.
> 　　What else? Yeah,
> I also got a roasted liver. If anyone can
> point to a single one of these items that's got a voice
> 　　or a soul,
> I'll admit I'm in the wrong and breaking the law.

So after all this—allow us to eat our dinner! Because,
look—while I have been talking to you, your inopportune
garrulity has made the pheasants sail by and ignore us![107]
Ulpian said: If you tell me, Myrtilus the pedant, where you
got the word *olbiogastōr* and whether any ancient authority mentions pheasants, it won't be a matter of my (*Il.*
9.360)

> sailing in early spring (to) the Hellespont

for you. But I *will* make a trip to the marketplace and buy a
pheasant, which we can eat together. Myrtilus responded:

[107] Cf. 9.387e with n.

ἔφη, ταῖς συνθήκαις λέγω. τοῦ μὲν ὀλβιογάστορος
Ἄμφις μέμνηται ἐν Γυναικομανίᾳ οὑτωσὶ λέγων·

Εὐρύβατε κνισολοιχέ, < . . . > οὐκ ἔσθ᾽ ὅπως
f   οὐκ ὀλβιογάστωρ | εἶ σύ.

φασιανικοῦ δὲ ὄρνιθος ὁ ἥδιστος Ἀριστοφάνης ἐν
δράματι Ὄρνισιν. Ἀττικοὶ δ᾽ εἰσὶ δύο πρεσβῦται ὑπὸ
ἀπραγμοσύνης πόλιν ζητοῦντες ἐν ᾗ κατοικήσουσιν
ἀπράγμονα· καὶ αὐτοῖς ἀρέσκει ὁ βίος ὁ μετ᾽ ὀρνίθων.
ἔρχονται οὖν ὡς τοὺς ὄρνιθας καὶ αἰφνίδιον αὐτοῖς
ἐπιπτάντος ἑνὸς τῶν ὀρνίθων ἀγρίου τὴν ὄψιν, δείσαν-
τες ἑαυτοὺς παραμυθούμενοι λέγουσι τά τ᾽ ἄλλα καὶ
τάδε· ||

387   (Θε.) ὁδὶ δὲ δὴ τίς ἐστιν ὄρνις; οὐκ ἐρεῖς;
       (Ευ.) ἐπικεχοδὼς ἔγωγε Φασιανικός.

καὶ τὸ ἐν Νεφέλαις δὲ ἐπὶ τῶν ὀρνίθων ἔγωγε ἀκούω
καὶ οὐκ ἐπὶ ἵππων ὡς πολλοί·

       τοὺς φασιανοὺς οὓς τρέφει Λεωγόρας.

δύναται γὰρ ὁ Λεωγόρας καὶ ἵππους τρέφειν καὶ
ὄρνεις φασιανούς· κωμῳδεῖται γὰρ ὁ Λεωγόρας ὡς
γαστρίμαργος ὑπὸ Πλάτωνος ἐν Περιαλγεῖ. Μνη-

I am answering your questions on those terms. Amphis uses the term *olbiogastōr* in *Crazy about Women* (fr. 10), where he says the following:

> Eurybates, you fat-licker; there's no way
> you're not *olbiogastōr*.

As for the pheasant (*phasianikos ornis*), the delightful Aristophanes (mentions it) in his play *Birds*. Two old men from Attica are tired of complications, and are looking for a city where they can settle that has none; and life with the birds appeals to them. They accordingly go visit the birds, and suddenly a wild-looking bird flies toward them. They are frightened and try to encourage one another by saying various things, including the following (Ar. *Av.* 67–8):[108]

> (Slave-bird) And what sort of a bird is this one? Tell me!
> (Euelpides) I'm a Phasian (*phasianikos*) shit-foot.

I also take the use of the word in *Clouds* (109) to refer to birds rather than to horses, as many authorities do:[109]

> the *phasianoi* that Leogoras is raising.

For Leogoras[110] could be raising either horses or pheasants; because Plato in *Perialges* (fr. 114.2) makes fun of

---

[108] The first speaker is in fact not one of the Athenian visitors, but the Hoopoe's doorkeeper.　　[109] The *scholia* to *Clouds* (perhaps drawing on Aristarchus) contain very similar material, including a more complete version of the passage from Plato Comicus alluded to below.　　[110] Leogoras (*PAA* 605075), a wealthy man mentioned several other times in comedy in the late 420s/early 410s BCE, was the father of the orator Andocides.

σίμαχος δ᾽ ἐν Φιλίππῳ (εἷς δὲ καὶ οὗτός ἐστι ⟨τῶν⟩[10]
τῆς μέσης κωμῳδίας ποιητῶν) φησί·

      καὶ τὸ λεγόμενον, |

b   σπανιώτατον πάρεστιν ὀρνίθων γάλα,
   καὶ φασιανὸς ἀποτετιλμένος καλῶς.

Θεόφραστος δὲ ὁ Ἐρέσιος, Ἀριστοτέλους μαθητής, ἐν
τῇ τρίτῃ Περὶ Ζῴων μνημονεύων αὐτῶν οὑτωσί πως
λέγει· ἐστὶ δὲ καὶ τοῖς ὄρνισι τοιαύτη διαφορά· τὰ μὲν
γὰρ βαρέα καὶ μὴ πτητικά, καθάπερ ἀτταγήν, πέρδιξ,
ἀλεκτρυών, φασιανός, εὐθὺς βαδιστικὰ καὶ δασέα.
καὶ Ἀριστοτέλης ἐν ὀγδόῃ Ζῴων Ἱστορίας γράφει
c τάδε· εἰσὶ δὲ τῶν ὀρνίθων οἱ μὲν κονιστικοί, | οἱ δὲ
λοῦνται, οἱ δὲ οὔτε κονιστικοὶ οὔτε λοῦνται. ὅσοι δὲ μὴ
πτητικοί, ἀλλ᾽ ἐπίγειοι, κονιστικοί, οἷον ἀλεκτορίς,
πέρδιξ, ἀτταγήν, φασιανός, κορυδαλλός. μνημονεύει
δ᾽ αὐτῶν καὶ Σπεύσιππος ἐν δευτέρῳ Ὁμοίων. φασιανὸν δὲ οὗτοι κεκλήκασιν αὐτὸν καὶ οὐ φασιανικόν.
Ἀγαθαρχίδης δ᾽ ὁ Κνίδιος ἐν τῇ τετάρτῃ καὶ τριακοστῇ τῶν Εὐρωπιακῶν περὶ τοῦ Φάσιδος ποταμοῦ
τὸν λόγον ποιούμενος γράφει καὶ ταῦτα· πλῆθος δ᾽
ὀρνίθων τῶν καλουμένων φασιανῶν φοιτᾷ τροφῆς
χάριν πρὸς τὰς ἐκβολὰς τῶν στομάτων. Καλλίξενος
d δ᾽ | ὁ Ῥόδιος ἐν τετάρτῃ Περὶ Ἀλεξανδρείας διαγρά-

10 add. Musurus

294

him for being a glutton. Mnesimachus (another Middle Comic poet) says in *Philip* (fr. 9):

> There's bird's milk,
> which is said to be the rarest food there is,
> and a nicely plucked pheasant (*phasianos*).

Theophrastus of Eresus, who was Aristotle's student, mentions them in Book III of *On Animals* (fr. 371 Fortenbaugh) and says something along the following lines: Birds fall into the following groups: some are heavy and do not depend primarily on their wings, such as the francolin, partridge, chicken (*alektruōn*), and pheasant (*phasianos*), and are able to walk and covered with down as soon as they hatch. Aristotle writes the following in Book VIII of the *Inquiry into Animals* (633ª29–ᵇ2): Some birds dust themselves; some bathe in water; and some neither dust themselves nor bathe in water. Those that do not depend primarily on their wings, but travel on the ground, dust themselves, for example the chicken (*alektoris*), partridge, francolin, pheasant (*phasianos*), and lark. Speusippus also mentions them in Book II of *Similar Things* (fr. 25 Tarán). These authorities refer to the bird as a *phasianos*, not a *phasianikos*. Agatharchides of Cnidus in Book XXXIV of his *History of Europe* (*FGrH* 86 F 15) writes the following in the course of his discussion of the Phasis River: Enormous numbers of the birds known as *phasianoi* come to feed at the river's mouths. Callixenus of Rhodes in Book IV of *On Alexandria* (*FGrH* 627 F 2d), describing the procession put on by the King Ptolemy known as Philadelphus,[111]

ATHENAEUS

φων τὴν γενομένην πομπὴν ἐν Ἀλεξανδρείᾳ Πτολεμαίου τοῦ Φιλαδέλφου καλουμένου βασιλέως ὡς μέγα
θαῦμα περὶ τῶν ὀρνίθων τούτων οὕτως γράφει· εἶτα
ἐφέροντο ἐν ἀγγείοις ψιττακοὶ καὶ ταῷ καὶ μελεαγρί-
δες καὶ φασιανοὶ καὶ ὄρνιθες Αἰθιοπικοὶ πλήθει πολλοί. Ἀρτεμίδωρος δὲ ὁ Ἀριστοφάνειος ἐν ταῖς ἐπιγρα-
e φομέναις Ὀψαρτυτικαῖς Γλώσσαις καὶ Πάμφιλος | ὁ
Ἀλεξανδρεὺς ἐν τοῖς Περὶ Ὀνομάτων καὶ Γλωσσῶν
Ἐπαίνετον παρατίθεται λέγοντα ἐν τῷ Ὀψαρτυτικῷ
ὅτι ὁ φασιανὸς ὄρνις τατύρας καλεῖται. Πτολεμαῖος δ᾽
ὁ Εὐεργέτης ἐν δευτέρῳ Ὑπομνημάτων τέταρόν φησιν
ὀνομάζεσθαι τὸν φασιανὸν ὄρνιν. τοσαῦτά σοι περὶ
τῶν φασιανικῶν ὀρνίθων ἔχων λέγειν, οὓς ἐγὼ διὰ σὲ
ὥσπερ οἱ πυρέσσοντες περιφερομένους εἶδον. σὺ δὲ
κατὰ τὰς συνθήκας ἂν μὴ αὔριον ἀποδῷς τὰ ὡμολο-
γημένα, οὐκ ἐξαπατήσεως δημοσίᾳ σε γράψομαι, |
f ἀλλὰ τὸν Φᾶσιν οἰκήσοντα ἀποπέμψω, ὡς Πολέμων ὁ
περιηγητὴς Ἴστρον τὸν Καλλιμάχειον συγγραφέα
εἰς τὸν ὁμώνυμον κατεπόντου ποταμόν.

Ἀτταγᾶς. Ἀριστοφάνης Πελαργοῖς·

ἀτταγᾶς ἥδιστον ἕψειν ἐν ἐπινικίοις κρέας.

---

111 Ptolemy II (reigned 285–246 BCE). Athenaeus preserves a
long extract from Callixenus' account of the procession at 5.196a–
203b; the section quoted here is found at 5.201b.

112 Cf. 1.5b with n. The Aristophanes in question is the grammarian Aristophanes of Byzantium, not the Athenian comic poet.

writes the following about these birds, which he treats as a great marvel: Then came an enormous number of parrots, peacocks, guinea-fowl, pheasants (*phasianoi*), and various Ethiopian birds, carried in cages. Aristophanes' student Artemidorus in his work entitled *Culinary Vocabulary*,[112] along with Pamphilus of Alexandria in his *On Names and Vocabulary* (fr. XXXIII Schmidt), cites Epaenetus as saying in his *Art of Cooking* that the pheasant (*phasianos ornis*) is referred to as a *taturas*[113]. But Ptolemy Euergetes in Book II of the *Commentaries* (*FGrH* 234 F 2b)[114] claims that the pheasant (*phasianos ornis*) is called a *tetaros*. This is what I can tell you about pheasants (*phasianikoi ornithes*), which—thanks to you—I saw going in circles around me, just as happens to people who are running a fever.[115] And if tomorrow you fail to offer me what we agreed on in our compact,[116] I have no intention of indicting you in the public courts for deceiving the people. Instead, I will send me off to the Phasis[117] as a colonist, in the same way the travel-writer Polemon (fr. LIV* Preller) wanted to drown Callimachus' student (*FGrH* 334 T 6), the prose-author Istrus, in the river that shared his name.

Francolin. Aristophanes in *Storks* (fr. 448):

Francolin-meat is quite delicious to stew at a victory
   celebration.

[113] A Median word, eventually adopted into Persian. Cf. Diggle on Thphr. *Char.* 5.9.   [114] Quoted at 14.654b–c.
[115] Cf. 6.245f (a *bon mot* by Lark, whence presumably Myrtilus has drawn his inspiration); 9.386d.
[116] Cf. 9.386e.
[117] Punning on the word for "pheasant" (*phasianos/phasianikos ornis*).

Ἀλέξανδρος δ᾽ ὁ Μύνδιός φησιν ὅτι μικρῷ μὲν μείζων
ἐστὶ πέρδικος, ὅλος δὲ κατάγραφος τὰ περὶ τὸν νῶτον,
κεραμεοῦς τὴν χρόαν, ὑποπυρρίζων μᾶλλον. θηρεύεται δ᾽ ὑπὸ κυνηγῶν διὰ τὸ βάρος καὶ τὴν τῶν πτερῶν
βραχύτητα. ἐστὶ δὲ κονιστικὸς πολύτεκνός τε καὶ
388   σπερμολόγος. Σωκράτης ‖ δ᾽ ἐν τῷ Περὶ Ὅρων καὶ
Τόπων καὶ Πυρὸς καὶ Λίθων, ἐκ τῆς Λυδίας μετακο-
μισθέντες, φησίν, εἰς Αἴγυπτον οἱ ἀτταγαῖ καὶ ἀφε-
θέντες εἰς τὰς ὕλας ἕως μέν τινος ὄρτυγος φωνὴν
ἀφίεσαν, ἐπεὶ δὲ τοῦ ποταμοῦ κοίλου ῥυέντος λιμὸς
ἐγένετο καὶ πολλοὶ τῶν κατὰ τὴν χώραν ἀπώλλυντο,
οὐ διέλιπον σαφέστερον τῶν παίδων τῶν τρανοτάτων
ἕως νῦν λέγοντες "τρὶς τοῖς κακούργοις κακά."
συλληφθέντες δὲ οὐ μόνον οὐ τιθασεύονται, ἀλλ᾽ οὐδὲ
φωνὴν ἔτι ἀφιᾶσιν· ἐὰν δὲ ἀφεθῶσι, φωνήεντες πάλιν
γίγνονται. μνημονεύει αὐτῶν Ἱππῶναξ οὕτως· |

b   οὐκ ἀτταγᾶς τε καὶ λαγοὺς καταβρύκων.

καὶ Ἀριστοφάνης ἐν Ὄρνισιν· ἐν δ᾽ Ἀχαρνεῦσιν καὶ
ὡς πλεοναζόντων αὐτῶν ἐν τῇ Μεγαρικῇ. περισπῶσι
δ᾽ οἱ Ἀττικοὶ παρὰ τὸν ὀρθὸν λόγον τοὔνομα· τὰ γὰρ
εἰς -ας λήγοντα ἐκτεταμένον ὑπὲρ δύο συλλαβὰς ὅτε
ἔχει τὸ ᾱ παραλῆγον, βαρύτονά ἐστιν, οἷον ἀκάμας,
Σακάδας, ἀδάμας. λεκτέον δὲ καὶ ἀτταγαῖ καὶ οὐχὶ
ἀτταγῆνες.

---

[118] Quoted again at 14.645c, along with two additional verses.
[119] The reference is in fact to Boeotia; Athenaeus (or his

Alexander of Myndus (fr. I.7 Wellmann) reports that (the francolin) is slightly larger than a partridge; has markings that cover its back; and is terracotta-colored and rather reddish. Dogs are used to hunt it, because it is heavy and has short wings. It dusts itself, lays a large number of eggs, and eats seeds. Socrates says in his *On Borders, Places, Fire, and Stones* (Socrates of Cos fr. 17, *FHG* iv.499–500): When francolins were imported into Egypt from Lydia and released in the woods, they produced a quail's cry for a while. But ever since the river's flow diminished, and a famine resulted and many of the inhabitants of the country died, they have never up to the present day stopped saying, more clearly than the most articulate children: "Troubles three times for the troublemakers!" Not only is it impossible to tame them if they are captured, but they stop producing any sound; once released, however, they recover their voice. Hipponax (fr. 37.1 Degani)[118] mentions them, as follows:

> eating no francolins or hares.

Also Aristophanes in *Birds* (249, 761); and in *Acharnians* (875) he alludes to their being abundant in Megarian territory.[119] Attic authors accent the word with a circumflex,[120] contrary to the correct rule; because words that are longer than two syllables and end in *-as* are barytone, if they have an *alpha* in the penult, for example *akámas* ("untiring"), *Sakádas*,[121] and *adámas* ("adamant"). In the plural, *attagai* rather than *attagēnes* should be used.

---

source) has confused the Boeotian trader with the Megarian who precedes him onstage.   [120] Sc. on the ultima, ἀτταγᾶς.
    [121] A personal name; cf. 13.610c with n.

ATHENAEUS

Πορφυρίων. ὅτι καὶ τούτου Ἀριστοφάνης μέμνηται
δῆλον. Πολέμων δ' ἐν πέμπτῳ τῶν Πρὸς Ἀντίγονον |
c καὶ Ἀδαῖον πορφυριωνά φησι τὸν ὄρνιν διαιτώμενον
κατὰ τὰς οἰκίας τὰς ὑπάνδρους τῶν γυναικῶν τηρεῖν
πικρῶς καὶ τοιαύτην ἔχειν αἴσθησιν ἐπὶ τῆς μοιχευο-
μένης, ὥσθ' ὅταν τοῦθ' ὑπονοήσῃ προσημαίνει τῷ
δεσπότῃ, ἀγχόνῃ τὸ ζῆν περιγράψας. οὐ πρότερόν τε,
φησίν, τροφῆς μεταλαμβάνει, εἰ μὴ περιπατήσει τόπον τινὰ ἐξευρὼν ἑαυτῷ ἐπιτήδειον· μεθ' ὃ κονισάμε-
νος λούεται, εἶτα τρέφεται. Ἀριστοτέλης δὲ σχιδανό-
ποδά φησιν αὐτὸν εἶναι ἔχειν τε χρῶμα κυάνεον,
σκέλη μακρά, ῥύγχος ἠργμένον ἐκ τῆς κεφαλῆς φοι-
d νικοῦν, μέγεθος | ἀλεκτρυόνος, στόμαχον δ' ἔχει
λεπτόν· διὸ τῶν λαμβανομένων εἰς τὸν πόδα ταμιεύ-
εται μικρὰς τὰς ψωμίδας. κύπτων[11] δὲ πίνει. πεντα-
δάκτυλός τε ὢν τὸν μέσον ἔχει μέγιστον. Ἀλέξανδρος
δ' ὁ Μύνδιος ἐν δευτέρᾳ Περὶ τῆς τῶν Πτηνῶν Ἱστορίας Λίβυν εἶναί φησι τὸν ὄρνιν καὶ τῶν κατὰ τὴν
Λιβύην θεῶν ἱερόν.

Πορφυρίς. Καλλίμαχος δ' ἐν τῷ Περὶ Ὀρνίθων
διεστάναι φησὶ πορφυρίωνα πορφυρίδος, ἰδίᾳ ἑκάτερον καταριθμούμενος· τὴν τροφήν τε λαμβάνειν τὸν
e πορφυρίωνα ἐν | σκότῳ καταδυόμενον, ἵνα μή τις
αὐτὸν θεάσηται· ἐχθραίνει γὰρ τοὺς προσιόντας αὐτοῦ τῇ τροφῇ. τῆς δὲ πορφυρίδος καὶ Ἀριστοφάνης ἐν
Ὄρνισιν μνημονεύει. Ἴβυκος δέ τινας λαθιπορφυρί-
δας ὀνομάζει διὰ τούτων·

Purple gallinule. That Aristophanes mentions this bird[122] is obvious. Polemon in Book V of his *Response to Antigonus and Adaeus* (fr. 59 Preller) claims that when the purple gallinule is domesticated, it keeps a close eye on the married women in the house, and feels so strongly about the situation, if one of them is seduced. that when it suspects that this is going on, it informs its master by hanging itself. It does not eat, he says, until it walks around and finds a place it likes; after this it takes a dust-bath and then finally feeds. Aristotle (fr. 255) reports that it has a divided foot; is a dark bluish-black; has long legs and a dark red beak that grows straight out of its head; is the size of a chicken; and has a small gullet, which is why it reduces any food it gets hold of with its feet to crumbs. It bends its head forward to drink. It has five toes, and the one in the middle is the longest. Alexander of Myndus in Book II of *On the Inquiry into Birds* (fr. I.8 Wellmann) reports that the bird is native to Libya and is sacred to the Libyan gods.

Porphuris. Callimachus in his *On Birds* (fr. 414 Pfeiffer) claims that the *porphuris* should be distinguished from the purple gallinule (*porphuriōn*), and catalogues the two separately. In addition, (he claims) that the purple gallinule goes down into dark places to feed, so that no one can see it; because it hates to have anyone come near when it is eating. Aristophanes mentions the *porphuris* in *Birds* (304). Ibycus (*PMG* 317a) refers to *lathiporphurides* in the following passage:

---

[122] Sc. in *Birds* (e.g. 707, 882); why there is no need to demonstrate this is unclear.

---

11 κύπτων Olson: κάπτων ACE

τοῦ μὲν πετάλοισιν ἐπ' ἀκροτάτοις
ἱζάνοισι ποικίλαι αἰολόδειροι
πανέλοπες λαθιπορφυρίδες ‹τε› καὶ
ἀλκυόνες τανυσίπτεροι.

ἐν ἄλλοις δέ φησιν·

αἰεί μ' ὦ φίλε θυμέ τανύπτερος ὡς ὅκα πορφυρίς.

f   Πέρδιξ. τούτων πολλοὶ μὲν | μέμνηνται, ὡς καὶ
Ἀριστοφάνης. τοῦ δὲ ὀνόματος αὐτῶν ἔνιοι συστέλ-
λουσι τὴν μέσην συλλαβήν, ὡς Ἀρχίλοχος·

‹ . . . › πτώσσουσαν ὥστε πέρδικα.

οὕτως καὶ ὄρτυγα καὶ χοίνικα· πολὺ δέ ἐστι τὸ ἐκτεινό-
μενον παρὰ τοῖς Ἀττικοῖς. Σοφοκλῆς Καμικοῖς·

ὄρνιθος ἦλθ' ἐπώνυμος
πέρδικος ἐν κλεινοῖς Ἀθηναίων πάγοις.

Φερεκράτης ἢ ὁ πεποιηκὼς τὸν Χείρωνα·

ἔξεισιν ἄκων δεῦρο πέρδικος τρόπον. ‖

389   Φρύνιχος Τραγῳδοῖς·

---

[123] Sc. in the oblique cases; the forms cited below are all accusative.

[124] A dry measure equivalent to about one quart.

[125] As in the first, third, and fourth quotations that follow; contrast Epich. fr. 73 (below), in which it is short, just as Athenaeus says.

On the highest branches of this tree
sit multicolored wild geese with
bright necks, and *lathiporphurides*, and
    long-winged halcyons.

And elsewhere he says (*PMG* 317b):

Heart, you are always as long-winged for me as when
    a *porphuris* . . .

Partridge. Many authors mention these birds, for example Aristophanes (e.g. *Av.* 297). Some shorten the middle syllable of their name,[123] for example Archilochus (fr. 224):

like a cowering partridge (*perdika*).

Compare *ortuga* ("quail") and *choinika*[124], although the syllable is often long in Attic authors.[125] Sophocles in *Camicians* (fr. 323):

    The man who shares the name of the partridge
in Athens' famous hills arrived.[126]

Pherecrates (fr. 160), or whoever the author of *Cheiron* is:[127]

He'll come out here unwillingly, like a partridge.[128]

Phrynichus in *Tragic Actors* (fr. 55):

[126] Perdix (literally "Partridge") was a brilliant mythical Athenian craftsman whom Daedalus murdered out of jealousy.

[127] For the disputed authorship of the play, see 8.364a n.

[128] The length of the syllable in question is ambiguous in this line.

τὸν Κλεόμβροτόν τε τοῦ
Πέρδικος υἱόν.

τὸ δὲ ζῷον ἐπὶ λαγνείας συμβολικῶς παρείληπται.
Νικοφῶν ἐν Ἐγχειρογάστορσι·[12]

< . . . > τοὺς ἑψητοὺς καὶ τοὺς πέρδικας ἐκείνους.

Ἐπίχαρμος δ' ἐν Κωμασταῖς βραχέως·

σηπίας τ' ἆγον νεούσας πέρδικάς τε πετομένους.

φησὶ δ' Ἀριστοτέλης περὶ τοῦ ζῴου τάδε· ὁ πέρδιξ
ἐστὶ μὲν χερσαῖος, σχιδανόπους, ζῇ δὲ ἔτη πεντεκαίδεκα, ἡ δὲ θήλεια καὶ πλείονα· πολυχρονιώτερα γὰρ ἐν
τοῖς ὄρνισι τῶν ἀρρένων τὰ θήλεα. ἐπῳάζει δὲ καὶ
b ἐκτρέφει | καθάπερ ἡ ἀλεκτορίς. ὅταν δὲ γνῷ ὅτι
θηρεύεται, προελθὼν τῆς νεοττιᾶς κυλινδεῖται παρὰ
τὰ σκέλη τοῦ θηρεύοντος, ἐλπίδα ἐμποιῶν τοῦ συλ-
ληφθήσεσθαι, ἐξαπατᾷ τε ἕως ἂν ἀποπτῶσιν οἱ νεοτ-
τοί· εἶτα καὶ αὐτὸς ἐξίπταται. ἐστὶ δὲ τὸ ζῷον κακόη-
θες καὶ πανοῦργον, ἔτι δὲ ἀφροδισιαστικόν. διὸ καὶ τὰ
ᾠὰ τῆς θηλείας συντρίβει, ἵνα ἀπολαύῃ τῶν ἀφροδισίων. ὅθεν ἡ θήλεια γιγνώσκουσα ἀποδιδράσκουσα
τίκτει. τὰ αὐτὰ ἱστορεῖ καὶ Καλλίμαχος ἐν τῷ Περὶ
c Ὀρνέων. μάχονται δὲ καὶ οἱ | χῆροι αὐτῶν πρὸς

---

[12] ἐν Χειρογάστορσι A

---

[129] *PAA* 577015; otherwise unknown.

and Cleombrotus the
son of Perdix.[129]

The animal is used to symbolize lust.[130] Nicopho in *Men Who Live from Hand to Mouth* (fr. 9):

the stewing-fish and those partridges.

But Epicharmus in *Revellers* (fr. 73) has it short:

They brought both swimming cuttlefish and flying
partridges.

Aristotle has the following to say about the creature (fr. 256): The partridge nests on the ground and has a divided foot. It lives for 15 years, the female even longer; because female birds outlive males. It broods on its eggs and raises its chicks in the same way a hen does.[131] When it realizes that it is being hunted, it leaves its nest and stumbles about under the hunter's feet, making him think that he is going to catch it, and fools him long enough for its chicks to fly away; at that point, it flies away itself. It is a nasty, mischievous creature, and also very fond of sex. It therefore smashes the female's eggs, so that it can enjoy having sex with her. As a result, the female, who recognizes the male's tendencies, runs away from him when she lays her eggs. Callimachus offers the same information in his *On Birds* (fr. 415 Pfeiffer). Male partridges that lack mates fight one

---

[130] An intrusive comment; the line from Nicopho that follows does not support it, but is instead another example of the word with a long *iota* in the penult in an Attic author. But the question of the partridge's alleged fondness for sex is taken up at length below.

[131] The material offered here appears to be a rough summary of Arist. *HA* 613^{b}13–14^{a}1.

ἀλλήλους καὶ ὁ ἡττηθεὶς ὀχεύεται ὑπὸ τοῦ νικήσαν-
τος· Ἀριστοτέλης δέ φησιν ὅτι τὸν ἡττηθέντα πάντες
ἐν μέρει ὀχεύουσιν. ὀχεύουσι δὲ καὶ οἱ τιθασοὶ τοὺς
ἀγρίους. ἐπειδὰν δὲ κρατηθῇ τις ὑπὸ τοῦ δευτέρου,
οὗτος λάθρᾳ ὀχεύεται ὑπὸ τοῦ κρατιστεύσαντος· γίνεται δὲ τοῦτο κατά τινα ὥραν τοῦ ἔτους, ὡς καὶ ὁ
Μύνδιός φησιν Ἀλέξανδρος. νεοττεύουσι δὲ ἐπὶ γῆς οἱ
ἄρρενες καὶ αἱ θήλειαι, διελόμενοι ἕκαστοι οἶκον. ἐπὶ
δὲ τὸν θηρεύοντα πέρδικα ὠθεῖται ὁ τῶν ἀγρίων ἡγε-
d   μὼν μαχούμενος· ἁλόντος δὲ | τούτου ἕτερος ἔρχεται
μαχούμενος. καὶ ὁπόταν μὲν ἄρρην ᾖ <ὁ>[13] θηρεύων,
τοῦτο ποιεῖ· ὅταν δὲ θήλεια ᾖ ἡ θηρεύουσα, ᾄδει ἕως
ἂν ἀπαντήσῃ ὁ ἡγεμὼν αὐτῇ· καὶ οἱ ἄλλοι ἀθροι-
σθέντες ἀποδιώκουσιν ἀπὸ τῆς θηλείας, ὅτι ἐκείνη,
ἀλλ᾽ οὐχ ἑαυτοῖς προσέχει. ὅθεν πολλάκις διὰ ταῦτα
σιγῇ προσέρχεται, ὅπως μὴ ἄλλος ἀκούσας τῆς φωνῆς ἔλθῃ μαχούμενος αὐτῷ· ἐνίοτε δὲ ἡ θήλεια τὸν
ἄρρενα προσιόντα κατασιγάζει. πολλάκις τε ἐπῳάζου-
σα ἐξίσταται, ὅταν προσερχόμενον ἐπαισθάνηται τὸν
e   ἄρρενα τῇ θηρευούσῃ, ὑπομένει τε | ὀχευθῆναι, ἵνα
αὐτὸν ἀποσπάσῃ τῆς θηρευούσης. ἐπὶ τοσοῦτον δ᾽
ἐπτόηνται περὶ τὴν ὀχείαν οἱ πέρδικες καὶ οἱ ὄρτυγες
ὡς εἰς τοὺς θηρεύοντας ἐμπίπτειν καθίζοντας ἐπὶ τῶν
κεφαλῶν. φασὶ δὲ καὶ τοὺς ἀγομένους θήλεις πέρδικας ἐπὶ θήραν, ὁπόταν ἴδωσιν ἢ ὄσφρωνται τῶν ἀρρένων κατ᾽ ἄνεμον στάντων ἢ περιπετομένων, ἐγκύους

13 add. Kaibel ex Aristotele

another, and the loser is buggered by the winner; according to Aristotle (*HA* 614ᵃ2–4), they all take turns bugger-
ing the loser. (*HA* 614ᵃ8–9) Domesticated partridges also
bugger wild ones.[132] When one of them defeats another,
the loser is discreetly buggered by the winner; this happens in all seasons of the year, according to Alexander of
Myndus (fr. I.9 Wellmann). Males and females both nest
on the ground, and each selects its own spot. (*HA* 614ᵃ10–
28, condensed) When a decoy partridge is used, the dominant bird in a flock of wild ones rushes out to fight it; when
it is caught, another bird comes out to fight. This is what
the dominant bird does when the decoy is a male. But
when the decoy is a female, it sings until the dominant bird
comes out to meet her; but the others form a group and
chase him away from the female, because he is paying attention to her, rather than to them. As a result, he often ap-
proaches her without making any noise because of this, to
keep any other male from hearing his song and coming out
to fight him; and sometimes the female silences the male
when he is coming to her. Often, when a female is brooding on a nest, she leaves it when she realizes that a male is
approaching a decoy, and lets him mate with her, so that
she can draw him away from the decoy. Partridges and
quail become so excited by the opportunity to mate that
they fall into the midst of the decoys[133] and sit on their
heads. People also say that when female partridges are
taken to be used as decoys, the moment they see or smell
the males that are standing or flying around upwind, they

[132] Sc. when wild ones are caught and introduced to their
cage.

[133] Or perhaps "the hunters".

ATHENAEUS

γίγνεσθαι, τινὲς δὲ καὶ παραυτίκα τίκτειν. πέτονταί τε
περὶ τὸν τῆς ὀχείας καιρὸν χάσκοντες καὶ τὴν γλῶσ-
σαν ἔξω ἔχοντες οἵ τε θήλεις καὶ οἱ ἄρρενες. Κλέαρ-
χος δ' ἐν τῷ Περὶ τοῦ Πανικοῦ, οἱ στρουθοί, | φησί,
χοἰ πέρδικες, ἔτι δὲ οἱ ἀλεκτρυόνες καὶ οἱ ὄρτυγες
προΐενται τὴν γονὴν οὐ μόνον ἰδόντες τὰς θηλείας,
ἀλλὰ κἂν ἀκούσωσιν αὐτῶν τὴν φωνήν. τούτου δὲ
αἴτιον ἡ τῇ ψυχῇ γινομένη φαντασία περὶ τῶν πλησι-
ασμῶν. φανερώτατον δὲ γίνεται περὶ τὰς ὀχείας, ὅταν
ἐξ ἐναντίας αὐτοῖς θῇς κάτοπτρον· προστρέχοντες
γὰρ διὰ τὴν ἔμφασιν ἁλίσκονταί τε καὶ προΐενται τὸ
σπέρμα, πλὴν τῶν ἀλεκτρυόνων. τούτους δ' ἡ τῆς
ἐμφάσεως αἴσθησις εἰς μάχην προάγεται μόνον.
ταῦτα μὲν ὁ Κλέαρχος. καλοῦνται δ' οἱ πέρδικες ὑπ'
ἐνίων κακκάβαι, ὡς καὶ ὑπ' Ἀλκμᾶνος ‖ λέγοντος
οὕτως·

   Ϝέπη τάδε καὶ μέλος Ἀλκμὰν
   εὗρε γεγλωσσαμέναν
   κακκαβίδων ὄπα συνθέμενος,

σαφῶς ἐμφανίζων ὅτι παρὰ τῶν περδίκων ᾄδειν ἐμάν-
θανε. διὸ καὶ Χαμαιλέων ὁ Ποντικὸς ἔφη τὴν εὕρεσιν
τῆς μουσικῆς τοῖς ἀρχαίοις ἐπινοηθῆναι ἀπὸ τῶν ἐν
ταῖς ἐρημίαις ᾀδόντων ὀρνίθων· ὧν κατὰ μίμησιν
λαβεῖν στάσιν τὴν μουσικήν. οὐ πάντες δ' οἱ πέρδικες, φησί, κακκαβίζουσιν· Θεόφραστος γοῦν ἐν τῷ
Περὶ Ἑτεροφωνίας τῶν Ὁμογενῶν, οἱ Ἀθήνησι, φη-
σίν, ἐπὶ τάδε | πέρδικες τοῦ Κορυδαλλοῦ πρὸς τὸ ἄστυ

308

become pregnant, and some actually lay eggs right on the spot. During mating-season, the females and the males both fly around with their mouths open and their tongues hanging out. Clearchus says in his *On Panic* (fr. 36 Wehrli): Sparrows and partridges, as well as roosters and quail, ejaculate not just when they see the hens, but even if they simply hear them calling. What causes this is the image of mating that forms in their mind. This becomes most obvious during mating-season, if you place a mirror in front of them; because they run up to their reflection, become entranced by it, and ejaculate. Roosters are the exception; when they see their reflection, they merely feel an urge to fight it. Thus Clearchus. Some authorities, however, refer to partridges as *kakkabai*. Alcman (*PMG* 39), for example, says the following:

> Alcman invented these
> verses and articulate song
> by arranging the sound made by partridges
>   (*kakkabides*),

making it clear that the partridges taught him how to sing. This is why Chamaeleon of Pontus (fr. 24 Wehrli) claimed that people in ancient times discovered how to make music by listening to the birds sing in deserted places; music developed through imitating them. But not all partridges, he claims, say "*kakkabē*". Theophrastus, at any rate, says in his *On the Diversity of Sounds Produced by Members of the Same Species* (fr. 355b Fortenbaugh): Athenian partridges on this side of Mt. Corydallus, toward the city,

κακκαβίζουσιν, οἱ δ᾽ ἐπέκεινα τιττυβίζουσιν. Βάσιλις
δ᾽ ἐν τῷ δευτέρῳ τῶν Ἰνδικῶν, οἱ μικροί, φησίν,
ἄνδρες οἱ ταῖς γεράνοις διαπολεμοῦντες πέρδιξιν ὀχή-
ματι χρῶνται. Μενεκλῆς δ᾽ ἐν πρώτῃ τῆς Συναγωγῆς,
οἱ Πυγμαῖοι, φησί, τοῖς πέρδιξι καὶ ταῖς γεράνοις
πολεμοῦσι. τῶν δὲ περδίκων ἐστὶν ἕτερον γένος ἐν
Ἰταλίᾳ ἀμαυρὸν τῇ πτερώσει καὶ μικρότερον τῇ ἕξει,
τὸ ῥύγχος οὐχὶ κινναβάρινον ἔχον. οἱ δὲ περὶ τὴν
Κίρραν πέρδικες ἄβρωτον ἔχουσι τὸ κρέας διὰ τὰς |
c νομάς. οἱ δὲ περὶ τὴν Βοιωτίαν ἢ οὐ διαβαίνουσιν
εἰς τὴν Ἀττικὴν ἢ διαβαίνοντες τῇ φωνῇ διάδηλοι
γίγνονται, καθάπερ προειρήκαμεν. τοὺς δὲ περὶ Πα-
φλαγονίαν γιγνομένους πέρδικάς φησι Θεόφραστος
δύο ἔχειν καρδίας. οἱ δ᾽ ἐν Σκιάθῳ τῇ νήσῳ κοχλίας
ἐσθίουσι. τίκτουσι δ᾽ ἐνίοτε καὶ πεντεκαίδεκα καὶ
ἑκκαίδεκα. πέτονται δὲ ἐπὶ βραχύ, ὥς φησι Ξενοφῶν
ἐν πρώτῳ Ἀναβάσεως γράφων οὕτως· τὰς δὲ ὠτίδας
ἄν τις ταχὺ ἀνιστῇ ἔστι λαμβάνειν· πέτονταί τε γὰρ
d βραχὺ ὥσπερ οἱ πέρδικες | καὶ ταχὺ ἀπαγορεύουσι.
τὰ δὲ κρέα αὐτῶν ἡδέα ἐστί. ἀληθῆ λέγειν φησὶ τὸν
Ξενοφῶντα ὁ Πλούταρχος περὶ τῶν ὠτίδων· φέρεσθαι
γὰρ πάμπολλα τὰ ζῷα ταῦτα εἰς τὴν Ἀλεξάνδρειαν
ἀπὸ τῆς παρακειμένης Λιβύης, τῆς θήρας αὐτῶν τοι-
αύτης γινομένης. μιμητικὸν δέ ἐστι τὸ ζῷον τοῦτο, ὁ
ὦτος, μάλιστα ὧν ἂν ἴδῃ ποιοῦντα ἄνθρωπον. ποιεῖ δ᾽
οὖν ταὐτὰ ὅσα ἂν ἴδῃ τοὺς κυνηγοῦντας πράττοντας.

---

134 For the hostility between Pygmies and cranes, cf. 9.393e–f.

say *"kakkabē"*, while those on the other side say *"tittubē"*. Basilis says in Book II of his *History of India* (*FGrH* 718 F 1): The tiny men who fight the cranes ride on partridge-back. And Menecles says in Book I of his *Collection* (*FGrH* 270 F 7): The Pygmies wage war on the partridges and the cranes.[134] There is a separate species of partridge in Italy that has dark feathers, is smaller in size, and has a beak that is not vermilion-colored. The partridges in Cirrha have inedible flesh because of what they eat. Boeotian partridges either do not cross over into Attica or can be recognized by their call if they do, as I noted earlier.[135] According to Theophrastus (fr. 356 Fortenbaugh), Paphlagonian partridges have two hearts. Those on the island of Sciathus eat snails. They sometimes produce 15 or 16 eggs. They can fly only a short distance, as Xenophon notes in Book I (5.3) of the *Anabasis*, where he writes as follows: If you start up bustards suddenly, you can catch them; because they can only fly a short distance, like partridges, and rapidly grow tired. Their meat is delicious. Plutarch[136] observes that Xenophon is right about bustards; because large numbers of these creatures are brought to Alexandria from the Libyan territory nearby, having been caught in the following way. This creature, the *ōtos*,[137] loves to imitate behavior, especially anything it sees a human being doing,

135 At 9.390a–b.

136 The character Plutarch, who is supposed to be from Alexandria (setting up the observation that follows), rather than the historical author, who was from Chaeronea.

137 Athenaeus (or his source) has become confused: an *ōtos* is a short-eared owl, whereas a bustard (a large terrestrial bird) is an *ōtis*.

ATHENAEUS

οἱ δὲ στάντες αὐτῶν καταντικρὺ ὑπαλείφονται φαρ-
μάκῳ τοὺς ὀφθαλμούς, παρασκευάσαντες ἄλλα φάρ-
e μακα | κολλητικὰ ὀφθαλμῶν καὶ βλεφάρων, ἅπερ οὐ
πόρρω ἑαυτῶν ἐν λεκανίσκαις βραχείαις τιθέασιν. οἱ
οὖν ὦτοι θεώμενοι τοὺς ὑπαλειφομένους τὸ αὐτὸ καὶ
αὐτοὶ ποιοῦσιν ἐκ τῶν λεκανίδων λαμβάνοντες καὶ
ταχέως ἁλίσκονται. γράφει δὲ περὶ αὐτῶν Ἀριστοτέλης οὕτως, ὅτι ἐστὶ μὲν τῶν ἐκτοπιζόντων καὶ σχιδανοπόδων καὶ τριδακτύλων, μέγεθος ἀλεκτρυόνος
μεγάλου, χρῶμα ὄρτυγος, κεφαλὴ προμήκης, ῥύγχος
ὀξύ, τράχηλος λεπτός, ὀφθαλμοὶ μεγάλοι, γλῶσσα
f ὀστώδης, πρόλοβον δ᾽ οὐκ ἔχει. | Ἀλέξανδρος δ᾽ ὁ
Μύνδιος καὶ προσαγορεύεσθαί φησιν αὐτὸν λαγω-
δίαν. φασὶ δ᾽ αὐτὸν καὶ τὴν τροφὴν ἀναμαρυκᾶσθαι
ἥδεσθαί τε ἵππῳ. εἰ γοῦν τις δορὰν ἵππων περιθοῖτο,
θηρεύσει ὅσους ἂν θέλῃ· προσίασι γάρ. ἐν ἄλλοις δὲ
πάλιν φησὶν ὁ Ἀριστοτέλης· ὁ ὦτός ἐστι μὲν παρ-
όμοιος τῇ γλαυκί, οὐκ ἔστι δὲ νυκτερινός. ἔχει τε περὶ
τὰ ὦτα πτερύγια, διὸ καὶ ὦτος καλεῖται· μέγεθος
περιστερᾶς, μιμητὴς ἀνθρώπων· ἀντορχούμενος γοῦν
ἁλίσκεται. ἀνθρωποειδὴς δ᾽ ἐστὶ τὴν μορφὴν καὶ πάντων μιμητὴς ὅσα ἄνθρωπος ποιεῖ. διόπερ καὶ τοὺς
391 ἐξαπατωμένους ῥᾳδίως ‖ ἐκ τοῦ τυχόντος οἱ κωμικοὶ
ὤτους καλοῦσιν. ἐν γοῦν τῇ θήρᾳ αὐτῶν ὁ ἐπιτη-
δειότατος ὀρχεῖται στὰς κατὰ πρόσωπον αὐτῶν, καὶ
τὰ ζῷα βλέποντα εἰς τὸν ὀρχούμενον νευροσπαστεῖ-
ται. ἄλλος δέ τις ὄπισθεν στὰς καὶ λαθὼν συλλαμβάνει τῇ περὶ τὴν μίμησιν ἡδονῇ κατεχομένους. τὸ δ᾽

BOOK IX

and it therefore does exactly what it sees the people who are hunting it doing. They stand in front of the birds and smear an oily substance in their eyes; before they do this, they prepare other compounds that make one's eyes and eyelids stick together, and set them nearby in shallow bowls. The *ōtoi*, at any rate, watch the men smear the first substance in their eyes, and then follow their example, taking what they use out the bowls, and are rapidly caught. Aristotle (fr. 257) writes as follows about them: This is a migratory bird, which has a divided foot and three toes. It is the size of a large chicken and the color of a quail; has an elongated head, a pointed beak, a slender neck, large eyes, and a bony tongue; and lacks a crop. Alexander of Myndus (fr. I.10 Wellmann) claims that it is also referred to as a *lagōdia*. People say that it chews the cud and likes horses; if you wrap a horseskin around yourself, therefore, you can catch as many as you like, because they come right up to you. Elsewhere again Aristotle (fr. 257, continued) says: The short-eared owl resembles the little owl, but is not nocturnal. It also has tufts around its ears (*ōta*), which is why it is referred to as an *ōtos*. It is the size of a pigeon and likes to imitate human beings; it is therefore caught when it imitates someone's dancing. It looks like a human being and imitates anything a person does. As a consequence, the comic poets (adesp. com. fr. 209) refer to individuals who are easily fooled by anyone who comes along as *ōtoi*. When they are being hunted, at any rate, the best dancer stands in front of them and performs, and the birds gawk at him and move around like marionettes. Someone else stands behind them and grabs them before they notice him, because they are so wrapped up in the pleasure they get from

αὐτὸ ποιεῖν λέγουσι καὶ τοὺς σκῶπας· καὶ γὰρ τούτους ὀρχήσει λόγος ἁλίσκεσθαι. μνημονεύει δ᾽ αὐτῶν
Ὅμηρος. γένος τε ὀρχήσεως ἀπ᾽ αὐτῶν καλεῖται
σκὼψ λαβὼν τοὔνομα ἀπὸ τῆς περὶ τὸ ζῷον ἐν τῇ
b κινήσει ποικιλίας. χαίρουσι δὲ οἱ | σκῶπες καὶ ὁμοι-
ότητι καὶ ἀπ᾽ αὐτῶν ἡμεῖς σκώπτειν καλοῦμεν τὸ
συνεικάζειν καὶ καταστοχάζεσθαι τῶν σκωπτομένων
διὰ τὸ τὴν ἐκείνων ἐπιτηδεύειν προαίρεσιν. πάντα δὲ
τὰ τῶν ζῴων εὔγλωττα καὶ διηρθρωμένα ἐστὶ τὴν
φωνὴν καὶ μιμεῖται τοὺς τῶν ἀνθρώπων καὶ τῶν ἄλλων ὀρνίθων ἤχους ὥσπερ ψιττακὸς καὶ κίττα. ὁ δὲ
σκώψ, ὥς φησιν Ἀλέξανδρος ὁ Μύνδιος, μικρότερός
ἐστι γλαυκὸς καὶ ἐπὶ μολυβδοφανεῖ τῷ χρώματι ὑπό-
λευκα στίγματα ἔχει δύο τε ἀπὸ τῶν ὀφρύων παρ᾽
c ἑκάτερον κρόταφον ἀναφέρει | πτερά. Καλλίμαχος δέ
φησι δύο γένη εἶναι σκωπῶν καὶ τοὺς μὲν φθέγγεσθαι, τοὺς δὲ οὔ, διὸ καὶ καλεῖσθαι τοὺς μὲν σκῶπας
αὐτῶν, τοὺς δ᾽ ἀείσκωπας. εἰσὶ δὲ γλαυκοί. ὁ δὲ
Μύνδιος Ἀλέξανδρός φησι τοὺς παρ᾽ Ὁμήρῳ χωρὶς
τοῦ ϛ̄ κῶπας εἶναι, καὶ Ἀριστοτέλη οὕτως αὐτοὺς
ὠνομακέναι. φαίνεσθαί τε τούτους ἀεὶ καὶ μὴ ἐσθί-
εσθαι· τοὺς δ᾽ ἐν τῷ φθινοπώρῳ φαινομένους δύο

---

[138] Cf. 14.629f; Ael. NA 15.28.

[139] A very unlikely etymology; both words may well be connected to skeptomai ("look at, inspect"; Indo-European).

[140] A garbled summary of Arist. HA 617b31–18a6, from which

314

imitation. People claim that the scops owl (*skōps*) acts the same way; the story is that dancing is used to catch them as well. Homer (*Od.* 5.66) mentions them. A dance-style known as the *skōps* gets its name from the variety of movements the creature makes.[138] Scops owls enjoy mimickry, and we get the term *skōptein*, meaning to copy and poke fun of the individuals we are mocking, from them, because we are behaving the way they tend to.[139] All animals with well-developed tongues are capable of producing articulate sounds and imitate the noises human beings and other birds produce; examples are the parrot and the jay. According to Alexander of Myndus (fr. I.11 Wellmann), the scops owl is smaller than the little owl, and has whitish spots on top of its lead-gray color, and two tufts that extend from its brow along each temple. Callimachus (fr. 418 Pfeiffer) claims that there are two varieties of scops owls, and that one produces a call, while the other does not, which is why some of them are referred to as *skōpes*, others as *aeiskōpes*.[140] They have bright eyes. Alexander of Myndus (fr. I.12 Wellmann) claims that the birds mentioned in Homer (*Od.* 5.66) are *kōpes*, without a *sigma*, and that Aristotle also refers to them this way.[141] The birds are seen in all seasons and are not eaten; but those that

the material that follows the quotation from Alexander of Myndus is also drawn.

141 The word (a *hapax legomenon* in Homer) stands at the head of the line at *Od.* 5.66, and either form is thus technically possible. But Alexander is presumably doing nothing more than ascribing unnecessary authority to a minor scribal error he found both there and in his copy of the *Historia Animalium*, and which Athenaeus (or another source) also found in Speusippus (below).

ἡμέραις ἢ μιᾷ, τούτους εἶναι ἐδωδίμους. διαφέρουσι
δὲ τῶν ἀεισκώπων τῷ τάχει[14] καί εἰσι παραπλήσιοι
d τρυγόνι καὶ φάττῃ. καὶ Σπεύσιππος δ' | ἐν δευτέρῳ
Ὁμοίων χωρὶς τοῦ ς̄ κῶπας αὐτοὺς ὀνομάζει. Ἐπί-
χαρμος·

  σκῶπας, ἔποπας, γλαύκας.

καὶ Μητρόδωρος δ' ἐν τῷ Περὶ Συνηθείας ἀντορχου-
μένους φησὶν ἁλίσκεσθαι τοὺς σκῶπας.

Ἐπεὶ δ' ἐν τῷ περὶ τῶν περδίκων λόγῳ ἐμνήσθημεν
ὅτι εἰσὶν ὀχευτικώτατοι, προσιστορήσθω ὅτι καὶ
ἀλεκτρυὼν ἀφροδισιαστικὸν τὸ ὄρνεον. Ἀριστοτέλης
γοῦν φησιν ὅτι τῶν ἀνατιθεμένων ἐν τοῖς ἱεροῖς
ἀλεκτρυόνων τὸν ἀνατεθέντα οἱ προόντες ὀχεύουσι
μέχρι ἂν ἄλλος ἀνατεθῇ· εἰ δὲ μὴ ἀνατεθείη, μάχον-
e ται | πρὸς ἀλλήλους καὶ ὁ ἡττήσας τὸν ἡττηθέντα διὰ
παντὸς ὀχεύει. ἱστορεῖται δὲ ὅτι καὶ ἀλεκτρυὼν εἰσιὼν
οἰανδήποτε θύραν ἐπικλίνει τὸν λόφον καὶ ὅτι τῆς
ὀχείας ἑτέρῳ δίχα μάχης οὐ παραχωρεῖ. ὁ δὲ Θεόφραστος τοὺς ἀγρίους φησὶν ὀχευτικωτέρους εἶναι τῶν
ἡμέρων. λέγει δὲ καὶ τοὺς ἄρρενας εὐθὺς ἐξ εὐνῆς
ἐθέλειν πλησιάζειν, τὰς δὲ θηλείας προβαινούσης
μᾶλλον τῆς ἡμέρας. καὶ οἱ στρουθοὶ δέ εἰσιν ὀχευ-
τικοί· διὸ καὶ Τερψικλῆς τοὺς ἐμφαγόντας φησὶν
f στρουθῶν ἐπικαταφόρους πρὸς ἀφροδίσια | γίνεσθαι.
μήποτε οὖν καὶ ἡ Σαπφὼ ἀπὸ τῆς ἱστορίας τὴν Ἀφρο-

[14] τάχει A: πάχει Aristotle, Aelian

appear in the fall for only a day or two are edible. The latter are faster than *aeiskōpes* and resemble turtledoves or ringdoves. Speusippus in Book II of *Similar Things* (fr. 26 Tarán) also refers to them as *kōpes*, without a *sigma*. Epicharmus (fr. 164):

scops owls, hoopoes, little owls.

Metrodorus in his *On Habit* (*FGrH* 184 F 3) also claims that scops owls are caught when they imitate people who are dancing.

Since I mentioned in the course of my discussion of partridges that they are highly sexed creatures (9.389a), I should also note that the rooster is a randy bird. Aristotle (fr. 259; cf. *HA* 614^{a}7–9), for example, claims that when roosters are dedicated in temples, those that are already there bugger the new rooster until yet another one is dedicated. If no new dedications are made, they fight one another, and the winner always buggers the loser. It is also reported that whenever a rooster enters a door of any kind, it raises its crest, and that no rooster ever lets another one bugger it without a fight. Theophrastus (fr. 381 Fortenbaugh) claims that wild birds are more interested in mating than domesticated birds are. He also says that the males are willing to have sex immediately after they wake up, but that the females become interested as it gets later in the day. Sparrows are also highly sexed; this is why Terpsicles claims that people who eat sparrows are prone to lust.[142] Perhaps, therefore, this is the basis on which Sappho (fr. 1.9–10) reports that Aphrodite's chariot

---

[142] Clearly a second fragment of *On Sex* (cf. 7.325d; 8.337b n.).

δίτην ἐπ᾽ αὐτῶν φησιν ὀχεῖσθαι· καὶ γὰρ ὀχευτικὸν τὸ
ζῷον καὶ πολύγονον. τίκτει γοῦν ὁ στρουθός, ὥς
φησιν Ἀριστοτέλης, καὶ μέχρι ὀκτώ. Ἀλέξανδρος δ᾽
ὁ Μύνδιος δύο γένη φησὶν εἶναι τῶν στρουθῶν, τὸ
μὲν ἥμερον, τὸ δ᾽ ἄγριον· τὰς δὲ θηλείας αὐτῶν
ἀσθενεστέρας τά τ᾽ ἄλλα εἶναι καὶ τὸ ῥύγχος κερατο-
ειδὲς μᾶλλον τὴν χρόαν, τὸ δὲ πρόσωπον οὔτε λίαν
λευκὸν ἐχούσας οὔτε μέλαν. Ἀριστοτέλης δέ φησι
392   τοὺς ἄρρενας τῷ χειμῶνι ἀφανίζεσθαι, διαμένειν ‖ δὲ
τὰς θηλείας, τεκμαιρόμενος ἐκ τῆς χρόας τὴν πιθανό-
τητα· ἀλλάττεσθαι γάρ, ὡς τῶν κοσσύφων καὶ φαλα-
ρίδων, ἀπολευκαινομένων κατὰ καιρούς. Ἠλεῖοι δὲ
καλοῦσι τοὺς στρουθοὺς δειρήτας, ὡς Νίκανδρός
φησιν ὁ Κολοφώνιος ἐν τρίτῳ Γλωσσῶν.

Ὄρτυγες. καθόλου ἐπὶ τῶν εἰς -υξ ληγόντων ὀνομάτων ἐζήτηται τί δή ποτε τῷ αὐτῷ οὐ χρῶνται ἐπὶ
γενικῆς συμφώνῳ τῆς τελευταίας συλλαβῆς τυπωτικῷ
(λέγω δὲ ὄνυξ καὶ ὄρτυξ), τὰ δὲ εἰς ξ ἀρσενικὰ ἁπλᾶ
b   δισσύλλαβα ὅταν τῷ ῡ | παρεδρεύηται, ἔχῃ δὲ τῆς
τελευταίας συλλαβῆς ἄρχον ἕν τι τῶν ἀμεταβόλων ἢ
δι᾽ ὧν ἡ πρώτη συζυγία τῶν βαρυτόνων λέγεται, διὰ
τοῦ κ̄ ἐπὶ γενικῆς κλίνεται, κήρυκος, πέλυκος, Ἔρυ-
κος, Βέβρυκος, ὅσα δὲ μὴ τοῦτον ἔχει τὸν χαρακτῆρα,
διὰ τοῦ ḡ, ὄρτυγος, ὄρυγος, κόκκυγος. σημειῶδες δὲ τὸ

---

143 Singular *ortux* (genitive *ortugos*).
144 I.e. what we would call a nasal or a liquid.
145 I.e. what we would call third-declension labial stems.

is drawn (*ocheisthai*) by sparrows; because the fact is that the bird likes to have sex (*ocheutikon*) and lays many eggs. According to Aristotle (fr. 260), at any rate, the sparrow lays up to eight eggs. Alexander of Myndus (fr. I.14 Wellmann) claims that there are two types of sparrows, the domesticated variety and the wild variety; the females are less powerful overall, and have a beak that is more horn-colored and a face that is neither particularly light nor particularly dark. Aristotle reports that the males disappear in the winter, but the females remain; he deduces this from their coloring, because certain birds (for example blackbirds and coots) change color and become lighter in particular seasons. The inhabitants of Elis refer to sparrows as *deirētai*, according to Nicander of Colophon in Book III of the *Glossary* (fr. 123 Schneider).

Quail.[143] In general, in the case of nouns that end in *-ux*, the question arises as to why they fail to use the same consonant in the genitive to form the final syllable (I refer to the words *onux* ["fingernail"] and *ortux*). As for simple disyllabic masculine nouns that end in a *xi*, when that letter is preceded by an *upsilon* and the final syllable begins with an unchangeable sound[144] or with one of the sounds used to form the so-called first barytone conjugation,[145] the word declines with *kappa* in the genitive: *kērukos* ("herald"), *pelukos* ("ax"), *Erukos*, *Bebrukos*.[146] Nouns that are not of this type, on the other hand, decline with *gamma*: *ortugos* ("quail"), *orugos* ("oryx"), *kokkugos*

---

[146] Formed, respectively, from the nominatives *kērux*, *pelux*, *Erux*, and *Bebrux*. Eryx was a place in western Sicily (cf. 9.394f), while the Bebrykes were an Iberian tribe.

ATHENAEUS

ὄνυχος. καθόλου τε τῇ πληθυντικῇ εὐθείᾳ ἑπομένη ἡ
ἑνικὴ γενικὴ χρῆται τῷ αὐτῷ συμφώνῳ τῆς τελευταίας
τυπωτικῷ, κἂν ἄνευ συμφώνου λέγηται, ὁμοίως. Ἀρι-
c στοτέλης δέ φησιν· ὁ ὄρτυξ ἐστὶ μὲν τῶν | ἐκτο-
πιζόντων καὶ σχιδανοπόδων, νεοττιὰν δὲ οὐ ποιεῖ,
ἀλλὰ κονίστραν· καὶ ταύτην σκεπάζει φρυγάνοις διὰ
τοὺς ἱέρακας, ἐν ᾗ ἐπῳάζει. Ἀλέξανδρος δ' ὁ Μύνδιος
ἐν δευτέρῳ Περὶ Ζῴων, ὁ θῆλυς, φησίν, ὄρτυξ λεπτο-
τράχηλός ἐστι τοῦ ἄρρενος οὐκ ἔχων τὰ ὑπὸ τῷ γενείῳ
μέλανα. ἀνατμηθεὶς δὲ πρόλοβον οὐχ ὁρᾶται μέγαν
ἔχων, καρδίαν δ' ἔχει μεγάλην, καὶ ταύτην τρίλοβον.
ἔχει δὲ καὶ ἧπαρ καὶ τὴν χολὴν ἐν τοῖς ἐντέροις
κεκολλημένην, σπλῆνα μικρὸν καὶ δυσθεώρητον, ὄρ-
d χεις δὲ | ὑπὸ τῷ ἥπατι ὡς ἀλεκτρυόνες. περὶ δὲ τῆς
γενέσεως αὐτῶν Φανόδημος ἐν δευτέρῳ Ἀτθίδος φη-
σίν· ὡς κατεῖδεν Ἐρυσίχθων Δῆλον τὴν νῆσον τὴν
ὑπὸ τῶν ἀρχαίων καλουμένην Ὀρτυγίαν παρ' ὃ τὰς
ἀγέλας τῶν ζῴων τούτων φερομένας ἐκ τοῦ πελάγους
ἱζάνειν εἰς τὴν νῆσον διὰ τὸ εὔορμον εἶναι < . . . >
Εὔδοξος δ' ὁ Κνίδιος ἐν πρώτῳ Γῆς Περιόδου τοὺς
Φοίνικας λέγει θύειν τῷ Ἡρακλεῖ ὄρτυγας διὰ τὸ τὸν
Ἡρακλέα τὸν Ἀστερίας καὶ Διὸς πορευόμενον εἰς
e Λιβύην ἀναιρεθῆναι μὲν | ὑπὸ Τυφῶνος, Ἰολάου δ'

147 Formed, respectively, from the nominatives *ortux*, *orux*,
and *kokkux*.
148 Sc. because the nominative *onux* declines with neither
kappa nor *gamma*, but instead yields genitive singular *onuchos*.

("cuckoo").[147] The form *onuchos* ("fingernail"; genitive singular) is worth noting.[148] In general, the genitive singular follows the nominative plural, using the same consonant to form the final syllable; this is true even if the noun is formed without a consonant. Aristotle (fr. 261) says: The quail is a migratory bird and has a divided foot. It does not build a nest, but does make a place to dust itself; it covers this with sticks to guard against hawks, and broods on its eggs there. Alexander of Myndus says in Book II of *On Animals* (fr. I.15 Wellmann): The female quail has a slender neck and lacks the black marks under the chin characteristic of the male. When dissected, it can be seen to lack a large crop; but it does have a large heart, and a three-lobed one at that. It also has a liver; a gall-bladder firmly attached to its intestines; a small spleen that is difficult to detect; and, like roosters, testicles located beneath its liver. As for their origin, Phanodemus reports in Book II of the *History of Attica* (FGrH 325 F 2): When Erysichthon[149] saw the island of Delos, which the ancients referred to as Ortygia ("Quail Island") because flocks of these creatures were carried there[150] from the sea and settled on the island, since it was a good place to put into . . . Eudoxus of Cnidus in Book I of the *Tour of the Earth* (fr. 284a Lasserre) claims that the Phoenicians sacrifice quail to Heracles because, when Heracles the son of Asteria and Zeus was on his way to Libya, he was killed by Typhon; but when Iolaus brought

---

[149] An Attic hero and the son of the mythical early king Cecrops; cf. [Apollod.] *Bib*. 3.14.2; Paus. 1.2.6. For another fragment of the (largely obscure) tale of his visit to Delos, see Paus. 1.31.2.

[150] Sc. by the wind.

αὐτῷ προσενέγκαντος ὄρτυγα καὶ προσαγαγόντος
ὀσφρανθέντα ἀναβιῶναι· ἔχαιρε γάρ, φησί, καὶ
περιὼν τῷ ζῴῳ τούτῳ. ὑποκοριστικῶς δὲ Εὔπολις ἐν
Πόλεσιν αὐτοὺς κέκληκεν ὀρτύγια λέγων οὕτως·

(A.) ὄρτυγας ἔθρεψας σύ τινας ἤδη πώποτε;
(B.) ἔγωγε μικρά γ' ὀρτύγια. κἄπειτα τί;

Ἀντιφάνης δ' ἐν Ἀγροίκῳ ὀρτύγιον εἴρηκεν οὕτως·

ὡς δὴ σύ τι
ποιεῖν δυνάμενος ὀρτυγίου ψυχὴν ἔχων.

Πρατίνας δ' ἐν Δυμαίναις ἢ Καρυάτισιν

< . . . > ἁδύφωνον

f ἰδίως καλεῖ τὸν ὄρτυγα, | πλὴν εἰ μή τι παρὰ τοῖς
Φλιασίοις ἢ τοῖς Λάκωσι φωνήεντες, ὡς καὶ οἱ πέρδικες. καὶ ἡ σιαλὶς δὲ ἀπὸ τούτου ἂν εἴη, φησὶν ὁ
Δίδυμος, ὠνομασμένη· σχεδὸν γὰρ τὰ πλεῖστα τῶν
ὀρνέων ἀπὸ τῆς φωνῆς ἔχει τὴν ὀνομασίαν. ἡ δὲ
ὀρτυγομήτρα καλουμένη, ἧς μνημονεύει Κρατῖνος ἐν
Χείρωσι λέγων· † Ἰθακησία ὀρτυγομήτρα †—λέγει δὲ
393 περὶ αὐτῆς ὁ || Μύνδιος Ἀλέξανδρος ὅτι ἐστὶ τὸ
μέγεθος ἡλίκη τρυγών, σκέλη δὲ μακρά, δυσθαλὴς
καὶ δειλή. περὶ δὲ τῆς τῶν ὀρτύγων θήρας ἰδίως

---

151 Diogenian. 4.49 (also citing Eudoxus) gives a more complete version of the story, in which the quail was burned alive and
the smoke it produced revived Heracles. For Asteria as Heracles'

him a quail and held it up close to him, he revived after
he caught the scent of it.[151] Because when he was alive,
Eudoxus says, he was fond of the creature. Eupolis in
Cities (fr. 226) refers to them with the diminutive *ortugia*,
saying the following:

> (A.) Did you ever breed any quail?
> (B.) I did—some little tiny quail (*ortugia*)! So what?

Antiphanes in *The Rustic* (fr. 5) also uses *ortugion*, as follows:

> As if you were, in fact,
> capable of doing anything, given that you have the
> courage of a little quail (*ortugion*)!

Pratinas in *Women of Dyme or Caryatids* (*TrGF* 4 F 1) refers in an odd way to the quail, as

> sweet-voiced,

unless perhaps Phliasian[152] or Spartan quail produce a
call, as partridges do. This must also be the source of the
name of the *sialis*[153], according to Didymus (fr. 46, pp. 76–
7 Schmidt); because almost all birds get their names from
their cries. The so-called *ortugomḗtra* ("corncrake"),[154]
which Cratinus mentions in *Cheirons* (fr. 264, unmetrical),
where he says: † an Ithacan *ortugomḗtra* † —Alexander of
Myndus (fr. I.16 Wellmann) claims that this bird is the size
of a turtledove, has long legs, and is thin and wary. As for

---

mother, cf. Cic. *ND* 3.42. Asteria is also supposed to have been an
early name for Delos; cf. West on Hes. *Th*. 409.
[152] Pratinus was from Phlius.   [153] Unidentified, but
probably a bird mentioned by one of the poets.

ἱστορεῖ Κλέαρχος ὁ Σολεὺς ἐν τῷ ἐπιγραφομένῳ Περὶ
τῶν Ἐν τῇ Πλάτωνος Πολιτείᾳ Μαθηματικῶς Εἰρημένων γράφων οὕτως· οἱ ὄρτυγες περὶ τὸν τῆς ὀχείας
καιρόν, ἐὰν κάτοπτρον ἐξ ἐναντίας τις αὐτῶν καὶ πρὸ
τούτου βρόχον θῇ, τρέχοντες πρὸς τὸν ἐμφαινόμενον
ἐν τῷ κατόπτρῳ ἐμπίπτουσιν εἰς τὸν βρόχον. καὶ περὶ
τῶν κολοιῶν δὲ καλουμένων τὰ ὅμοια ἱστορεῖ ἐν |
b τούτοις· καὶ τοῖς κολοιοῖς δὲ διὰ τὴν φυσικὴν φιλο-
στοργίαν, καίπερ τοσοῦτον πανουργίᾳ διαφέρουσιν,
ὅμως ὅταν ἐλαίου κρατὴρ τεθῇ πλήρης, οἱ στάντες
αὐτῶν ἐπὶ τὸ χεῖλος καὶ καταβλέψαντες ἐπὶ τὸν ἐμφαινόμενον καταράττουσι. διόπερ ἐλαιοβρόχων γενομένων ἡ τῶν πτερῶν αὐτοῖς συγκόλλησις αἰτία γίνεται
τῆς ἁλώσεως. τὴν μέσην δὲ τοῦ ὀνόματος συλλαβὴν
ἐκτείνουσιν Ἀττικοὶ ὡς δοίδυκα καὶ κήρυκα, ὡς ὁ
Ἰξίων φησὶ Δημήτριος ἐν τῷ Περὶ τῆς Ἀλεξανδρέων
c Διαλέκτου. Ἀριστοφάνης | δ᾽ ἐν Εἰρήνῃ συνεσταλ-
μένως ἔφη διὰ τὸ μέτρον·

ὄρτυγες οἰκογενεῖς.

τῶν δὲ καλουμένων χεννίων (μικρὸν δ᾽ ἐστὶν ὀρτύγιον)
μνημονεύει Κλεομένης ἐν τῇ Πρὸς Ἀλέξανδρον Ἐπιστολῇ γράφων οὕτως· φαληρίδας ταριχηρὰς μυρίας,

---

154 Referred to briefly here because its name contains the ele-
ment ortugo- ("quail-").
155 The upsilon is short in the nominative forms of all three
words (doidux, kērux, and ortux), and long in the oblique cases of

how quail are hunted, Clearchus of Soli offers unusual information in his work entitled *On the Mathematical Sections in Plato's Republic* (fr. 3 Wehrli), where he writes as follows: During mating-season, if you set a mirror in front of them, and a noose before the mirror, they rush toward the image in the mirror and are snared by the noose. He makes similar comments about what are referred to as *koloioi* ("jackdaws"), in the following passage (fr. 3 Wehrli, continued): Because jackdaws are naturally gregarious— and despite the fact that they are quite clever—when a basin full of olive oil is set out, if they stand on the rim and look down at their image, they fall in. As a consequence, their wings become soaked with oil and stick together, which leads to their being captured. Attic authors lengthen the middle syllable of the word in the same way they do with *doiduka* ("pestle") and *kēruka* ("herald"), according to Demetrius Ixion in his *On the Alexandrian Dialect* (fr. 40 Staesche).[155] But Aristophanes in *Peace* (788) pronounces it short for the sake of the meter:

domestically-bred quail (*ortuges*).

What are known as *chennia* (this is a tiny variety of quail) are mentioned by Cleomenes in his *Letter to Alexander*, where he writes as follows:[156] 10,000 salted coots, 5000

the first two. But the claim that it is long in the oblique cases of *ortux* appears to be incorrect, as the example from Aristophanes cited below makes clear.

156 Cleomenes of Naucratis (Berve i #431) was Alexander the Great's chief financial officer in Egypt; this passage presumably comes from a cover letter that accompanied a large shipment of supplies sent to the king.

τυλάδας πεντακισχιλίας, χέννια ταριχηρὰ μύρια. καὶ
Ἵππαρχος ἐν τῇ Αἰγυπτίᾳ Ἰλιάδι·

οὐ<δέ> μοι Αἰγυπτίων βίος ἤρεσεν οἷον ἔχουσι,
χέννια τίλλοντες † καλκατιαδεισαλέοντα. †

Οὐκ ἀπελείποντο δὲ ἡμῶν τοῦ συμποσίου πολ-
d λάκις | οὐδὲ κύκνοι, περὶ ὧν φησιν ὁ Ἀριστοτέλης· ὁ
κύκνος εὔτεκνός ἐστι καὶ μάχιμος· ἀλληλοκτονεῖ γοῦν
ὁ μάχιμος. μάχεται δὲ καὶ τῷ ἀετῷ, αὐτὸς μάχης μὴ
προαρξάμενος. εἰσὶ δ' ᾠδικοὶ καὶ μάλιστα περὶ τὰς
τελευτάς· διαίρουσι δὲ καὶ τὸ πέλαγος ᾄδοντες. ἔστιν
δὲ τῶν στεγανοπόδων καὶ ποηφάγων. ὁ δὲ Μύνδιός
φησιν Ἀλέξανδρος πολλοῖς τελευτῶσιν παρακολου-
θήσας οὐκ ἀκοῦσαι ᾀδόντων. ὁ δὲ τὰ Κεφαλίωνος
ἐπιγραφόμενα Τρωικὰ συνθεὶς Ἡγησιάναξ ὁ Ἀλεξαν-
e δρεὺς καὶ τὸν | Ἀχιλλεῖ μονομαχήσαντα Κύκνον φησὶ
τραφῆναι ἐν Λευκόφρυι πρὸς τοῦ ὁμωνύμου ὄρνιθος.
Βοῖος δ' ἐν Ὀρνιθογονίᾳ ἢ Βοιώ, ὥς φησι Φιλόχορος,
ὑπὸ Ἄρεως τὸν Κύκνον ὀρνιθωθῆναι καὶ παραγενό-
μενον ἐπὶ τὸν Σύβαριν ποταμὸν πλησιάσαι γεράνῳ.
λέγει δὲ καὶ ἐντίθεσθαι αὐτὸν τῇ νεοττιᾷ πόαν τὴν
λεγομένην λυγαίαν. καὶ περὶ τῆς γεράνου δέ φησιν ὁ
Βοῖος ὅτι ἦν τις παρὰ τοῖς Πυγμαίοις γυνὴ διάσημος,
ὄνομα Γεράνα. αὕτη κατὰ θεὸν τιμωμένη πρὸς τῶν

---

157 *tuladas*; cf. 2.65a (citing Alexander of Myndus).
158 Much of the material that follows (to 9.395a) is preserved
in slightly different form at Ael. *VH* 1.14–15 (perhaps drawn

thrushes[157], 10,000 salted *chennia*. Also Hipparchus in his
Egyptian Iliad (*SH* 497):

> I didn't like the sort of life the Egyptians lead,
> plucking *chennia* [corrupt].

Even swans were not generally absent from our
party.[158] Aristotle (fr. 262) says about them: The swan takes
good care of its young and is belligerent—belligerent
enough, at any rate, that they kill one another. It even
fights the eagle, although it does not initiate the fight. They
like to sing, especially when dying; they even sing as they
cross the sea. They are web-footed and herbivorous. Alexander of Myndus (fr. I.17 Wellmann), on the other hand,
claims to have followed many dying swans and not heard
them singing. Hegesianax of Alexandria, the author of
the work entitled *Cephalion's History of Troy* (*FGrH* 45 F
1), claims that Cycnus[159], who fought a duel with Achilleus,
was raised in Leucophrys by the bird whose name he
shared. According to Philochorus (*FGrH* 328 F 214),
Boeus (or Boeo) in the *Origin of Birds*[160] claims that
Cycnus was transformed into a bird by Ares and, when he
came to the Sybaris River, had sex with a crane; he adds
that Cycnus put the grass referred to as *lugaia*[161] in his
nest. As for the crane (*geranos*), Boeus says that there was
an important Pygmy woman named Gerana, who was hon-

---

straight from Alexander of Myndus, with the additional material
in Athenaeus coming from other sources).

[159] Literally "Swan".   [160] Boeus' *Origin of Birds* (Powell
pp. 24–5) was known to Ovid. For Boeo of Delphi, see Paus.
10.5.7–8 (citing four dactylic hexameter lines from a *Hymn for the
Delphians*, = Powell p. 24).   [161] Literally "gloomy, dark".

f πολιτῶν αὐτὴ τοὺς ὄντως θεοὺς ταπεινῶς | ἦγε, μάλι-
στα δὲ Ἥραν τε καὶ Ἄρτεμιν. ἀγανακτήσασα οὖν ἡ
Ἥρα εἰς ἀπρεπῆ τὴν ὄψιν ὄρνιν μετεμόρφωσε πολέ-
μιόν τε καὶ στυγητὴν κατέστησε τοῖς τιμήσασιν
αὐτὴν Πυγμαίοις, γενέσθαι τε λέγει ἐξ αὐτῆς καὶ
Νικοδάμαντος τὴν χερσαίαν χελώνην. καθόλου δὲ ὁ
ποιήσας ταῦτα τὰ ἔπη πάντα τὰ ὄρνεα ἀνθρώπους
ἱστορεῖ πρότερον γεγονέναι.

Φάσσαι. Ἀριστοτέλης φησὶ περιστερῶν μὲν εἶναι
ἓν γένος, εἴδη δὲ πέντε, γράφων οὕτως· περιστερά,
394 οἰνάς, φάψ, φάσσα, || τρυγών. ἐν δὲ πέμπτῳ Περὶ
Ζῴων Μορίων τὴν φάβα οὐκ ὀνομάζει, καίτοι Αἰσχύλου ἐν τῷ σατυρικῷ Πρωτεῖ οὕτω μνημονεύοντος τοῦ
ὄρνιθος·

σιτουμένην δύστηνον ἀθλίαν φάβα
μέσακτα πλευρὰ πρὸς πτύοις πεπληγμένην.

κἂν Φιλοκτήτῃ δὲ κατὰ γενικὴν κλίσιν

φαβῶν

εἴρηκεν. ἡ μὲν οὖν οἰνάς, φησὶν ὁ Ἀριστοτέλης, μείζων ἐστὶ τῆς περιστερᾶς, χρῶμα δ᾽ ἔχει οἰνωπόν, ἡ δὲ
φὰψ μέσον περιστερᾶς καὶ οἰνάδος, ἡ δὲ φάσσα
ἀλέκτορος τὸ μέγεθος, χρῶμα δὲ σποδιόν, ἡ δὲ τρυ-
γὼν πάντων ἐλάττων, χρῶμα δὲ τεφρόν. αὕτη δὲ
b θέρους φαίνεται, τὸν δὲ χειμῶνα φωλεύει. | ἡ δὲ φὰψ
καὶ ἡ περιστερὰ αἰεὶ φαίνονται, ἡ δ᾽ οἰνὰς φθινοπώρῳ

ored like a goddess by her fellow-citizens, but herself held the real gods, especially Hera and Artemis, in contempt. Hera accordingly became upset and transformed Gerana into an ugly-looking bird, and made the Pygmies (who worshipped Hera) hate and loathe her.[162] He also claims that Gerana and Nicodamas were the parents of the tortoise. Nearly all birds, the author of this poem reports, were previously human beings.

Ringdoves. Aristotle (fr. 263), writing as follows, says that these constitute a single group with five sub-types: pigeon, rock-pigeon, *phaps*, ringdove, turtledove. He fails to mention the *phaps* in Book V of *On Parts of Animals*, even though Aeschylus refers to the bird in his satyr play *Proteus* (fr. 210), as follows:

> an unhappy, miserable, feeding *phaps*,
> whose middle ribs were broken when it was struck by
>   the winnowing shovels.

He also uses the word in *Philoctetes* (fr. 257), in the genitive case:

> *phabōn.*

According to Aristotle (fr. 264; cf. *HA* 544^{b}6–7), the rock-pigeon (*oinas*) is larger than the pigeon and reddish colored (*oinōpos*); the *phaps* falls mid-way between the pigeon and the rock-pigeon; the ringdove is the size of a chicken, and a dirty white color; and the turtledove is the smallest of them all, and ash-gray. The turtledove is seen in the summer, but goes into hiding in the winter. The *phaps* and the pigeon are visible all year round, whereas the rock-

---

162 For the hostility between Pygmies and cranes, cf. 9.390b.

μόνῳ. πολυχρονιωτέρα δὲ εἶναι λέγεται τούτων ἡ
φάσσα· καὶ γὰρ τριάκοντα καὶ τεσσαράκοντα ζῇ ἔτη.
οὐκ ἀπολείπουσι δ' ἕως θανάτου οὔτε οἱ ἄρρενες τὰς
θηλείας οὔτε αἱ θήλειαι τοὺς ἄρρενας, ἀλλὰ καὶ τελευτήσαντος χηρεύει ὁ ὑπολειπόμενος. τὸ δ' αὐτὸ ποιοῦσι
καὶ κόρακες καὶ κορῶναι καὶ κολοιοί. ἐπῳάζει δ' ἐκ
διαδοχῆς πᾶν τὸ περιστεροειδὲς γένος, καὶ γενομένων
τῶν νεοττῶν ὁ ἄρρην ἐμπτύει αὐτοῖς, ὡς μὴ βασκαν-
c θῶσι. | τίκτει δὲ ᾠὰ δύο, ὧν τὸ μὲν πρῶτον ἄρρεν
ποιεῖ, τὸ δὲ δεύτερον θῆλυ. τίκτουσι δὲ πᾶσαν ὥραν
τοῦ ἔτους· διὸ δὴ καὶ δεκάκις τοῦ ἐνιαυτοῦ τιθέασιν, ἐν
Αἰγύπτῳ δὲ δωδεκάκις· τεκοῦσα γὰρ τῇ ἐχομένῃ
ἡμέρᾳ συλλαμβάνει. ἔτι ἐν τῷ αὐτῷ φησιν Ἀριστοτέλης ὅτι περιστερὰ ἕτερον, πελειὰς δ' ἔλαττον, καὶ
ὅτι ἡ πελειὰς τιθασὸν γίνεται, περιστερὰ δὲ καὶ μέλαν
καὶ μικρὸν καὶ ἐρυθρόπουν καὶ τραχύπουν· διὸ οὐδεὶς
τρέφει. ἴδιον δὲ λέγει τῆς περιστερᾶς τὸ κυνεῖν αὐτὰς
ὅταν μέλλωσιν ἀναβαίνειν ἢ οὐκ ἀνέχεσθαι τὰς θη-
d λείας. ὁ δὲ πρεσβύτερος, | φησί, καὶ προαναβαίνει καὶ
μὴ κύσας· οἱ δὲ νεώτεροι αἰεὶ τοῦτο ποιήσαντες ὀχεύουσιν. καὶ αἱ θήλειαι δ' ἀλλήλας ἀναβαίνουσιν, ὅταν
ἄρρην μὴ παρῇ, κυνήσασαι· καὶ οὐδὲν προϊέμεναι εἰς
ἀλλήλας τίκτουσιν ᾠά, ἐξ ὧν οὐ γίνεται νεοττός. οἱ δὲ
Δωριεῖς τὴν πελειάδα ἀντὶ περιστερᾶς τιθέασιν, ὡς
Σώφρων ἐν Γυναικείοις. Καλλίμαχος δ' ἐν τῷ Περὶ
Ὀρνέων ὡς διαφορὰς ἐκτίθεται φάσσαν, πυραλλίδα,

pigeon is seen only in the fall. The ringdove is said to be longer-lived than the others; in fact, it lives 30 or 40 years. The males do not desert the females or *vice versa* until they die; if one member of the pair dies, the other is left alone. Ravens, crows, and jackdaws behave the same way. All pigeon-varieties take turns brooding on their eggs, and when the chicks hatch, the male spits on them to keep off the evil eye. The pigeon lays two eggs; the first produces a male chick, the second a female chick. They lay eggs in every season of the year. As a consequence, they produce them ten times a year, or 12 times a year in Egypt; because after the female lays her eggs, she conceives again the next day. Aristotle goes on to say in the same section that the pigeon is different,[163] and that the dove is smaller and can be domesticated, whereas the pigeon is tiny and dark-colored, and has rough, red feet; as a result, no one breeds them. He claims that a peculiar characteristic of the pigeon is that the males kiss the females when they are about to mount them, and that otherwise the females do not put up with them. An older bird, he says, can mount a female first, without kissing her; but the younger ones always kiss her before they mate. The females also mount one another, if no male is available, after kissing first; although they ejaculate nothing into one another, they produce eggs, which are, however, infertile. The Dorians, for example Sophron in the *Women's Mimes*,[164] use the word *peleias* ("dove") rather than *peristera* ("pigeon"). Callimachus in his *On Birds* (fr. 416 Pfeiffer) explains that the ringdove, *purallis*, pigeon, and turtledove are different

---

163 Sc. from the dove (*peleias*).
164 The fragment is omitted by Kassel–Austin.

περιστεράν, τρυγόνα. ὁ δὲ Μύνδιος Ἀλέξανδρος οὐ
e πίνειν φησὶ τὴν φάσσαν ἀνακύπτουσαν | ὡς τὴν
τρυγόνα καὶ τοῦ χειμῶνος μὴ φθέγγεσθαι, εἰ μὴ
εὐδίας γενομένης. λέγεται δὲ ὅτι ἡ οἰνὰς ἐὰν φαγοῦσα
τὸ τῆς ἰξίας σπέρμα ἐπί τινος ἀφοδεύσῃ δένδρου,
ἰδίαν ἰξίαν φύεσθαι. Δαίμαχος δ' ἐν τοῖς Ἰνδικοῖς
ἱστορεῖ περιστερὰς μηλίνας γίνεσθαι ἐν Ἰνδοῖς.
Χάρων δ' ὁ Λαμψακηνὸς ἐν τοῖς Περσικοῖς περὶ Μαρ-
δονίου ἱστορῶν καὶ τοῦ διαφθαρέντος στρατοῦ Περ-
σικοῦ περὶ τὸν Ἄθω γράφει καὶ ταῦτα· καὶ λευκαὶ
περιστεραὶ τότε πρῶτον εἰς Ἕλληνας ἐφάνησαν,
πρότερον οὐ γιγνόμεναι. ὁ δ' Ἀριστοτέλης φησὶν ὡς
f αἱ περιστεραὶ γινομένων | τῶν νεοττῶν τῆς ἁλμυρι-
ζούσης γῆς διαμασησάμεναι ἐμπτύουσιν αὐτοῖς διοι-
γνῦσαι τὸ στόμα, διὰ τούτου παρασκευάζουσαι αὐτοὺς πρὸς τὴν τροφήν. τῆς δὲ Σικελίας ἐν Ἔρυκι
καιρός τις ἐστίν, ὃν καλοῦσιν Ἀναγωγάς, ἐν ᾧ φασι
τὴν θεὸν εἰς Λιβύην ἀνάγεσθαι. τότ' οὖν αἱ περὶ τὸν
τόπον περιστεραὶ ἀφανεῖς γίνονται ὡς δὴ τῇ θεῷ
συναποδημοῦσαι. καὶ μεθ' ἡμέρας ἐννέα ἐν τοῖς λεγο-
395 μένοις Καταγωγίοις ‖ μιᾶς προπετασθείσης ἐκ τοῦ
πελάγους περιστερᾶς καὶ εἰς τὸν νεὼν εἰσπτάσης
παραγίνονται καὶ αἱ λοιπαί. ὅσοι οὖν τότε περιουσίας
εὖ ἥκουσι τῶν περιοίκων εὐωχοῦνται, οἱ δὲ λοιποὶ
κροταλίζουσιν μετὰ χαρᾶς, ὄζει τε πᾶς ὁ τόπος τότε

creatures. Alexander of Myndus (fr. I.18 Wellmann) claims that the ringdove does not put its head back to drink, as the turtledove does, and does not call during the winter, except when the weather is good. People say that if a rock-pigeon eats mistletoe-seed and defecates on a tree, another shoot of mistletoe grows there. Daimachus in his *History of India* (*FGrH* 716 F 4) reports that pigeons the color of quinces are found in India. When Charon of Lampsacus in his *History of Persia* (*FGrH* 262 F 3a) discusses Mardonius and the Persian fleet that was destroyed in the vicinity of Mt. Athos,[165] he writes the following: This was the first time that white pigeons were seen in Greece, having previously not been found there. Aristotle (*HA* 613^{a}2–5)[166] reports that when their chicks hatch, pigeons chew up a bit of salty earth, open the chicks' beaks, and spit it in, as a way of preparing them to accept food. In Eryx in Sicily there is a time of year known as the Festival of Departure when, they claim, the goddess[167] leaves for Libya. The pigeons in the area disappear at that point, as if they were accompanying the goddess on her journey abroad. After nine days, at the so-called Festival of Return, a single pigeon flies in from the sea in advance of the others and alights in the temple, and afterward the rest arrive. At that point, the rich people in the region have a feast; the rest use clappers to express their joy; and the whole area smells

165 In 492 BCE; cf. Hdt. 6.44.2–3. Ael. *VH* 1.15 cites the same fragment of Charon.

166 = Gigon's fr. 265.

167 Aphrodite, according to Ael. *NA* 4.2, who offers a more complete version of the anecdote.

βουτύρου[15], ᾧ δὴ τεκμηρίῳ χρῶνται τῆς θείας ἐπανόδου. Αὐτοκράτης ἐν τοῖς Ἀχαϊκοῖς καὶ τὸν Δία ἱστορεῖ μεταβαλεῖν τὴν μορφὴν εἰς περιστερὰν ἐρασθέντα παρθένου Φθίας ὄνομα ἐν Αἰγίῳ. Ἀττικοὶ δὲ ἀρσενικῶς περιστερὸν καλοῦσιν. Ἄλεξις Συντρέχουσιν·

λευκὸς Ἀφροδίτης εἰμὶ γὰρ περιστερός. |
b   ὁ δὲ Διόνυσος οἶδε τὸ μεθύσαι μόνον·
εἰ δὲ νέον ἢ παλαιόν, οὐ πεφρόντικεν.

ἐν δὲ Δορκίδι ἢ Ποππυζούσῃ θηλυκῶς εἴρηκε καὶ ὅτι αἱ Σικελικαὶ διάφοροί εἰσι·

περιστερὰς
ἔνδον τρέφω τῶν Σικελικῶν τούτων πάνυ
κομψάς.

Φερεκράτης ἐν Γραυσί φησιν·

ἀπόπεμψον ἀγγέλλοντα τὸν περιστερόν.

ἐν δὲ Πετάλῃ·

ἀλλ' ὦ περιστέριον ὁμοῖον Κλεισθένει, |
c   πέτου, κόμισον δέ μ' ἐς Κύθηρα καὶ Κύπρον.

15 βουτύρου Olson: βούτυρον ACE

---

168 The word may refer instead to a plant of some sort; cf. Hsch. β 1000.
169 Apparently a fragment of a foundation-myth for the region of Achaean Phthiotis in Thessaly.

like butter[168], which they regard as evidence that the goddess has returned. Autocrates in his *History of Achaea* (*FGrH* 297 F 2) reports that Zeus transformed himself into a pigeon when he fell in love with a girl named Phthia in Aegium.[169] Attic authors use the word as a masculine, *peristeros*. Alexis in *Men Who Agree* (fr. 217):

> I'm Aphrodite's white pigeon (*peristeros*).
> All Dionysus understands is getting drunk;
> he doesn't notice if the wine's new or old.

In *Dorcis or The Girl Who Popped Her Lips* (fr. 58), on the other hand, he uses it as a feminine form and claims that Sicilian pigeons are particularly good:

> Inside my house
> I'm breeding some really nice pigeons (*peristerai*) of
>   this Sicilian
> variety.

Pherecrates says in *Hags* (fr. 38):

> Send the pigeon (*peristeros*) off as a messenger!

And in *Petale* (fr. 143):

> O little pigeon (*peristerion*) who resemble
>   Cleisthenes[170]—
> fly away and take me to Cythera and Cyprus!

---

[170] Cleisthenes (*PAA* 575540) is repeatedly mocked by the comic poets for his alleged effeminacy (cf. Olson on Ar. *Ach.* 118), and the point is presumably that the pigeon—which is being asked to carry the speaker off to several of Aphrodite's favorite haunts— is as soft and white as he is.

Νίκανδρος δὲ ἐν δευτέρῳ Γεωργικῶν τῶν Σικελικῶν
μνημονεύων πελειάδων φησί·

καί τε σύ γε θρέψαιο Δρακοντιάδας διτοκεύσας
ἢ Σικελὰς μεγάροισι πελειάδας· οὐδέ φιν ἅρπαι
οὐδ᾿ ὄφις ὀστρακέοις λωβήσιμοι ἐξενέπονται.

Νῆτται. τούτων, ὥς φησιν Ἀλέξανδρος ὁ Μύνδιος,
ὁ ἄρρην μείζων καὶ ποικιλώτερος. τὸ δὲ λεγόμενον
d γλαυκίον διὰ τὴν τῶν ὀμμάτων | χρόαν μικρῷ ἔλαττόν
ἐστι νήττης. τῶν δὲ βοσκάδων καλουμένων ὁ μὲν
ἄρρην κατάγραφος < . . . > νήττης. ἔχουσι δὲ οἱ
ἄρρενες σιμά τε καὶ ἐλάττονα τῇ συμμετρίᾳ τὰ ῥύγχη.
ἡ δὲ μικρὰ κολυμβίς, πάντων ἐλαχίστη τῶν ἐνύδρων,
ῥυπαρομέλαινα τὴν χροιὰν καὶ τὸ ῥύγχος ὀξὺ ἔχει
σκέπον τε τὰ ὄμματα, τὰ δὲ πολλὰ καταδύεται. ἔστι δὲ
καὶ ἄλλο γένος βοσκάδων μεῖζον μὲν νήττης, ἔλαττον
δὲ χηναλώπεκος. αἱ δὲ λεγόμεναι φασκάδες μικρῷ
μείζονες οὖσαι τῶν μικρῶν κολυμβίδων τὰ λοιπὰ
νήτταις εἰσὶ παραπλήσιοι. ἡ δὲ λεγομένη οὐρία οὐ |
e πολὺ λείπεται νήττης, τῷ χρώματι δὲ ῥυπαροκέραμός
ἐστι, τὸ δὲ ῥύγχος μακρόν τε καὶ στενὸν ἔχει. ἡ δὲ
φαλαρὶς καὶ αὐτὴ στενὸν ἔχουσα τὸ ῥύγχος στρογγυ-
λωτέρα τὴν ὄψιν οὖσα ἔντεφρος τὴν γαστέρα, μικρῷ
μελαντέρα τὸν νῶτον. τῆς δὲ νήττης καὶ κολυμβάδος,
ἀφ᾿ ὧν καὶ τὸ νήχεσθαι καὶ κολυμβᾶν εἴρηται, μνημο-

Nicander in Book II of the *Georgics* (fr. 73 Schneider) mentions Sicilian doves, saying:

> You might also raise Dracontiad doves, which lay
> two eggs, in your house, or else the Sicilian variety.
>   Kites
> and snakes are said not to harm their eggs.

Ducks. According to Alexander of Myndus (fr. I.20 Wellmann), the male duck is larger and more variegated in color. The bird known as the *glaukion*, because of the color of its eyes,[171] is slightly smaller than a duck. As for the so-called *boskades*[172], the male has conspicuous markings . . . than a duck. The males have snubbed beaks that are disproportionately small. The little grebe, the smallest of all aquatic birds, is a dirty black color; has a pointed beak that shields its eyes; and dives frequently below the surface of the water. There is also another variety of *boskas* that is larger than a duck, but smaller than an Egyptian goose. What are referred to as *phaskades* are slightly larger than little grebes, but otherwise resemble ducks. What is referred to as an *ouria* is not much smaller than a duck; is a dirty terracotta color; and has a long, narrow beak. The coot too has a narrow beak; appears rather round; and has an ash-gray belly and a slightly darker back. Aristophanes in *Acharnians* (875–6) mentions the duck (*nēttē*) and the grebe (*kolumbas*), from which the verbs *nēchesthai* ("to

---

171 Which must thus have been *glaukos* ("light blue, gray" *vel sim.*).

172 Literally "feeders". The words that have been lost below probably included something to the effect of "and is smaller"; cf. Arist. *HA* 593b17–18.

νεύει μετὰ καὶ ἄλλων λιμναίων πολλῶν Ἀριστοφάνης
ἐν Ἀχαρνεῦσι διὰ τούτων·

νάσσας κολοιὼς ἀτταγᾶς φαλαρίδας |
f   τροχίλως κολύμβως.

μνημονεύει αὐτῶν καὶ Καλλίμαχος ἐν τῷ Περὶ Ὀρνέων.

Παρῆσαν δὲ πολλάκις ἡμῖν καὶ οἱ καλούμενοι
παραστάται, ὧν μνημονεύει Ἐπαίνετος ἐν Ὀψαρτυτικῷ καὶ Σιμάριστος ἐν τρίτῳ Συνωνύμων καὶ τετάρτῳ.
εἰσὶ δ᾽ οἱ ὄρχεις οὕτω καλούμενοι.

Συγκεκνισωμένων δέ τινων κρεῶν ζωμῷ[16] παραφερομένων ἐπεί τις ἔφη, τῶν πνικτῶν κρεᾳδίων δός. ὁ
396   τῶν ὀνομάτων Δαίδαλος Οὐλπιανός, ‖ αὐτὸς ἐγώ,
φησίν, ἀποπνιγήσομαι, εἰ μὴ εἴπῃς ὅπου καὶ σὺ εὗρες
τὰ τοιαῦτα κρεᾴδια. οὐ μὴ γὰρ ὀνομάσω πρὶν μαθεῖν.
ὁ δέ, Στράττις εἶπεν, ἔφη, ἐν Μακεδόσιν ἢ Παυσανίᾳ·

πνικτόν τι τοίνυν < . . . > ἔστω σοι συχνὸν
τοιοῦτον.

καὶ Εὔβουλος Κατακολλωμένῳ·

καὶ πνικτὰ Σικελὰ πατανίων σωρεύματα.

Ἀριστοφάνης τ᾽ εἴρηκεν ἐν Σφηξίν·

[16] ζωμῷ καὶ A: καὶ del. Schweighäuser

[173] In fact, there is probably no etymological relationship be-

swim") and *kolumban* ("to dive") are derived,[173] along with many other marsh-birds, in the following passage:

> ducks (*nassai*), jackdaws, francolins, coots,
> plovers, grebes (*kolumboi*).

Callimachus also mentions them in his *On Birds* (fr. 417 Pfeiffer).

We often had what are known as *parastatai*[174], which Epaenetus mentions in the *Art of Cooking*, as does Simaristus in Books III and IV of *Synonyms*. Testicles are referred to this way.

Chunks of meat that had been stewed in broth were being served, when someone said: Give me some hunks of smothered meat! Ulpian, the Daedalus[175] of vocabulary, responded: I'll smother myself, unless you tell me where you found a reference to meat of that sort! And I refuse to use the term until I get an answer. The other man said: Strattis used the word in *Macedonians or Pausanias* (fr. 30):

> Make sure you have a lot of smothered . . .
> like this!

Also Eubulus in *The Man Who Was Glued to the Spot* (fr. 46):

> and smothered Sicilian-style heaps of cook-pans.

Aristophanes too uses the word in *Wasps* (511):

tween *nēttē* and *nēchesthai*, while *kolumbas* is derived from *kolumban*, rather than the other way around.

[174] Literally "witnesses". For eating testicles, cf. 9.384e–f.
[175] I.e. "the inventive genius"; cf. 9.399d.

< . . . > ἐν λοπάδι πεπνιγμένον.

Κρατῖνος δ' ἐν Δηλιάσι·

b   τῷ δ' ὑποτρίψας | τι μέρος πνῖξον καθαρύλλως.

Ἀντιφάνης δ' ἐν Ἀγροίκῳ·

                (A.) καὶ πρῶτα μὲν
αἴρω ποθεινὴν μᾶζαν, ἣν φερέσβιος
Δηὼ βροτοῖσι χάρμα δωρεῖται φίλον·
ἔπειτα πνικτὰ τακερὰ μηκάδων μέλη,
χλόην καταμπέχοντα σάρκα νεογενῆ.
(B.) τί λέγεις; (A.) τραγῳδίαν περαίνω
   Σοφοκλέους.

c   Γαλαθηνῶν δὲ χοίρων ποτὲ περιενεχθέντων | καὶ
περὶ τούτων ἐζήτησαν οἱ δαιταλεῖς εἰ τὸ ὄνομα εἴρηται. καί τις ἔφη· Φερεκράτης Δουλοδιδασκάλῳ·

   γαλαθήν' ἔκλεπτον, οὐ τέλεα.

ἐν δὲ Αὐτομόλοις·

   οὐ γαλαθηνὸν ἄρ' ὖν θύειν μέλλεις.

Ἀλκαῖος Παλαίστρᾳ·

   ὁδὶ γὰρ αὐτός ἐστιν· εἴ τι γρύξομαι
   ὧν σοι λέγω πλέον τι γαλαθηνοῦ μυός.

smothered in a casserole-dish.

Cratinus in *Delian Women* (fr. 29):

Grind a bit up and smother it daintily with this!

Antiphanes in *The Rustic* (fr. 1):

(A.) And first of all
I'm fetching a luscious barley-cake, which Deo,
the giver of life, grants mortals as a welcome source
    of joy.
Then tender smothered goat-haunches,
new-born flesh clad in greens.
(B.) What are you talking about? (A.) I'm reciting a
    tragedy by Sophocles.[176]

At one point suckling pigs were served, and the guests
at the banquet took up the question of whether the word is
used.[177] Someone said: Pherecrates in *The Slave-Teacher*
(fr. 49):

I stole a suckling pig that wasn't full-grown.

And in *Deserters* (fr. 33):

You're not going to be sacrificing a suckling pig, then!

Alcaeus in *The Wrestling-School* (fr. 22):

Here's the man himself. If anything I say to you
amounts to more than a squeek of a suckling
    mouse . . .

---

[176] Probably a reference to Sophocles II (*TrGF* 62; active in
the first half of the 4th century BCE).

Ἡρόδοτος δ' ἐν τῇ πρώτῃ φησὶν ὅτι ἐν Βαβυλῶνι ἐπὶ τοῦ χρυσοῦ βωμοῦ οὐκ ἔξεστι θύειν ὅτι μὴ γαλαθηνὰ μοῦνα. Ἀντιφάνης Φιλεταίρῳ·

d   κομψός γε μικρὸς κρωμακίσκος | οὑτοσὶ
    γαλαθηνός.

Ἡνίοχος Πολυεύκτῳ·

    ὁ βοῦς <ὁ> χαλκοῦς ἦν ἂν ἑφθὸς δεκάπαλαι,
    ὁ δ' ἴσως γαλαθηνὸν τέθυκε τὸν χοῖρον λαβών.

καὶ Ἀνακρέων δέ φησιν·

         οἷά τε νεβρὸν νεοθηλέα
    γαλαθηνὸν ὅς τ' ἐν ὕλῃ κεροέσσης
    ἀπολειφθεὶς ἀπὸ μητρὸς ἐπτοήθη.

Κράτης Γείτοσι·

    νῦν μὲν γὰρ ἡμῖν † παιδικῶν δαις †
    ὅκωσπερ ἀρνῶν ἐστι γαλαθηνῶν τε καὶ
    χοίρων.

e Σιμωνίδης δ' ἐπὶ τοῦ | Περσέως τὴν Δανάην ποιεῖ λέγουσαν·

         ὦ τέκος, οἷον ἔχω πόνον·
    σὺ δ' ἀωτεῖς, γαλαθηνῷ
    δ' ἤθεϊ κνοώσσεις.

Herodotus in his Book I (183.2) claims that nothing can be sacrificed on the gold altar in Babylon except sucklings. Antiphanes in *The Man Who Loved His Comrades* (fr. 214):

This here is a dainty little suckling
piglet.

Heniochus in *Polyeuctus* (fr. 2):

The bronze bull[178] would've been stewed ages ago;
maybe he's taken the suckling pig and sacrificed it.

Anacreon (*PMG* 408.1–3) as well says:

Just like a newborn suckling
fawn, which was abandoned in the woods
by its horned mother and is frightened.

Crates in *Neighbors* (fr. 1):

Because now for us † of sex with boys [corrupt] †
just as it is of lambs and sucklings and
pigs.

Simonides (*PMG* 543.7–9) represents Danae as saying about Perseus:[179]

Oh child, what grief I have!
But you are asleep, and you slumber
as a suckling does.

177 Sc. in what Athenaeus and his characters would have regarded as ancient literature.

178 See 9.396e n.

179 Sc. after her father Acrisius set her adrift with her baby in the sea to die.

καὶ ἐν ἄλλοις ἐπ᾽ Ἀρχεμόρου εἴρηκεν·

ἰοστεφάνου γλυκεῖαν ἐδάκρυσαν
ψυχὰν ἀποπνέοντα γαλαθηνὸν τέκος.

Κλέαρχος δ᾽ ἐν τοῖς Περὶ Βίων εἰς τοῦτό φησιν ὠμό-
τητος Φάλαριν τὸν τύραννον ἐλάσαι ὡς γαλαθηνὰ
θοινᾶσθαι βρέφη. θῆσθαι δ᾽ ἐστὶ τὸ θηλάζειν τὸ
f γάλα. | Ὅμηρος·

Ἕκτωρ μὲν θνητός τε γυναῖκά τε θήσατο μαζόν.

διὰ τὸ ἐντίθεσθαι τὰς θηλὰς εἰς τὰ στόματα τὰ βρέφη, καὶ ὁ τιτθὸς ἐνθένδε διὰ τὸ ἐντίθεσθαι τὰς θηλάς.

νεβροὺς κοιμήσασα νεηγενέας γαλαθηνούς. ‖

397   Περιενεχθεισῶν δέ ποτε καὶ δορκάδων ὁ Ἐλεατικὸς
Παλαμήδης <ὁ> ὀνοματολόγος ἔφη· οὐκ ἄχαρι κρέας
τὸ τῶν δορκώνων. πρὸς ὃν ὁ Μυρτίλος ἔφη· μόνως
δορκάδες λέγονται, δόρκωνες δὲ οὔ. Ξενοφῶν Ἀναβάσεως πρώτῳ· ἐνῆσαν δὲ καὶ ὠτίδες καὶ δορκάδες.

---

180 Archemorus, the son of the king and queen of Nemea, died
after his nurse Hypsipyle set him on the ground to show the Seven
Against Thebes the way to a spring, and the snake that guarded it
struck him; the Nemean Games were founded in his honor. Cf.
Hyg. *fab.* 74.

181 An early 6th-century BCE tyrant of Acragas in Sicily, whose
name became a byword for cruelty, and to whom the bronze bull
alluded to above belonged.

And in another passage (*PMG* 553) he says about Archemorus:[180]

> They wept for the suckling child of a violet-crowned mother, as it breathed out its sweet life.

Clearchus in his *On Lives* (fr. 61 Wehrli) claims that the tyrant Phalaris[181] became so savage that he dined on suckling babies. The verb *thēsthai* means to suck milk (*gala*) from a teat.[182] Homer (*Il.* 24.58):

> Hector is mortal and sucked (*thēsato*) on a mortal woman's breast.

Because babies put the nipples into (*entithesthai*) their mouths, this is the source of the word *tithos* ("breast"), that is, the fact that they put the nipples in their mouths.[183]

> putting her newborn suckling fawns to bed (*Od.* 4.336).[184]

At one point gazelles were served, and the lexicographer Palamedes of Elis said: Gazelle meat (*kreas dorkōnōn*) is quite nice. Myrtilus responded: *Dorkades* is the only form of the word that is used; *dorkōnes* is not. Xenophon in Book I of the *Anabasis* (5.2): and bustards and gazelles (*dorkades*) were also found in it.

---

182 Hence *galathēnos*, "suckling."

183 A false etymology.

184 Another example of the adjective *galathēnos* ("suckling"), which has been separated from the poetic quotations above (with which it belongs) via the insertion of the reference to Clearchus and some etymological material.

Ταώς. ὅτι σπάνιος οὗτος ὁ ὄρνις δηλοῖ Ἀντιφάνης ἐν Στρατιώτῃ ἢ Τύχωνι λέγων οὕτως·

> τῶν ταῶν μὲν ὡς ἅπαξ τις ζεῦγος ἤγαγεν μόνον,
> σπάνιον ὂν τὸ χρῆμα, πλείους εἰσὶ νῦν τῶν
> ὀρτύγων.

καὶ Εὔβουλος ἐν Φοίνικι· |

b   καὶ γὰρ ὁ ταῶς διὰ τὸ σπάνιον θαυμάζεται.

ὁ ταώς, φησὶν Ἀριστοτέλης, σχιδανόπους ἐστὶ καὶ ποιολόγος καὶ τίκτει τριέτης γενόμενος, ἐν οἷς[17] καὶ τὴν ποικιλίαν τῶν πτερῶν λαμβάνει. ἐπῳάζει δ᾽ ἡμέρας πρὸς τριάκοντα. τίκτει τε ἅπαξ τοῦ ἔτους ᾠὰ δώδεκα· ταῦτα δὲ οὐκ εἰς ἅπαξ, ἀλλὰ παρ᾽ ἡμέρας δύο· αἱ δὲ πρωτοτόκοι ὀκτώ. τίκτει δὲ καὶ ὑπηνέμια, ὡς ἡ ἀλεκτορίς, οὐ πλείω δὲ τῶν δύο. ἐκλέπει δὲ καὶ ἐπῳάζει καθάπερ ἡ ἀλεκτορίς. Εὔπολις δ᾽ ἐν Ἀστρατεύτοις c   φησὶ περὶ | αὐτοῦ οὕτως·

> μή ποτε θρέψω
> παρὰ Φερσεφόνῃ τοιόνδε ταῶν, ὃς τοὺς εὔδοντας
> ἐγείρει.

Ἀντιφῶντι δὲ τῷ ῥήτορι λόγος μὲν γέγραπται ἔχων ἐπίγραμμα Περὶ Ταῶν, καὶ ἐν αὐτῷ τῷ λόγῳ οὐδεμία

---

[17] οἷς χρόνοις ACE: χρόνοις del. Rose (om. Arist.)

Peacock. Antiphanes in *The Soldier or Tycho* (fr. 203.1–2)[185] makes it clear that the bird was rare, when he says the following:

> When someone imported a single pair of peacocks
>   only once,
> they were rare. But nowadays they're more common
>   than quail.

Also Eubulus in *Phoenix* (fr. 113):

> For the peacock's treated like a curiosity because it's
>   so rare.

According to Aristotle (fr. 266), the peacock has a divided foot; is herbivorous; and lays eggs when it is three years old, at which point it also acquires its elaborate plumage. It broods on its eggs for up to 30 days. It lays a dozen eggs once a year. The eggs are not produced all at once, but over the course of two days; the first time they lay eggs, they produce only eight. It also produces infertile eggs,[186] as hens do, although not more than two. It hatches and broods on its eggs just as a hen does. Eupolis in *Draft-Dodgers* (fr. 41) says the following about it:

>   so that I never breed
> a peacock (*tahōs*) like this, which wakes up anyone
>   who's sleeping, in Persephone's house.[187]

The orator Antiphon wrote a speech with the title *On the Peacocks*, although he never uses the word in the speech

---

[185] Quoted at greater length at 14.654e.
[186] Literally "wind-eggs"; cf. 9.374c n.
[187] I.e. the Underworld.

μνεία τοῦ ὀνόματος γίνεται, ὄρνεις δὲ ποικίλους πολλάκις ἐν αὐτῷ ὀνομάζει, φάσκων τούτους τρέφειν
Δῆμον τὸν Πυριλάμπους καὶ πολλοὺς παραγίνεσθαι
κατὰ πόθον τῆς τῶν ὀρνίθων θέας ἔκ τε Λακεδαίμονος
καὶ Θετταλίας καὶ σπουδὴν ποιεῖσθαι τῶν ᾠῶν μετα-
d λαβεῖν. περὶ δὲ τῆς ἰδέας | αὐτῶν λέγων γράφει· εἴ τις
ἐθέλοι καταβαλεῖν εἰς πόλιν τοὺς ὄρνιθας, οἰχήσονται
ἀναπτόμενοι. ἐὰν δὲ τῶν πτερύγων ἀποτέμῃ, τὸ κάλλος ἀφαιρήσεται· τὰ πτερὰ γὰρ αὐτῶν τὸ κάλλος
ἐστίν, ἀλλ’ οὐ τὸ σῶμα. ὅτι δὲ καὶ περισπούδαστος ἦν
αὐτῶν ἡ θέα ἐν τῷ αὐτῷ λόγῳ πάλιν φησίν· ἀλλὰ τὰς
μὲν νουμηνίας ὁ βουλόμενος εἰσῄει, τὰς δ’ ἄλλας
ἡμέρας εἴ τις ἔλθοι βουλόμενος θεάσασθαι, οὐκ ἔστιν
ὅστις ἔτυχε. καὶ ταῦτα οὐκ ἐχθὲς οὐδὲ πρώην, ἀλλ’ ἔτη
e πλέον ἢ τριάκοντά ἐστιν. ταῶς | δὲ λέγουσιν Ἀθη-
ναῖοι, ὥς φησι Τρύφων, τὴν τελευταίαν συλλαβὴν
περισπῶντες καὶ δασύνοντες. καὶ ἀναγιγνώσκουσι
μὲν οὕτως παρ’ Εὐπόλιδι ἐν Ἀστρατεύτοις—πρόκειται
δὲ τὸ μαρτύριον—καὶ ἐν Ὄρνισιν Ἀριστοφάνους·

Τηρεὺς γὰρ εἶ σύ; πότερον ὄρνις ἢ ταῶς;

καὶ πάλιν·

---

188 For the speech, cf. Plu. *Mor.* 833d; Ael. *NA* 5.21.
189 *PAA* 317910. The family was distinguished and thus most likely wealthy. Plato reports that Pyrilampes travelled repeatedly as an ambassador to the Great King (*Chrm.* 158a), and the peacocks were almost certainly given to him in Persia, perhaps in the 440s BCE. Antiphon was related to the family by marriage.

itself, and instead refers repeatedly in the course of it to "brightly colored birds" (fr. 57 Blass–Thalheim).[188] He alleges that Demos the son of Pyrilampes[189] bred them, and that large numbers of people came from Sparta and Thessaly, wanting to see the birds and eager to get some eggs. When he discusses their appearance, he says: If someone tries to keep the birds in town, they'll fly away. But if he lops their wings, they'll be less beautiful; because their plumage is what's attractive, not their body. He also notes in the same speech that people were extremely eager to see them: But anyone who was interested was allowed in on the first of the month;[190] whereas on other days, if someone came and wanted to see them, he was out of luck. And this didn't happen yesterday or the day before; instead, it's now more than 30 years. According to Tryphon (fr. 5 Velsen), the Athenians say *tahōs*,[191] putting a circumflex accent and a rough breathing on the final syllable. This is the reading in Eupolis' *Draft-Dodgers* (fr. 41.2)—I cited the passage earlier (9.397c)[192]—and in Aristophanes' *Birds* (102):

You're Tereus? Are you a bird—or a peacock (*tahōs*)?

And again (*Av.* 269):

[190] Literally "on new-moon days".

[191] Sc. rather than *taōs*.

[192] The implication would seem to be that this was *not* the manuscript reading, on the other hand, in Antiphanes fr. 203.1, with which this section begins (9.397a).

< . . . > ὄρνις δῆτα. τίς ποτ᾽ ἐστίν; οὐ δήπου
ταῶς;

λέγουσι δὲ καὶ τὴν δοτικὴν ταῶνι, ὡς ἐν τῷ αὐτῷ
Ἀριστοφάνης. ἀμήχανον δὲ παρὰ Ἀττικοῖς καὶ Ἴωσιν
ἐν τοῖς ὑπὲρ μίαν συλλαβὴν ὀνόμασι τὴν τελευτῶ-
f σαν | ἀπὸ φωνήεντος ἀρχομένην δασύνεσθαι· πάντως
γὰρ εἶναι ψιλὴν αὐτὴν παρηκολούθηκεν, οἷον νεώς,
λεώς, Τυνδάρεως, Μενέλεως, λειπόνεως, εὔνεως, Νεί-
λεως, πρᾶος, υἱός, Κεῖος, Χῖος, δῖος, χρεῖος, πλεῖος,
λεῖος, λαιός, βαιός, φαιός, πηός, γόος, θοός, ῥόος,
ζωός. φίλαρχος γὰρ οὖσα καὶ ἡγεμονικὴ τὴν φύσιν ἡ
δασύτης τοῖς τελευταίοις μέρεσι τῶν ὀνομάτων οὐδα-
μῶς ἐγκαθείργνυται. ὠνόμασται δὲ ταῶς ἀπὸ τῆς
398 τάσεως τῶν πτερῶν. ‖ Σέλευκος δ᾽ ἐν τῷ πέμπτῳ Περὶ
Ἑλληνισμοῦ· ταῶς· παραλόγως δ᾽ οἱ Ἀττικοὶ καὶ
δασύνουσι καὶ περισπῶσι. τοῖς δὲ πρώτοις τῶν
φωνηέντων κατὰ τὰς ἁπλᾶς τῶν ὀνομάτων ἐκφορὰς
συνεκφέρεσθαι ἐθέλει καὶ ἐνταυθοῖ προάττουσα καὶ
τάχιον ἐκθέουσα δι᾽ ἐπιπολῆς ἐστι τῶν λέξεων.
τεκμαιρόμενοι οὖν Ἀθηναῖοι καὶ διὰ τῆς τάξεως τὴν
ἐνοῦσαν τῇ προσῳδίᾳ φύσιν οὐκ ἐπὶ τῶν φωνηέντων
αὐτὴν τιθέασιν ὥσπερ τὰς ἄλλας, πρὸ δὲ τούτων
τάσσουσιν. οἶμαι δὲ καὶ διὰ τοῦ Η στοιχείου τυπώ-
σασθαι τοὺς παλαιοὺς τὴν δασεῖαν· διόπερ καὶ Ῥω-

---

[193] An epic, not an Attic form.
[194] A desperate and misguided etymology; *tahōs* is in fact an
Oriental loan-word.

It's obviously a bird. But what bird is it? I don't
suppose it's a peacock (*tahōs*)?

Moreover, they pronounce the dative *tahōni*, as Aristophanes does in the same play (*Av.* 884). In the case of
words of more than one syllable, Attic- and Ionic-speakers
find it impossible to put a rough breathing on the final
syllable when it begins with a vowel. This is because con-
sistency absolutely requires that the breathing be smooth;
compare *neōs* ("temple"), *leōs* ("people"), *Tyndareōs*,
Meneleōs, *leiponeōs* ("one who deserts his ship"), *euneōs*
("well-supplied with ships"), *Neileōs*, *praos* ("mild"), *huios*
("son"), *Keios*, *Chios*, *dios* ("bright"), *chreios* ("needy"),
pleios[193] ("full"), *leios* ("smooth"), *laios* ("left"), *baios*
("small, few"), *phaios* ("gray"), *pēos* ("son-in-law"), *goos*
("lamentation"), *thoos* ("swift"), *rhoos* ("stream"), and *zōos*
("life"). For it is in the nature of the rough breathing to
stand at the beginning of words and come first, and it is not
included in the final portion of a word under any circumstances. The bird got the name *tahōs* from the pattern
(*taseōs*) in which its feathers are arranged.[194] Seleucus in
Book V of *On Greek Style* (fr. 70 Müller): *Tahōs* ("peacock"); contrary to the normal rule, Attic authors put a
rough breathing and a circumflex accent on the word. In
the simple pronunciation of words, (the rough breathing)
tends to be pronounced along with initial vowels, and darts
forward from there and races off rapidly over the surface of
the words. As a way of acknowledging the inherent character of the breathing mark by where it is placed, therefore,
the Athenians do not put it over vowels (as they do with
other such marks), but in front of them. In my opinion, the
ancients also indicated a rough breathing with the letter H;

b μαῖοι | πρὸ πάντων τῶν δασυνομένων ὀνομάτων τὸ Η̄
προγράφουσι, τὸ ἡγεμονικὸν αὐτῆς διασημαίνοντες.
εἰ δὲ τοιαύτη ἡ δασύτης, μήποτ᾽ ἀλόγως κατὰ τὴν
τελευτῶσαν συλλαβὴν ὁ ταῶς πρὸς τῶν Ἀττικῶν·
προσπνεῖται.

Πολλῶν οὖν καὶ ἄλλων ἐν τῷ συμποσίῳ περὶ
ἑκάστου τῶν εἰσκομιζομένων ῥηθέντων, ἀλλὰ κἀγώ,
φησὶν ὁ Λαρήνσιος, κατὰ τὸν πάντα ἄριστον Οὐλπι-
ανὸν προτείνω τι καὶ αὐτὸς ὑμῖν· ζητήσεις γὰρ σιτού-
μεθα· τὸν τέτρακα τί νομίζετε; καί τινος εἰπόντος,
c εἶδος ὀρνέου (ἔθος δὲ γραμματικῶν | παισὶν περὶ
πάντων τῶν προβαλλομένων λέγειν, "εἶδος φυτοῦ,
εἶδος ὀρνέου, εἶδος λίθου"), ὁ Λαρήνσιος ἔφη· καὶ
αὐτός, ἀνδρῶν λῷστε, ὅτι ὁ χαρίεις Ἀριστοφάνης ἐν
τοῖς Ὄρνισι μνημονεύει ἐν τούτοις οἶδα·

πορφυρίωνι καὶ πελεκᾶντι
καὶ πελεκίνῳ καὶ φλέξιδι
καὶ τέτρακι καὶ ταῶνι.

ζητῶ δ᾽ ἐγὼ παρ᾽ ὑμῶν μαθεῖν εἰ καὶ παρ᾽ ἄλλῳ τινὶ
αὐτοῦ τις γίνεται μνήμη. Ἀλέξανδρος γὰρ ὁ Μύνδιος
ἐν δευτέρῳ Περὶ Πτηνῶν Ζῴων οὐ τοῦ ὄρνιθος τοῦ
μεγάλου μνημονεύει, ἀλλά τινος τῶν σμικροτάτων.
λέγει γὰρ οὕτως· τέτραξ τὸ μέγεθος ἴσος σπερ-
d μολόγῳ, τὸ χρῶμα | κεραμεοῦς, ῥυπαραῖς στιγμαῖς
καὶ μεγάλαις γραμμαῖς ποικίλος, καρποφάγος. ὅταν

this is why the Romans put an H at the beginning of all their aspirated words, as a way of marking the tendency of the rough breathing to come first.[195] If this is the character of the rough breathing, the Attic pronunciation of *taōs* with such a breathing on the final syllable may be irrational.

After many additional remarks were made at our party about the various items we were served, Larensius said: I too have something to offer you, in the style of the marvellous Ulpian, since we are being fed questions. What do you think a *tetrax*[196] is? When someone responded: A type of bird—no matter what the question is, the grammarians' habit is to say, "It's a type of plant, or a type of bird, or a type of stone"!—Larensius replied: I myself am aware, best of men, that the witty Aristophanes mentions the creature in his *Birds* (882–4):

> to the purple gallinule and both types
> of pelican and the *phlexis*
> and the *tetrax* and the peacock.

But what I would like to learn from you, is whether any other author mentions it. Because Alexander of Myndus in Book II of *On Winged Creatures* (fr. I.21 Wellmann) does not refer to this as a large bird, but as one of the very smallest. For he says the following: The *tetrax* is the same size as a rook; is terracotta-colored, with variegated markings that consist of dirty-looking spots and long stripes; and

---

[195] *to hēgemonikon*, whence supposedly the Roman H.

[196] Identified by Dunbar (on Ar. *Av.* 884, quoted below) as an Asian sandgrouse of some sort.

ᾠοτοκῇ δέ, τετράζει τῇ φωνῇ. καὶ Ἐπίχαρμος ἐν
Ἥβας Γάμῳ·

> λαμβάνοντι γὰρ
> ὄρτυγας στρουθούς τε κορυδαλλάς ⟨τε⟩
>   φιλοκονείμονας
> τέτραγάς τε σπερματολόγους κἀγλαὰς
>   συκαλλίδας.

καὶ ἐν ἄλλοις δέ φησιν·

> ἦν δ᾽ ἐρῳδιοί τε πολλοὶ μακροκαμπυλαύχενες
> τέτραγές τε σπερματολόγοι.

ἐπεὶ δὲ ὑμεῖς οὐδὲν ἔχετε (σιωπᾶτε γάρ), ἐγὼ καὶ τὸ
ὄρνεον ὑμῖν ἐπιδείξω. ἐπιτροπεύων γὰρ ἐν Μυσίᾳ τοῦ
κυρίου αὐτοκράτορος | καὶ προϊστάμενος τῶν τῆς
ἐπαρχίας ἐκείνης πραγμάτων τεθέαμαι ἐπὶ τῇ χώρᾳ
ἐκείνῃ τοὔρνεον. καὶ μαθὼν οὕτω καλούμενον παρὰ
τοῖς Μυσοῖς καὶ Παίοσιν ὑπεμνήσθην ἐκ τῶν ὑπ᾽
Ἀριστοφάνους εἰρημένων τὸν ὄρνιθα. νομίζων δὲ καὶ
παρὰ τῷ πολυμαθεστάτῳ Ἀριστοτέλει μνήμης ἠξιῶ-
σθαι τὸ ζῷον ἐν τῇ πολυταλάντῳ πραγματείᾳ (ὀκτα-
κόσια γὰρ εἰληφέναι τάλαντα παρ᾽ Ἀλεξάνδρου τὸν
Σταγιρίτην λόγος ἔχει εἰς τὴν Περὶ τῶν Ζῴων Ἱστορίαν) ὡς οὐδὲν εὗρον περὶ αὐτοῦ λεγόμενον, ἔχαιρον

---

197 Clearly intended to serve as an etymology of the name.
198 The final two words of the fragment are quoted also at
2.65b, where they are again followed immediately by Epich. fr. 85
(in slightly more complete form).

feeds on fruit. When it lays its eggs, it cackles (*tetrazei*).[197] Epicharmus in *The Wedding of Hebe* (fr. 42):[198]

> Because they get
> quail, and sparrows, and larks that love to dust
>   themselves,
> and seed-gathering *tetrages*, and colorful warblers.

He also says in another passage (fr. 85.1–2):[199]

> There were many herons with long curved necks
> and seed-gathering *tetrages*.

Since none of you have anything to contribute—I see that you are keeping quiet—I will offer you an account of the bird myself. Because when I was serving as procurator for our lord the Emperor in Mysia and was in charge of the provincial government there, I saw a *tetrax* in that country; and when I learned that this was the name the Mysians and Paeonians have for it, I remembered it from the remarks offered by Aristophanes.[200] I assumed that the deeply learned Aristotle would have thought that the creature deserved some mention in his enormously expensive treatise—since the story goes that the Stagirite got 800 talents from Alexander to support work on his *Research on Animals*[201]—but when I found no reference to it there, I

[199] Quoted also, with a gap in the first verse but more of the second, at 2.65b.

[200] *Av.* 884 (quoted at 9.398c).   [201] I.e. the *Historia Animalium*. Aristotle (called "the Stagirite" after his native city of Stagira in Chalcidice) was Alexander's tutor (Berve i #135). Whether Alexander later supported his research is unclear; but 800 talents is in any case a preposterously large amount of money.

f ἔχων ἐχεγγυώτατον μάρτυρα τὸν χαρίεντα | Ἀριστο-
φάνη. ἅμα δὲ ταῦτα λέγοντος αὐτοῦ εἰσῆλθέ τις
φέρων ἐν τῷ ταλάρῳ τὸν τέτρακα. ἦν δὲ τὸ μὲν
μέγεθος ὑπὲρ ἀλεκτρυόνα τὸν μέγιστον, τὸ δὲ εἶδος
πορφυρίωνι παραπλήσιος· καὶ ἀπὸ τῶν ὤτων ἑκατέρωθεν εἶχε κρεμάμενα ὥσπερ οἱ ἀλεκτρυόνες τὰ κάλ-
399 λαια· βαρεῖα δ᾽ ἦν ἡ φωνή. ‖ θαυμασάντων οὖν ἡμῶν
τὸ εὐανθὲς τοῦ ὄρνιθος μετ᾽ οὐ πολὺ καὶ ἐσκευασμένος
παρηνέχθη, καὶ τὰ κρέα αὐτοῦ ἦν παραπλήσια τοῖς
τῆς μεγάλης στρουθοῦ, ἣν καὶ αὐτὴν πολλάκις κατ-
εδαισάμεθα.

Ψύαι. ὁ τὴν τῶν Ἀτρειδῶν Κάθοδον πεποιηκὼς ἐν
τῷ τρίτῳ φησίν·

Ἶσον δ᾽ Ἑρμιονεὺς ποσὶ καρπαλίμοισι
     μετασπῶν
ψύας ἔγχεϊ νύξε.

Σιμάριστος δ᾽ ἐν τρίτῳ Συνωνύμων οὕτως γράφει· |
b ὀσφύος αἱ ἐκ πλαγίων σάρκες ἐπανεστηκυῖαι ψύαι. τὰ
δ᾽ ἑκατέρωθεν κοιλώματα λέγουσι † κύβους γαλλίας †.
Κλέαρχος δ᾽ ἐν δευτέρῳ Περὶ Σκελετῶν οὕτως φησί·
σάρκες μυωταὶ καθ᾽ ἑκάτερον μέρος, ἃς οἱ μὲν ψύας, οἱ
δὲ ἀλώπεκας, οἱ δὲ νευρομήτρας καλοῦσι. μνημονεύει
δὲ τῶν ψύων καὶ Ἱπποκράτης ὁ ἱερώτατος. ὠνομάσθη-
σαν δ᾽ οὕτως διὰ τὸ ῥᾳδίως ἀποψᾶσθαι ἢ οἷόν τις
ἐπιψαύουσα[18] σὰρξ καὶ ἐπιπολῆς τοῖς ὀστέοις ὑπάρ-

---

[18] τις οὖσα ACE: οὖσα del. Wilamowitz

was delighted to have the witty Aristophanes as an utterly reliable witness. As he was in the middle of these remarks, someone came in, carrying the *tetrax* in its cage. It was larger than the largest rooster; looked a great deal like a purple gallinule; had wattles hanging below its ears on both sides, like a rooster; and produced a low-pitched call. We expressed amazement at the bird's beautiful coloring, and a few minutes later it was cooked and served; its meat resembled ostrich, which we also dined on frequently.

Loin-muscles. The author of the *Return of the Atreidae* says in Book III (*Nost*. fr. 11 Bernabé):

Hermioneus used his swift feet to pursue Isos,
and pierced his loin-muscles with a spear.

Simaristus writes as follows in Book III of *Synonyms*: The sections of flesh that sit sideways over the tailbone are loin-muscles. The hollow sections on either side of it, on the other hand, are referred to as [corrupt]. Clearchus says the following in Book II of *On Skeletons*[202] (fr. 106a Wehrli): the muscles on either side, which various authorities refer to as loin-muscles (*psuai*), *alōpekes*, and *neuromētrai*. The venerable Hippocrates (e.g. *Morb. Sacr.* 6.366.14 Littré) also mentions loin-muscles. They got this name from the fact that they can easily be wiped clean (*apopsasthai*), or because they represent a bit of flesh that sits on top of the bones and barely touches (*epipsauousa*) them.[203] The

---

[202] Or *On Dried Bodies, Mummies*.
[203] Desperate and impossible etymologies.

c χουσα. μνημονεύει αὐτῶν καὶ Εὔφρων ὁ κωμικὸς | ἐν Θεωροῖς·

> λοβός τις ἐστι καὶ ψύαι καλούμεναι·
> ταύτας ἐπιτεμὼν πρὶν θεωρῆσαι μαθών.

Οὖθαρ. Τηλεκλείδης Στερροῖς·

> ὡς οὖσα θῆλυς εἰκότως οὖθαρ φορῶ.

Ἡρόδοτος δ᾽ ἐν τῇ τετάρτῃ τῶν Ἱστοριῶν φησιν < . . . >. σπανίως δ᾽ ἔστιν εὑρεῖν τὸ οὖθαρ ἐπὶ τῶν ἄλλων ζῴων λεγόμενον· ὑπογάστριον δὲ μόνον ὡς ἐπὶ τῶν ἰχθύων λέγεται. Στράττις Ἀταλάντῃ·

d ὑπογάστριον | θύννου τι κἀκροκώλιον.

Θεόπομπος Καλλαίσχρῳ·

> ἰχθύων δὲ δὴ
> ὑπογάστρι᾽, ὦ Δάματερ.

ἐν δὲ Σειρῆσιν ὑπήτρια καλεῖ τὰ ὑπογάστρια λέγων οὕτως·

> θύννων τε λευκὰ Σικελικῶν ὑπήτρια·

Λαγῶς. περὶ τούτου ὁ μὲν ὀψοδαίδαλος Ἀρχέστρατος οὕτως φησί·

---

204 The quotation (from an account of how the Scythians milk their horses) has fallen out of the text. Teleclides fr. 33 (above) is quoted also at 14.656e, where see n.

comic author Euphro refers to them in *Sacred Ambassadors* (fr. 7):

> There's a lobe, as well as what are called loin-
>   muscles;
> make a gash in them before you leave on your
>   embassy, after you learn . . .

Udder. Teleclides in *Tough Guys* (fr. 33):

> I'm a female, so naturally I've got an udder.

Herodotus says in Book IV (2.1) of his *History*: . . . [204] The word udder (*outhar*) is rarely attested referring to any other animal, while *hupogastrion* ("underbelly") is only used of fish. Strattis in *Atalante* (fr. 5.1):[205]

> a tuna-underbelly and a trotter.

Theopompus in *Callaeschrus* (fr. 24):[206]

> > underbellies
> of fish indeed, O Demeter!

But in *Sirens* (fr. 52) he refers to underbellies as *hupētria* ("underpaunches"), saying the following:

> and white underpaunches (*hupētria*) of Sicilian tuna.

Hare. Archestratus (fr. 57 Olson–Sens = *SH* 188), the Daedalus[207] of fancy dishes, says the following about this creature:

---

[205] A slightly longer version of the fragment is preserved at 7.302d–e.

[206] Quoted also at 7.302e.

[207] See 9.396a n.

τοῦ δὲ λαγὼ πολλοί τε τρόποι πολλαί τε
    θέμιστες
σκευασίης εἰσίν. κεῖνος δ᾽ οὖν ἐστιν ἄριστος,
ἂν πίνουσι μεταξὺ φέρῃς κρέας ὀπτὸν ἑκάστῳ, |
e   θερμόν, ἁπλῶς ἁλίπαστον, ἀφαρπάζων
    ὀβελίσκου
μικρὸν ἐνωμότερον. μὴ λυπείτω δέ σ᾽ ὁρῶντα
ἰχῶρα στάζοντα κρεῶν, ἀλλ᾽ ἔσθιε λάβρως.
αἱ δ᾽ ἄλλαι περίεργοι ἔμοιγ᾽ εἰσὶν διὰ παντὸς
σκευασίαι, γλοιῶν καταχύσματα καὶ κατάτυρα
καὶ κατέλαια λίην, ὥσπερ γαλῇ ὀψοποιούντων.

Ναυσικράτης δ᾽ ὁ κωμῳδιοποιὸς ἐν Περσίδι, σπα-
f   νίως, | φησίν, ἔστιν εὑρεῖν δασύποδα περὶ τὴν Ἀττι-
κήν. λέγει δὲ ὧδε·

εν τῇ γὰρ Ἀττικῇ τίς εἶδε πώποτε
λέοντας ἢ τοιοῦτον ἕτερον θηρίον;
οὗ δασύποδ᾽ εὑρεῖν ἐστιν οὐχὶ ῥᾴδιον.

Ἀλκαῖος δ᾽ ἐν Καλλιστοῖ καὶ ὡς πολλῶν ὄντων ἐμφανίζει διὰ τούτων·

(Α). κορίαννον ἵνα τί λεπτόν; (Β.) ἵνα τοὺς
    δασύποδας
οὓς ἂν λάβωμεν ἁλσὶ διαπάττειν ἔχῃς. ||

400   Τρύφων δέ φησι· τὸν λαγὼν ἐπ᾽ αἰτιατικῆς ἐν Δαναί-
σιν Ἀριστοφάνης ὀξυτόνως καὶ μετὰ τοῦ ν λέγει·

Diverse are the manners and settled customs of
the hare's preparation. But it is best
if, while the others are drinking, you serve each man
    roasted meat,
hot and seasoned with salt only, pulling it off the spit
when it is still a bit on the rare side. Do not let it
    trouble you when you see
the juice dripping from the meat, but eat it greedily!
The other ways of preparing it are, in my opinion,
    much
too elaborate—sauces made of sticky ingredients and
    over-rich
in oil and cheese, as if they were preparing a dish for
    a weasel.

The comic poet Nausicrates in *The Girl from Persia* (fr. 2)
claims that hares are seldom found in Attica. He puts it as
follows:

Because who's ever seen lions
or any other beast like that in Attica?
It's not even easy to find a hare there!

But Alcaeus in *Callisto* (fr. 17) suggests that there were
plenty of them, in the following passage:

(A.) What's the powdered coriander for? (B.) So you
    can
sprinkle any hares we catch with salt.

Tryphon (fr. 19 Velsen) says: Aristophanes in *Danaids* (fr.
263) uses the accusative form *lagōn* ("hare") with an acute
accent on the final syllable and a *nu*:

λύσας ἴσως ἂν τὸν λαγὼν ξυναρπάσειεν ὑμῶν.

καὶ ἐν Δαιταλεῦσιν·

ἀπόλωλα· τίλλων τὸν λαγὼν ὀφθήσομαι.

Ξενοφῶν δ' ἐν Κυνηγετικῷ χωρὶς τοῦ ῡ λαγῶ καὶ
περισπωμένως, ἐπεὶ τὸ καθ' ἡμᾶς ἐστι λαγός, ὥσπερ
δὲ ναὸν λεγόντων ἡμῶν ἐκεῖνοί φασιν νεὼν καὶ λαὸν
λεών, οὕτω λαγὸν ὀνομαζόντων ἐκεῖνοι λαγῶν ἐροῦσι.
b τῇ δὲ τὸν λαγὸν ἑνικῇ αἰτιατικῇ | ἀκόλουθός ἐστιν ἡ
παρὰ Σοφοκλεῖ ἐν Ἀμύκῳ σατυρικῷ πληθυντικὴ ὀνο-
μαστική·

γέρανοι, χελῶναι, γλαῦκες, ἰκτῖνοι, λαγοί.

τῇ δὲ λαγὼν ἡ διὰ τοῦ ῶ παραπλησίως προσαγορευομένη λαγῷ παρ' Εὐπόλιδι ἐν Κόλαξιν·

ἵνα πάρα μὲν < . . . > βατίδες καὶ λαγῷ
καὶ γυναῖκες εἰλίποδες.

εἰσὶν δ' οἳ καὶ ταῦτ' ἀλόγως κατὰ τὴν τελευτῶσαν
συλλαβὴν περισπωμένως προφέρονται. δεῖ δὲ ὀξυτο-
νεῖν τὴν λέξιν, ἐπειδὴ τὰ εἰς -ος λήγοντα τῶν ὀνο-
c μάτων ὁμότονά ἐστι, κἂν μεταληφθῇ | εἰς τὸ ῶ παρ'

---

208 Probably a proverbial expression (or a comic adaptation
thereof).

209 I.e. Attic-speakers.

210 Quoted again below, in a slightly different form (and thus
presumably from a different source).

362

He might let the hare (*lagōn*) go and then join you in
  stealing it.

And in *Banqueters* (fr. 218):

I've had it; I'm going to be seen plucking the hare
  (*lagōn*)![208]

Xenophon in the *Art of Hunting* (e.g. 4.10), on the other
hand, has *lagō* without the *nu* and with a circumflex accent
on the final syllable. Because our form of the word is *lagos*;
and just as we say *naos* ("temple") and *laos* ("people"),
whereas they[209] say *neōs* and *leōs*, so too we say *lagos*,
whereas they say *lagōs*. The form of the nominative plural
used in Sophocles' satyr play *Amycus* (fr. 111)[210] is consis-
tent with the accusative singular *lagon*:

cranes, tortoises, little owls, kites, hares (*lagoi*).

The form *lagōi* pronounced with an *omega* and analogous
with *lagōn*, on the other hand, is found in Eupolis' *Flatterers* (fr. 174.2–3):[211]

where skate and hares (*lagōi*) are present,
as well as shambling-footed[212] women.

Some authorities accent these forms irrationally, placing a
circumflex on the final syllable. But the word ought to take
an acute there, since nouns that end in *-os* have the same
pitch throughout, even if they change to an *omega* in Attic:

211 A slightly longer version of the fragment is quoted at
7.286b.
212 A Homeric epithet of cattle.

ATHENAEUS

Ἀττικοῖς· ναὸς νεώς, κάλος κάλως. οὕτως δ' ἐχρήσατο τῷ ὀνόματι καὶ Ἐπίχαρμος καὶ Ἡρόδοτος καὶ ὁ τοὺς Εἵλωτας ποιήσας. εἶτά ἐστι τὸ μὲν Ἰακὸν λαγός·

λαγὸν ταράξας πῖθι τὸν θαλάσσιον,

τὸ δὲ λαγὼς Ἀττικόν. λέγουσι δὲ καὶ Ἀττικοὶ λαγός, ὡς Σοφοκλῆς·

γέρανοι, κορῶναι, γλαῦκες, ἰκτῖνοι, λαγοί.

τὸ μέντοι

< . . . > ἢ πτῶκα λαγωὸν

εἰ μέν ἐστιν Ἰωνικόν, πλεονάζει τὸ ω, εἰ δ' Ἀττικόν, τὸ
d ō. λαγῷα δὲ λέγεται | κρέα. Ἡγήσανδρος δ' ὁ Δελφὸς
ἐν Ὑπομνήμασι κατὰ τὴν Ἀντιγόνου τοῦ Γονατᾶ
φησιν βασιλείαν τοσοῦτον πλῆθος γενέσθαι λαγῶν
ἐν Ἀστυπαλαίᾳ, ὡς τοὺς Ἀστυπαλαιεῖς περὶ αὐτῶν
μαντεύσασθαι· καὶ τὴν Πυθίαν εἰπεῖν κύνας τρέφειν
καὶ κυνηγετεῖν· ἁλῶναί τε ἐν ἐνιαυτῷ πλείους τῶν
ἑξακισχιλίων. ἐγένετο δὲ τὸ πλῆθος τοῦτο Ἀναφαίου
τινὸς ἐμβαλόντος δύο λαγωοὺς εἰς τὴν νῆσον· ὡς καὶ
πρότερον Ἀστυπαλαιέως τινὸς ἀφέντος δύο πέρδικας

---

213 The first form is the common one, the second form the Attic.

214 Sc. the common form *lagos*.

215 Quoted repeatedly by Athenaeus (7.286f, 287b–c, 305c).

216 For doubts about the authorship of this play (attributed to
Eupolis by Polemon at 4.138f), see 14.638e.

naós neōs ("temple"), *kálos kálōs* ("rope, line").[213] This[214] is the form of the word used by Epicharmus (fr. 53.2)[215], Herodotus (e.g. 1.123.4, 124.1), and the author of *Helots* (Eup. fr. 153).[216] Next, the Ionian form is *lagos*:

> Stir up the sea-hare (*lagos*) and drink it! (Amips. fr. 17),[217]

whereas *lagōs* is the Attic form. But even Attic authors use *lagos*, as for example Sophocles (fr. 111):[218]

> cranes, crows, little owls, kites, hares (*lagoi*).

But as for the phrase (*Il.* 22.310)

> or a cowering hare (*lagōon*),

if this is an Ionic form, the *omega* is superfluous, whereas if it is Attic, the *omicron* is. Hare-meat is referred to as *lagōia*. Hegesander of Delphi in his *Commentaries* (fr. 42, *FHG* iv.421) claims that during the reign of Antigonus Gonatas[219] there were so many hares in Astypalaea that the local residents consulted an oracle about them. The Pythia told them (Delphic Oracle Q233 Fontenrose) to raise dogs and hunt them; that year more than 6000 were caught. This explosion in their numbers occurred when someone from Anaphe released two hares on the island; so too earlier, after an Astypalaean let two partridges go on Anaphe,

---

[217] Attributed to Amipsias' *Sling* at 10.446d; the speaker is presumably either a physician or someone imitating medical language. The material that follows appears to come from a different source than the preceding.

[218] Cf. 9.400b with n.

[219] King of Macedon *c.*277/6–239 BCE.

εἰς τὴν Ἀνάφην τοσοῦτον πλῆθος ἐγένετο περδίκων ἐν
e   τῇ Ἀνάφῃ, | ὡς κινδυνεῦσαι ἀναστάτους γενέσθαι
τοὺς κατοικοῦντας. κατ' ἀρχὰς δ' ἡ μὲν Ἀστυπάλαια
οὐκ εἶχεν λαγώς, ἀλλὰ πέρδικας. πολύγονον δ' ἐστὶ τὸ
ζῷον ὁ λαγώς, ὡς Ξενοφῶν εἴρηκεν ἐν τῷ Κυνηγετικῷ.
καὶ Ἡρόδοτος δ' οὕτως φησίν· τοῦτο μὲν ὅτι ὁ λαγὼς
ὑπὸ πάντων θηρεύεται, καὶ θηρίου καὶ ὄρνιθος καὶ
ἀνθρώπου, οὕτω δή τι πολύγονόν ἐστιν, ἐπικυΐσκει τε
μόνον πάντων θηρίων, καὶ τὸ μὲν δασὺ τῶν τέκνων ἐν
τῇ γαστρί, τὸ δὲ ψιλόν, τὸ δὲ ἄρτι ἐν τῆς μήτρῃσι
f   πλάσσεται, τὸ δ' ἐπαναιρέεται. Πολύβιος δ' ἐν | τῇ
δωδεκάτῃ τῶν Ἱστοριῶν γίγνεσθαί φησι παρόμοιον
τῷ λαγῷ ζῷον τὸν κούνικλον καλούμενον, γράφων
οὕτως· ὁ δὲ κούνικλος καλούμενος πόρρωθεν μὲν ὁρώμενος εἶναι δοκεῖ λαγὼς μικρός· ὅταν δ' εἰς τὰς χεῖρας
λάβῃ τις, μεγάλην ἔχει διαφορὰν καὶ κατὰ τὴν ἐπι-
φάνειαν καὶ κατὰ τὴν βρῶσιν. γίνεται δὲ τὸ πλεῖον
401   κατὰ γῆς. μνημονεύει δ' αὐτῶν καὶ Ποσειδώνιος ‖ ὁ
φιλόσοφος ἐν τῇ Ἱστορίᾳ· καὶ ἡμεῖς εἴδομεν πολλοὺς
κατὰ τὸν ἀπὸ Δικαιαρχείας πλοῦν ἐπὶ Νέαν πόλιν·
νῆσος γάρ ἐστιν οὐ μακρὰν τῆς γῆς κατὰ τὰ τελευ-
ταῖα μέρη τῆς Δικαιαρχείας ὑπ' ὀλίγων μὲν κατοι-
κουμένη, πολλοὺς δὲ ἔχουσα τοὺς κουνίκλους τούτους.
καλοῦνται δέ τινες καὶ χελιδονίαι λαγοί. μνημονεύει
Δίφιλος ἢ Καλλιάδης ἐν Ἀγνοίᾳ οὕτως·

there were so many partridges there that the inhabitants almost had to abandon the place. Astapalaea originally had no hares, but did have partridges. According to Xenophon in his *Art of Hunting* (5.13), the hare is a prolific creature. Herodotus (3.108.3) as well says the following:[220] Because, first of all, the hare is hunted by everything—animals, birds, and humans—it is accordingly prolific, and is the only animal that carries a number of pregnancies simultaneously: one set of young is covered with fur in its belly, while a second set is fur-less, a third is just beginning to take shape in its womb, and a fourth is being conceived. Polybius in Book XII (3.10) of his *History* reports that the so-called *kouniklos* ("rabbit") is a creature that resembles the hare. He writes as follows: When seen from a distance, the so-called *kouniklos* appears to be a small hare; but when you get one in your hands, it both looks and tastes quite different. It is generally found underground. The philosopher Posidonius also mentions them in his *History* (*FGrH* 87 F 61 = fr. 52 Edelstein–Kidd): We saw many of these on our voyage from Dicaearcheia to Neapolis; because there is an island not far from shore, at the very edge of Dicaearcheian territory, that has only a few human inhabitants, but large numbers of these *kounikloi*. Certain varieties of hare are also known as *chelidoniai*[221]. Diphilus (fr. 1) or Calliades[222] mentions them in *Ignorance*, as follows:

[220] Some Ionicisms have been removed from the text.

[221] Presumably cognate with *chelidōn*, "swallow".

[222] Otherwise known only from his presence in the catalogue of victors at the Lenaia festival (*IG* II² 2325.166; one victory near the end of the 4th century BCE).

ATHENAEUS

(A.) τί τοῦτο; ποδαπὸς οὗτος;
(B.) χελιδόνειος ὁ δασύπους, γλυκεῖα δ' ἡ
μίμαρκυς.

b Θεόπομπος δὲ ἐν τῇ εἰκοστῇ τῶν Ἱστοριῶν | περὶ τὴν
Βισαλτίαν φησὶ λαγωοὺς γίγνεσθαι δύο ἥπατα ἔχοντας.

Συὸς δὲ ἀγρίου ἐπεισενεχθέντος, ὃς κατ' οὐδὲν ἦν
ἐλάττων τοῦ καλοῦ γραφομένου Καλυδωνίου, προ-
βάλλω, τὶς ἔφη, σοὶ ζητεῖν, φροντιστὰ καὶ λογιστὰ
Οὐλπιανέ, τίς ἱστόρηκε τὸν Καλυδώνιον σῦν θήλειάν
τε γεγονέναι καὶ λευκὸν τὴν χρόαν. ὁ δὲ σφόδρα
φροντίσας καὶ τὸ προβληθὲν ἀποδιοπομπησάμενος,
ἀλλ' ὑμεῖς γε, ἔφη, ἄνδρες γάστρωνες, εἰ μὴ κόρον
ἤδη ἔχετε τοσούτων ἐμπλησθέντες, ὑπερβάλλειν μοι
c δοκεῖτε πάντας | τοὺς ἐπὶ πολυφαγίᾳ διαβοήτους γε-
νομένους· καὶ τίνες εἰσὶν οὗτοι ζητεῖτε. προφέρεσθαι
δὲ δίκαιόν ἐστιν ὑμᾶς σὺν τῷ ς̄ σῦς ἐτυμώτερον· παρὰ
τὸ σεύεσθαι γὰρ καὶ ὁρμητικῶς ἔχειν τὸ ζῷον εἴρηται.
τέτριπται δὲ καὶ τὸ λέγειν χωρὶς τοῦ κατ' ἀρχὰς ς̄ ὗς.
οἱ δὲ σὺν εἰρῆσθαι οἱονεὶ θῦν, τὸν εἰς θυσίαν εὐθε-
τοῦντα. νῦν δέ, εἰ δοκεῖ, ἀποκρίνασθέ μοι τίς μνημονεύει κατὰ τὸ σύνθετον ὁμοίως ἡμῖν συάγρου ἐπὶ τοῦ

---

223 A dish made from the blood and entrails of a hare; see
Olson on Ar. *Ach*. 1112. 224 The object of the famous hunt
in the generation before the Trojan War, which led to the death of
the hero Meleager and was a popular topic in art from the 6th century BCE on; cf. *Il*. 9.529–99; Bacch. 5; A. *Ch*. 602–11.

368

> (A.) What's this? What type's this one?
> (B.) The hare's a *chelidoneios*; but the *mimarkus*[223] is
>   delicious!

Theopompus in Book XX of his *History* (*FGrH* 115 F 126a) reports that there are hares in Bisaltia that have two livers.

After a wild boar (*sus agrios*) no smaller than the fine Calydonian boar[224] seen in paintings was served, someone said: I invite you, (adesp. com. fr. *116, unmetrical) my thoughtful and precise Ulpian, to take up the question of who reports that the Calydonian boar (*sus*) was both a sow and white. He thought hard and set the matter aside,[225] and said: Potbellies, unless you are so full of topics like this that you are satisfied, you appear to me to outdo anyone who was ever notorious for gluttony. The question you must explore is: Who are these individuals?[226] You ought properly to pronounce the word *sus*, with a *sigma*, which is closer to its origin; because the creature gets its name from the fact that it moves rapidly (*seuesthai*) and tends to attack.[227] But pronouncing it *hus*, without the initial *sigma*, has become common usage. Some authorities claim that it is pronounced *sus* because this is, as it were, a *thus*, since the creature is appropriate for sacrifice (*thusia*).[228] But now, if you will, tell me who refers to a wild boar (*sus agrios*) with the compound form *suagros*, as we do. For

225 The question is taken up at 9.402a.

226 Gluttons are the main topic of Books 10 and especially 11, but the question is ignored in what follows.

227 A false etymology. Most likely *sus* and *hus* are simply variant forms of the same, originally Indo-European word.

228 Another false etymology.

συὸς τοῦ ἀγρίου. Σοφοκλῆς μὲν γὰρ ἐν Ἀχιλλέως
d Ἐρασταῖς ἐπὶ κυνὸς ἔταξε τοὔνομα ἀπὸ | τοῦ σῦς
ἀγρεύειν, λέγων·

σὺ δ᾽, ὦ Σύαγρε, Πηλιωτικὸν τρέφος.

παρ᾽ Ἡροδότῳ δὲ ὄνομα κύριον Σύαγρος Λάκων γένος, ὁ πρὸς Γέλωνα τὸν Συρακόσιον πρεσβεύσας περὶ
τῆς πρὸς τοὺς Μήδους συμμαχίας ἐν τῇ ἑβδόμῃ. καὶ
Αἰτωλῶν δὲ οἶδα στρατηγὸν Σύαγρον, οὗ μνημονεύει
Φύλαρχος ἐν τετάρτῃ Ἱστοριῶν. καὶ ὁ Δημόκριτος
ἔφη· ἀεί ποτε σύ, ὦ Οὐλπιανέ, οὐδενὸς μεταλαμβάνειν
εἴωθας τῶν παρασκευαζομένων πρὶν μαθεῖν εἰ ἡ χρῆ-
e σις μὴ εἴη τῶν ὀνομάτων | παλαιά. κινδυνεύεις οὖν
ποτε διὰ ταύτας τὰς φροντίδας ὥσπερ ὁ Κῷος Φιλη-
τᾶς ζητῶν τὸν καλούμενον ψευδολόγον τῶν λόγων
ὁμοίως ἐκείνῳ διαλυθῆναι. ἰσχνὸς γὰρ πάνυ τὸ σῶμα
διὰ τὰς ζητήσεις γενόμενος ἀπέθανεν, ὡς τὸ πρὸ τοῦ
μνημείου αὐτοῦ ἐπίγραμμα δηλοῖ·

ξεῖνε, Φιλίτας εἰμί· λόγων ὁ ψευδόμενός με
ὤλεσε καὶ νυκτῶν φροντίδες ἑσπέριοι.

ἵν᾽ οὖν μὴ καὶ σὺ ζητῶν τὸν σύαγρον ἀφανανθῇς,
f μάθε ὅτι Ἀντιφάνης μὲν ἐν Ἁρπαζομένῃ οὕτως | ὠνό-
μασε·

Sophocles in *The Lovers of Achilleus* (fr. 154) gave the name to a dog, since it hunts boars (*sus agreuein*), saying:

> and you, Suagros, whom Pelion produced.

In Herodotus Book VII (153.1), Suagros is a proper name that belongs to a Spartan who was sent to Gelon in Syracuse about the question of forming an alliance against the Medes.[229] I also know of an Aetolian general named Suagros[230], who is mentioned by Phylarchus in Book IV of the *History* (*FGrH* 81 F 5). Democritus responded: Ulpian, you always make it your practice not to taste any of the food prepared for us, until you learn whether an ancient author uses the word. Your concern for such matters may be putting you at risk of wasting away like Philetas of Cos, when he tried to identify what he referred to as the lying word. He became extremely emaciated as a result of his research and died, as the epigram inscribed on his tomb makes clear (adesp. *FGE* 1612–13 = Philet. test. 21 Spanoudakis = test. 7 Sbardella):

> I am Philitas, stranger. The lying word brought about my
> death, along with hard work at night after the sun
> went down.

So to keep you from shriveling up as a result of your inquiry into the term *suagros*, allow me to inform you that Antiphanes used it in *The Girl Who Was Kidnapped* (fr. 44), as follows:

229 In 480 BCE. Suagros (otherwise unknown) is Poralla #677.
230 Grainger p. 313 (Suagros 1); he was general in 226/5 BCE.

λαβὼν ἐπανάξω σύαγρον εἰς τὴν οἰκίαν
τῆς νυκτὸς αὐτῆς καὶ λέοντα καὶ λύκον.

Διονύσιος δὲ ὁ τύραννος ἐν τῷ Ἀδώνιδι·

νυμφῶν ὑπὸ σπήλυγγα † τὸν † αὐτόστεγον
σύαγρον ἐκβόλειον † εὔθηρον κλύειν †
ὁπλάς τ᾽ ἀπαρχὰς ἀκροθινιάζομαι.

Λυγκεὺς δ᾽ ὁ Σάμιος ἐν τῇ Πρὸς Ἀπολλόδωρον Ἐπι-
402 στολῇ γράφει οὕτως· ἵνα τὰ μὲν αἴγεια ‖ τοῖς παισί,
τὰ δὲ συάγρεια μετὰ τῶν φίλων αὐτὸς ἔχῃς. καὶ
Ἱππόλοχος δὲ ὁ Μακεδών, οὗ ἐμνημονεύσαμεν ἐν τοῖς
πρὸ τούτων, ἐν τῇ πρὸς τὸν προειρημένον Λυγκέα
ἐπιστολῇ ἐμνήσθη συάγρων πολλῶν. ἐπεὶ δὲ σὺ καὶ
τὸ προβληθέν σοι ἀποπροσπεποίησαι περὶ τῆς χρόας
τοῦ Καλυδωνίου συός, εἴ τις αὐτὸν ἱστορεῖ λευκὸν τὴν
χρόαν γεγονότα, ἐροῦμεν ἡμεῖς τὸν εἰπόντα· τὸ δὲ
μαρτύριον ἀνίχνευσον σύ. πάλαι γὰρ τυγχάνω ἀν-
εγνωκὼς τοὺς Κλεομένους τοῦ Ῥηγίνου διθυράμβους,
ὧν ἐν τῷ ἐπιγραφομένῳ Μελεάγρῳ τοῦτο ἱστόρηται.
b οὐκ | ἀγνοῶ δ᾽ ὅτι οἱ περὶ τὴν Σικελίαν κατοικοῦντες
ἀσχέδωρον καλοῦσι τὸν σύαγρον. Αἰσχύλος γοῦν ἐν
Φορκίσι παρεικάζων τὸν Περσέα τῷ ἀγρίῳ τούτῳ συΐ
φησιν·

ἔδυ δ᾽ ἐς ἄντρον ἀσχέδωρος ὥς.

---

[231] Presumably a high-style way of referring to a sow's womb
(for which, cf. 3.100b–1c).

Tonight I'm going to get a wild boar (*suagros*), a lion, and a wolf, and bring them into the house too!

The tyrant Dionysius in his *Adonis* (*TrGF* 76 F 1):

Within the cave of the nymphs † here † with its
    natural roof
I take as first-fruit spoils for myself the hooves and
and wild-boar (*suagron*) expulsion[231] † easily caught
    to hear about. †

Lynceus of Samos in his *Letter to Apollodorus* (fr. 18 Dalby) writes as follows: so that you can have goat-meat for your slaves, but wild-boar meat (*ta suagreia*) to enjoy yourself, along with your friends. Hippolochus of Macedon, whom we discussed earlier, also referred repeatedly to *suagroi* in his letter to the Lynceus mentioned above.[232] But since you have deferred the question posed for you (9.401b) about the color of the Calydonian boar and whether anyone describes it as white, I will tell you who said this; but you can track down the reference yourself. For I read the dithyrambs of Cleomenes of Rhegium long ago, and this claim is put forward in the one entitled *Meleager* (*PMG* 838). I am well aware that the Sicilians refer to the wild boar (*suagros*) as an *aschedōros*. Aeschylus in *The Children of Phorcys*[233] (fr. 261), for example, compares Perseus to this wild boar and says:

He descended into the cave like an *aschedōros*.

---

[232] I.e. in the letter describing the wedding feast of Caranus of Macedon quoted at 4.128a–30d.

[233] I.e. the Graeae and the Gorgons (including Medusa).

καὶ Σκίρας (εἷς δ᾽ ἐστὶν οὗτος τῆς Ἰταλικῆς καλουμένης κωμῳδίας ποιητής, γένος Ταραντῖνος) ἐν Μελεάγρῳ φησίν·

ἔνθ᾽ οὔτε ποιμὴν ἀξιοῖ νέμειν βοτὰ
οὔτ᾽ ἀσχέδωρος νεμόμενος καπρώζεται. |

c ὅτι δὲ Αἰσχύλος διατρίψας ἐν Σικελίᾳ πολλαῖς κέχρηται φωναῖς Σικελικαῖς οὐδὲν θαυμαστόν.

Περιεφέροντο καὶ ἔριφοι πολλάκις ποικίλως ἐσκευ-
ασμένοι· ἄλλοι δὲ καὶ πολὺ τοῦ ὀποῦ ἔχοντες, οἵτινες
οὐ τὴν τυχοῦσαν ἡδονὴν παρεῖχον ἡμῖν. καὶ γὰρ τὸ
τοῦ αἰγὸς κρέας τροφιμώτατόν ἐστι. Κλειτόμαχος
γοῦν ὁ Καρχηδόνιος οὐδενὸς δεύτερος τῶν ἀπὸ τῆς
νέας Ἀκαδημείας κατὰ τὴν θεωρίαν ὢν Θηβαῖόν τινα
ἀθλητὴν ὑπερβαλεῖν ἰσχύι φησὶ τοὺς καθ᾽ ἑαυτὸν
κρέασιν αἰγείοις χρώμενον· εὔτονοι γὰρ καὶ γλίσχροι
d ⟨οἱ⟩[19] χυμοὶ καὶ πολὺν χρόνον | ὑπομένειν ἐν τοῖς
ὄγκοις δυνάμενοι. ἐσκώπτετο δὲ ὁ ἀθλητὴς διὰ τὴν
ἀπὸ τῶν ἱδρώτων δυσωδίαν. τὰ δ᾽ ὕεια καὶ ἄρνεια κρέα
ἀδιαπόνητα ταῖς ἕξεσιν ὑπάρχοντα ῥᾷστα φθείρεται
διὰ τὴν πιμελήν.

Τὰ δὲ παρὰ τοῖς κωμῳδιοποιοῖς λεγόμενα δεῖπνα
ἡδίστην ἀκοὴν παρέχει τοῖς ὠσὶ μᾶλλον ἢ τῇ φάρυγ-
γι, ὥσπερ τὰ παρὰ Ἀντιφάνει μὲν ἐν Ἀκεστρίᾳ·

[19] add. Kaibel

And Sciras—(test. 1) he wrote what is referred to as Italian comedy, and his family was from Tarentum—says in *Meleager* (fr. 1):

> In that spot neither does any shepherd think it right
> to graze his flocks,
> nor does an *aschedōros* rut there as it grazes.

It comes as no surprise that Aeschylus (test. 92a) uses a considerable amount of Sicilian vocabulary, given that he spent time on the island.[234]

Fancily-prepared kids were often served; some were made with a large amount of silphium juice, and we found them exceptionally tasty. Goat-meat is in fact extremely nourishing. Cleitomachus of Carthage,[235] at any rate, who is second to no one in the New Academy in his theoretical work, claims that a Theban athlete overpowered all his opponents by eating nothing except goat-meat; because the humours it produces are strong and sticky, and capable of remaining in one's flesh for a long time. But people made fun of the athlete because his sweat smelled bad. Pork and mutton, on the other hand, are quite easily broken down while still in an undigested state, because of the fat they contain.

The accounts of dinner parties offered by the comic poets provide more pleasure for one's ears than one's throat, as for example the passage in Antiphanes' *The Seamstress* (fr. 21):

---

234 Aeschylus made at least two trips to Sicily, once in the late 470s BCE (to Syracuse) and again in the mid-450s (to Gela, where he died in 456/5). 235 Head of the New Academy c.128–c.110 BCE (*PAA* 575900); none of his writings are preserved.

(A.) κρέας δὲ τίνος ἥδιστ᾽ ἂν ἐσθίοις (φησίν);
   (B.) τίνος;
εἰς εὐτέλειαν. τῶν προβάτων μὲν οἷς ἔνι |

e   μήτ᾽ ἔρια μήτε τυρός, ἀρνός, φίλτατε.
τῶν δ᾽ αἰγιδίων κατὰ ταῦθ᾽ ἃ μὴ τυρὸν ποεῖ,
ἐρίφου· διὰ τὴν ἐπικαρπίαν γὰρ τῶν ἁδρῶν
ταῦτ᾽ ἐσθίων τὰ φαῦλ᾽ ἀνέχομαι.

ἐν δὲ Κύκλωπί φησι·

  τῶν χερσαίων δ᾽ ἡμῖν[20] ἥξει
  παρ᾽ ἐμοῦ ταυτί·
  βοῦς ἀγελαῖος, τράγος ὑλιβάτης,
  αἲξ οὐρανία, κριὸς τομίας,
  κάπρος ἐκτομίας, ὗς οὐ τομίας,
  δέλφαξ, δασύπους, ἔριφοι, < . . . >
  τυρὸς χλωρός, τυρὸς ξηρός,
  τυρὸς κοπτός, τυρὸς ξυστός,
  τυρὸς τμητός, τυρὸς πηκτός.

Μνησίμαχος δ᾽ ἐν Ἱπποτρόφῳ τοιαῦτα παρασκευάζει·

  βαῖν᾽ ἐκ θαλάμων κυπαρισσορόφων |

f   ἔξω, Μάνη· στεῖχ᾽ εἰς ἀγορὰν
  πρὸς τοὺς Ἑρμᾶς,
  οὗ προσφοιτῶσ᾽ οἱ φύλαρχοι,

[20] ἡμῖν Nesselrath: ὑμῖν ACE (followed by K–A)

(A.) What kind of meat's your favorite (he says)? (B.)
    What kind?
The cheap kind! The type of sheep that doesn't
    produce
any wool or cheese, which is to say a lamb, my friend.
Likewise the type of goat that doesn't produce any
    cheese,
that is, a kid. Since there's money to be made from
    the full-grown ones,
I don't mind eating lousy food like this.

And in *The Cyclops* (fr. 131)[236] he says:

I'll furnish us with the following
mainland items:
a cow from my herd, a mud-trodding he-goat,
a heavenly she-goat, a castrated ram,
a castrated boar, an uncastrated pig,
a hog, a hare, kids,
fresh cheese, dried cheese,
chopped cheese, grated cheese,
sliced cheese, cottage cheese.

Mnesimachus in *The Horse-Groom* (fr. 4) prepares food of
the following sort:

Leave our cypress-roofed chambers,
Manes! Go to the marketplace,
to the Herms,
where the cavalry commanders spend their time,

---

[236] The love-smitten Cyclops lists the provisions he will offer
for their wedding banquet, if the sea-nymph Galateia will have
him as her husband.

377

τούς τε μαθητὰς τοὺς ὡραίους,
οὓς ἀναβαίνειν ἐπὶ τοὺς ἵππους
μελετᾷ Φείδων καὶ καταβαίνειν.
οἶσθ᾽ οὓς φράζω;
τούτοις τοίνυν ἄγγελλ᾽ ὁτιὴ
ψυχρὸν τοὔψον, τὸ ποτὸν θερμόν,
ξηρὸν φύραμ᾽, ἄρτοι ξηροί· ‖

403 σπλάγχν᾽ ὀπτᾶται, χναῦμ᾽ ἥρπασται,
κρέας ἐξ ἅλμης ἐξῄρηται,
τόμος ἀλλᾶντος, τόμος ἠνύστρου,
χορδῆς ἕτερος, φύσκης ἕτερος
διαλαιμοτομεῖθ᾽ ὑπὸ τῶν ἔνδον.
κρατὴρ ἐξερροίβδητ᾽ οἴνου·
πρόποσις χωρεῖ· λέπεται κόρδαξ·
ἀκολασταίνει νοῦς μειρακίων·
πάντ᾽ ἔστ᾽ ἔνδον τὰ κάτωθεν ἄνω.
μέμνησ᾽ ἃ λέγω, πρόσεχ᾽ οἷς φράζω.
χάσκεις οὗτος;
βλέψον δευρί· πῶς αὐτὰ φράσεις;
αὐτίκ᾽ ἐρῶ σοι πάλιν ἐξ ἀρχῆς.

b ἥκειν ἤδη καὶ | μὴ μέλλειν,
τῷ τε μαγείρῳ μὴ λυμαίνεσθ᾽,
ὡς τῶν ὄψων ἐφθῶν ὄντων,

---

237 *PA* 14178; cf. Shear, *Hesperia* 42 (1973) 178–9 (several clay seals found in a well in the Agora that read "Pheidon of the deme Thriasus, hipparch for Lemnos").

and to the handsome young pupils
Pheidon[237] is training to mount
and dismount from their horses.
Do you know who I'm talking about?
Well, then—announce to them that
the fish is cold, the wine's warm,
the barley-cake's dry, and the bread's baked.
Entrails are roasting; snacks have been pulled from
      the fire;
meat's been removed from the stewing-brine;
a slice of sausage, and a slice of fourth-stomach
      sausage,
and one of gut-sausage, and one of large-intestine
      sausage,
are having their throats slit by the people working
      inside.
A mixing-bowl's gulped down some wine;
a toast's going around; a wild dance[238] is being
      thrashed out;
the boys are having dirty thoughts;
and everything in the house is upside-down.
Remember what I'm saying! Pay attention to what
      I'm telling you!
Hey! Are you ignoring me?
Look at me! How are you going to give them the
      message?
I'll start over and tell you again.
They should come immediately and not wait;
and they shouldn't mistreat the cook,
because there's stewed fish,

237 A *kordax*; see 14.630e, 631d.

ὀπτῶν ὄντων, ψυχρῶν ὄντων,
καθ᾿ ἕκαστα λέγων· βολβός, ἐλαία,
σκόροδον, καυλός, κολοκύντη, ἔτνος,
θρῖον, φυλλάς, θύννου τεμάχη,
γλάνιδος, γαλεοῦ, ῥίνης, γόγγρου,
φοξῖνος ὅλος, κορακῖνος ὅλος,
μεμβράς, σκόμβρος,
θυννίς, κωβιός, ἠλακατῆνες,
κυνὸς οὐραῖον τῶν καρχαριῶν,
νάρκη, βάτραχος, πέρκη, σαῦρος,
τριχίας, φυκίς, βρίγκος, τρίγλη,
κόκκυξ, τρυγών, σμύραινα, φάγρος,
c   μύλλος, λεβίας, | σπάρος, αἰολίας,
θρᾷττα, χελιδών, καρίς, τευθίς,
ψῆττα, δρακαινίς,
πουλυπόδειον, σηπία, ὀρφώς,
κάραβος, ἔσχαρος, ἀφύαι, βελόναι,
κεστρεύς, σκορπίος, ἔγχελυς, ἄρκτοι,
κρέα τ᾿ ἄλλα (τὸ πλῆθος ἀμύθητον)
χηνός, χοίρου, βοός, ἀρνός, οἰός,
κάπρου, αἰγός, ἀλεκτρυόνος, νήττης,
κίττης, πέρδικος, ἀλωπεκίου.
καὶ μετὰ δεῖπνον θαυμαστὸν ὅσ᾿ ἔστ᾿
ἀγαθῶν πλήθη.
πᾶς δὲ κατ᾿ οἴκους μάττει, πέττει,
τίλλει, κόπτει, τέμνει, δεύει,
χαίρει, παίζει, πηδᾷ, δειπνεῖ,

roasted fish, and cold fish—
give them the whole list! Hyacinth-bulbs, olives,
garlic, silphium stalk, gourds, pea-soup,
fig-leaf pastries, grape-leaf pastries, tuna steaks,
cuts of sheatfish, dogfish, monkfish, and conger eel,
a whole *phoxinos*, a whole *korakinos*,
a smelt, a mackerel,
a *thunnis*, a goby, *ēlakatēnes*,
a tail of one of the jagged-toothed sharks,
an electric ray, a fishing-frog, a perch, a horse-
      mackerel,
a pilchard, a *phukis*-wrasse, a *brinkos*, a red mullet,
a gurnard, a stingray, a moray eel, a sea-bream,
a *mullos*, a *lebias*, a *sparos*-bream, an *aiolias*,
a *thraitta*, a flying-fish, a shrimp, a squid,
a flounder, a weever-fish,
an octopus, a cuttlefish, a sea-perch,
a crayfish, an *escharos*, small-fry, garfish,
a gray mullet, a bullhead, an eel, and bear-crabs.
Also other kinds of meat (in unbelievable quantities):
goose, pork, beef, lamb, mutton,
boar, goat, chicken, duck,
jay, partridge, thresher shark.
As for after dinner, it's amazing how much
good food there is!
Everyone in the house is kneading, baking,
plucking, chopping, slicing, soaking,
enjoying, goofing off, jumping around, eating dinner,

ATHENAEUS

d   πίνει, σκιρτᾷ, | λορδοῖ, κεντεῖ²¹.
σεμναὶ δ᾽ αὐλῶν ἀγαναὶ φωναί,
μολπά, κλαγγὰ θράττει, πνεῖται²²
κούρα κασίας
ἀπὸ γᾶς ἁγίας ἁλίας Συρίας,
ὀσμὴ σεμνὴ μυκτῆρα δονεῖ
λιβάνου, μάρου, σμύρνης, καλάμου,
στύρακος, βάρου,
λίνδου, κίνδου, κισθοῦ, μίνθου.
τοιάδε δόμους ὀμίχλη κατέχει
    πάντων ἀγαθῶν ἀνάμεστος.

Ἐπὶ τούτοις λεγομένοις παρηνέχθη ἡ ῥοδουντία
καλουμένη λοπάς· περὶ ἧς ἐξετραγῴδησεν ὁ σοφὸς
e ἐκεῖνος | μάγειρος, πρὶν καὶ ἐπιδεῖξαι ὅ τι φέρει.
διεχλεύαζέ τε τοὺς πάνυ μαγείρους γενομένους, ὧν καὶ
μνημονεύων ἔφη· τί τοιοῦτον ἐξεῦρεν ὁ παρὰ Ἀναξίπ-
πῳ²³ τῷ κωμικῷ μάγειρος, <ὃς>²⁴ ἐν τῷ Ἐγκαλυπτο-
μένῳ τοιάδε ὠγκώσατο·

    (Α.) Σόφων Ἀκαρνὰν καὶ Ῥόδιος Δαμόξενος
    ἐγένονθ᾽ ἑαυτῶν συμμαθηταὶ τῆς τέχνης· |

²¹ κεντει βινει ACE: βινεῖ del. Meineke
²² νεῖται πνεῖται A: νεῖται del. Meineke
²³ Ἀναξίππῳ Valcknaer: Ἀνθίππῳ A: ξανθίππῳ CE
²⁴ add. Schweighäuser

382

drinking, hopping up and down, lying on their back,
    driving it in.[239]
The sacred, gentle voices of pipes,
song, and music resound; the daughter
of cassia, from the holy
land of maritime Syria, breathes forth;
and nostrils are set awhirl by the sacred scent
of frankincense, sage, myrrh, sweet-flag,
storax, *baros*,
lindos, *kindos*, rock-rose, and mint.
That's the sort of cloud, packed with everything
    good, that fills the house.

As he was still speaking, we were offered the so-called
rhodountia ("rose-flavored") casserole-dish; our clever
cook provided us with an extravagant description of it before showing us what he was serving.[240] He also made fun
of the famous cooks of the past,[241] referring to them individually and saying: What did the cook in the comic author
Anaxippus invent that resembled this? He bragged as follows in *The Man Who Tried to Hide His Face* (fr. 1):

(A.) Sophon of Acarnania and Damoxenus of Rhodes
were fellow-students when they got their training;[242]

---

[239] I.e. having sex with the (women) just referred to, who are
lying on their backs.

[240] Cf. 9.406a, where the dish is referred to as a *rhodōnia*.

[241] Continuing the catalogue of long comic fragments dealing
with cooks broken off abruptly at 9.383e.   [242] Sophon is also
mentioned at Bato fr. 4.4 (quoted at 14.662c–d), and Damoxenus
may be referred to in adesp. com. fr. 1057.9. Both men are otherwise unknown, as is their teacher Labdacus.

f   ἐδίδασκε δ᾽ αὐτοὺς Σικελιώτης Λάβδακος.
οὗτοι τὰ μὲν παλαιὰ καὶ θρυλούμενα
ἀρτύματ᾽ ἐξήλειψαν ἐκ τῶν βιβλίων
καὶ τὴν θυείαν ἠφάνισαν ἐκ τοῦ μέσου,
οἷον λέγω κύμινον, ὄξος, σίλφιον,
τυρόν, κορίαννον, οἷς ὁ Κρόνος ἀρτύμασιν
ἐχρῆτο, πάντ᾽ ἀφεῖλον εἶναί θ᾽ ὑπέλαβον ‖

404   τὸν τοῖς ⟨τοιούτοις⟩ παντοπώλην χρώμενον.
αὐτοὶ δ᾽ ἔλαιον καὶ λοπάδα καινήν, πάτερ,
πῦρ τ᾽ ὀξὺ καὶ μὴ πολλάκις φυσώμενον
ἐπόουν· ἀπὸ τούτου πᾶν τὸ δεῖπνον εὐτρεπές.
οὗτοί τε πρῶτοι δάκρυα καὶ πταρμὸν πολὺν
ἀπὸ τῆς τραπέζης καὶ σίαλον ἀπήγαγον,
τῶν τ᾽ ἐσθιόντων ἀνεκάθηραν τοὺς πόρους.
ὁ μὲν οὖν Ῥόδιος πιών τιν᾽ ἄλμην ἀπέθανεν·

b   παρὰ τὴν φύσιν γὰρ τὸ ποτὸν ἦν. μάλ᾽ εἰκότως.
ὁ Σόφων δὲ πᾶσαν τὴν Ἰωνίαν ἔχει,
ἐμὸς γενόμενος, ὦ πάτερ, διδάσκαλος.
καὐτὸς φιλοσοφῶ καταλιπεῖν συγγράμματα
σπεύδων ἐμαυτοῦ καινὰ τῆς τέχνης. (Β.) παπαῖ·
ἐμὲ κατακόψεις, οὐχ ὃ θύειν μέλλομεν.
(Α.) τὸν ὄρθρον ἐν ταῖς χερσί μ᾽ ὄψει βιβλία

their teacher was Labdacus of Sicily.
These guys erased the famous old
seasonings from the cookbooks
and got the mortar out of sight—
I'm talking, for example, about cumin, vinegar,
    silphium,
cheese, and coriander, the spices Cronus
used to cook with. They got rid of them all and
    became convinced
that anyone who used ingredients like that was just a
    grocer.
They themselves went in for olive oil and a new
    casserole-dish,
honored sir, and a hot fire that wasn't blown on
too much; any meal can be prepared with this
    equipment.
They were the first to remove tears and a lot of
sneezing and runny noses from the dinner table,
and they cleaned out the pores of the people who ate
    their food.
The Rhodian drank some stewing-brine and died;
because drinking it was contrary to his nature. Just as
    you might expect!
Sophon, on the other hand, is the master of all Ionia;
and he, honored sir, was my teacher.
I'm also a philosopher, and I'm eager to leave behind
my own original treatises on my line of work. (B.)
    Damn!
You'll be the death of *me*, not the animal we're going
    to sacrifice!
(A.) First thing in the morning, you'll see me with
    books

ἔχοντα καὶ ζητοῦντα ⟨τὰ⟩ κατὰ τὴν τέχνην. |
c οὐθὲν Διοδώρου διαφέρω τἀσπενδίου.
γεύσω δ', ἐὰν βούλῃ, σε τῶν εὑρημένων.
οὐ ταὐτὰ προσάγω πᾶσιν ἀεὶ βρώματα,
τεταγμέν' εὐθύς ἐστί μοι πρὸς τὸν βίον·
ἕτερ' ἐστὶ τοῖς ἐρῶσι καὶ τοῖς φιλοσόφοις
καὶ τοῖς τελώναις. μειράκιον ἐρωμένην
ἔχον πατρῴαν οὐσίαν κατεσθίει·
τούτῳ παρέθηκα σηπίας καὶ τευθίδας
καὶ τῶν πετραίων ἰχθύων τῶν ποικίλων,
ἐμβαμματίοις γλαφυροῖσι κεχορηγημένα· |
d ὁ γὰρ τοιοῦτός ἐστιν οὐ δειπνητικός,
πρὸς τῷ φιλεῖν δὲ τὴν διάνοιάν ἐστ' ἔχων.
τῷ φιλοσόφῳ παρέθηκα κωλῆν ἢ πόδας·
ἀδηφάγον τὸ ζῷον εἰς ὑπερβολὴν
ἔστιν. τελώνῃ γλαῦκον, ἔγχελυν, σπάρον·
ὅταν ἐγγὺς ᾖ δ' ὁ Δύστρος, ἀρτύω φακῆν
καὶ τὸ περίδειπνον τοῦ βίου λαμπρὸν ποῶ.
τὰ τῶν γερόντων στόματα διαφορὰν ἔχει,
νωθρότερα πολλῷ δ' ἐστὶν ἢ τὰ τῶν νέων. |
e σίναπι παρατίθημι τούτοις καὶ ποῶ
χυλοὺς ἐχομένους δριμύτητος, τὴν φύσιν
ἵνα διεγείρας πνευματῶ τὸν ἀέρα.

---

243 A Pythagorean philosopher (probably late 5th or early 4th century BCE) said to have been the first to adopt what eventually became distinctly Cynic mannerisms, by growing his hair and beard long, declining to bathe, and dressing like a beggar. Cf. 4.163e–4a.

in my hands, doing research on my trade;
I'm no different from Diodorus of Aspendus.[243]
If you want, I'll give you a sample of my discoveries.
I don't offer everyone the same food all the time.
Instead, I organize what I serve from the beginning,
        to suit their lifestyle;
lovers, philosophers, and tax-collectors
require different menus. Suppose a young man's got a
girlfriend, and is gobbling up his inheritance;
I serve him cuttlefish, squid,
and some variegated rockfish,
all immersed in elegant sauces.
Because someone like that isn't interested in dinner;
his attention's fixed on being in love.
I serve the philosopher a ham or pigs' feet;
that's a really gluttonous
creature. The tax-collector gets *glaukos*, eel, and
        sparos-bream;[244]
and when it's almost Dustros[245], I fix lentil-soup
and make his funeral meal a brilliant one.
Old men's palates are different;
they're much more sluggish than young men's.
I serve them mustard, and I produce
sauces that have some zing, so I can wake
their body up and pump air into it.

[244] Presumably because all three fish—like the tax-collector who is going to eat them—are characterized by vicious, voracious greed.

[245] A month in the Macedonian calendar.

ἰδὼν τὸ πρόσωπον γνώσομ' οὗ ζητεῖ φαγεῖν
ἕκαστος ὑμῶν.

καὶ ὁ παρὰ Διονυσίῳ δὲ ἐν Θεσμοφόρῳ μάγειρος,
ἄνδρες δαιταλεῖς (οὐ χεῖρον γὰρ καὶ τούτου μνησθῆ-
ναι), τί φησίν;

(A.) σφόδρα μοι κεχάρισαι, Σιμία, νὴ τοὺς
       θεούς,
ταυτὶ προείπας· τὸν μάγειρον εἰδέναι |

f   πολὺ δεῖ γὰρ αἰεὶ πρότερον οἷς μέλλει ποεῖν
τὸ δεῖπνον ἢ τὸ δεῖπνον ἐγχειρεῖν ποεῖν.
ἂν μὲν γὰρ ἕν τις τοῦτ' ἐπιβλέψῃ μόνον,
τοὔψον ποῆσαι κατὰ τρόπον πῶς δεῖ, τίνα
τρόπον παραθεῖναι δ' ἢ πότ' ἢ πῶς σκευάσαι
< . . . > μὴ προΐδηται τοῦτο μηδὲ φροντίσῃ,
οὐκέτι μάγειρος, ὀψοποιός ἐστι δέ.
οὐ ταὐτὸ δ' ἐστὶ τοῦτο, πολὺ διήλλαχεν. ‖

405   <ὡς γὰρ> στρατηγὸς πᾶς καλεῖθ' ὃς ἂν λάβῃ
δύναμιν, ὁ μέντοι δυνάμενος κἂν πράγμασιν
ἀναστραφῆναι καὶ διαβλέψαι τί που
στρατηγός ἐστιν, ἡγεμὼν δὲ θάτερον,
οὕτως ἐφ' ἡμῶν σκευάσαι μὲν ἢ τεμεῖν
ἡδύσμαθ' ἑψῆσαί τε καὶ φυσᾶν τὸ πῦρ
ὁ τυχὼν δύναιτ' ἄν· ὀψοποιὸς οὖν μόνον
ἐστὶν ὁ τοιοῦτος, ὁ δὲ μάγειρος ἄλλο τι. |

b   συνιδεῖν τόπον, ὥραν, τὸν καλοῦντα, τὸν πάλιν

388

When I see your faces, I'll know what each of you
wants to eat.

As for the cook in Dionysius' *Lawgiver* (fr. 2),
banqueters—because there's no harm in mentioning
him—what does he have to say?

(A.) By the gods, Simias, you've done me quite a
     favor
by telling me this ahead of time! A cook always really
needs to know in advance who he's going to be
     making
dinner for—or trying to make dinner for.
Because if all someone worries about
is how to prepare the fish properly, but as for
how to serve it, or when or how to fix
. . . , if he doesn't look ahead to this or give it some
     consideration,
he's no longer a cook; he's just a guy who prepares
     fish.
This isn't the same; it's very different.
Because just as anyone who gets an army is *called* a
     general,
but the man who can recover when he's
in trouble, and can somehow see the situation clearly
is a *real* general, whereas the other guy's just a
     commander,
so too in our case. Any warm body could
fix food, or mince spices, or stew meat,
or blow on the fire. But someone like that
just prepares fish; a real cook is a different matter.
To understand the site and the season, the host as
     well

δειπνοῦντα, πότε δεῖ καὶ τίν' ἰχθὺν ἀγοράσαι,
<   . . .   > πάντα μὲν λήψει σχεδὸν
αἰεὶ γάρ· οὐκ αἰεὶ δὲ τὴν τούτων χάριν
ἔχεις ὁμοίαν οὐδ' ἴσην τὴν ἡδονήν.
Ἀρχέστρατος γέγραφέ τε καὶ δοξάζεται
παρά τισιν οὕτως ὡς λέγων τι χρήσιμον.
τὰ πολλὰ δ' ἠγνόηκε κοὐδὲ ἓν λέγει.|

c   μὴ πάντ' ἄκουε μηδὲ πάντα μάνθανε
† τῶν βιαίων ἐσθ' ἕνεκα τὰ γεγραμμένα,
κενὰ μᾶλλον ἢ ὅτε ἦν οὐδέπω γεγραμμένα· †
οὐδ' ἔστιν εἰπεῖν περὶ μαγειρικῆς, ἐπεὶ
εἶπ' ἀρτίως < . . . >
ὅρον γὰρ οὐκ ἔσχηκεν † οὗ ὁ καιρὸς †
αὐτὴ δ' ἑαυτῆς ἐστι δεσπότης. ἐὰν δ'
εὖ μὲν σὺ χρήσῃ τῇ τέχνῃ, τὸν τῆς τέχνης
καιρὸν δ' ἀπολέσῃς, παραπόλωλεν ἡ τέχνη.
(Σιμ.) ἄνθρωπε, μέγας εἶ. (Α.) τουτονὶ δ', ὃν
      ἀρτίως |

d   ἔφης ἔχοντα πεῖραν ἥκειν πολυτελῶν
πολλῶν τε δείπνων, ἐπιλαθέσθαι, Σιμία,
πάντων ποήσω, θρῖον ἂν δείξω μόνον
παραθῶ <τε> δεῖπνον ὄζον αὔρας Ἀττικῆς.
ἐξ ἀντλίας ἥκοντα καὶ γέμοντ' ἔτι
φορτηγικῶν μοι βρωμάτων ἀγωνίαις
τῇ μῇ ποήσω νυστάσαι παροψίδι.

as the guest; when to buy the fish, and what kind
. . . Because you can almost always
get anything; but you don't always get the same
joy or an equal amount of pleasure out of these items.
Archestratus (test. 1 Olson–Sens) has done some
      writing, and there are people
who think he's got something useful to say.
But he's mostly ignorant, and he talks nonsense.
Don't listen to everything or try to learn everything
† because of violent actions what's been written is
more hollow than when it hadn't been written. †
You can't just talk about cooking, since
he said just now . . .
Because it didn't have any limit † where the right
      moment †
Our craft's its own master. And if
you make good use it, but don't do so
at precisely the right moment, it's ruined.
(Simias) You're really something, mister. (A.) And this
      guy, who you said
arrived just now with lots of experience in
expensive dinner parties—I'll make him
forget them all, Simias, if I simply show him a fig-leaf
      pastry
and serve him a dinner that smells like the Attic
      breezes!
When he emerges from the hold of his ship and
      comes to me, still
full of the tortures inflicted by the food they serve on
      merchant-ships,
I'll put him to sleep with my side-dish.

Πρὸς ταῦτα Αἰμιλιανὸς ἔφη·

βέλτιστε, πολλοῖς πολλὰ περὶ μαγειρικῆς |
e εἰρημέν᾽ ἐστίν,

κατὰ τοὺς Ἡγησίππου Ἀδελφούς· σὺ οὖν ἢ δρῶν τι
φαίνου

καινὸν παρὰ τοὺς ἔμπροσθεν ἢ μὴ κόπτε με,

καὶ δεῖξον ὃ φέρεις καὶ λέγε τί ἐστι. καὶ ὅς· κατα-
φρονεῖς ὅτι μάγειρός εἰμι ἴσως·

ὅσον ἀπὸ ταύτης τῆς τέχνης εἴργασμ᾽ ἐγώ,

κατὰ τὸν κωμικὸν Δημήτριον, ὃς ἐν τῷ ἐπιγραφομένῳ
Ἀρεοπαγίτῃ ταῦτ᾽ εἴρηκεν·

ὅσον ἀπὸ ταύτης τῆς τέχνης εἴργασμ᾽ ἐγώ,
οὐδεὶς ὑποκριτής ἐσθ᾽ ὅλως εἰργασμένος.
καπνιζομένη τυραννὶς αὕτη 'σθ᾽ ἡ τέχνη. |
f ἀβυρτακοποιὸς παρὰ Σέλευκον ἐγενόμην,
παρ᾽ Ἀγαθοκλεῖ ⟨δὲ⟩ πρῶτος εἰσήνεγκ᾽ ἐγὼ
τῷ Σικελιώτῃ ⟨τὴν⟩ τυραννικὴν φακῆν.
τὸ μέγιστον οὐκ εἴρηκα· Λαχάρους † τινος †,
ὅτ᾽ ἦν ὁ λιμός, ἑστιῶντος τοὺς φίλους,
ἀνάληψιν ἐποίησ᾽ εἰσενέγκας κάππαριν.

---

246 Quoted at much greater length at 7.290b–e. Aemilianus'
next few words are a slightly adapted version of the rest of the second verse.

247 *Aburtakē* was a "barbarian" sour sauce made of ingredients

Aemilianus responded:

> My good sir, many people have had a lot to say
> about the art of cooking,

to quote Hegesippus' *Brothers* (fr. 1.1–2).[246] So either
make it clear that you are doing (Hegesipp. Com. fr. 1.3)

> something different from your predecessors, or don't
>   waste my time;

show us what you are serving and identify it for us! (The
cook) replied: Perhaps you feel contempt for me because I
am a cook.

> As for what I've accomplished through my trade,

to quote the comic author Demetrius, who says the following in his play entitled *The Areopagite* (fr. 1):

> As for what I've accomplished through my trade,
> there's not a single actor who's done as much.
> This business is a smoky tyranny.
> I was an *aburtakē*-maker[247] in Seleucus' court,
> as well as the first person to introduce royal
> lentil-soup in the court of Agathocles[248] in Sicily.
> But I haven't mentioned my greatest
>   accomplishment. † A certain † Lachares
> was giving a dinner party for some friends when the
>   famine was going on,
> and I made everything alright by serving capers.

such as garlic, mustard, leeks, and pomegranate seeds (Phot. *a* 66;
Suda a 103).   [248] Tyrant of Syracuse from the mid-310s to
289/8 BCE. The Seleucus mentioned above must accordingly be
Seleucus I Nicator (d. 281 BCE).

γυμνὴν ἐποίησεν Ἀθηνᾶν Λαχάρης, οὐδὲν ἐνοχλοῦ-
406 σαν· <σὲ>[25] δ᾽ ἐνοχλοῦντα νῦν ἐγώ, ‖ ὁ Αἰμιλιανὸς
ἔφη, εἰ μὴ δείξεις ὅ τι φέρεις. καὶ ὃς μόλις ἔφη·
ῥοδωνιὰν καλῶ μὲν τὴν λοπάδα ταύτην ἐγώ, ἐσκεύ-
ασται δ᾽ οὕτως, ἵνα καὶ ἥδυσμα στεφανωτικὸν μὴ
μόνον ἐπὶ τῆς κεφαλῆς λαβὼν σχῇς, ἀλλὰ καὶ ἔνδον
σεαυτοῦ καὶ πανδαισίᾳ τὸ σωμάτιον πᾶν ἑστιάσῃς.
ῥόδα τὰ εὐοσμότατα ἐν ἴγδει τρίψας ἐπέβαλον ἐγκε-
φάλους ὀρνίθων τε καὶ χοίρων ἑφθοὺς σφόδρα ἐξινια-
σθέντας καὶ τῶν ᾠῶν τὰ χρυσᾶ, μεθ᾽ ἃ ἔλαιον, γάρον,
πέπερι, οἶνον. καὶ ταῦτα διατρίψας ἐπιμελῶς ἐνέβαλον
b εἰς λοπάδα καινήν, ἁπαλὸν καὶ συνεχὲς διδοὺς[26] ǀ τὸ
πῦρ. καὶ ἅμα λέγων ἀναπετάσας τὴν λοπάδα τοσαύ-
την εὐωδίαν παρέσχε τῷ συμποσίῳ, ὡς ἀληθῶς τινα
τῶν παρόντων εἰπεῖν·

τοῦ καὶ † κινυμένοιο Διὸς κατὰ χαλκοβατὲς δῶ
ἔμπης ἐς γαῖάν τε καὶ οὐρανὸν ἵκετ᾽ αὐτμή.

τοσαύτη διεχύθη ἀπὸ τῶν ῥόδων εὐωδία.

[25] add. Schweighäuser
[26] Casaubon's text lacks an indication of where 9.406a ends
and 9.406b begins, but the division appears to fall approximately
here.

---

[249] Identified by Dindorf (followed by Meineke, but not
by Kassel–Austin) as an adespota comic fragment (fr. XXIb
Meineke). Lachares (*PAA* 602090) was an Athenian general who

BOOK IX

Lachares stripped Athena naked,[249] and she did nothing to stop him, said Aemilianus; and I will now do the same to you for pestering me, unless you identify what you have there. (The cook) finally said (adesp. com. fr. *117, unmetrical): I call this dish a *rhodōnia*,[250] and it has been prepared as follows, allowing you not only to take the sauce and wear it on your head like a garland,[251] but also to have it inside you and entertain your entire body with an amazing feast. I ground up exceptionally fragrant roses in a mortar; threw in chickens' heads and pigs' heads that had been stewed for a long time and had had their stringy parts removed, along with some egg-yolks; and added olive oil, fermented fish-sauce, pepper, and wine. I ground these ingredients up thoroughly; tossed them into a new casserole-dish; and set it all over a constant, low fire. As he was making these remarks, he took the lid off the dish, and what the group smelled was so delicious that one of the men present actually said (*Il.* 14.173–4):[252]

the smell of which, when it was † shaken in the
        bronze-floored
house of Zeus, went out over earth and heaven alike.

This is how fragrant the roses were.

in 296 BCE used the gold from Athena's statue on the Acropolis to pay his mercenary troops (Paus. 1.25.7–8, 29.16; Plu. *Mor.* 379d).

[250] Cf. 9.406a, where the dish is referred to as a *rhodōnia*.

[251] Sc. because roses (the most important ingredient in the dish) were routinely used in garlands.

[252] Also quoted at 1.17b.

Μετὰ ταῦτα περιενεχθεισῶν ὀρνίθων τε ὀπτῶν φακῆς τε καὶ πισῶν αὐταῖς χύτραις, ἔτι δὲ τῶν τοιούτων
c περὶ ὧν Φαινίας | ὁ Ἐρέσιος ἐν τοῖς Περὶ Φυτῶν τάδε
γράφει· πᾶσα γὰρ χεδροπώδης ἥμερος φύσις ἐνσπέρματος. ἡ μὲν ἑψήσεως ἕνεκα σπείρεται, οἷον κύαμος,
πισός· ἔτνηρὸν γὰρ ἐκ τούτων ἕψημα γίνεται. τὰ δὲ
πάλιν αὖθις λεκιθώδη, καθάπερ ἄρακος· τὸ δὲ φακῆς,
οἷον φακός.[27] τὸ δὲ χόρτου ἕνεκα τῶν τετραπόδων
ζῴων, οἷον ὄροβος μὲν ἀροτήρων βοῶν, ἀφάκη δὲ
προβάτων. πισοῦ δὲ τοῦ ὀσπρίου μνημονεύει καὶ Εὔπολις ἐν Χρυσῷ Γένει. Ἡλιόδωρος δ᾽ ὁ περιηγητὴς ἐν
πρώτῳ Περὶ Ἀκροπόλεως, τῆς τῶν πυρῶν, φησίν,
d ἑψήσεως ἐπινοηθείσης | οἱ μὲν παλαιοὶ πύανον, οἱ δὲ
νῦν ὁλόπυρον προσαγορεύουσιν. τοιούτων ἔτι πολλῶν
λεγομένων ὁ Δημόκριτος ἔφη· ἀλλὰ κἂν τῆς φακῆς
ἐάσητε[28] ἡμᾶς μεταλαβεῖν ἢ αὐτῆς γε τῆς χύτρας, μὴ
καὶ λίθοις τις ὑμῶν βεβλήσεται, κατὰ τὸν Θάσιον
Ἡγήμονα. καὶ ὁ Οὐλπιανὸς ἔφη· τίς δ᾽ αὕτη ἡ λιθίνη
βαλλητύς; Ἐλευσῖνι γὰρ τῇ ἐμῇ οἶδά τινα πανήγυριν
ἀγομένην καὶ καλουμένην Βαλλητύν· περὶ ἧς οὐκ ἄν
τι εἴποιμι μὴ παρ᾽ ἑκάστου μισθὸν λαβών. ἀλλ᾽ ἔγωγε, φησὶν ὁ Δημόκριτος, οὐκ ὢν

[27] ἀφάκη φακός A: ἀφάκη del. Olson
[28] ἐάσητε Olson: ἐάσατε A

After this, roasted chickens, lentil-soup, and peas were brought around, cookpots and all,[253] along with items of the sort discussed by Phaenias of Eresos in his *On Plants* (fr. 48 Wehrli), where he writes the following: Because all domesticated leguminous plants produce seeds. One type is sown in order to be cooked (for example beans and peas, which are boiled to make soup), while other varieties are more suited to producing gruel (for example *arakos*) or for porridge (for example lentils). The second type is planted to provide forage for four-legged animals (for example bitter vetch for plow-oxen, and tare for sheep and goats). Eupolis in *The Golden Age* (fr. 323) mentions the pulse-variety known as the pea.[254] The travel-writer Heliodorus says in Book I of *On the Acropolis* (*FGrH* 373 F 3): After the idea of boiling wheat arose, the ancients referred to the dish as *puanos*, whereas people nowadays call it *holopuros*[255]. Many remarks like these were still being made, when Democritus said: Well, I wish you would let us have a bit of this lentil-soup, or even part of the cookpot itself, so that none of you (cooks) gets pelted with stones, like Hegemon of Thasos. And Ulpian responded: What sort of pelting (*ballētus*) with stones are you referring to? For I know that a festival celebrated in my own city of Eleusis is referred to as the *Ballētus*; but I decline to say anything about it, unless each of you pays me for doing so. Whereas I for my part, said Democritus, since I am no

253 Identified by Kock (not followed by Kassel–Austin) as an adespota comic fragment (fr. 416 Kock).
254 A quotation has perhaps fallen out of the text.
255 Literally "whole-wheat".

< . . . > λαβάργυρος ὡρολογητής,

e κατὰ τὸν Τίμωνος | Πρόδικον, λέξω τὰ περὶ τοῦ
Ἡγήμονος. Χαμαιλέων ὁ Ποντικὸς ἐν ἕκτῳ Περὶ τῆς
Ἀρχαίας Κωμῳδίας· Ἡγήμων ὁ Θάσιος <ὁ> τὰς
Παρῳδίας γράψας Φακῆ ἐπεκαλεῖτο καὶ ἐποίησεν ἔν
τινι τῶν Παρῳδιῶν·

> ταῦτά μοι ὁρμαίνοντι παρίστατο Παλλὰς Ἀθήνη,
> χρυσῆν ῥάβδον ἔχουσα, καὶ ἤλασεν εἶπέ τε
> μῦθον· |

f > "δεινὰ παθοῦσα, Φακῆ βδελυρή, χώρει 's τὸν
> ἀγῶνα."
> καὶ τότ' ἐγὼ θάρσησα.

εἰσῆλθε δέ ποτε καὶ εἰς τὸ θέατρον διδάσκων κωμῳ-
δίαν λίθων ἔχων πλῆρες τὸ ἱμάτιον, οὓς βάλλων εἰς
τὴν ὀρχήστραν διαπορεῖν ἐποίησε τοὺς θεατάς. καὶ
ὀλίγον διαλιπὼν εἶπε· ||

407 > λίθοι μὲν οἵδε· βαλλέτω δ' εἴ τις θέλει·
> ἀγαθὸν δὲ κἂν χειμῶνι κἂν θέρει φακή.

εὐδοκίμει δ' ὁ ἀνὴρ μάλιστα ἐν ταῖς παρῳδίαις καὶ
περιβόητος ἦν λέγων τὰ ἔπη πανούργως καὶ ὑπο-
κριτικῶς καὶ διὰ ταῦτα σφόδρα παρὰ τοῖς Ἀθηναίοις
εὐδοκίμει. ἐν δὲ τῇ Γιγαντομαχίᾳ οὕτω σφόδρα τοὺς
Ἀθηναίους ἐκήλησεν, ὡς ἐν ἐκείνῃ τῇ ἡμέρᾳ πλεῖστα

---

256 Quoted at much greater length at 15.698d–9a.

money-grubbing speaker-by-the-hour,

like Timo's Prodicus (*SH* 792), will tell you what I know about Hegemon. Chamaeleon of Pontus in Book VI of *On Old Comedy* (fr. 44 Wehrli): Hegemon of Thasos, the author of the *Parodies*, was nicknamed Lentil-Soup and wrote in one of his *Parodies*:[256]

> And as I was pondering these things, Pallas Athena
>   stood beside me
> with a gold wand in her hand, and she struck me with
>   it and made a speech:
> "Although you have suffered terribly, wretched
>   Lentil-Soup, enter the contest."
> And then I got my courage up.

Once when he was staging a comedy (test. 4), he entered the Theater with his robe full of stones, and puzzled the audience by tossing them into the orchestra. But a few minutes later he said:

> Here are some stones, and anyone who likes can
>   throw them.
> But Lentil-Soup is a fine dish in winter and summer
>   alike.

He was particularly admired for his parodies and had a reputation for reciting his poems stylishly, like an actor; as a consequence, the Athenians had an extremely high opinion of him. They were so captivated by his *Gigantomachy* that they laughed a great deal that day, even though the di-

[257] In 413 BCE, when a huge Athenian expeditionary force to the island was almost entirely destroyed.

αὐτοὺς γελάσαι, καίτοι ἀγγελθέντων αὐτοῖς ἐν τῷ
θεάτρῳ τῶν γενομένων περὶ Σικελίαν ἀτυχημάτων.

b οὐδεὶς ἀπέστη καίτοι σχεδὸν πᾶσι τῶν οἰκείων | ἀπο-
λωλότων. ἔκλαιον οὖν ἐγκαλυψάμενοι, οὐκ ἀνέστησαν
δ᾽, ἵνα μὴ γένωνται διαφανεῖς τοῖς ἀπὸ τῶν ἄλλων
πόλεων θεωροῦσιν ἀχθόμενοι τῇ συμφορᾷ· διέμειναν
δ᾽ ἀκροώμενοι καίτοι καὶ αὐτοῦ τοῦ Ἡγήμονος, ὡς
ἤκουσε, σιωπᾶν διεγνωκότος. καθ᾽ ὃν δὲ χρόνον θα-
λασσοκρατοῦντες Ἀθηναῖοι ἀνῆγον εἰς ἄστυ τὰς
νησιωτικὰς δίκας, γραψάμενός τις καὶ τὸν Ἡγήμονα
δίκην ἤγαγεν εἰς τὰς Ἀθήνας. ὁ δὲ παραγενόμενος καὶ
συναγαγὼν τοὺς περὶ τὸν Διόνυσον τεχνίτας προσ-

c ῆλθε μετ᾽ | αὐτῶν Ἀλκιβιάδῃ βοηθεῖν ἀξιῶν. ὁ δὲ
θαρρεῖν παρακελευσάμενος εἰπών τε πᾶσιν ἕπεσθαι
ἧκεν εἰς τὸ Μητρῷον, ὅπου τῶν δικῶν ἦσαν αἱ γραφαί,
καὶ βρέξας τὸν δάκτυλον ἐκ τοῦ στόματος διήλειψε
τὴν δίκην τοῦ Ἡγήμονος. ἀγανακτοῦντες δ᾽ ὅ τε
γραμματεὺς καὶ ὁ ἄρχων τὰς ἡσυχίας ἤγαγον δι᾽
Ἀλκιβιάδην, φυγόντος δι᾽ εὐλάβειαν καὶ τοῦ τὴν
δίκην γραψαμένου. αὕτη παρ᾽ ἡμῶν, Οὐλπιανέ, ἡ
βαλλητύς· σὺ δ᾽ ὅταν βουληθῇς ἐρεῖς περὶ τῆς Ἐλευ-

d σῖνι. καὶ ὁ Οὐλπιανός· ἀλλά με ἀνέμνησας, | καλὲ
Δημόκριτε, μνησθεὶς χύτρας ποθοῦντα μαθεῖν πολ-

---

258 Sc. of the Empire.   259 Alcibiades son of Cleinias of
the deme Scambonidae (*PAA* 121630) was an enormously wealthy
and influential political and social loose cannon throughout the
410s and 400s BCE, and was *inter alia* one of the original commanders of the Sicilian Expedition (above).

sasters that had occurred in Sicily[257] were announced to
them in the Theater. No one got up to leave, despite the
fact that almost everyone had lost family-members. So
they covered their faces and cried, but did not leave their
seats, because they did not want it to be obvious to the
spectators from the other cities[258] that they were upset
about what had happened. Instead, they stayed there and
listened to the recital, even though Hegemon himself had
decided not to perform when he heard the news. The
Athenians were the masters of the sea in this period and required all legal cases involving islanders to be heard in
their city. Someone filed a suit against Hegemon and sum-
moned him to Athens, and when he got there, he gathered
everyone involved in the theater business and went with
them to see Alcibiades,[259] in the expectation that he could
be of assistance. Alcibiades encouraged him to keep his
spirits up; told them all to follow him; went to the
Metroon, where the records having to do with lawsuits
were kept; and licked his finger and erased Hegemon's
trial from the list. The secretary and the magistrate in
charge were unhappy about this, but kept quiet, because it
was Alcibiades and because the man who brought the suit
had discreetly disappeared. This is what I have to offer,
Ulpian, about the *ballētus*; and whenever you like, you may
tell us about what goes on in Eleusis.[260] Ulpian said: But,
my good Democritus, when you mentioned a cookpot
(9.406d), you reminded me that I often wanted to learn

[260] Cf. 9.406d. Ulpian never takes the point up, and our only
other information about the *Ballētus* festival is preserved at Hsch.
β 167: "an Athenian festival, celebrated in honor of Demophon
son of Celeus" (sc. in connection with the mystery-cult at Eleusis).

λάκις τίς ἡ Τηλεμάχου καλουμένη χύτρα καὶ τίς ὁ
Τηλέμαχος. καὶ ὁ Δημόκριτος ἔφη· Τιμοκλῆς ὁ τῆς
κωμῳδίας ποιητὴς (ἦν δὲ καὶ τραγῳδίας) ἐν μὲν δράματι Λήθῃ φησί·

   μετὰ τοῦτον αὐτῷ Τηλέμαχος συνετύγχανε.
   καὶ τοῦτον ἀσπασάμενος ἡδέως πάνυ
   ἔπειτα "χρῆσόν μοι σύ," φησί, "τὰς χύτρας |
e   ἐν αἷσιν ἕψεις τοὺς κυάμους." καὶ ταῦτά τε
   εἴρητο καὶ παριόντα Φείδιππον πάνυ
   τὸν Χαιρεφίλου πόρρωθεν ἀπιδὼν τὸν παχὺν
   ἐπόππυσ᾽, εἶτ᾽ ἐκέλευσε πέμπειν σαργάνας.

ὅτι δὲ καὶ τῶν δήμων Ἀχαρνεὺς ὁ Τηλέμαχος ὁ αὐτὸς
ποιητής φησιν ἐν Διονύσῳ οὕτως·

   (Α.) ὁ δ᾽ Ἀχαρνικὸς Τηλέμαχος ἔτι δημηγορεῖ;
   (Β.) οὗτος δ᾽ ἔοικε τοῖς νεωνήτοις Σύροις.
   (Α.) πῶς; ἢ τί πράττων; βούλομαι γὰρ εἰδέναι.
   (Β.) θάργηλον ἀγκάλῃ χύτραν φέρει. |

f ἐν δ᾽ Ἰκαρίοις Σατύροις φησίν·

---

261 Telemachus (*PA* 13562) was active in Athenian politics in
the 320s BCE, but most of what is known about him comes from
the fragments quoted below.

262 The tragic poet by this name (*TrGF* 86; victorious at the
City Dionysia in 340 and 329 BCE) is almost certainly someone
else. The confusion may be due in part to the title *Icarian Satyrs*
(below), which almost certainly belongs to a comedy, but might

what the so-called "cookpot of Telemachus" is and who this Telemachus might be.[261] And Democritus replied: The comic poet Timocles, who also wrote tragedies (test. 2),[262] says in his play *Forgetfulness* (fr. 23):

> After this guy, Telemachus bumped into him.
> He gave him a warm greeting and
> then said, "Loan me the pots
> you cook your beans in!" That's what
> he said; and then from a long distance off he spied
> Chaerephilus' fat son Pheidippus[263] passing by,
> and he whistled him over and told him to send
>   baskets.

The same poet, in the following passage from *Dionysus* (fr. 7), claims that Telemachus was from the deme Acharnae:

> (A.) Is Telemachus of Acharnae still a leading
>   politician?
> (B.) He's like newly-purchased Syrian slaves.
> (A.) How so? What's he do? I want to know.
> (B.) He's carrying a *thargēlos* cookpot around under
>   his arm.[264]

And in *Icarian Satyrs* (fr. 18) he says:

easily have been mistaken for a satyr play by Hellenistic scholars with only a few small scraps of the text at their disposal.

263 *PA* 14163; also mentioned in Alex. fr. 221 (quoted at 3.120b).

264 Newly-purchased slaves were greeted with a shower of small gifts when they first entered the house (Ar. *Pl.* 768–9), and Hsch. *θ* 106 glosses *thargēlos* as "a cookpot for stewing sacred food" (cf. 3.114a); but the point of the remark remains obscure.

ATHENAEUS

ὥστ᾽ ἔχειν οὐδὲν παρ᾽ ἡμῖν. νυκτερεύσας δ᾽
  ἀθλίως
πρῶτα μὲν σκληρῶς καθηῦδον, εἶτα Θούδιππος
  βδέων
παντελῶς ἔπνιξεν ἡμᾶς, εἶθ᾽ ὁ λιμὸς ἥπτετο.
† ἐφέρετο † πρὸς Δίωνα τὸν διάπυρον· ἀλλὰ γὰρ
οὐδ᾽ ἐκεῖνος οὐθὲν εἶχε. πρὸς δὲ τὸν χρηστὸν
  δραμὼν
Τηλέμαχον Ἀχαρνέα σωρόν τε κυάμων
  καταλαβὼν
ἁρπάσας τούτων ἐνέτραγον. ⟨ὁ⟩ δ᾽ ὄνος ἡμᾶς ὡς
  ὁρᾷ
ὁ ⟨ . . . ⟩ Κηφισόδωρος περὶ τὸ βῆμ᾽ ἐπέρδετο.

408 ἐκ τούτων δῆλόν ἐστιν ὅτι Τηλέμαχος ‖ κυάμων χύτρας ἀεὶ σιτούμενος ἦγε Πυανέψια πορδὴν ἑορτήν.
ἔτνους δὲ κυαμίνου μνημονεύει Ἡνίοχος ὁ κωμικὸς ἐν
Τροχίλῳ λέγων οὕτως·

(A.) πρὸς ἐμαυτὸν ἐνθυμούμενος, νὴ τοὺς θεούς,
ὅσῳ διαφέρει σῦκα καρδάμων. σὺ δὲ
Παύσωνι φῂς τὸ δεῖνα προσλελαληκέναι;
(B.) καὶ πρᾶγμά ⟨γ᾽⟩ ἠρώτα με δυστράπελον
  πάνυ,
ἔχον δὲ πολλὰς φροντίδων διεξόδους. |

---

265 Thudippus (*PAA* 514700) was a member of a wealthy and
politically active family (cf. J. K. Davies, *Athenian Propertied
Families 600–300 B.C.* [Oxford, 1971] 228–30), and was executed
as an associate of Phocion in 318 BCE.

404

so that we wouldn't have anything. I spent a
    miserable night.
First of all, I was sleeping on a hard bed; then
    Thudippus[265] kept farting
and absolutely suffocated us; and on top of that I was
    starving.
† It was taken † to the red-hot Dion[266]; but even he
didn't have anything. I ran to the noble
Telemachus of Acharnae, got a pile of beans,
and grabbed some of them and ate them. But when
    that donkey
Cephisodorus[267] saw us, he started farting around the
    speaker's stand.

It is clear from these passages that (adesp. com. fr. *118)
because Telemachus was always consuming cookpots full
of beans, he celebrated the Pyanepsia[268] as a festival of
farts. The comic author Heniochus mentions bean-soup in
Trochilus (fr. 4), saying the following:

(A.) thinking to myself, by the gods,
how much better figs are than cress. But you
claim you've said something or other to Pauson[269]?
(B.) And he asked me about an extremely
    problematic matter,
which involves many intellectual ins-and-outs.

265 *PAA* 369570; otherwise unknown.
267 *PAA* 568060; otherwise unknown.
268 Literally the "Bean-Boiling (Festival)"; celebrated in Athens in late October.
269 *PAA* 770375; perhaps a Pythagorean philosopher (thus Meineke).

b   (Α.) λέγ᾽ αὐτό· καὶ γὰρ οὐκ ἀγέλοιόν ἐστ᾽ ἴσως.
(Β.) ἔτνος κυάμινον διότι τὴν μὲν γαστέρα
φυσᾷ, τὸ δὲ πῦρ οὔ. (Α.) χάριεν οἷς γινώσκεται
τὸ πρᾶγμα τοῦ Παύσωνος. ὡς δ᾽ ἀεί ποτε
περὶ τοὺς κυάμους ἔσθ᾽ οὗτος ὁ σοφιστὴς †
τέλος †.

Τοιούτων οὖν πολλάκις λεγομένων ὕδωρ ἐφέρετο
κατὰ χειρῶν. καὶ πάλιν ὁ Οὐλπιανὸς ἐζήτει εἰ τὸ
χέρνιβον εἴρηται, καθάπερ ἡμεῖς λέγομεν ἐν τῇ συνη-
θείᾳ. καί τις αὐτῷ ἀπήντησεν λέγων τὸ ἐν Ἰλιάδι· |

c   ἦ ῥα, καὶ ἀμφίπολον ταμίην ὤτρυν᾽ ὁ γεραιὸς
χερσὶν ὕδωρ ἐπιχεῦαι ἀκήρατον· ἡ δὲ παρέστη
χέρνιβον ἀμφίπολος πρόχοόν θ᾽ ἅμα χερσὶν
ἔχουσα.

Ἀττικοὶ δὲ χερνίβιον λέγουσιν, ὡς Λυσίας ἐν τῷ Κατὰ
Ἀλκιβιάδου λέγων οὕτως· τοῖς χρυσοῖς χερνιβίοις
d καὶ θυμιατηρίοις. | χειρόνιπτρον δ᾽ Εὔπολις ἐν Δή-
μοις·

κἄν τις τύχῃ πρῶτος βαλών, εἴληφε
χειρόνιπτρον,
ἀνὴρ δ᾽ ὅταν τις ἀγαθὸς ᾖ καὶ χρήσιμος
πολίτης,
νικᾷ τε ‹πάντας› χρηστὸς ὤν, οὐκ ἔστι
χειρόνιπτρον.

406

(A.) Tell me about it; maybe it's kind of funny.
(B.) Why is it that bean-soup pumps air into
your belly, but not into the fire? (B.) It's nice how you
    can
recognize Pauson's work; since this clever thinker's
always involved with beans † end †.

As numerous remarks along these lines were being
made, water was brought and poured over our hands (*kata
cheirōn*); and Ulpian attempted to raise another question,
as to whether the word *chernibon* ("washing-basin") is attested in the sense in which we are accustomed to using it.
Someone responded to him by quoting the passage in the
Iliad (24.302–4):

> Thus he spoke; and the old man ordered a serving-
>   woman
> to pour pure water over his hands. The servant stood
> beside him, holding a *chernibon*, along with a pitcher,
>   in her hands.

But Attic authors use *chernibion*, as for example Lysias in
his *Against Alcibiades*, where he says the following:[270] the
gold washing-basins (*chernibioi*) and censers. Eupolis uses
cheironiptron in *Demes* (fr. 129):

> Whoever's the first to hit it gets a *cheironiptron*.
> But if someone's a good, effective citizen,
> and beats everyone else for honesty, there's no
>   *cheironiptron* for him.

[270] The quotation is in fact drawn not from Lysias, but from
And. 4.29.

Ἐπίχαρμος δ᾽ ἐν Θεαροῖς εἴρηκε χειρόνιβα διὰ τού-
των·

κιθάραι, τρίποδες, ἅρματα, τράπεζαι χάλκιαι,
χειρόνιβα, λοιβάσια, λέβητες χάλκιοι.

e ἡ πλείων δὲ χρῆσις κατὰ χειρὸς ὕδωρ | εἴωθε λέγειν,
ὡς Εὔπολις ἐν Χρυσῷ Γένει καὶ Ἀμειψίας Σφενδόνῃ
Ἀλκαῖός τε ἐν Ἱερῷ Γάμῳ. πλεῖστον δ᾽ ἐστὶ τοῦτο.
Φιλύλλιος δὲ ἐν Αὔγῃ κατὰ χειρῶν εἴρηκεν οὕτως·

καὶ δὴ δεδειπνήκασιν αἱ γυναῖκες· ἀλλ᾽ ἀφαιρεῖν
ὥρα ᾽στὶν ἤδη τὰς τραπέζας, εἶτα παρακορῆσαι,
ἔπειτα κατὰ χειρῶν ἑκάστῃ καὶ μύρον τι δοῦναι.

Μένανδρος Ὑδρίᾳ·

οἱ δὲ κατὰ χειρῶν λαβόντες περιμένουσι, |
f   φίλτατοι.

Ἀριστοφάνης δὲ ὁ γραμματικὸς ἐν τοῖς Πρὸς τοὺς
Καλλιμάχου Πίνακας χλευάζει τοὺς οὐκ εἰδότας τὴν
διαφορὰν τοῦ τε κατὰ χειρὸς καὶ τοῦ ἀπονίψασθαι.
παρὰ γὰρ τοῖς παλαιοῖς τὸ μὲν πρὸ ἀρίστου καὶ
δείπνου λέγεσθαι κατὰ χειρός, τὸ δὲ μετὰ ταῦτα
ἀπονίψασθαι. ἔοικε δ᾽ ὁ γραμματικὸς τοῦτο πεφυλα-
409 χέναι παρὰ τοῖς Ἀττικοῖς, || ἐπεί τοι Ὅμηρός πῃ μέν
φησι·

---

271 Several additional verses of the fragment are quoted and
the context supplied at 8.362b–c.

Epicharmus in *Sacred Envoys* (fr. 68.1–2)[271] uses the plural *cheironiba* in the following passage:

> lyres, tripods, chariots, bronze tables,
> *cheironiba*, libation vessels, bronze basins.

Normal usage was to say "water over the hand" (*kata cheiros*), for example Eupolis in *The Golden Age* (fr. 320), Amipsias in *The Sling* (fr. 20), and Alcaeus in *The Sacred Marriage* (fr. 16). This is the most common usage. But Philyllius in *Auge* (fr. 3) says "over the hands" (*kata cheirōn*), as follows:

> The women have in fact finished dinner. Now it's
> time to remove the tables, then to sweep,
> and then to give them all (water) over their hands
>   (*kata cheirōn*) and some perfume.

Menander in *The Water-Jar* (fr. 360):

> They got (water) over their hands (*kata cheirōn*) and
>   are waiting around, my friends.

The grammarian Aristophanes in his *Response to Callimachus' Tablets* (fr. 368 Slater) makes fun of people who do not know the difference between "(water) over the hand" (*kata cheiros*) and "to wash up" (*aponipsasthai*); because in ancient authors "(water) over the hand" was used to refer to what went on before lunch or dinner, whereas what went on after meals is described as "washing up". The grammarian has apparently made this observation on the basis of Attic authors, since Homer in fact says somewhere (e.g. *Od.* 1.138):

409

νίψασθαι· παρὰ δὲ ξεστὴν ἐτάνυσσε τράπεζαν.

πῇ δέ·

τοῖσι δὲ κήρυκες μὲν ὕδωρ ἐπὶ χεῖρας ἔχευαν,
σῖτον δὲ δμῳαὶ παρενήνεον ἐν κανέοισι.

καὶ Σώφρων ἐν Γυναικείοις· τάλαινα Κοικόα, κατὰ
χειρὸς δοῦσα ἀπόδος πόχ᾽ ἁμῖν τὰν τράπεζαν. παρὰ
μέντοι τοῖς τραγικοῖς καὶ τοῖς κωμικοῖς παροξυτόνως
ἀνέγνωσται χερνίβα· παρ᾽ Εὐριπίδῃ ἐν Ἡρακλεῖ· |

b   ἐς χερνίβ᾽ ὡς βάψειεν Ἀλκμήνης τόκος.[29]

ἀλλὰ καὶ παρ᾽ Εὐπόλιδι ἐν Αἰξίν·

αὐτοῦ τὴν χερνίβα παύσεις.

ἐστὶ δὲ ὕδωρ εἰς ὃ ἀπέβαπτον δαλὸν ἐκ τοῦ βωμοῦ
λαμβάνοντες ἐφ᾽ οὗ τὴν θυσίαν ἐπετέλουν· καὶ τούτῳ
περιρραίνοντες τοὺς παρόντας ἥγνιζον. χρὴ μέντοι
προπαροξυτόνως προφέρεσθαι· τὰ γὰρ τοιάδε ῥη-
ματικὰ σύνθετα εἰς ψ λήγοντα γεγονότα παρὰ τὸν
παρακείμενον τὴν παραλήγουσαν τοῦ παρακειμένου
φυλάσσουσιν, ἄν τε ἔχῃ τοῦτον διὰ τῶν δύο μ̄ λεγόμε-

---

[29] The Euripidean text has a comma at hepthemimeral caesura, and Ἀλκμήνης τόκος is actually the subject of the verb that
follows in the next line.

---

[272] Sc. in the accusative singular.
[273] The line ought in fact to be divided by a comma at the
hepthemimeral caesura.

410

> to wash themselves (*nipsasthai*); and she stretched
> out a polished table beside them.

But in another place (*Od.* 1.146–7):

> and heralds poured (water) over their hands (*epi
> cheiras*) for them,
> and slave-women heaped up bread in baskets.

Also Sophron in the *Women's Mimes* (fr. 15): Coicoa, you idiot—after you give us (water) over our hand (*kata cheiros*), *then* bring us the table! Again, in the tragic and comic poets, the word[272] is read with an acute on the penultimate syllable, *cherníba*. In Euripides' *Heracles* (929):

> so that Alcmene's child might dip it into the
> *cherníba*.[273]

Also in Eupolis' *Nanny-Goats* (fr. 14):

> You'll keep the *cherníba* from him.

This is the water into which they dipped a burning piece of wood, after they removed it from the altar where they were making a sacrifice; they sprinkled the individuals present with it to sanctify them. The word should in fact be accented with an acute on the antepenult.[274] Because compounds of this sort that end in *psi* and are derived from the perfect retain the penultimate syllable of the perfect, and if this syllable is pronounced with a double *mu*, it gets an

---

[274] I.e. *chérniba* (from nominative *chérnips*); the discussion that follows is apparently intended to correct the position on the accentuation of the word attributed to the tragic and comic poets above.

c νον, βαρύνεται, λέλειμμαι | αἰγίλιψ, τέτριμμαι οἰκό-
τριψ, κέκλεμμαι βοίκλεψ, παρὰ Σοφοκλεῖ Ἑρμῆς,
‹βέβλεμμαι›[30] κατῶβλεψ, παρὰ Ἀρχελάῳ τῷ Χερρο-
νησίτῃ ἐν τοῖς Ἰδιοφυέσιν. ἐν δὲ ταῖς πλαγίοις τὰ
τοιαῦτα ἐπὶ τῆς αὐτῆς συλλαβῆς φυλάττειν τὴν
τάσιν. Ἀριστοφάνης δ᾽ ἐν Ἥρωσι χερνίβιον εἴρηκεν.
ἐχρῶντο δ᾽ εἰς τὰς χεῖρας ἀποπλύνοντες αὐτὰς καὶ
σμήματι ἀπορρύψεως χάριν, ὡς παρίστησιν Ἀντιφάνης ἐν Κωρύκῳ·

(A.) ἐν ὅσῳ δ᾽ ἀκροῶμαί σου κέλευσόν ‹μοι›
τινὰ |
d φέρειν ἀπονίψασθαι. (B.) δότω τις δεῦρ᾽ ὕδωρ
καὶ σμῆμα.

ἔτι δὲ καὶ εὐώδεσι τὰς χεῖρας κατεχρίοντο τὰς ἀπο-
μαγδαλίας ἀτιμάσαντες, ἃς Λακεδαιμόνιοι ἐκάλουν
κυνάδας, ὥς φησι Πολέμων ἐν τῇ Περὶ Ὀνομάτων
Ἀδόξων ἐπιστολῇ. περὶ δὲ τοῦ εὐώδεσι χρίεσθαι τὰς
χεῖρας Ἐπιγένης ἢ Ἀντιφάνης φησὶν ἐν Ἀργυρίου
Ἀφανισμῷ οὕτως·

30 hab. Eustathius p. 1401.16

---

275 Whence (according to the argument articulated here) accusative singular *aigílipa*, like *oikótriba*, *boíklepa*, and *katóblepa*
(below). *aigilips* is attested in Homer and Aeschylus; for *oikotrips*,
cf. Ar. *Th.* 426 with Austin–Olson ad loc.
276 Cf. 5.221b (citing Alexander of Myndus) with n.

acute accent: thus *léleimmai* ("I have been left") and *aigílips*[275] ("destitute of goats"); *tétrimmai* ("I have been ruined") and *oikótrips* ("a home-bred slave"); *kéklemmai* ("I have been deceived") and *boíkleps* ("cattle-thief"), which is used by Sophocles (fr. *318) of Hermes; *béblemmai* ("I have been seen") and *katōbleps* ("downward-looking"), which is used by Archelaus of the Chersonese in his *Strange Creatures* (fr. 7 Giannini).[276] In the oblique cases, words of this type retain the accent on the same syllable. Aristophanes uses the form *chernibion* in *Heroes* (fr. 330).[277] They put soap on their hands when they washed them, in order to get them clean, as Antiphanes establishes in *The Beggar's-Bag* (fr. 134):

(A.) While I'm listening to you, please order someone
to bring me water to wash up. (B.) Someone bring
water and
soap here!

In addition, they applied lotions with a pleasant fragrance to their hands, and did not bother with hand-wiping bread, which the Spartans referred to as *kunades* ("dog-bits"),[278] according to Polemon in his letter *On Unusual Words* (fr. 77 Preller). As for applying lotions with a pleasant fragrance to their hands, Epigenes or Antiphanes (fr. 41)[279] says the following in *Vanished Money*:

[277] The quotation has perhaps fallen out of the text.

[278] Because after they were used, they were thrown to the household's dogs to eat.

[279] This is the only reference to a play with this title by either man.

413

καὶ τότε

† περιπατήσεις † κἀπονίψει κατὰ τρόπον |

e   τὰς χεῖρας εὐώδη λαβὼν τὴν γῆν.

καὶ Φιλόξενος δ᾽ ἐν τῷ ἐπιγραφομένῳ Δείπνῳ φησίν·

ἔπειτα δὲ παῖ-
  δες νίπτρ᾽ ἔδοσαν κατὰ χειρῶν
σμήμασιν ἰρινομίκ-
  τοις χλιεροθαλπὲς ὕδωρ
    ἐπεγχέοντες
τόσσον ὅσον ⟨τις⟩ ἔχρῃζ᾽,
  ἐκτρίμματά τ(ε) ⟨ . . . ⟩ λαμπρὰ
σινδονυφῆ, δίδοσαν
  ⟨δὲ⟩ χρίματά τ᾽ ἀμβροσίο-
    δμα καὶ στεφάνους ἰοθαλέας.

Δρόμων δ᾽ ἐν Ψαλτρίᾳ·

ἐπεὶ δὲ θᾶττον ἦμεν ἠριστηκότες,
⟨ . . . ⟩ περιεῖλε τὰς τραπέζας, νίμματα
f   ἐπέχει τις, | ἀπενιζόμεθα, τοὺς στεφάνους πάλιν
† δὲ σπορίνους † λαβόντες ἐστεφανούμεθα.

ἐκάλουν δ᾽ ἀπόνιπτρον τὸ ἀπόνιμμα τῶν χειρῶν καὶ
τῶν ποδῶν. Ἀριστοφάνης·

ὥσπερ ἀπόνιπτρον ἐκχέοντες ἑσπέρας.

and then
† you'll walk around † and you'll get the nice-smelling
soap[280] and wash your hands the right way.

Philoxenus as well says in his poem entitled *The Dinner
Party* (*PMG* 836(b).40–3):[281]

then slaves
poured washing-water over our hands (*kata
cheirōn*),
spilling as much
lukewarm water mixed with iris-scented
soaps over them
as anyone needed;
and (they . . .) clean towels (*ektrimmata*)[282]
woven of linen, and gave us
lotions that smelled like ambrosia,
and garlands full of violets.

Dromo in *The Female Harp-Player* (fr. 2):

And then, as soon as we were done with lunch,
. . . removed the tables; someone poured us
washing-water, and we washed up; and again we got
[corrupt] garlands and put them on our heads.

They referred to the water used to wash their hands and
feet as *aponiptron*. Aristophanes (*Ach.* 616):

just like people who dump *aponiptron* in the evening.

---

[280] Literally "earth"; cf. 8.351e with n.
[281] A large number of additional verses from the fragment
(overlapping at the very end with the material preserved here) are
quoted at 4.146f–7e.   [282] See 9.410b.

415

ἴσως δὲ καὶ τὴν λεκάνην οὕτως ἔλεγον, ἐν ᾧ τρόπῳ καὶ χειρόνιπτρον. ἰδίως δὲ καλεῖται παρ' Ἀθηναίοις ἀπόνιμμα ἐπὶ τῶν εἰς τιμὴν τοῖς νεκροῖς γινομένων καὶ ἐπὶ τῶν τοὺς ἐναγεῖς καθαιρόντων, ὡς καὶ Κλείδημος ‖

410 ἐν τῷ ἐπιγραφομένῳ Ἐξηγητικῷ. προθεὶς γὰρ περὶ ἐναγισμῶν γράφει τάδε· ὄρυξαι βόθυνον πρὸς ἑσπέραν τοῦ σήματος. ἔπειτα παρὰ τὸν βόθυνον πρὸς ἑσπέραν βλέπε, ὕδωρ κατάχεε λέγων τάδε· "ὑμῖν ἀπόνιμμα οἷς χρὴ καὶ οἷς θέμις." ἔπειτα αὖθις μύρον κατάχεε. παρέθετο ταῦτα καὶ Δωρόθεος, φάσκων καὶ ἐν τοῖς τῶν Εὐπατριδῶν πατρίοις τάδε γεγράφθαι

b περὶ τῆς τῶν ἱκετῶν καθάρσεως· | ἔπειτα ἀπονιψάμενος αὐτὸς καὶ οἱ ἄλλοι οἱ σπλαγχνεύοντες ὕδωρ λαβὼν κάθαιρε, ἀπόνιζε τὸ αἷμα τοῦ καθαιρομένου καὶ μετὰ τὸ ἀπόνιμμα ἀνακινήσας εἰς ταὐτὸ ἔγχεε. χειρόμακτρον δὲ καλεῖται ᾧ τὰς χεῖρας ἀπεμάττοντο ὠμολίνῳ· ὅπερ ἐν τοῖς προκειμένοις Φιλόξενος ὁ Κυθήριος ὠνόμασεν ἔκτριμμα. Ἀριστοφάνης Ταγηνισταῖς·

φέρε παῖ ταχέως κατὰ χειρὸς ὕδωρ,
παράπεμπε τὸ χειρόμακτρον.

---

283 Cf. Eup. fr. 129.1, 3 (quoted at 9.408d).
284 I.e. those that involved washing the corpse.
285 The name ought perhaps to be emended to Autocleides (thus Stiehle), as also at 11.473b.
286 Presumably Dorotheus of Ascalon or Sidon, quoted by Athenaeus also at e.g. 7.329d; 11.481d, 497e.

They may also have referred to the basin this way, as they did with the word *cheironiptron*.[283] The Athenians alone use the term *aponimma* to refer to the rituals intended to show respect for dead bodies[284] and those that serve to purify individuals subject to a curse, for example Cleidemus[285] in his work entitled *The Art of Interpretation*. After some initial remarks about offerings to the dead, he writes the following: Dig a hole to the west of the grave. Then stand beside the hole, look to the west, and pour water into it as you say the following: "This is *aponimma* intended for you who need and ought to receive it." Then, after that, pour perfume in. This passage is cited by Dorotheus[286], who claims that the following is included in the traditional texts of the Eupatridae[287] on the subject of the cleansing-ceremony for suppliants: Then after you and the others who tasted the entrails wash up, take water and cleanse him. Wash the blood off the individual being cleansed, and after the cleansing ceremony (*aponimma*), stir the water and dump it in the same place. The coarse linen towel they used to wipe their hands was referred to as a *cheiromaktron*; in the passage cited above (*PMG* 836(b).42, cited at 9.409e), Philoxenus of Cythera called it an *ektrimma*. Aristophanes in *Frying-Pan Men* (fr. 516):

Slave! Hurry up and bring us water to wash our
      hands (*kata cheiros*)!
And bring the *cheiromaktron* too!

[287] The Eupatridae were Athens' traditional pre-Solonian aristocracy, whose formal powers gradually shrank to include only a few ritual functions, including the ones referred to in the passage cited here.

417

σημειωτέον δὲ ὅτι καὶ μετὰ τὸ δειπνῆσαι κατὰ χειρὸς
c ἔλεγον, οὐχ ὡς Ἀριστοφάνης ὁ γραμματικός | φησιν
ὅτι πρὶν φαγεῖν οἱ Ἀττικοὶ κατὰ χειρὸς ἔλεγον, μετὰ
δὲ τὸ δειπνῆσαι ἀπονίψασθαι. Σοφοκλῆς Οἰνομάῳ·

Σκυθιστὶ χειρόμακτρον ἐκκεκαρμένος.

καὶ Ἡρόδοτος ἐν δευτέρᾳ. Ξενοφῶν δ᾽ ἐν πρώτῳ Παιδείας γράφει· ὅταν δὲ τούτων τινὸς θίγῃς, εὐθὺς ἀπο-
καθαίρῃ τὴν χεῖρα εἰς τὰ χειρόμακτρα, ὡς πάνυ ἀχθόμενος ὅτι κατάπλεά σοι ἀπ᾽ αὐτῶν ἐγένετο. Πολέμων
δ᾽ ἐν ἕκτῳ τῶν Πρὸς Ἀντίγονον καὶ Ἀδαῖον περὶ τῆς
d διαφορᾶς λέγει τοῦ | κατὰ χειρὸς πρὸς τὸ νίψασθαι.
Δημόνικος δ᾽ ἐν τῷ Ἀχελῴῳ τὸ πρὸ τοῦ δείπνου κατὰ
χειρός φησι διὰ τούτων·

ἐσπουδάκει δ᾽ ἕκαστος ὡς ἂν ἑστιῶν
ἅμα τ᾽ ὀξύπεινον ἄνδρα καὶ Βοιώτιον.
τὸ γοῦν κατὰ χειρὸς περιέγραψ᾽, εἴπας ὅτι
μετὰ δεῖπνον αὐτῷ τοῦτο γίνεται λαβεῖν.

ὠμολίνου δὲ μέμνηται Κρατῖνος ἐν Ἀρχιλόχοις·

ὠμολίνοις κόμη βρύουσ᾽ ἀτιμίας πλέως.

---

288 This sentence is clearly out of place here.
289 Quoted at 9.410e.
290 The Boeotians had a reputation for gluttony; cf. 10.417b–
18b.

It should also be noted that they said *kata cheiros* ("[water] over the hand") in reference to what went on after dinner, and that it is not the case, as the grammarian Aristophanes (fr. 368 Slater, cited at 9.408f) claims, that Attic authors said *kata cheiros* to refer to what went on before they ate, but *aponipsasthai* ("to wash up") to refer to what went on after dinner.[288] Sophocles in *Oenomaus* (fr. 473):

> with his head sheared so that it looked like a
> > *cheiromaktron*, Scythian style.

Also Herodotus in Book II (122.1).[289] Xenophon writes in Book I of the *Education* (*Cyr.* 1.3.5): When you touch any of these foods, you immediately wipe your hand clean on your napkins, as if you were quite upset because you had picked up an infection from them. Polemon in Book VI of his *Response to Antigonus and Adaeus* (fr. 62 Preller) discusses the difference between *kata cheiros* and *nipsasthai* ("to wash oneself"). Demonicus in his *Acheloüs* (fr. 1) refers to what goes on before dinner as *kata cheiros*, in the following passage:

> Everyone was as busy as if he were entertaining
> an individual who was simultaneously extremely
> > hungry and a Boeotian.[290]
> He rejected the (water) *kata cheiros*, for example,
> > saying
> he preferred to have this after dinner.

Cratinus mentions rough linen in *Archilochuses* (fr. 10):

> hair teeming with strips of rough linen and full of
> > disgrace.

Σαπφὼ δ᾽ ὅταν λέγῃ ἐν τῷ πέμπτῳ τῶν Μελῶν πρὸς τὴν Ἀφροδίτην·

e   χερρόμακτρα δὲ | † καγγόνων †
πορφύρᾳ † καταυταμενά-
τατιμάσεις † ἔπεμψ᾽ ἀπὺ Φωκάας
δῶρα τίμια † καγγόνων †,

κόσμον λέγει κεφαλῆς τὰ χειρόμακτρα, ὡς καὶ Ἑκαταῖος δηλοῖ ἢ ὁ γεγραφὼς τὰς Περιηγήσεις ἐν τῇ Ἀσίᾳ ἐπιγραφομένῃ· γυναῖκες δ᾽ ἐπὶ τῆς κεφαλῆς ἔχουσι χειρόμακτρα. Ἡρόδοτος δ᾽ ἐν τῇ δευτέρῃ φησί· μετὰ δὲ ταῦτα ἔλεγον τοῦτον τὸν βασιλέα ζωὸν καταβῆναι κάτω εἰς ὃν οἱ Ἕλληνες Ἅιδην νομίζουσι κἀκεῖθι συγκυβεύειν τῇ Δήμητρι, καὶ τὰ μὲν νικᾶν
f   αὐτήν, τὰ δὲ ἐσσοῦσθαι ὑπ᾽ αὐτῆς· καί μιν | πάλιν ἀναφικέσθαι δῶρον ἔχοντα παρ᾽ αὐτῆς χειρόμακτρον χρύσεον. τὸν δὲ τῷ χερνίβῳ ῥάναντα παῖδα διδόντα κατὰ χειρὸς Ἡρακλεῖ ὕδωρ, ὃν ἀπέκτεινεν ὁ Ἡρακλῆς κονδύλῳ, Ἑλλάνικος μὲν ἐν ταῖς Ἱστορίαις Ἀρχίαν φησὶ καλεῖσθαι· δι᾽ ὃν καὶ ἐξεχώρησε Καλυδῶνος. ἐν δὲ τῷ δευτέρῳ τῆς Φορωνίδος Χερίαν αὐτὸν ὀνομάζει. Ἡρόδωρος δ᾽ ἐν ἑπτακαιδεκάτῃ τοῦ καθ᾽ Ἡρακλέα
411a λόγου Εὔνομον. καὶ Κύαθον ‖ δὲ τὸν Πύλητος μὲν υἱόν, ἀδελφὸν δὲ Ἀντιμάχου ἀπέκτεινεν ἄκων Ἡρακλῆς οἰνοχοοῦντα αὐτῷ, ὡς Νίκανδρος ἱστορεῖ ἐν

---

291 Cf. D.S. 4.36.2–3; [Apollod.] *Bib.* 2.7.6 (where the boy is called Eunomus).

When Sappho in Book V of her *Lyric Poems* (fr. 101) tells Aphrodite:

> and towels (*cherromaktra*) [corrupt]
> with purple [corrupt]
> [corrupt] he sent from Phocaea
> as a gift full of honor [corrupt],

she is using *cheiromaktra* to refer to something worn on one's head, as Hecataeus (or whoever wrote his *Tours*) makes clear in his work entitled *Asia* (*FGrH* 1 F 358): Women wear *cheiromaktra* on their heads. Herodotus says in Book II (122.1): Afterward, they claimed, this king descended alive to the place the Greeks regard as Hades, and shot dice there with Demeter; sometimes he beat her, and sometimes he lost to her. They also claimed that he emerged again with a gold *cheiromaktron* as a gift from her. The slave who spilled washing-water (*chernibos*) on Heracles when he was offering it to him to wash his hands, and whom Heracles killed with a punch, was named Archias, according to Hellanicus in his *History* (*FGrH* 4 F 2, including the reference to Book II that follows); he was the reason that Heracles left Calydon.[291] But in Book II of the *History of Phoroneus*, Hellanicus refers to him as Cherias.[292] Herodorus in Book XVII of his *Story of Heracles* (*FGrH* 31 F 3), on the other hand, (calls him) Eunomus. Heracles also killed Cyathus the son of Pyles and brother of Antimachus accidentally, when Cyathus was pouring wine for him, according to Nicander in Book

[292] Most likely one name is a corruption of the other (thus Casaubon).

421

δευτέρῳ Οἰταικῶν, ᾧ καὶ ἀνεῖσθαί φησι τέμενος ὑπὸ τοῦ Ἡρακλέους ἐν Προσχίῳ, ὃ μέχρι νῦν προσαγορεύεσθαι Οἰνοχόου.

Ἡμεῖς δ᾽ ἐνταῦθα καταπαύσαντες τὸν λόγον ἀρχὴν ποιησόμεθα τῶν ἑξῆς ἀπὸ τῆς τοῦ Ἡρακλέους ἀδηφαγίας.

II of his *Oetaica* (fr. 17 Schneider = *FGrH* 271–2 F 14); he claims that Heracles dedicated a sanctuary in Cyathus' honor in Proschion which is referred to even today as the sanctuary of Oinochoous ("the Winepourer").[293]

I will break off my account at this point and begin what follows with the question of Heracles' gluttony.

[293] Cf. Paus. 2.13.8.

I

411b   Ἀλλ' ὥσπερ δείπνου γλαφυροῦ ποικίλην εὐωχίαν
    τὸν ποιητὴν δεῖ παρέχειν τοῖς θεαταῖς τὸν
      σοφόν,
    ἵν' ἀπίῃ τις τοῦτο φαγὼν καὶ πιών, ὅπερ λαβὼν
    χαίρει <τις>, καὶ σκευασία μὴ μί' ᾖ τῆς
      μουσικῆς,

  Ἀστυδάμας ὁ τραγικὸς ἐν Ἡρακλεῖ σατυρικῷ, ἑταῖρε,
φησί, Τιμόκρατες. φέρε εἴπωμεν ἐνταῦθα τοῖς προειρημένοις τὰ ἀκόλουθα ὅτι ἦν καὶ ὁ Ἡρακλῆς ἀδηφάγος. ἀποφαίνονται δὲ τοῦτο σχεδὸν πάντες ποιηταὶ
καὶ συγγραφεῖς. Ἐπίχαρμος μὲν ἐν Βουσίριδι λέ-
γων· |

c   πρᾶτον μὲν αἴ κ' ἔσθοντ' ἴδοις νιν, ἀποθάνοις·
  βρέμει μὲν ὁ φάρυγξ ἔνδοθ', ἀραβεῖ δ' ἁ
    γνάθος,
  ψοφεῖ δ' ὁ γομφίος, τέτριγε δ' ὁ κυνόδων,
  σίζει δὲ ταῖς ῥίνεσσι, κινεῖ δ' οὔατα.

424

BOOK X

A clever poet should supply his audience with
a rich feast that resembles an elegant dinner,
so everyone eats and drinks whatever he likes before
he leaves, and the entertainment doesn't consist of a
    single course,

says the tragic poet Astydamas in his satyr play *Heracles*
(*TrGF* 60 F 4),[1] my friend Timocrates. So let me describe
the discussions that followed those I told you about earlier,
and which concerned Heracles being a glutton. Almost
every poet and prose-author makes this clear. Epicharmus
in *Bousiris*[2] (fr. 18), saying:

If you saw him eating, first of all, you'd die.
His throat emits a roar, his jaw rattles,
his molars resound, his canine teeth squeak,
he snorts loudly, and he wiggles his ears.

---

[1] The quotation is relevant to the theme of this Book, in that it
involves Heracles and feasting, but is also programmatic for the
Learned Banqueters as a whole; cf. Metag. fr. 15 (quoted at
10.459b–c, at the very end of the Book).

[2] Bousiris, the king of Egypt—who is most likely being ad-
dressed here—misguidedly attempted to sacrifice Heracles to
Zeus when Heracles visited Egypt; cf. 10.420e with n.; [Apollod.]
Bib. 2.5.11.

425

Ἴων δ᾽ ἐν Ὀμφάλῃ ἐμφανίσας αὐτοῦ τὴν ἀδηφαγίαν
ἐπιφέρει·

> ὑπὸ δὲ τῆς εὐφημίας
> κατέπινε καὶ τὰ κᾶλα καὶ τοὺς ἄνθρακας.

d   παρὰ | Πινδάρου δὲ τοῦτ᾽ εἴληφεν εἰπόντος·

> δοιὰ βοῶν
> θερμὰ πρὸς ἀνθρακιὰν
> στέψαν πυρὶ δεῖπνον
> σώματα. καὶ τότ᾽ ἐγὼ
> σαρκῶν τ᾽ ἐνοπὰν < . . . > ἠδ᾽ ὀ-
> στέων στεναγμὸν βαρύν·
> ἦν διακρῖναι ἰδόντα πολλὸς ἐν καιρῷ χρόνος.

τοιοῦτον οὖν αὐτὸν ὑποστησάμενοι ταῖς ἀδηφαγίαις
καὶ τῶν ὀρνέων ἀποδεδώκασιν αὐτῷ τὸν λάρον τὸν
προσαγορευόμενον βουφάγον. εἰσάγεται δὲ ὁ Ἡρακλῆς καὶ Λεπρεῖ περὶ πολυφαγίας ἐρίζων ἐκείνου
412 προκαλεσαμένου, καὶ νενίκηκεν. Ζηνόδοτος || δ᾽ ἐν
δευτέρῳ Ἐπιτομῶν Καύκωνός φησι τοῦ Ποσειδῶνος
καὶ Ἀστυδαμείας τῆς Φόρβαντος γενέσθαι τὸν Λεπρέα, ὃν τὸν Ἡρακλέα κελεῦσαι δεθῆναι, ὅτε Αὐγέαν

---

[3] Omphale was a Lydian queen whom Heracles served as a
slave for a number of years; cf. S. *Tr.* 248–53, 274–8; Pherecyd.
FGrH 3 F 82b.

[4] The fragment as preserved in Athenaeus is desperately
corrupt and is printed here in substantially emended form;
Athenaeus (or his source) apparently thought that Pindar meant

But Ion in *Omphale*[3] (*TrGF* 19 F 29) first describes his gluttony and then continues:

> while the order for silence was being given,
> he began gulping down the firewood and the
> charcoal.

He borrowed this from Pindar (fr. 168b), who said:[4]

> They surrounded
> two hot bull-carcasses
> with fire, along with charcoal,
> to be his dinner. And then I
> . . . the cry of flesh and the
> heavy groan of bones.
> There was considerable time available to watch and
> evaluate.

Because they believe that he is such an extraordinary glutton, they have given him the sea-gull, also known as the *bouphagos*[5], to be his bird. Heracles is also represented as having an eating-contest with Lepreus, after Lepreus challenged him, and as winning. Zenodotus in Book II of the *Epitomes*[6] (*FGrH* 19 F 1) reports that Lepreus was the son of Caucon the son of Poseidon and Astydameia the daughter of Phorbas, and that he suggested that Heracles be put in chains after he asked Augeas for his pay.[7] After

that Heracles intended to have the charcoal as well as the bulls for dinner.   [5] Literally "bull-eater." For the association of the sea-gull with Heracles, see Ar. *Av.* 567.

[6] Sc. *"of the Epic Sagas"*.   [7] Sc. for cleaning Augeas' stables. For the story of Heracles and Lepreus, cf. Ael. *VH* 1.24 (apparently drawing on the same source); Paus. 5.5.4.

τὸν μισθὸν ἀπῄτει. Ἡρακλῆς δ᾽ ἐκτελέσας τοὺς
ἄθλους ἔρχεται ἐπὶ Καύκωνας καὶ δεηθείσης Ἀστυδαμείας διαλύεται πρὸς τὸν Λεπρέα. καὶ μετὰ ταῦτα ὁ
Λεπρεὺς Ἡρακλεῖ ἐρίζει δίσκῳ καὶ ὕδατος ἀντλήσει
καὶ ὅστις ἀναλώσει θᾶττον ταῦρον, καὶ λείπεται πάν-
b   τα. | εἶτα θωρηχθεὶς προκαλεῖται Ἡρακλέα καὶ θνή-
σκει ἐν τῇ μάχῃ. Μᾶτρις δ᾽ ἐν τῷ τοῦ Ἡρακλέους
Ἐγκωμίῳ καὶ εἰς πολυποσίαν φησὶ τὸν Ἡρακλέα
προκληθῆναι ὑπὸ τοῦ Λεπρέως, καὶ πάλιν νικηθῆναι.
τὰ αὐτὰ ἱστορεῖ καὶ ὁ Χῖος ῥήτωρ Καύκαλος, ὁ
Θεοπόμπου τοῦ ἱστοριογράφου ἀδελφός, ἐν τῷ τοῦ
Ἡρακλέους Ἐγκωμίῳ.

Καὶ τὸν Ὀδυσσέα δὲ Ὅμηρος πολυφάγον καὶ
λαίμαργον παραδίδωσιν ὅταν λέγῃ·

ἀλλ᾽ ἐμὲ μὲν δορπῆσαι ἐάσατε κηδόμενόν περ· |
c   οὐ γάρ τι στυγερῇ ἐπὶ γαστέρι κύντερον ἄλλο
ἔπλετο, ἥ τ᾽ ἐκέλευσεν ἕο μνήσασθαι ἀνάγκῃ
καὶ μάλα τειρόμενον καὶ ἐνιπλησθῆναι ἀνώγει.[1]

ὑπερβάλλουσα γὰρ ἐν τούτοις φαίνεται αὐτοῦ λαι-
μαργία μετὰ τοῦ μηδὲ ἐν δέοντι τὰ περὶ τῆς γαστρὸς
γνωμολογεῖν· ἐχρῆν γάρ, εἰ καὶ ἐλίμωττεν, διακαρ-
τερεῖν ἢ μετριάζειν τὰ περὶ τὴν τροφήν. τὸ δὲ τελευ-
ταῖον καὶ τὴν τελειοτάτην αὐτοῦ παρίστησι λαιμαρ-
γίαν καὶ γαστριμαργίαν· |

[1] The traditional text of Homer has καὶ ἐνὶ φρεσὶ πένθος
ἔχοντα; for the text preserved here, cf. *Od.* 7.221 (quoted below).

428

Heracles completed his labors, he visited the Cauconians and, at Astydameia's request, gave up his hostility toward Lepreus. Afterward, Lepreus competed against Heracles in the discus, in bailing water, and to see who could eat a bull more rapidly, and lost every time. Then he put on his breastplate, challenged Heracles to a fight, and died in the duel. Matris in his *Eulogy of Heracles* (*FGrH* 39 F 1) claims that Lepreus also challenged Heracles to a drinking-contest and lost there as well. The Chian orator Caucalus, who was the brother of the historian Theopompus (*FGrH* 38 T 1 = 115 T 4), tells the same story in his *Eulogy of Heracles*.

Homer presents Odysseus as well as a greedy gourmand, when he says (*Od.* 7.215–18):

> But let me eat my dinner, unhappy as I am.
> For nothing is more shameless than the miserable
> belly, which orders us to pay attention to it and gives
> us no choice,
> even when we are worn out, and demands to be
> filled.

For in this passage Odysseus' greed is shown to be excessive, and he offers an unnecessary sentencious discussion of his belly; because even if he was famished, he should have put up with the situation, or have eaten a modest amount. But his conclusion establishes his extreme greed and gluttony (*Od.* 7.219–21):

d ὡς καὶ ἐγὼ πένθος μὲν ἔχω φρεσίν, ἡ δὲ μάλ᾽
  αἰεὶ
 ἐσθέμεναι κέλεται καὶ πινέμεν, ἐκ δέ με πάντων
 ληθάνει ὅσσ᾽ ἔπαθον, καὶ ἐνιπλησθῆναι ἀνώγει.

ταῦτα γὰρ οὐδ᾽ ἂν ἐκεῖνος ὁ Σαρδανάπαλλος εἰπεῖν
ποτε ἂν ἐτόλμησεν. γέρων τε ὢν

 ἤσθιεν ἁρπαλέως κρέα τ᾽ ἄσπετα καὶ μέθυ ἡδύ.

Θεαγένης δ᾽ ὁ Θάσιος ἀθλητὴς ταῦρον μόνος κατ-
έφαγεν, ὡς Ποσείδιππός φησιν ἐν Ἐπιγράμμασι· |

e καὶ περὶ συνθεσίης ἔφαγόν ποτε Μηόνιον βοῦν,
  πάτρη γὰρ βρώμην οὐκ ἂν ἐπέσχε Θάσος
 Θευγένει, ὅσσα φαγὼν ἔτ᾽ ἐπῄτεον· οὕνεκεν οὕτω
  χάλκεος ἕστήκω χεῖρα προϊσχόμενος.

Μίλων δ᾽ ὁ Κροτωνιάτης, ὥς φησιν ὁ Ἱεραπολίτης
Θεόδωρος ἐν τοῖς Περὶ Ἀγώνων, ἤσθιε μνᾶς κρεῶν
εἴκοσι καὶ τοσαύτας ἄρτων οἴνου τε τρεῖς χοᾶς ἔπινεν.
f ἐν δὲ Ὀλυμπίᾳ ταῦρον ἀναθέμενος τοῖς ὤμοις | τετρα-
έτη καὶ τοῦτον περιενέγκας τὸ στάδιον μετὰ ταῦτα

---

8 Cf. 8.335f–6d with n.

9 The second half of the line occurs at *Od.* 9.162 (describing
Odysseus' men on Goat Island, before the visit to the land of the
Cyclopes).

10 Theagenes (more likely Theogenes; the poets call him
Theugenes for metrical reasons) was one of the dominant boxers
and pancratiasts of the 480s and 470s BCE (Moretti #201).

Since I feel pain in my heart; but my belly
      relentlessly
insists that I eat and drink, and makes me forget
all my sufferings, and demands to be filled.

Not even the famous Sardanapallus would have dared to
say this.[8] And although he was an old man,

he ravenously consumed boundless meat and
      delicious wine.[9]

The Thasian athlete Theagenes[10] ate a bull all by himself, according to Posidippus in the *Epigrams* (120 Austin-
Bastianinni = *HE* 3126–9):

I once ate a Meionian bull on a bet;
      because my native land, Thasos, could not supply
      enough food for
Theugenes; however much I ate, I still asked for
      more. I accordingly stand
      here, made of bronze, with my hand stretched
      out.

According to Theodorus of Hierapolis in his *On Contests*
(fr. 1, *FHG* iv.513), Milo of Croton[11] used to eat 20 *minas*[12]
of meat, along with an equal amount of bread, and would
drink three pitchers of wine. At Olympia he put a four-
year-old bull on his shoulders and walked around the sta-
dium carrying it, and afterward he butchered it and ate

---

[11] A famous wrestler, victorious six times at the Olympic
games in the late 6th century BCE (Moretti #115, etc.), as well six
times at the Pythian games, ten times at the Isthmian games, and
nine times at the Nemean games.

δαιτρεύσας μόνος αὐτὸν κατέφαγεν ἐν μιᾷ ἡμέρᾳ.
Τίτορμός τε ὁ Αἰτωλὸς διηριστήσατο αὐτῷ βοῦν, ὡς
ἱστορεῖ ὁ Αἰτωλὸς Ἀλέξανδρος. Φύλαρχος δέ φησιν
ἐν τῇ τρίτῃ τῶν Ἱστοριῶν τὸν Μίλωνα ταῦρον καταφαγεῖν κατακλιθέντα πρὸ τοῦ βωμοῦ τοῦ Διός, διὸ καὶ
ποιῆσαι εἰς αὐτὸν Δωριέα τὸν ποιητὴν τάδε·

> τοῖος ἔην Μίλων, ὅτ᾽ ἀπὸ χθονὸς ἤρατο βρῖθος,
> τετραετῆ δαμάλην, ἐν Διὸς εἰλαπίναις, ‖
413   ὤμοις δὲ κτῆνος τὸ πελώριον ὡς νέον ἄρνα
> ἤνεγκεν δι᾽ ὅλης κοῦφα πανηγύρεως.
> καὶ θάμβος μέν, ἀτὰρ τοῦδε πλέον ἤνυσε θαῦμα
> πρόσθεν Πισαίου, ξεῖνε, θυηπολίου·
> ὃν γὰρ ἐπόμπευσεν βοῦν ἄζυγον, εἰς κρέα τόνδε
> κόψας πάντα κατ᾽ οὖν μοῦνος ἐδαίσατό νιν.

Ἀστυάναξ δ᾽ ὁ Μιλήσιος τρὶς Ὀλύμπια νικήσας ‖
b κατὰ τὸ ἑξῆς παγκράτιον, κληθείς ποτε ἐπὶ δεῖπνον
ὑπὸ Ἀριοβαρζάνου τοῦ Πέρσου καὶ ἀφικόμενος ὑπ-
έσχετο φαγεῖν πάντα τὰ πᾶσι παρασκευασθέντα καὶ
κατέφαγε. τοῦ Πέρσου δ᾽ αὐτὸν ἀξιώσαντος, ὡς ὁ
Θεόδωρος ἱστορεῖ, ἄξιόν τι ποιῆσαι τῶν κατὰ τὴν
ἰσχὺν φακὸν τῆς κλίνης περίχαλκον ὄντα κλάσας
ἐξέτεινε μαλάξας. τελευτήσαντος δ᾽ αὐτοῦ καὶ κατα-

---

12 Roughly 20 pounds (on the Attic standard).
13 I.e. Olympia.   14 In 324, 320, and 316 BCE (Moretti
#470, 474, 479).   15 Several important Persians from this
period bore the name Ariobarzanes (Berve i #115–16), and precisely who is being referred to is unclear.

the whole thing in a single day, all by himself. According to
Alexander Aetolus (fr. 14 Magnelli), Titormus of Aetolia
competed with Milo in eating an ox for lunch. Phylarchus
in Book III of his *History* (*FGrH* 81 F 3) claims that Milo
lay down in front of the altar of Zeus and consumed a bull,
which is why the poet Dorieus (*SH* 396 = *FGE* 159–66)
wrote the following about him:

> This is what Milo was like, when he lifted the weight
>   of a four-year-old
>   heifer from the earth at Zeus' feast,
> and carried the enormous beast lightly on his
>   shoulders
>   through the entire crowd, as if it were a new-born
>   lamb.
> This was astonishing; but he did something more
>   amazing than this,
>   stranger, before the altar in Pisa[13];
> for he cut up this unyoked cow he carried around
>   into chunks of meat
>   and ate the entire thing all by himself.

Astyanax of Miletus, who took the prize in the pancration
three times in a row at Olympia,[14] was invited to dinner at
one point by Ariobarzanes of Persia;[15] when he got there,
he claimed that he could eat all the food that had been
prepared for the entire party—and did so. According to
Theodorus (fr. 2, *FHG* iv.513), when the Persian asked him
to do something to show how strong he was, he broke a
bronze-plated ornament off of his couch, kneaded it until
it was soft, and pressed it flat. When he died and was cre-

κανθέντος οὐκ ἐχώρησε μία ὑδρία τὰ ὀστέα, μόλις δὲ
δύο. καὶ τὰ τοῖς ἐννέα ἀνδράσι παρεσκευασμένα παρὰ
c   τῷ Ἀριοβαρζάνῃ | εἰς τὸ δεῖπνον μόνον καταφαγεῖν.

Καὶ οὐδὲν παράδοξον τούτους τοὺς ἄνδρας ἀδηφά-
γους γενέσθαι· πάντες γὰρ οἱ ἀθλοῦντες μετὰ τῶν
γυμνασμάτων καὶ ἐσθίειν πολλὰ διδάσκονται. διὸ καὶ
Εὐριπίδης ἐν τῷ πρώτῳ Αὐτολύκῳ λέγει·[2]

κακῶν γὰρ ὄντων μυρίων καθ᾽ Ἑλλάδα
οὐδὲν κάκιόν ἐστιν ἀθλητῶν γένους.
οἳ πρῶτα μὲν ζῆν[3] οὔτε μανθάνουσιν εὖ
οὔτ᾽ ἂν δύναιντο· πῶς γὰρ ὅστις ἔστ᾽ ἀνὴρ
γνάθου τε δοῦλος νηδύος θ᾽ ἡσσημένος |
d   κτήσαιτ᾽ ἂν ὄλβον εἰς ὑπερβολὴν πατρός;
οὐδ᾽ αὖ πένεσθαι κἀξυπηρετεῖν τύχαις
οἷοί τ᾽· ἔθη γὰρ οὐκ ἐθισθέντες καλὰ
σκληρῶς διαλλάσσουσιν εἰς τἀμήχανα.[4]
λαμπροὶ δ᾽ ἐν ἥβῃ καὶ πόλεως ἀγάλματα
φοιτῶσ᾽· ὅταν δὲ προσπέσῃ γῆρας πικρόν,
τρίβωνες ἐκβαλόντες οἴχονται κρόκας.
ἐμεμψάμην δὲ καὶ τὸν Ἑλλήνων νόμον,
οἳ τῶνδ᾽ ἕκατι σύλλογον ποιούμενοι
τιμῶσ᾽ ἀχρείους ἡδονὰς δαιτὸς χάριν. |

[2] Verses 1–6 are also preserved in *POxy.* liii 3699, while verses
1–9, 16–22 are also preserved by Galen, *Protrept.* 10.
[3] *POxy.* liii 3699 and Galen (followed by Kannicht in *TrGF*)
have πρῶτον οἰκεῖν.

mated, a single jar was not big enough to hold his bones, and two barely were. All by himself he ate the food that had been prepared for nine men's dinner at Ariobarzanes' house.

It comes as no surprise that these men were gluttons; because all athletes in the course of their training are taught to eat a large amount of food. This is why Euripides in *Autolycus I* (fr. 282) says:

Because although Greece has more problems than
      you can count,
there's none worse than the athletes.
First of all, they don't learn to live decently,
and they couldn't anyway. For how could a man
who's enslaved to his jaws and weaker than his belly
accumulate more wealth than his father?
They're also incapable of being poor or coping with
adversity; because the bad habits they develop mean
      that
they have trouble adapting to difficult circumstances.
They're famous when they're young, and they're the
      city's stars
wherever they go. But when bitter old age hits them,
they disappear like cheap robes that lose their nap.
I also disapprove of how the Greeks behave
when they call an assembly because of these people
and shower them with worthless pleasures in order to
      have a feast.

---

4 Galen (followed by Kannicht in *TrGF*) has σκληρῶς μεταλλάσσουσιν εἰς τἀμήχανον.

ATHENAEUS

e   τί γὰρ παλαίσας εὖ, τί⁵ δ᾽ ὠκύπους ἀνὴρ
ἢ δίσκον ἄρας ἢ γνάθον παίσας καλῶς
πόλει πατρᾴα στέφανον ἤρκεσεν λαβών;
πότερα μαχοῦνται πολεμίοισιν ἐν χεροῖν
δίσκους ἔχοντες ἢ δι᾽ ἀσπίδων χερὶ
θείνοντες ἐκβαλοῦσι πολεμίους πάτρας;
οὐδεὶς σιδήρου ταῦτα μωραίνει πέλας
† στάς. ἄνδρας χρὴ σοφούς τε κἀγαθοὺς
φύλλοις στέφεσθαι, χὤστις ἡγεῖται πόλει |
f   κάλλιστα σώφρων καὶ δίκαιος ὢν ἀνήρ,
ὅστις τε μύθοις ἔργ᾽ ἀπαλλάσσει κακά
μάχας τ᾽ ἀφαιρῶν καὶ στάσεις. τοιαῦτα γὰρ
πόλει τε πάσῃ πᾶσί θ᾽ Ἕλλησιν καλά.

Ταῦτ᾽ εἴληφεν ὁ Εὐριπίδης ἐκ τῶν τοῦ Κολοφωνίου Ἐλεγείων Ξενοφάνους οὕτως εἰρηκότος·

ἀλλ᾽ εἰ μὲν ταχυτῆτι ποδῶν νίκην τις ἄροιτο
ἢ πενταθλεύων, ἔνθα Διὸς τέμενος ‖
414   πὰρ Πίσαο ῥοῆς ἐν Ὀλυμπίῃ, εἴτε παλαίων
ἢ καὶ πυκτοσύνην ἀλγινόεσσαν ἔχων

⁵ Galen (followed by Kannicht in *TrGF*) has τίς . . . τίς.

If someone's a good wrestler, or runs fast,
or has a talent for throwing a discus or punching
      another person in the jaw—
what good does he do his native city by winning a
      garland?
Are they planning to fight the enemy with discuses
in their hands? Or do they intend to expel hostile
      forces from
their country by punching their fist through shields?
No one indulges in this kind of foolishness when he's
      † standing
close to iron. We ought to wreathe the heads of
good, wise men, and of anyone who's sensible and
      just,
and does an excellent job of leading the city,
or who uses eloquence to put a stop to bad behavior,
or to extricate us from battles and political strife.
      Because actions like those
are good for the entire city and for the Greeks
      generally.

Euripides borrowed these remarks from the *Elegies* of
Xenophanes of Colophon (fr. B 2 West²), who says the following:

But if someone wins a victory by the speed of his
      feet,
   or by competing in the pentathlon, where Zeus'
      sacred precinct lies
alongside the streams of the Pisa in Olympia, or by
      wrestling,
   or through his control of the painful skill of boxing

εἴτε τὸ δεινὸν ἄεθλον ὃ παγκράτιον καλέουσιν,
   ἀστοῖσίν κ' εἴη κυδρότερος προσορᾶν,
καί κε προεδρίην φανερὴν ἐν ἀγῶσιν ἄροιτο,
   καί κεν σῖτ' εἴη δημοσίων κτεάνων
ἐκ πόλεως, καὶ δῶρον ὅ οἱ κειμήλιον εἴη—
   εἴτε καὶ ἵπποισιν· ταῦτά κε πάντα λάχοι,
οὐκ ἐὼν ἄξιος ὥσπερ ἐγώ· ῥώμης γὰρ ἀμείνων |
b   ἀνδρῶν ἠδ' ἵππων ἡμετέρη σοφίη.
ἀλλ' εἰκῇ μάλα τοῦτο νομίζεται, οὐδὲ δίκαιον
   προκρίνειν ῥώμην τῆς ἀγαθῆς σοφίης.
οὔτε γὰρ εἰ πύκτης ἀγαθὸς λαοῖσι μετείη
   οὔτ' εἰ πενταθλεῖν οὔτε παλαισμοσύνην,
οὐδὲ μὲν εἰ ταχυτῆτι ποδῶν, τόπερ ἐστὶ
     πρότιμον,
   ῥώμης ὅσσ' ἀνδρῶν ἔργ' ἐν ἀγῶνι πέλει,
τοὔνεκεν ἂν δὴ μᾶλλον ἐν εὐνομίῃ πόλις εἴη |
c   σμικρὸν δ' ἄν τι πόλει χάρμα γένοιτ' ἐπὶ τῷ,
εἴ τις ἀεθλεύων νικῷ Πίσαο παρ' ὄχθας·
   οὐ γὰρ πιαίνει ταῦτα μυχοὺς πόλεως.

πολλὰ δὲ καὶ ἄλλα ὁ Ξενοφάνης κατὰ τὴν ἑαυτοῦ
σοφίαν ἐπαγωνίζεται, διαβάλλων ὡς ἄχρηστον καὶ
ἀλυσιτελὲς τὸ τῆς ἀθλήσεως εἶδος. καὶ ὁ Ἀχαιὸς[6] δὲ ὁ
Ἐρετριεὺς περὶ τῆς εὐεξίας τῶν ἀθλητῶν διηγούμενός
φησι·

     [6] Ἀχαιὸς Casaubon: ἀχίλλιος A

438

or the awful contest known as the pancration;
>   and if his fellow-citizens regard him as more
>   distinguished,
and he is awarded a prominent front-row seat at
>   competitions,
>   and the city grants him maintenance at public
expense, as well as a gift he can keep as a treasure—
>   or even if he is victorious in chariot-racing—he
>   could get all these rewards
and not deserve them as much as I do. For my
>   wisdom
>   is better than the strength of men or of horses.
This is very bad practice, and it is wrong to prefer
>   physical strength to my good wisdom.
For the fact that one of the people is a good boxer,
>   or good at the pentathlon or in wrestling,
or in the speed of his feet, which is the most
>   respected
>   of all the contests of physical strength in which
>   men engage,
could not make a city better governed.
>   A city would get only minimal joy from the fact
that someone takes the prize when he competes
>   beside the banks of the Pisa;
>   for this is not what enriches a city internally.

Xenophanes also offers many other contentious comments
about his own wisdom, attacking the idea of athletics as
useless and worthless. So too Achaeus of Eretria (*TrGF* 20
F *4) says in his description of the fine living conditions
athletes enjoy:

ATHENAEUS

γυμνοὶ γὰρ † ὤθουν † φαιδίμους βραχίονας |
d ἥβῃ σφριγῶντες ἐμπορεύονται, νέῳ
στίλβοντες ἄνθει καρτερὰς ἐπωμίδας·
ἄδην δ᾽ ἐλαίου στέρνα καὶ † ποδῶν † κύτος
χρίουσιν ὡς ἔχοντες οἴκοθεν τρυφήν.

Ἡράκλειτος δ᾽ ἐν τῷ Ξενίζοντι Ἑλένην φησί τινα
γυναῖκα πλεῖστα βεβρωκέναι. Ποσείδιππος δ᾽ ἐν
Ἐπιγράμμασι Φυρόμαχον, εἰς ὃν καὶ τόδ᾽ ἐπέγραψε·

Φυρόμαχον, τὸν πάντα φαγεῖν βορόν, οἷα
κορώνην |
e παννυχικήν, αὕτη ῥωγὰς ἔχει κάπετος
χλαίνης ἐν τρύχει Πελληνίδος. ἀλλὰ σὺ τούτου
καὶ χρῖε στήλην, Ἀττικέ, καὶ στεφάνου,
εἴ ποτέ σοι προκύων συνεκώμασεν. ἦλθε δ᾽
ἀμαυρὰ
βλέψας ἐκ πελιῶν νωδὸς ἐπισκυνίων,
† ὁ τριχιδιφθερίας⁷ † μονολήκυθος· ἐκ γὰρ
ἀγώνων
τῶν τότε Ληναϊκὴν ἦλθ᾽ ὑπὸ Καλλιόπην.

Ἀμάραντος δὲ ὁ Ἀλεξανδρεὺς ἐν τοῖς Περὶ Σκηνῆς |

⁷ ὁ τρεχέδειπνος ἀεὶ Austin

---

16 An otherwise unknown (comic?) poet; see K–A vol. V s.v.
17 Calliope was the leader of the Muses, and the point (admittedly obscure) is presumably that Phyromachus was routinely referred to in the comedies staged at the Lenaia festival in Athens.

440

Because naked † they were pushing † they travel
    around, their
gorgeous arms bursting with adolescent strength,
    their powerful
shoulders glistening with the glow of youth;
and they anoint their chest and the trunk † of their
    feet † with
plenty of oil, as if they had been raised in the lap of
    luxury.

Heracleitus[16] in his *The Host* claims that a woman named Helen ate more than anyone else could. Posidippus in the *Epigrams* (121 Austin–Bastianinni = *HE* 3134–41) (mentions) Phyromachus, about whom he composed the following poem:

This crudely dug trench contains Phyromachus, who
    was as voraciously
    eager to eat everything as a raven at an all-night
      festival,
in the ragged remnants of a Pellenian robe. It is for
    you,
    resident of Athens, to anoint his stele and garland
      it,
if he ever joined you as a hanger-on at a party. He
    went there, toothless and
casting a blind glance from his black-and-blue
    brow,
† the one with a hairy robe made of skin † with a
    single oil-flask; for he came from the contests
    held in those days, escorted by Lenaian Calliope.[17]

Amarantus of Alexandria in his *On the Stage* claims that

f Ἡρόδωρόν φησι τὸν Μεγαρέα σαλπιγκτὴν γενέσθαι
τὸ μὲν μέγεθος πηχῶν τριῶν καὶ ἡμίσους, εἶναι δὲ καὶ
τὰς πλευρὰς ἰσχυρόν· ἐσθίειν δὲ ἄρτων μὲν χοίνικας
ἕξ, κρεῶν δὲ λίτρας εἴκοσιν οἵων ἂν εὑρήκῃ, πίνειν δὲ
χοᾶς δύο καὶ σαλπίζειν ἅμα σάλπιγξι δυσί. κοι-
μᾶσθαι δὲ ἔθος εἶχεν ἐπὶ λεοντῆς μόνης. ἐσήμαινε δὲ
σαλπίζων μέγιστον. Ἄργος γοῦν πολιορκοῦντος Δη-
415 μητρίου ‖ τοῦ Ἀντιγόνου καὶ οὐ δυναμένων τῶν στρατιωτῶν τὴν ἑλέπολιν προσαγαγεῖν τοῖς τείχεσι διὰ τὸ
βάρος, ταῖς δύο σάλπιγξι σημαίνων ὑπὸ τῆς ἁδρότη-
τος τοῦ ἤχου τοὺς στρατιώτας ἠνάγκασε προθυμη-
θέντας προσαγαγεῖν τὴν μηχανήν. ἐνίκησε δὲ τὴν
περίοδον δεκάκις καὶ ἐδείπνει καθήμενος, ὡς ἱστορεῖ
Νέστωρ ἐν τοῖς Θεατρικοῖς Ὑπομνήμασι. καὶ γυνὴ δὲ
ἐσάλπισεν Ἀγλαῒς ἡ Μεγακλέους ἐν τῇ πρώτῃ ἀχθεί-
σῃ μεγάλῃ πομπῇ ἐν Ἀλεξανδρείᾳ τὸ πομπικόν, περι-
b θέτην ἔχουσα καὶ λόφον | ἐπὶ τῆς κεφαλῆς, ὡς δηλοῖ
Ποσείδιππος ἐν Ἐπιγράμμασιν. ἤσθιε δὲ καὶ αὐτὴ
λίτρας μὲν κρεῶν δώδεκα, ἄρτων δὲ χοίνικας τέσσαρας, καὶ ἔπινεν οἴνου χοᾶ.

---

18 Literally "three-and-a-half cubits".

19 A *choinix* was a dry measure equivalent (on the Attic standard, at least) to about one quart.

20 Literally "and 20 *litrai*".

21 Demetrius Poliorcetes. The siege of Argos perhaps took
place in 303 BCE; cf. Plu. *Demetr.* 25.1–2 (although there the city
is liberated via bribery); Poll. 4.89 (who tells a similar story, but
does not name the city).

the Megarian trumpeter Herodorus was only about five feet[18] tall, but had a powerful chest. He used to eat six *choinikes*[19] of bread and 20 pounds[20] of any meat he could find, and drank two pitchers of wine; blew two trumpets at the same time; and made it a practice to sleep on a lion-skin and nothing else. He produced extremely loud signals when he blew the trumpet. When Demetrius the son of Antigonus[21] was besieging Argos, at any rate, and the weight of the siege-engine was preventing the soldiers from bringing it up to the walls, Herodorus used two trumpets to give the signals, and the noise was so loud that the soldiers had no choice but to get their courage up and move the machine forward. He was victorious ten times on the circuit,[22] and used to eat his meals sitting down, according to Nestor in his *Theatrical Commentaries*. So too, a woman named Aglaïs the daughter of Megacles gave the trumpet-signals at the first great procession held in Alexandria, wearing a wig and a crest on top of her head, according to Posidippus in the *Epigrams* (143 Austin–Bastianinni = *SH* 702).[23] She also used to eat 12 pounds[24] of meat and four *choinikes*[25] of bread, and could drink a full pitcher of wine.

[22] I.e. he took the prize at all four of the major games: the Olympic (Moretti #468, etc.), Pythian, Nemean, and Isthmian.

[23] Cf. Ael. *VH* 1.26 (drawing on the same source). The procession is most likely the one organized by Ptolemy II Philadelphus (reigned 285/3–246 BCE) and described at great length by Callixeinus of Rhodes (quoted at 5.197c–203b).

[24] Literally "12 *litrai*".

[25] See 10.414f n.

Λιτυέρσας δὲ ἦν μὲν υἱὸς Μίδου νόθος, Κελαινῶν δὲ τῶν ἐν Φρυγίᾳ βασιλεύς, ἄγριος ἰδέσθαι καὶ ἀνήμερος ἄνθρωπος, ἀδηφάγος δ' ἰσχυρῶς. λέγει δὲ περὶ αὐτοῦ Σωσίθεος ὁ τραγῳδιοποιὸς ἐν δράματι Δάφνιδι ἢ Λιτυέρσᾳ οὕτως·

ἔσθει μὲν ἄρτους[8], τρεῖς ὅλους[9] κανθηλίους,
τρὶς τῆς βραχείας ἡμέρας· πίνει δ', ἕνα |
c καλῶν μετρητήν, τὸν δεκάμφορον πίθον.

τοιοῦτός ἐστι καὶ ὁ παρὰ Φερεκράτει ἢ Στράττιδι ἐν Ἀγαθοῖς, περὶ οὗ φησιν·

(Α.) ἐγὼ κατεσθίω μόλις τῆς ἡμέρας
πένθ' ἡμιμέδιμν', ἐὰν βιάζωμαι. (Β.) μόλις;
ὡς ὀλιγόσιτος ἦσθ' ἄρ', ὃς κατεσθίεις
τῆς ἡμέρας μακρᾶς τριήρους σιτία.

Ξάνθος δ' ἐν τοῖς Λυδιακοῖς Κάμβλητά φησι τὸν βασιλεύσαντα Λυδῶν πολυφάγον γενέσθαι καὶ πολυπότην, ἔτι δὲ γαστρίμαργον. τοῦτον οὖν ποτε νυκτὸς |
d τὴν ἑαυτοῦ γυναῖκα κατακρεουργήσαντα καταφαγεῖν,

[8] ἄρτους C: αὐτοὺς A: αὐτὸς E
[9] ὅλους A: ὄνους CE

[26] For Lityersas, whose name is apparently drawn from the refrain of a traditional reaping song, and who is said to have forced passers-by to reap with him and then to have cut off their heads, see Gow on Theoc. 10.41. He was eventually killed by Heracles.
[27] A much fuller version of this fragment is quoted at Stob.

Lityersas was an illegitimate son of Midas, and was king of the Celaenai in Phrygia; he was a cruel and savage-looking individual, and a devoted glutton.[26] The tragic poet Sositheus says the following about him in his play *Daphnis or Lityersas* (*TrGF* 99 F 2.6–8):[27]

> He eats "bread"—three entire loaves as big as a
>   donkey could carry!—
> three times in one short day. And he drinks a 10-
>   amphora
> jar of wine—which he refers to as "just one jarful".

The man in Pherecrates' (fr. 1) or Strattis' *Good Men*[28], about whom the poet says the following, is the same sort:

> (A.) I can barely consume two-and-a-half *medimnoi*[29]
> per day, if I'm forced to. (B.) "Barely"?
> What a tiny appetite you have, then—a man who
>   consumes
> enough rations for a large trireme every day!

Xanthus in his *History of Lydia* (*FGrH* 765 F 18) claims that Cambles, the king of Lydia,[30] ate and drank large amounts, and was a glutton on top of that. At one point, in fact, he chopped his own wife up into pieces during

---

4.10.18. Ael. *VH* 1.27 appears to be a condensed version of 10.415b–16e or the source from which it is drawn.

[28] Athenaeus expresses similar doubts about the authorship of the play at 6.248c (where he quotes vv. 3–4) and 15.685b (quoting Pherecr. fr. 2). But Pollux twice assigns the play unambiguously to Pherecrates (7.198; 10.47).   [29] A *medimnos* was a dry measure equivalent to about six gallons.

[30] A mythological rather than an historical figure.

ἔπειτα πρωὶ εὑρόντα τὴν χεῖρα τῆς γυναικὸς ἐνοῦσαν
ἐν τῷ στόματι ἑαυτὸν ἀποσφάξαι, περιβοήτου τῆς
πράξεως γενομένης. περὶ δὲ Θυὸς τοῦ Παφλαγόνων
βασιλέως ὅτι καὶ αὐτὸς ἦν πολυφάγος προειρήκαμεν,
παραθέμενοι Θεόπομπον ἱστοροῦντα ἐν τῇ πέμπτῃ καὶ
τριακοστῇ. Ἀρχίλοχος δ᾽ ἐν Τετραμέτροις Χαρίλαν
εἰς τὰ ὅμοια διαβέβληκεν, ὡς οἱ κωμῳδιοποιοὶ Κλεώ-
νυμον καὶ Πείσανδρον. περὶ δὲ Χαιρίππου φησὶ Φοι-
e νικίδης | ἐν Φυλάρχῳ οὕτως·

> τρίτον δὲ πρὸς τούτοισι τὸν σοφώτατον
> Χαίριππον. οὗτος, ὥσπερ οἶδας, ἐσθίει
> μέχρι ἂν διδῷ τις ἢ λάθῃ διαρραγείς.
> τοιοῦτ᾽ ἔχει ταμιεῖον ὥσπερ οἰκίας.

Νικόλαος δ᾽ ὁ περιπατητικὸς ἐν τῇ τρίτῃ πρὸς ταῖς
ἑκατὸν τῶν Ἱστοριῶν Μιθριδάτην φησὶ τὸν Ποντικὸν
βασιλέα προθέντα ἀγῶνα πολυφαγίας καὶ πολυπο-
σίας (ἦν δὲ τὸ ἆθλον τάλαντον ἀργυρίου) ἀμφότερα
νικῆσαι. τοῦ μέντοι ἄθλου ἐκστῆναι τῷ μετ᾽ αὐτὸν
κριθέντι Καλαμόδρυϊ τῷ Κυζικηνῷ ἀθλητῇ. καὶ Τιμο-
f κρέων δ᾽ ὁ Ῥόδιος | ποιητὴς καὶ ἀθλητὴς πένταθλος

---

31 At 4.144e–5a, where see n.

32 Also mentioned in Archil. fr. 168, where the poet addresses
him (ironically?) as "far and away the dearest of my companions".

33 Cleonymus (*PAA* 579410) and Peisander (*PAA* 771270)
were prominent late 5th-century BCE Athenian politicians.

the night and ate her; then the next morning, when he found her hand in his mouth, he committed suicide, since rumors about what he had done had already spread. I noted earlier[31] that Thys the king of the Paphlagonians also ate large amounts, citing Theopompus, who discusses him in Book XXXV (*FGrH* 115 F 179). Archilochus in the *Tetrameters* (fr. 167 West²) makes similarly hostile remarks about Charilas,[32] as the comic poets do about Cleonymus and Peisander (adesp. com. fr. 119).[33] Phoenicides in *The Tribal Cavalry Commander* (fr. 3) says the following about Chaerippus:[34]

> and third, in addition to them, the brilliant
> Chaerippus. As you know, this guy eats for
> as long as anyone offers him food—or until he stops
>   paying attention and explodes!
> He's got a storeroom inside him as big as one in a
>   house.

Nicolaus the Peripatetic in Book CIII of his *History* (*FGrH* 90 F 73) claims that Mithridates, the king of Pontus,[35] held an eating- and drinking-contest—the prize was a talent[36] of silver—and won in both categories, although he yielded the prize to the Cyzicene athlete Calamodrys, who took second place behind him. The poet Timocreon of Rhodes, who competed in the pentathlon,

[34] Otherwise unknown. Phoenicides dates to the early 3rd century BCE.

[35] Given the location of the anecdote in Book CIII, this must be a reference to Mithradates VI Eupator Dionysos (reigned 120–63 BCE).

[36] About 60 pounds.

ἄδην ἔφαγε καὶ ἔπιεν, ὡς τὸ ἐπὶ τοῦ τάφου αὐτοῦ
ἐπίγραμμα δηλοῖ·

πολλὰ πιὼν καὶ πολλὰ φαγὼν καὶ πολλὰ κάκ᾽
εἰπὼν
ἀνθρώπους κεῖμαι Τιμοκρέων Ῥόδιος. ‖

416   Θρασύμαχος δ᾽ ὁ Χαλκηδόνιος ἔν τινι τῶν Προοιμίων
τὸν Τιμοκρέοντά φησιν ὡς μέγαν βασιλέα ἀφικόμε-
νον καὶ ξενιζόμενον παρ᾽ αὐτῷ πολλὰ ἐμφορεῖσθαι.
πυθομένου δὲ τοῦ βασιλέως ὅ τι ἀπὸ τούτων ἐργά-
ζοιτο, εἶπε Περσῶν ἀναριθμήτους συγκόψειν. καὶ τῇ
ὑστεραίᾳ πολλοὺς καθ᾽ ἕνα νικήσας μετὰ τοῦτο ἐχει-
ρονόμησε. πυνθανομένου δὲ τὴν πρόφασιν ὑπολεί-
b   πεσθαι ἔφη τοσαύτας, εἰ προσίοι | τις, πληγάς. Κλέ-
αρχος δ᾽ ἐν πέμπτῳ Βίων Καντιβάρι φησὶ τῷ Πέρσῃ,
ὁπότε κοπιάσειε τὰς σιαγόνας ἐσθίων, κεχηνότι
καθάπερ εἰς ἄψυχον ἀγγεῖον εἰσαντλεῖν τὴν τροφὴν
τοὺς οἰκείους. Ἑλλάνικος δ᾽ ἐν πρώτῃ Δευκαλιωνείας
Ἐρυσίχθονά φησι τὸν Μυρμιδόνος, ὅτι ἦν ἄπληστος
βορᾶς, Αἴθωνα κληθῆναι. Πολέμων δ᾽ ἐν πρώτῳ τῶν
c   Πρὸς | Τίμαιον παρὰ Σικελιώταις φησὶν Ἀδηφαγίας
ἱερὸν εἶναι καὶ Σιτοῦς Δήμητρος ἄγαλμα, οὗ πλησίον
ἱδρῦσθαι καὶ Ἱμαλίδος, καθάπερ ἐν Δελφοῖς † ερμού-

---

37 A satirical (rather than a genuine sepulchral) epigram.

38 For Timocreon's (late 6th/early 5th centuries BCE) attrac-
tion to Persia, cf. *PMG* 729.   39 For Erysichthon (whose insatiable appetite was a curse imposed upon him when he cut down
a sacred grove belonging to Demeter), cf. Callimachus' *Hymn to*

also ate and drank enormous amounts, as the epigram on his tomb (*FGE* 831–2)[37] attests:

> After drinking much, and eating much, and making
> many nasty remarks
> about others, I lie here, Timocreon of Rhodes.

Thrasymachus of Chalcedon in one of his *Preludes* (85 B 4 D–K) claims that Timocreon visited the Great King[38] and consumed a large amount of food when they had dinner together. When the King asked what this was going to give him energy for, he said he intended to beat up more Persians than you could count. The next day he defeated numerous opponents, one after another, and did some shadow-boxing afterward. When the King asked why, he said that that was how many punches he had left, if anyone else wanted to fight him. Clearchus in Book V of the *Lives* (fr. 52 Wehrli) claims that whenever Cantibaris the Persian was eating and his jaws got tired, he would open his mouth and his servants would pour the food in, as if he were an inanimate jar. Hellanicus in Book I of the *Story of Deucalion* (*FGrH* 4 F 7) says that because Erysichthon the son of Myrmidon could eat endless amounts, he was called Aethon.[39] Polemon in Book I of his *Response to Timaeus* (fr. 39 Preller)[40] reports that in Sicily there is a temple of Gluttony and statue of Demeter Sitō ("Goddess of Grain"), near to which is another statue of (Demeter) Himalis,[41]

Demeter with Hopkinson's Introduction pp. 18–31, and on verse 67 (on the name Aethon, here perhaps imagined to be derived from *aiei* ["always"] and a participial form of *esthō* ["eat"]).

[40] Quoted also at 3.109a–b.

[41] "Goddess of Abundance" *vel sim.*; cf. 14.618d.

χου †, ἐν δὲ Σκώλῳ τῷ Βοιωτιακῷ Μεγαλάρτου καὶ
Μεγαλομάζου. καὶ Ἀλκμὰν δ᾽ ὁ ποιητὴς ἑαυτὸν ἀδηφάγον εἶναι παραδίδωσιν ἐν τῷ τρίτῳ διὰ τούτων·

    καί ποκά τοι δώσω τρίποδος κύτος
    † ὠκένιλεα Γείρης †
    ἀλλ᾽ ἔτι νῦν γ᾽ ἄπυρος, τάχα δὲ πλέος
    ἔτνεος, οἷον ὁ παμφάγος Ἀλκμὰν
    ἠράσθη χλιαρὸν πεδὰ τὰς τροπάς·
    οὔτι γὰρ † οὐ τετυμμένον † ἔσθει,
    ἀλλὰ τὰ κοινὰ γάρ, ὥπερ ὁ δᾶμος,
    ζατεύει.

κἀν τῷ πέμπτῳ δὲ ἐμφανίζει αὐτοῦ τὸ ἀδηφάγον
d λέγων | οὕτως·

    ὥρας δ᾽ ἔσηκε τρεῖς, θέρος
    καὶ χεῖμα κὠπώραν τρίταν
    καὶ τέτρατον τὸ Ϝῆρ, ὄκα
    σάλλει μέν, ἐσθίην δ᾽ ἄδαν
    οὐκ ἔστι.

Ἀναξίλας δ᾽ ὁ κωμικὸς περὶ Κτησίου τινὸς διαλεγό-
μενος ἐν Χρυσοχόῳ δράματί φησιν·

    ἤδη σχεδόν τι πάντα σοι πλὴν Κτησίου.
    δεῖπνον γὰρ οὗτος, ὡς λέγουσιν οἱ σοφοί,
    ἀρχήν, τελευτὴν δ᾽ οὐκ ἐπίσταται μόνος.

---

[42] *PAA* 586680 (also mentioned in Is. 4.9, along with Cranaus,
referred to below).

like that of † *ermouchos* † in Delphi, and those of Mega-lartos ("Large Loaf of Bread") and Megalomazos ("Large Barley-Cake") in Boeotian Scolus. The poet Alcman also presents himself as a glutton in Book III (*PMG* 17), in the following passage:

And someday I'll give you a hollow tripod
[corrupt]
but has not yet been placed on a fire, and soon it will
      be full
of bean-soup of the kind the gluttonous Alcman
loves to eat hot after the solstice.
Because he never eats any [corrupt],
but looks for ordinary food, what normal people
like.

He also brings out his own gluttony in Book V (*PMG* 20), where he says the following:

He added three seasons: summer,
and winter, and autumn third,
and spring fourth, when
everything's growing, but there's not enough
to eat.

The comic author Anaxilas says in his discussion of a certain Ctesias[42] in his play *The Goldsmith* (fr. 30):

You've now got almost everything except Ctesias;
because the clever people say he understands how
      dinner
begins, but he's the only one who doesn't know how it
      ends.

451

κἀν Πλουσίοις·

(Α.) διαρραγήτω χἄτερος δειπνῶν τις εὖ, |
μὴ Κτησίας μόνος. (Β.) τί γάρ σε κωλύει;
(Α.) δείπνου γὰρ οὗτος, ὡς λέγουσιν οἱ σοφοί,
ἀρχήν, τελευτὴν δ᾽ ἔμαθεν οὐδεπώποτε.

κἀν Χάρισι δὲ Κραναόν τινα συγκαταλέγει οὕτως
αὐτῷ·

οὐκ ἐτὸς ἐρωτῶσίν ‹με› προσιόντες τινές·
"ὄντως ὁ Κραναὸς Κτησίου κατεσθίει
ἔλαττον, ἢ δειπνοῦσιν ἀμφότεροι συχνά;"

Φιλέταιρος δ᾽ ἐν Ἀταλάντῃ·

κἂν δέῃ, τροχάζω στάδια πλείω Σωτάδου, |
τὸν Ταυρέαν δὲ τοῖς πόνοις ὑπερβαλῶ,
τὸν Κτησίαν τε τῷ φαγεῖν ὑπερδραμῶ.

Ἀνάξιππος Κεραυνῷ·

(Α.) ὁρῶ γὰρ ἐκ παλαίστρας τῶν φίλων
προσιόντα μοι Δάμιππον. (Β.) ‹ἢ› τοῦτον λέγεις

---

43 Sc. "from exploding".
44 *PAA* 583465; cf. on Ctesias, above.
45 Literally "more stades".
46 Victorious in the long run at Olympia in 384 and 380 BCE
(Moretti #390, 398); see Paus. 6.18.6.

And in *Rich Men* (fr. 25):

(A.) I hope anyone else who eats well explodes,
and not just Ctesias! (B.) Well, what's stopping you?[43]
(A.) The fact that, as the clever people say, he
        understands how dinner
begins, but he's the only one who's never learned how
        it ends.

And in *The Graces* (Anaxil. fr. 29) he includes someone named Cranaus[44] in the same category as Ctesias, as
follows:

It's not for nothing that certain people come up to me
        and ask:
"Does Cranaus actually consume less food
than Ctesias, or do they both eat huge dinners?"

Philetaerus in *Atalanta* (fr. 3):

And if necessary, I run further[45] than Sotades;[46]
and I'll work harder than Taureas[47],
and I'll beat Ctesias when it comes to eating!

Anaxippus in *The Lightning-Bolt* (fr. 3):

(A.) Because I see one of my friends, Damippus,[48]
        coming out of
the wrestling school to meet me. (B.) Are you talking
        about this guy,

---

[47] Presumably to be identified with the glutton referred to at
Antiph. frr. 50.3 (preserved at 8.343d); 188.4 (preserved at
8.342f).
[48] *PAA* 301110.

453

417   τὸν † πέτρινον; ‖ † (Α.) τοῦτον οἱ φίλοι καλοῦσί
         σοι
       νυνὶ δι᾽ ἀνδρείαν Κεραυνόν. (Β.) εἰκότως.
       ἀβάτους ποεῖν γὰρ τὰς τραπέζας οἴομαι
       αὐτόν, κατασκήπτοντα † αὐταῖς † τῇ γνάθῳ.

       ἐν τούτοις ἐδήλωσεν ὁ κωμικὸς διότι καὶ τὸ δρᾶμα
       Κεραυνὸν ἀπ᾽ αὐτοῦ ἐπιγέγραφε. Θεόφιλος δ᾽ ἐν Ἐπι-
       δαύρῳ·

           Ἀτρεστίδας τις Μαντινεὺς λοχαγὸς ἦν,
           ἀνδρῶν ἁπάντων πλεῖστα δυνάμενος φαγεῖν.

       ἐν δὲ Παγκρατιαστῇ παραγαγὼν τὸν ἀθλητὴν ὡς |
  b   πολλὰ ἐσθίοντά φησιν·

                              (Α.) ἐφθῶν μὲν σχεδὸν
       τρεῖς μνᾶς. (Β.) λέγ᾽ ἄλλο. (Α.) ῥυγχίον, κωλῆν,
           πόδας
       τέτταρας ὑείους. (Β.) Ἡράκλεις. (Α.) βοὸς δὲ
           τρεῖς,
       ὄρνιθ᾽. (Β.) Ἄπολλον. λέγ᾽ ἕτερον. (Α.) σύκων
           δύο
       μνᾶς. (Β.) ἐπέπιες δὲ πόσον; (Α.) ἀκράτου
           δώδεκα
       κοτύλας. (Β.) Ἄπολλον, Ὧρε καὶ Σαβάζιε.

       Καὶ ἔθνη δὲ ὅλα εἰς πολυφαγίαν ἐκωμῳδεῖτο, ὡς τὸ

       _____

       49 Spots that had been struck by lightning were regarded as sa-
       cred; cf. E. *Ba*. 6–12 with Dodds' n.

the † rocky one † ? (A.) Nowadays your friends call
        him
Lightning-Bolt, because he's so brave. (B.) That
        makes sense;
because I imagine he makes their tables sacred
ground, by descending † on them † with his jaws.[49]

The author made it clear in this passage that his play *Lightning-Bolt* gets its title from this individual. Theophilus in
Epidaurus (fr. 3):

A certain Atrestidas of Mantinea was a company-
        commander,
a man who was better than anyone else—at eating.

And in *The Pancratiast* (Theophil. fr. 8)[50] he introduces
the athlete as someone who eats large quantities, saying:

                                (A.) Almost three pounds[51]
of stewed meat— (B.) Keep going. (A.) a little snout,
        a ham, four
pigs' feet— (B.) Heracles! (A.) and three cows' feet,
poultry— (B.) Apollo![52] Tell me the rest! (A.) two
        pounds[53]
of figs— (B.) And how much did you drink on top of
        this? (A.) 12 cups
of unmixed wine. (B.) Apollo, Horus, and Sabazius!

Entire ethnic groups were also mocked for being glut-

---

[50] The first three verses are quoted also at 3.95a–b.
[51] Literally "three *minas*".
[52] Cf. 9.386a n.
[53] Literally "two *minas*".

c   Βοιωτόν. Εὔβουλος γοῦν ἐν Ἀντιόπῃ | φησί·

πώνειν μὲν ἁμὲς καὶ φαγεῖν μάλ᾽ ἀνδρικοὶ
καὶ καρτερεῖμεν † τοῖς δ᾽ Ἀθηναίοις λέγειν
καὶ μικρὰ φαγέμεν, τοὶ δὲ Θηβαῖοι μέγα. †

καὶ ἐν Εὐρώπῃ·

κτίζε Βοιωτῶν πόλιν,
ἀνδρῶν ἀρίστων ἐσθίειν δι᾽ ἡμέρας.

καὶ ἐν Ἴωνι·

οὕτω σφόδρ᾽ ἐστὶ τοὺς τρόπους Βοιώτιος,
ὥστ᾽ οὐδὲ δειπνῶν, ὡς λέγουσ᾽, ἐμπίμπλαται.

ἐν δὲ Κέρκωψι· |

d   μετὰ ταῦτα Θήβας ἦλθον, οὗ τὴν νύχθ᾽ ὅλην
τήν θ᾽ ἡμέραν δειπνοῦσι καὶ κοπρῶν᾽ ἔχει
ἐπὶ ταῖς θύραις ἕκαστος, οὗ πλήρει βροτῷ
οὐκ ἔστι μεῖζον ἀγαθόν· ὡς χεζητιῶν
μακρὰν βαδίζων, πολλὰ δ᾽ † ἐσθίων † ἀνήρ,
δάκνων τὰ χείλη παγγέλοιός ἐστ᾽ ἰδεῖν.

ἐν δὲ τοῖς Μυσοῖς πρὸς τὸν Ἡρακλέα ποιεῖ τινα τάδε
λέγοντα·

---

54 The lines are in a dialect apparently intended to approxi-
mate Boeotian.

tons, for example the Boeotians. Thus Eubulus says in
Antiope (fr. 11):[54]

> We're very brave, when it comes to eating and
>   drinking
> and enduring † whereas it's the Athenians' job to not
>   talk
> or eat much, while the Thebans a lot. †

And in *Europa* (Eub. fr. 33):

> Found the city of the Boeotians,
> the men who are best at eating all day long!

And in *Ion* (Eub. fr. 38):

> His behavior's so thoroughly Boeotian
> that people say he doesn't feel full even during
>   dinner.

And in *Cercopes* (Eub. fr. 52):

> After that I went to Thebes, where they eat dinner all
>   night long
> and all day, and where everyone has his own
>   outhouse
> right next to his door. There's nothing better
> for a mortal whose belly's full of food. Because
>   someone who
> needs to take a shit and has a long way to go, and †
>   who's eating † a lot
> and biting his lips, is an extremely amusing sight.

And in his *Mysians* (Eub. fr. 66) he presents someone as
saying the following to Heracles:

σὺ μὲν τὸ Θήβης, ὡς λέγεις, πέδον λιπών,
ἀνδρῶν ἀρίστων ἐσθίειν δι᾽ ἡμέρας |
e   ὅλης τραχήλους, καὶ κοπρῶνας πλησίον.

Δίφιλος δὲ ἐν Βοιωτίῳ·

οἷος ἐσθίειν πρὸ ἡμέρας
ἀρξάμενος ἢ πάλιν πρὸς ἡμέραν.

Μνησίμαχος Βουσίριδι·

(Α.) εἰμὶ γὰρ Βοιώτιος
ὀλίγα μὲν λαλῶν, (Β.) δίκαια ταῦτα. (Α.) πολλὰ
δ᾽ ἐσθίων.

Ἄλεξις Τροφωνίῳ·

νῦν δ᾽ ἵνα μὴ παντελῶς Βοιώτιοι
φαίνησθ᾽ εἶναι τοῖς διασύρειν ὑμᾶς εἰθισμένοις,
ὡς ἀκίνητοι † νῦν εἶναι † βοᾶν καὶ πίνειν
μόνον |
f   καὶ δειπνεῖν ἐπιστάμενοι διὰ τέλους τὴν νύχθ᾽
ὅλην,
γυμνοῦθ᾽ αὑτοὺς θᾶττον ἅπαντες.

Ἀχαιὸς δ᾽ ἐν Ἄθλοις·

(Α.) πότερα θεωροῖς εἴτ᾽ ἀγωνισταῖς λέγεις; ‖

*   *   *

418   (Β.) πόλλ᾽ ἐσθίουσιν, ὡς ἐπασκούντων τρόπος.

---

55 Speaker A is presumably Heracles; cf. 10.411a–b with n.

As for you, after you left the Theban plain, as you say,
which belongs to the best men in the world at eating
shellfish-necks all day long, and the outhouses
      nearby.

Diphilus in *The Boeotian* (fr. 22):

            the type who starts eating before
the sun's up, or on the other hand (continues) until
      the crack of dawn.

Mnesimachus in *Bousiris* (fr. 2):[55]

                  (A.) Because I'm a Boeotian:
I don't talk much— (B.) That's true. (A.) But I eat a
      lot.

Alexis in *Trophonius* (fr. 239):

            But now, so you don't look like complete
Boeotians to the people who are used to making fun
      of you
for being stolid † now to be † and not knowing
      anything except how
to shout, and drink, and eat dinner endlessly all night
      long—
hurry up, all of you, and take off your clothes!

Achaeus in *The Competitions* (*TrGF* 20 F 3):

(A.) Are you speaking to the sacred ambassadors or
      the contestants?

                  *   *   *

(B.) They eat a lot—as men in training do!

* * *

(Α.) ποδαποὶ γάρ εἰσιν οἱ ξένοι; (Β.) Βοιώτιοι.

ἐκ τούτων εἰκός ἐστι καὶ Ἐρατοσθένη ἐν ταῖς Ἐπιστο-
λαῖς Πρεπέλαον φῆσαι ἐρωτηθέντα τί αὐτῷ δοκοῦσιν
εἶναι Βοιωτοὶ εἰπεῖν· "τί γὰρ ἄλλο ἢ τοιαῦτα ἐλάλουν,
οἷα ἂν καὶ τὰ ἀγγεῖα φωνὴν λαβόντα, ὁπόσον ἕκαστος χωρεῖ." Πολύβιος δ' ὁ Μεγαλοπολίτης ἐν τῇ
εἰκοστῇ τῶν Ἱστοριῶν φησιν ὡς Βοιωτοὶ μεγίστην
δόξαν λαβόντες κατὰ τὰ Λευκτρικὰ κατὰ μικρὸν ἀν-
b έπεσον ταῖς ψυχαῖς καὶ ὁρμήσαντες | ἐπ' εὐωχίας καὶ
μέθας διέθεντο καὶ κοινωνείᾳ τοῖς φίλοις. πολλοὶ δὲ
καὶ τῶν ἐχόντων γενεὰς ἀπεμέριζον τοῖς συσσιτίοις
τὸ πλέον μέρος τῆς οὐσίας, ὥστε πολλοὺς εἶναι Βοιωτῶν οἷς ὑπῆρχε δεῖπνα τοῦ μηνὸς πλείω τῶν εἰς τὸν
μῆνα διατεταγμένων ἡμερῶν. διόπερ Μεγαρεῖς μισή-
σαντες αὐτῶν τὴν τοιαύτην κατάστασιν ἀπένευσαν εἰς
τοὺς Ἀχαιούς.

Καὶ Φαρσάλιοι δὲ κωμῳδοῦνται ὡς πολυφάγοι.
Μνησίμαχος γοῦν ἐν Φιλίππῳ φησί·

(Α.) τῶν Φαρσαλίων |
c ἥκει τις, ἵνα ⟨καὶ⟩ τὰς τραπέζας καταφάγῃ;

---

56 One of Cassander's generals (late 4th/early 3rd century
BCE).

57 What follows is a garbled summary of phrases and ideas borrowed from Plb. 20.4.2, 6–7; 20.6.5.

* * *

(A.) So where are the strangers from? (B.) They're
   Boeotians.

These passages explain why Eratosthenes in his *Letters*
(*FGrH* 241 F 18) claims that when Prepelaus[56] was asked
his opinion of the Boeotians, he said: "Well, what else except that they say what pots would if they could talk, and
each of them announces how much he can hold?" Polybius
of Megalopolis in Book XX of his *History*[57] says that after
the Boeotians got a great reputation for what happened at
Leuctra,[58] they gradually allowed themselves to relax, began having feasts and drinking parties, and made arrange-
ments in their wills for their friends to have parties.[59] Even
many of those who had families divided up the majority of
their property among their messmates, the result being
that large numbers of Boeotians had more dinners to at-
tend each month than there were days in it. This is why the
Megarians, who despised the situation in Boeotia, revolted
to the Achaeans.[60]

   The inhabitants of Pharsalus are also mocked in comedy for being gluttons. Mnesimachus, for example, says in
Philip (fr. 8):

                    (A.) Did any of the Pharsalians
come in order to eat the tables?

[58] Where the Boeotians, led by Epameinondas of Thebes,
defeated the Spartans in 371 BCE.

[59] Sc. in their memory.

[60] In the 240s BCE, when Megara joined the Achaean League.

461

(B.) οὐδεὶς πάρεστιν. (A.) εὖ γε δρῶντες. ἆρά
   που
ὀπτὴν κατεσθίουσι πόλιν Ἀχαϊκήν;

ὅτι δὲ καὶ πάντες Θετταλοὶ ὡς πολυφάγοι διεβάλ-
λοντο Κράτης φησὶν ἐν Λαμίᾳ·

   ἔπη τριπήχη Θετταλικῶς τετμημένα.

τοῦτο δ᾽ εἶπεν ὡς τῶν Θετταλῶν μεγάλα κρέα τεμνόν-
των. Φιλέταιρος δ᾽ ἐν Λαμπαδηφόροις·

   καὶ χειροβαρὲς σαρκὸς ὑείας Θετταλότμητον
      κρέας.

ἔλεγον δὲ καὶ Θετταλικὴν ἔνθεσιν τὴν μεγάλην. Ἕρ-
μιππος Μοίραις· |

d   ὁ Ζεὺς δὲ τούτων οὐδὲν ἐνθυμούμενος
      μύων ξυνέπλαττε Θετταλικὴν τὴν ἔνθεσιν.

ταῦτα δὲ καπανικὰ εἴρηκεν Ἀριστοφάνης ἐν Ταγη-
νισταῖς·

   (A.) τί πρὸς τὰ Λυδῶν δεῖπνα καὶ τὰ Θετταλῶν;
   (B.) τὰ Θετταλικὰ μὲν πολὺ καπανικώτερα.

οἷον τὰ ἁμαξιαῖα· Θετταλοὶ γὰρ τὰς ἀπήνας καπάνας
ἔλεγον. Ξέναρχος Σκύθαις· |

(B.) None of them's here. (A.) Good for them. Maybe they're gobbling down a roasted Achaean city?

Crates in his *Lamia* (fr. 21) claims that the Thessalians generally[61] were attacked for being gluttons:

> five-foot[62] words cut Thessalian-style.

He said this because the Thessalians cut meat into large chunks. Philetaerus in *Torch-Bearers* (fr. 10):

> and a piece of pork, heavy in your hand, cut
> Thessalian-style.

They also referred to a large mouthful of food as "Thessalian". Hermippus in *Fates* (fr. 42):

> Zeus paid no attention to any of this,
> but closed his eyes and began to mould a Thessalian
> mouthful.[63]

Aristophanes in *Frying-Pan Men* (fr. 507) refers to these as *kapanika*:

> (A.) How about compared to Lydian or Thessalian
> dinners?
> (B.) Thessalian dinners are a lot more *kapanika*.

This means "as much as a wagon can carry"; because the Thessalians referred to wagons as *kapanai*. Xenarchus in *Scythians* (fr. 11):

---

[61] I.e. rather than the inhabitants of Pharsalus alone.

[62] Literally "three-cubit".

[63] Despite Athenaeus (or his source), this might just as well be a high-style way of referring to a barley-cake made of Thessalian grain.

e   (Α.) ἑπτὰ δὲ καπάνας ἔτρεφον εἰς Ὀλύμπια.

    (Β.) τί λέγεις; ‹καπάνας; πῶς;› (Α.) καπάνας
      Θετταλοὶ

πάντες καλοῦσι τὰς ἀπήνας. (Β.) μανθάνω.

Αἰγυπτίους δὲ Ἑκαταῖος ἀρτοφάγους φησὶν εἶναι
κυλλήστιας ἐσθίοντας, τὰς δὲ κριθὰς εἰς ποτὸν κατα-
λέοντας. διὰ ταῦτα καὶ Ἀλεξῖνος[10] ἐν τῷ Περὶ Αὐταρ-
κείας ἔφη μετρίᾳ τροφῇ κεχρῆσθαι τὸν Βόκχοριν καὶ
τὸν πατέρα αὐτοῦ Νεόχαβιν. καὶ Πυθαγόρας δ᾽ ὁ
Σάμιος μετρίᾳ τροφῇ ἐχρῆτο, ὡς ἱστορεῖ Λύκων ὁ
Ἰασεὺς ἐν τῷ Περὶ Πυθαγορείου ‹Βίου›[11]· οὐκ ἀπεί-
χετο δὲ ἐμψύχων, ὡς Ἀριστόξενος εἴρηκεν. Ἀπολ-
f λόδωρος | δὲ ὁ ἀριθμητικὸς καὶ θῦσαί φησιν αὐτὸν
ἑκατόμβην ἐπὶ τῷ εὑρηκέναι ὅτι τριγώνου ὀρθογωνίου
‹ἡ› τὴν ὀρθὴν γωνίαν ὑποτείνουσα ἴσον δύναται ταῖς
περιεχούσαις·

ἡνίκα Πυθαγόρης τὸ περικλεὲς εὕρετο γράμμα,
κλεινὸς ἐφ᾽ ᾧ κλεινὴν ἤγαγε βουθυσίην. ‖

419 ἦν δὲ καὶ ὀλιγοπότης ὁ Πυθαγόρας καὶ εὐτελέστατα
διεβίου, ὡς καὶ πολλάκις μέλιτι μόνῳ ἀρκεῖσθαι. τὰ
παραπλήσια δ᾽ ἱστορεῖται καὶ περὶ Ἀριστείδου καὶ
Ἐπαμεινώνδου καὶ Φωκίωνος καὶ Φορμίωνος τῶν

---

[10] Ἀλεξῖνος Meineke: Ἄλεξις A   [11] add. Kaibel

---

[64] Very similar material is cited at 10.447c.
[65] Cf. 3.114c–d.   [66] Beer; cf. 1.34a–b.

(A.) They were stabling seven *kapanai* for the
    Olympic games.
(B.) What are you talking about? *Kapanai*? Huh? (A.)
    The Thessalians all
refer to wagons as *kapanai*. (B.) I get it.

Hecataeus (*FGrH* 1 F 323b)[64] reports that the Egyptians consume bread, in that they eat *kullēstiai*[65], but that they grind up barley to produce a substance that can be drunk.[66] This is why Alexinus in his *On Self-Sufficiency* (*SSR* IIc F 19) claimed that Bocchoris[67] and his father Neochabis consumed a modest diet. Pythagoras of Samos also ate moderately, according to Lycon of Iasos in his *On the Pythagorean Lifestyle* (57.3 D–K); but he did not avoid meat, according to Aristoxenus (fr. 28 Wehrli). The mathematician Apollodorus claims that Pythagoras sacrificed a hecatomb when he discovered that the hypotenuse of a right-triangle is equal to the sides that enclose it:[68]

When Pythagoras discovered his famous theorem,
    celebrating which the famous man offered a
    famous sacrifice of bulls.

Pythagoras also did not drink much, and lived a very simple life, to the extent that he was often satisfied with honey and nothing else.[69] Similar stories are told about the generals Aristides, Epameinondas, Phocion, and

[67] Bocchoris was the last Pharaoh of the 24th Egyptian Dynasty (reigned 726/5–720 BCE?); his father was named Stephinates (Tefnacht).
[68] Sc. when the numbers are squared.
[69] Cf. 2.46e–f (Democritus).

στρατηγῶν. Μάνιος δὲ Κούριος ὁ Ῥωμαίων στρατηγὸς ἐπὶ γογγυλίσι διεβίω πάντα τὸν χρόνον· καὶ
Σαβίνων αὐτῷ πολὺ χρυσίον προσπεμπόντων οὐκ ἔφη
δεῖσθαι χρυσίου, ἕως ἂν τοιαῦτα δειπνῇ. ἱστορεῖ δὲ
ταῦτα Μεγακλῆς ἐν τῷ Περὶ Ἐνδόξων Ἀνδρῶν.

Τῶν δείπνων δὲ πολλοὶ τὰ μέτρια ἀσπάζονται, ὡς
Ἄλεξις ἐν Φιλούσῃ παραδίδωσιν· |

b   ἀλλ' ἔγωγε τοῦ τὰ δέοντ' ἔχειν
τὰ περιττὰ μισῶ· τοῖς ὑπερβάλλουσι γὰρ
τέρψις μὲν οὐκ ἔνεστι, πολυτέλεια δέ.

⟨ἐν⟩[12] Ψευδομένῳ·

τὰ περιττὰ μισῶ· τοῖς ὑπερβάλλουσι γὰρ
δαπάνη πρόσεστιν, ἡδονὴ δ' οὐδ' ἡτισοῦν.

ἐν δὲ Συντρόφοις·

ὡς ἡδὺ πᾶν τὸ μέτριον· οὔθ' ὑπεργέμων |
c ἀπέρχομαι νῦν οὔτε κενός, ἀλλ' ἡδέως
ἔχων ἐμαυτοῦ. Μνησίθεος γάρ φησι δεῖν
φεύγειν ἁπάντων τὰς ὑπερβολὰς ἀεί.

Ἀρίστων δ' ὁ φιλόσοφος ἐν Ἐρωτικῶν Ὁμοίων δευτέρῳ Πολέμωνά φησι τὸν Ἀκαδημαϊκὸν παραινεῖν

[12] add. Olson

---

[70] The Athenian politicians and generals Aristides (*PAA*
165170), Phocion "the Good" (*PA* 15076), and Phormio (*PA*

Phormio.[70] The Roman general Manius Curius survived on turnips for his entire life; when the Sabines sent him a large amount of gold,[71] he said that he had no need for gold, as long as he had turnips for dinner. Megacles preserves this information in his *On Famous Men* (*FHG* iv.443).

Many people take a positive attitude toward modest dinners, as Alexis informs us in *Philousa* (fr. 256):

> But as for me, I despise having
> more than I need; because there's no pleasure
> in extravagance, and it costs lots of money.

In *The Liar* (Alex. fr. 261):

> I despise excess; because extravagance
> involves expense, and there's no pleasure in it at all.

And in *Foster-Brothers* (fr. 219):

> Moderation's always nice. I'm leaving now, and
> I'm neither too full nor empty; I just
> feel good. Because Mnesitheus[72] says you should
> always avoid excess in everything.

The philosopher Ariston in Book II of the *Erotic Comparisons* (fr. 24 Wehrli) reports that Polemon of the Academy[73]

14958) date to the early 5th century, the 4th century, and the 440s–430s BCE, respectively. For Epameinondas (d. 362 BCE), see 10.418b n.   [71] During his first consulship, in 290 BCE.
[72] = fr. 21 Bertier. Mnesitheus was a well-known 4th-century BCE Athenian physician with a particular interest in diaetetic matters, and is cited by Athenaeus at e.g. 8.355a, 357a–8c.
[73] *PAA* 776720; cf. 2.44e n.

τοῖς ἐπὶ δεῖπνον πορευομένοις φροντίζειν ὅπως ἡδὺν
πότον ποιῶνται μὴ μόνον εἰς τὸ παρόν, ἀλλὰ καὶ εἰς
τὴν αὔριον. Τιμόθεος δ᾽ ὁ Κόνωνος ἐκ τῶν πολυτελῶν
d καὶ στρατηγικῶν δείπνων παραληφθεὶς ὑπὸ | Πλά-
τωνος εἰς τὸ ἐν Ἀκαδημείᾳ συμπόσιον καὶ ἑστιαθεὶς
ἀφελῶς καὶ μουσικῶς ἔφη ὡς οἱ παρὰ Πλάτωνι
δειπνοῦντες καὶ τῇ ὑστεραίᾳ καλῶς γίνονται. ὁ δ᾽
Ἡγήσανδρος ἐν τοῖς Ὑπομνήμασιν ἔφη ὡς καὶ τῇ
ὑστεραίᾳ ὁ Τιμόθεος ἀπαντήσας τῷ Πλάτωνι εἶπεν·
"ὑμεῖς, ὦ Πλάτων, εὖ δειπνεῖτε μᾶλλον εἰς τὴν ὑστε-
ραίαν ἢ τὴν παροῦσαν ἡμέραν." Πύρρων δ᾽ ὁ Ἠλεῖος
τῶν γνωρίμων τινὸς αὐτὸν ὑποδεξαμένου πολυτελῶς
<μέν, ...>[13] δέ, ὡς <ὁ>[14] αὐτὸς ἱστορεῖ, "εἰς τὸ
e λοιπόν," εἶπεν, "οὐχ ἥξω πρὸς σέ, ἂν | οὕτως ὑποδέχῃ,
ἵνα μήτε ἐγὼ σὲ ἀηδῶς ὁρῶ καταδαπανώμενον οὐκ
ἀναγκαίως μήτε σὺ θλιβόμενος κακοπαθῇς. μᾶλλον
γὰρ ἡμᾶς τῇ μεθ᾽ ἑαυτῶν συνουσίᾳ προσῆκόν ἐστιν
εὐεργετεῖν ἢ τῷ πλήθει τῶν παρατιθεμένων, <ὧν>[15] οἱ
διακονοῦντες τὰ πλεῖστα δαπανῶσιν." Ἀντίγονος δ᾽ ὁ
Καρύστιος ἐν τῷ Μενεδήμου Βίῳ τὴν διάταξιν διηγούμενος τοῦ παρὰ τῷ φιλοσόφῳ συμποσίου φησὶν ὅτι
ἠρίστα μὲν δεύτερος ἢ τρίτος καθ᾽ αὑτόν· κᾆτ᾽ ἔδει καὶ
f τοὺς λοιποὺς παρεῖναι δεδειπνηκότας· ἦν γὰρ | τὸ τοῦ
Μενεδήμου τοιοῦτον ἄριστον. μετὰ δὲ ταῦτα εἰσ-

13 lac. not. Kaibel
14 add. Dobree
15 add. Casaubon

advised people who were on their way to dinner to think about how they could make the drinking enjoyable not only at the moment, but on the next day as well.[74] Timotheus son of Conon,[75] who was accustomed to expensive dinners of the sort given by generals, was invited by Plato to a drinking party in the Academy; after he was entertained in a frugal, but sophisticated style, he said that people who had dinner with Plato were happy the next day as well. Hegesander in his *Commentaries* (fr. 34, *FHG* iv.420) reported that when Timotheus met Plato the next day, he said: "Plato, you people get more pleasure out of your dinner the next day than you do on the day of the party itself!" When one of his disciples entertained him lavishly, but . . . , according to the same authority, Pyrrho of Elis said: "I'm not going to visit you in the future, if you entertain me that way, so that I don't feel bad when I see you wasting your money unnecessarily, and so that you don't run short of funds and suffer. Because it's better to favor one another with our company than with a large number of dishes, most of which the servants consume." Antigonus of Carystus in his *Life of Menedemus* (pp. 99–101 Wilamowitz = fr. 26A Dorandi),[76] when he describes how the philosopher's drinking parties were organized, says that he used to have the equivalent of lunch along with one or two guests; he adds that the others needed to have had their dinner before they got there, because this was how light a meal Menedemus served. Afterward they

[74] I.e. by avoiding a hangover.

[75] *PA* 13700; he was active politically in the 370s–mid-350s BCE.

[76] Parallel material is preserved at D.L. 2.139–40.

εκάλουν τοὺς παραγινομένους· ὧν, ὡς ἔοικεν, ὅτε
προτερήσειαν ἔνιοι τῆς ὥρας, ἀνακάμπτοντες παρὰ
τὰς θύρας ἀνεπυνθάνοντο τῶν ἐξιόντων παίδων τί τὸ
παρακείμενον εἴη καὶ πῶς ἔχοι τῆς τοῦ χρόνου συμ-
μετρίας τὸ ἄριστον. ὅτε μὲν οὖν ἀκούσειαν λάχανον ἢ
τάριχος, ἀνεχώρουν, ὅτε δ᾿ ὅτι κρεάδιον, εἰσῇεσαν εἰς
420   τὸν ἐπὶ τοῦτο παρεσκευασμένον οἶκον. ‖ ἦν δὲ τοῦ
μὲν θέρους ἡτοιμασμένη ψίαθος ἐφ᾿ ἑκάστης κλίνης,
τοῦ δὲ χειμῶνος κώδιον· προσκεφάλαιον δὲ αὐτὸν
φέρειν ἕκαστον ἔδει. τὸ δὲ περιαγόμενον ποτήριον οὐ
μεῖζον ἦν κοτυλιαίου, τράγημα δὲ θέρμος μὲν ἢ κύαμος συνεχῶς, ποτὲ δὲ καὶ τῶν ὡρίων εἰσεφέρετό τι, τοῦ
μὲν θέρους ἄπιος ἢ ῥόα, τοῦ δ᾿ ἔαρος ὦχροι, κατὰ δὲ
τὴν χειμερινὴν ὥραν ἰσχάδες. μαρτυρεῖ δὲ καὶ περὶ
τούτων Λυκόφρων ὁ Χαλκιδεὺς γράψας σατύρους Με-
νέδημον, ἐν οἷς φησιν ὁ Σιληνὸς πρὸς τοὺς σατύρους·

παῖδες κρατίστου πατρὸς ἐξωλέστατοι, |
b   ἐγὼ μὲν ὑμῖν, ὡς ὁρᾶτε, στρηνιῶ·
δεῖπνον γὰρ οὔτ᾿ ἐν Καρίᾳ, μὰ τοὺς θεούς,
οὔτ᾿ ἐν Ῥόδῳ τοιοῦτον οὔτ᾿ ἐν Λυδίᾳ
κατέχω δεδειπνηκώς. Ἄπολλον, ὡς καλόν.

καὶ προελθών·

ἀλλὰ κυλίκιον
ὑδαρὲς ὁ παῖς περιῆγε τοῦ πεντωβόλου,

---

77 The final two verses are quoted also at 2.55d.

would invite in anyone who was there. As one might expect, any of them who arrived early would walk back and forth in front of the doors and ask the slaves as they were coming out what was being served and how far along the schedule the meal had got. When they heard that (the main course was) a vegetable or some saltfish, they left, whereas when they heard it was a cut of meat, they went into the room that had been prepared for the occasion. In the summer, a rush mat was set on each couch ahead of time, whereas during the winter there was a sheepskin; but everyone had to bring his own pillow. The cup that was passed around held less than a ladleful, and the snack that was offered was normally lupine-seeds or beans, although occasionally seasonal fruit was served, pears or pomegranates in the summer, bird's-pease in the spring, or figs in the wintertime. Lycophron of Chalcedon also attests to these facts in the satyr play *Menedemus* (*TrGF* 100 F 2, encompassing both quotations) he wrote, in which Silenus says to the satyrs:

> Vile children of a powerful father,
> I'm running rough-shod over you, as you can see;
> because, by the gods, I don't recall having eaten
> a dinner like this in Caria, or Rhodes,
> or Lydia. Apollo! How nice it was!

And further on:[77]

> But the slave brought
> around a cup full of water and some five-obol[78] wine

[78] I.e. extremely inexpensive.

ἀτρέμα παρεξεστηκός· ὅ τ᾿ ἀλιτήριος
καὶ δημόκοινος ἐπεχόρευε δαψιλὴς
θέρμος, πενήτων καὶ τρικλίνου συμπότης. |

c   ἑξῆς δέ φησιν ὅτι ζητήσεις ἦσαν παρὰ πότον·

τράγημα δὲ
ὁ σωφρονιστὴς πᾶσιν ἐν μέσῳ λόγος.

ἱστορεῖται δὲ καὶ ὅτι

πολλάκις
συνόντας αὐτοὺς

ἐπὶ πλεῖον ὁ ὄρνις κατελάμβανε

τὴν ἕω καλῶν,
< . . . > τοῖσι δὲ οὐδέπω κόρος.

Ἀρκεσίλαος δ᾿ ἑστιῶν τινας, καὶ ἐλλιπόντων τῶν ἄρτων νεύσαντος τοῦ παιδὸς ὡς οὐκ ἔτ᾿ εἰσίν, ἀνα-
καγχάσας καὶ τὼ χεῖρε συγκροτήσας, "οἷόν τι", ἔφη,
"τὸ συμπόσιόν ἐστιν ἡμῶν, ἄνδρες φίλοι· ἄρτους ἐπι-
λελήσμεθ᾿ ἀρκοῦντας πρίασθαι. τρέχε δή, παῖ." καὶ
d   τοῦτ᾿ ἔλεγεν αὐτὸς γελῶν· | καὶ τῶν παρόντων δ᾿
ἄθρους ἐξεχύθη γέλως καὶ διαγωγὴ πλείων ἐνέπεσεν
καὶ διατριβή, ὥστε ἥδυσμα γενέσθαι τῷ συμποσίῳ
τὴν τῶν ἄρτων ἔνδειαν. ἄλλοτε δὲ ὁ Ἀρκεσίλαος
Ἀπελλῇ τῷ γνωρίμῳ προστάξας καθυλίσαι τὸν οἶνον,

---

79 A longer version of the fragment is preserved at D.L. 2.140.

that had already gone a bit bad. And the criminal
and plentiful common lupine, which drinks
with poor men at their parties, came dancing in.

Immediately after this he says that they posed questions
for one another as they were drinking (*TrGF* 100 F 3.2–
3):[79]

> Because our snack
> was the moralizing conversation we all engaged in.

It is also reported that (*TrGF* 100 F 4, encompassing both
quotations)

> often,
> when they were together

for a long time, the rooster overtook them

> summoning the dawn,
> and they had by no means had enough.

When Arcesilaus[80] had some people to dinner, and the
bread ran out and the slave shook his head to signal that it
was all gone, he burst out in laughter, clapped his hands,
and said: "What a party we're having, my friends—we for-
got to buy enough bread! Run, slave!" He was laughing
as he said this, and all the guests also began to laugh, and
the party became happier and more enjoyable, the result
being that the shortage of bread added zest to the occasion. On another occasion Arcesilaus assigned his student
Apelles to strain the wine, and when Apelles' lack of expe-

---

[80] Arcesilaus of Pitane (316/5–242/1 BCE; *PAA* 202740) was
the founder of the Middle Academy. Apelles and Arideices (below) are *PAA* 140190 and 162020, respectively.

ἐπειδὴ διὰ τὴν ἀπειρίαν ἐκεῖνος τὰ μὲν ἐτάραττεν, τὰ δ' ἐξέχει, καὶ πολὺ θολώτερος ἐφαίνετο ὁ οἶνος, ὑπομειδιάσας ἔφη· "ἐγὼ δὲ καθυλίσαι προσέταξα ἀνθρώπῳ μηδὲν ἑωρακότι ἀγαθὸν ὥσπερ οὐδ' ἐγώ. ἀνάστηθι

e οὖν σύ, Ἀρίδεικες· σὺ δὲ ἀπελθὼν † τὰ | ἑκτὰ τρύπα †." ταῦτα δ' οὕτως εὔφραινε καὶ ἐξιλάρου τοὺς παρόντας ὡς εὐθυμίας πληροῦσθαι.

rience caused him to make some of it cloudy, and to spill the rest, and when the wine actually looked much murkier than it did before, Arcesilaus smiled gently and said: "I assigned someone to strain the wine who has no more idea of what the Good is than I do. So get off of your couch, Arideices! And as for you, go away † the qualities pierce!" † These remarks delighted and amused the other guests so much that they were in a very good mood.

INDEX

INDEX

INDEX

INDEX

482

INDEX